DISTANT THUNDER

Canada's Citizen Soldiers on the Western Front

To Roy
with best wishes
Joyce Kennedy
August 2000

Lest we forget...

DISTANT THUNDER

Canada's Citizen Soldiers on the Western Front

by
Joyce M. Kennedy, Ph.D.

Sunflower University Press®

1531 Yuma • P. O. Box 1009 • Manhattan, Kansas 66505-1009 USA

Cover art, Mike Boss, Hill City, Kansas

Technical Editor, Sonie Liebler

Layout by Lori L. Daniel

ISBN 0-89745-243-7

Sunflower University Press is a wholly-owned subsidiary
of the non-profit 501(c)3 Journal of the West, Inc.

www.sunflower-univ-press.org

Blow out, you bugles,
over the rich Dead!
There's none of these so lonely
and poor of old,
But, dying, has made us
rarer gifts than gold.

1914, by Rupert Brooke

To the memory of my father
Robert James Kennedy
A Soldier of the Great War

Contents

Preface   xiii

Acknowledgment   xv

Chapter 1   Genesis — Call to Colors   1
             The Gathering War Clouds
             Signs of German Preparations for War
             The Flashpoint
             The North Sea Cables

Chapter 2   Canada's Military Preparedness   11

Chapter 3   Chaos in Quebec   17

Chapter 4   The Western Front   28
             The Battle of Mons
             The Miracle of the Marne

Chapter 5   Digging In   39
             The First Battle of Ypres
             Trench Development
             The German Trenches
             Trench Routine

Chapter 6   The Atlantic Crossing   52

Chapter 7   On Salisbury Plain — Winter 1915   57

Chapter 8   To the Front   66
                    Neuve Chapelle

Chapter 9   Gas — And the Second Battle of Ypres   77
                    Gas Attack
                    The Deadly Counterattacks
                    The Battle Continues
                    In Flanders Fields
                    In Retrospect

Chapter 10   The HMS *Lusitania*   102

Chapter 11   Festubert and Givenchy   105

Chapter 12   The Gathering War Clouds   111
                    Trench Raids
                    Life in the Trenches

Chapter 13   The Battle of Verdun — 1916   125

Chapter 14   Outgunned and Outfought in the Mud of St. Eloi   136
                    A New Assignment

Chapter 15   Vindication and Victory at Mount Sorrel   146
              and Observatory Ridge

Chapter 16   Slaughter on the Somme   151
                    Why the Somme?
                    The Battle Begins
                    The Lads from Newfoundland

Chapter 17   The Battle of the Somme Continues —   169
              August-November 1916
                    Pozières Ridge
                    The New Weapon
                    Courcelette
                    Regina Trench

Chapter 18   German Plans Revealed,   187
              American Neutrality Ends — 1917
                    The Turnip Winter
                    The Zimmerman Telegram
                    Unrestricted Submarine Warfare
                    Operation Alberich
                    The United States Enters the War

Chapter 19   The Ill-Omened Vimy Ridge,   196
              and the Birth of a Nation
                    Plans and Preparations
                    So Loud the Silence
                    The Outcome

Chapter 20   The Artillery Comes of Age   224
                    Allied Attacks Along the Scarpe River
                    Messines Ridge, 7-15 June 1917
                    The Killing Fields of Lens, Loos, and Hill 70

Chapter 21   Gethsemane — The Flanders Offensive —   248
              The Third Battle of Ypres — 1917
                    Passchendaele — The Tragic Victory

Chapter 22   Cambrai and the Armada of Tanks   263
                    Other Disturbing Developments in Late 1917

Chapter 23   The Winter of Discontent — 1918   270
                    Operation Michael

Chapter 24   Germany's Spring Offensives — 1918   277
                    "With Our Backs to the Wall"

Chapter 25   Amiens and the Turning of the Tide   283
                    Inter-Allied Attacks
                    German Morale Plunges
                    Drocourt-Quéant Line

Chapter 26   The Collapse of the Central Powers   292
                   The Franco-American Assault —
                       Meuse-Argonne
                   The British Assault — Verdun to the
                       English Channel
                   The Canadians Take Cambrai

Chapter 27   The Distant Thunder Ceases   301
                   The Americans Advance
                   Valenciennes

Epilogue   309

Sources   312

Glossary   318

Chronology   321

Index   329

Preface

*T*HE GREAT WAR has been the subject of more books and
articles that any other event in the history of writing. More
than 5,000 titles, many of them now out of print, have been
published on some aspect of that world cataclysm. Why then would
anyone want to write yet another?

My reasons were twofold, one building on the other.

My first impetus came from the discovery of my father's frayed
war diaries, and a dusty certificate that recorded his being Mentioned
in Despatches "for gallant and distinguished services in the Field" on
9 April 1917, the day that Canada took Vimy Ridge, France, the first
major Allied offensive victory of the war. He had never mentioned it.

That led — approximately 80 years after the fact — to my tran-
scribing his diaries for my sister and brothers. Because I failed to
understand some of the terms he used, I began to accumulate books
on the war, specifically on the Western Front where he served.
Illuminating discoveries brought satisfaction — but more questions.
And it was still a personal voyage.

The second reason to write was born of frustration. As I read more and more books on the First World War, I experienced a dearth of material regarding Canadian participation and sacrifices in that war. In their listing of casualties, for example, some books never mentioned Canada. Why? Her wounded and dead were, understandably, subsumed under British Empire casualties. Thus, for example, in the *History of the World War, An Authentic Narrative of the World's Greatest War* (1919), Francis March mentions the "twenty eight nations entering the war and their populations," which included San Marino (population 10,000) and Panama (400,000), but not Canada, with a population of nearly eight million. Great Britain was, of course, listed with a population of 440,000,000 with an asterisk "including colonies." I felt that Canada, and of course Australia and New Zealand, deserved more than an asterisk.

One day when corresponding by E-mail with a young college student, who was writing his thesis on the war, I mentioned my difficulty in finding material on Canada. "That's because Canada didn't do much," he responded. I cringed and wondered why Canada's contributions were still, nearly a century later, so often overlooked. I resolved then and there to stop wondering and start writing.

There is really a third reason, of course, for writing this book. No one who has read of the unspeakable horrors of World War I can ever take for granted the extraordinary sacrifices made by the men and women who fought in it. This book is, therefore, also an attempt to honor all who served, by reaching out to new, younger audiences to retell a true but tragic story about times past . . . lest we forget.

Acknowledgment

*T*HERE ARE MANY TO whom I have become indebted during the writing of this book. Among them are my brothers, Robert and "Hap," for their corrections, suggestions, and encouragement; the staff of the National Archives of Canada in Ottawa and the Imperial War Museum in London for their gracious assistance; Sonie Liebler for her editing expertise and encouragement; Loretta Wagoner of the California State University at Northridge, Ventura Campus Library and the staff of Ventura's E. P. Foster Library for their endless patience in tracking down out-of-print and other military books; Marianne Ratcliff for proofreading; Tom Gudmestad of the Pacific Coast Branch of the Western Front Association for his insightful comments; Polis Associates for computer assistance; Karl Murray for long-term, trans-Atlantic moral support; and most of all to Maria Maginnis, who though unable to witness the final outcome, gave the first encouragement. I am indebted to them all.

The focus on Canadian valor and casualties in this book should in no way diminish the magnificent contributions of other nations.

Any inaccuracies or misinterpretaions of what happened so long ago are mine alone.

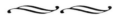

The diplomatic origins, so-called, of the Great War are only the fever chart of the patient; they do not tell us what caused the fever.
　　　— Barbara Tuchman, *The Proud Tower*

Chapter 1

Genesis — Call to Colors

NEVER BEFORE HAD there been such a sight in Canada. On this glorious Fall day, as the morning mists lifted off the Gaspé Harbor, there they lay at anchor, like a phantom navy.

Thirty ships had rendezvoused in the colorful bay of Eastern Canada the night before, the first day of October 1914, to wait for British warships that would escort them in convoy 2,500 miles across the Atlantic. On board the motley assortment of the hastily painted, gray ships were more than 30,000 green troops of the First Canadian Division.

It was really something of a wonder. Just two short months before, the men had been ordinary citizens from the nine provinces and two territories of Canada — farmers, miners, newspapermen, lumberjacks, fishermen, doctors, bankers, lawyers, prospectors, ranchers, salesmen.[1] They still were, of course. But now they were something more. They were soldiers of the Crown. And they had all volunteered to serve in the distant war that would ultimately involve most nations on earth.

It had all happened with remarkable speed, especially for the peaceful country that had achieved nationhood only 47 years before. Now its young sons were off to war. (However, one "son" was noticeably missing. Mackenzie King, a future Prime Minister of Canada, left for New York on 13 August 1914, where he became head of the Rockefeller Foundation's Department of Industrial Relations. He spent the war years in the United States.)

As has been so frequently documented, it all began in foreign fields so far away.

The Gathering War Clouds[2]

Historians frequently fix the years 1870-1871 as a significant framing point for the building of conditions that led to the "Great War." It was then that Germany crushed and humiliated its nemesis France, thereby ending more than 200 years of French domination of Europe. As part of the spoils, Germany grabbed the easterly French provinces of Alsace and Lorraine. Adding insult to injury, Wilhelm I of Prussia was proclaimed Emperor of Germany on French soil, in the Hall of Mirrors at Versailles. The French would not soon forget the humiliation. They would *never* forget the loss of Alsace-Lorraine! As the French patriot Leon Gambeth urged at the time, "Think of it always, speak of it never." Victor Hugo echoed similar sentiments, warning that France would "nourish her sacred anger" and someday, with a new generation, retake Alsace-Lorraine.

And thus a small but malignant war cloud appeared over France.

For a time, events went along somewhat placidly in Germany under the guidance of Otto von Bismarck. It was he, in fact, as chief minister of Prussia, who had orchestrated not only the crushing victory over France, but the bringing together of 25 German states to form a new united Germany — Prussia being the most powerful state, and its king becoming the Kaiser of the new Germany, with almost dictatorial powers.

After Germany became unified as an empire, her industrial and economic (as well as her political) power began to rise. With the impact of the Industrial Revolution and von Bismarck's skillful guidance, Germany surged to new heights of prosperity and power. German pride swelled as massive new steamships took to the High Seas and airplanes to the skies. Electric lights lengthened the days; telephones made them more productive. Nonetheless, Germany found it an anathema to be surrounded by other powers. And for some reason (possibly because it didn't have colonies like Great Britain, France, and even "little" Belgium), there was an undercurrent of feeling among its countrymen that it was not being accorded its due place on the world's stage. One historian, John Laffin, goes so far as to say that Germans "had an inferiority complex, which showed itself in the arrogance of the troops and the hero worship the civilian populace gave to them."[3] Not surprisingly, the military began to grow in importance.

Von Bismarck, for all his success, did not crave more territory for Germany. Content with land power, he was more interested in security than in expansion, and to this end aimed to keep France isolated. Thus came the alliance between Germany and Austria-Hungary in 1879. With remarkable diplomatic skills, von Bismarck even made a friend of Russia in spite of its antipathy toward Germany's partner, Austria-Hungary. It was a delicate balance. Then Italy joined Germany and Austria-Hungary in 1882, to form the Triple Alliance. Although not immediately evident, another nettlesome cloud formed on the European horizon. Others were about to appear.

In March 1888, the aging Emperor Wilhelm I of Germany died. As fate would have it, his son and heir, Frederick III, bedridden and incurably ill with throat cancer, lived only three months, most of them in a coma. Thus, by midyear, Frederick's 29-year-old son, Wilhelm II, ascended the throne.

Seldom described in tender terms by historians, young Wilhelm was alternately arrogant, ambitious, stubborn, paranoid, and anti-Semitic, among other things. He also could be vicious and intemperate. It was only a question of time (March 1890) until he dismissed von Bismarck, characteristically preferring to oversee much of the policy-making role himself. Suddenly, therefore, the world's strongest army had a new leader, far more bellicose than von Bismarck. Worse yet, Wilhelm lacked von Bismarck's talent and diplomacy, and without the statesman's political skills, Russia, like a giant iceberg, was allowed to drift away into unchartered waters.

Signs of German Preparations for War

By now, other nations were taking anxious note of the emerging power of the Triple Alliance members, particularly Germany and its self-aggrandizing Kaiser. It would have been hard not to notice.

For one thing, Germany had a standing army of more than 840,000 well-trained men. (For more than a century, she had had a system of conscription whereby young men, called up at the age of 20, were given two years of military training by seasoned professionals.) Further, the army was well organized, and "possessed the most perfect machinery in the world for swift and efficient mobilization . . . for the simple reason that everything is in perpetual preparation for war."[4] Even long before the war, the German General Staff issued to most of its officers a copy of the handbook of war, *Kriegsbrauch im Landkriege*, which warned that no one, including civilians, could escape the burdens, sacrifices, and inconveniences of war, and cautioned officers not to be too humane. Laffin states:

> By steeping himself in military history, an officer will be able to guard himself against excessive humanitarian notions. It will teach him that certain severities are indispensable in war, that the only true humanity very often lies in a ruthless application of them.[5]

France was apprehensive. Obviously, something would be needed to counter Germany's growing power and the Triple Alliance. Not surprisingly, therefore, by 1891 Russia and France "found" each other, and agreed to "consult if either were menaced by aggression." The countries took more formal steps in 1893 by promising to mobilize should they be threatened by a member of the Triple Alliance. Armed with her new ally, France grew more confident.

But by the same token, a festering "balance of power" was emerging. And another, larger thundercloud began to form.

While Germany was enhancing its military might on land, naval strength was by no means neglected. By 1898, the construction of warships was escalating under Admiral Alfred von Tirpitz, ostensibly to strengthen the German High Seas Fleet "for defense," though most historians argue that Germany's limited coastline called for coastal artillery, not ships. Moreover, the Kiel Canal would be finished in 1914, enabling German vessels to glide from the Baltic Sea to the North Sea and the Atlantic Ocean with greater speed and security. Wilhelm took pride in his growing navy, so much so that he had a royal stateroom on every ship.

There was yet another telltale indication of war preparation. German military maps of France showed new roads, which had not yet appeared in official French maps.[6] Inevitably, by the turn of the century, the virus of militarism was multiplying rapidly.

By 1912, there were more disturbing omens of war. A retired Prussian cavalry officer, General Friedrich von Bernhardi, claimed in *Germany and the Next War*[7] that war was a biological necessity, and that Germany would need to make war or lose the struggle for world power.

Baron von Stengel, then a Professor at Munich and one of Germany's delegates at the Hague Conference, disclosed a similar arrogant sentiment. He later wrote:

> . . . We, the Germans, have been chosen by Providence, from among all earth's peoples, to put ourselves at the head of all civilized nations . . . . For this we possess not only the necessary power and force, but also, in the highest degree, the intellectual gifts requisite, and we are the flower of the entire creation's *Kultur.*[8]

In December, Kaiser Wilhelm called a "war council" in which he exhibited no aversion to a European war. Inexorably, dark clouds were spreading all over the face of Europe.

The Flashpoint

Some say it was simply a wrong turn. Some say it was superbly planned. Some say it was a tragic succession of errors. Some say it was all of those factors. It was an assassination. And it was the spark that changed the world.

Archduke Francis Ferdinand, in 1914, was next in line to his uncle, 84-year-old Franz Josef I, for the throne of Austria-Hungary. (The old monarch's only son had committed suicide in 1889 and the mantle of the crown thus fell to his nephew, Archduke Ferdinand.) Ferdinand wasn't exactly popular. Historian S. L. A. Marshall describes him as a man "swollen with pride, dangerously thin-skinned, a misanthrope, religious bigot, and miser . . . loved only by his wife and children. There was no moderation in him."[9]

For all his faults, however, Ferdinand had at least married for love, though his choice of a wife was to plague him throughout their marriage. Sophie Chotek was a "mere Countess" when he courted her over the objections of his uncle, Emperor Franz Josef. The marriage, nonetheless, took place on 28 June 1900, but only after Ferdinand made a number of concessions, including renouncing the right of succession for his children. And Sophie would not be able to ride in the royal coach with her husband, except in his role as Inspector General of the Army.

The 28th of June 1914, would be different, however. It would be their 14th wedding anniversary. Ferdinand could take his beloved Sophie with him to Bosnia-Herzegovina to review the troops and tour Sarajevo, the capital city of Bosnia, a Balkan province that had been annexed by Austria in 1908 after 30 years of occupancy. Moreover, she could ride with him in an open coach and be treated with the royal respect Ferdinand thought she deserved.

But fate would intervene.

Seven young schoolboy assassins, trained by a Serbian terrorist organization known as the Black Hand, also prepared for the morning of 28 June. With various instruments of death at their disposal, they waited for the Archduke and his wife along scattered parts of the route. Most had the opportunity to become forever infamous, but in a strange twist of circumstances, wrote themselves out of history. One assassin simply froze when the opportunity came. One changed his mind. Some did nothing. One threw a bomb that actually hit the Archduke, but bounced off his arm into the street, wounding members of the crowd, as he protected his Sophie.

The Archduke, unhurt but understandably furious at the lack of protection, apparently calmed down long enough to express a desire to visit the hospital to meet with the victims. However, en route, the chauffeur took a wrong turn. As fate would have it, Gavrilo Princip, the seventh assassin, was nearby — so close in fact that he was able to jump onto the open coach's running board. He fired at pointblank range, first at the Archduke and then at his wife. Both died almost immediately.

Surprisingly, there was no immediate outcry or upheaval. But, like a time-bomb with a delayed fuse, the outcry would indeed come. And still another cloud joined the weightiness in the heavens.

Enter onto the world stage General Franz Conrad von Hötzendorf, Chief of the Austrian General Staff. He saw a unique opportunity to capitalize on the Archduke's death and position Austria higher on the political rung of Europe. He was confident that Russia would not interfere in the Balkans in spite of its support of Serbian ambitions. Nonetheless, von Hötzendorf needed "insurance" support, so his thoughts turned to Germany. On 5 July, the Austrian Ambassador met with the German Kaiser who immediately promised to back Austria if Russia entered the picture to support Serbia. He went even further, in an agreement that would change history; the German Kaiser, in fact, gave Austria a "blank check."

With an investigation into the assassination showing some Serbian connection, von Hötzendorf was able to convince the Austrian cabinet to confront Serbia for the dire deed. Austria then gave Serbia a humiliating, 48-hour ultimatum. Although Serbia agreed to most of the demands, it was impossible to meet every condition without complete surrender of sovereignty.[10] (Austria had deliberately planned it that way.) Even before responding to the ultimatum, however, Serbia began to mobilize.

Meanwhile, Russia, the large iceberg that had drifted away from Germany with the departure of von Bismarck, now floated back onto the horizon. Alarmed that Serbia might be attacked and absorbed into Austria, Russia, on 25 July (partially but only partially bluffing), ordered "preparatory measures" for mobilization in several military districts. Maybe the *threat* of mobilization would be enough to reverse the growing confrontation! But events were already beginning to snowball. On the same day, France reaffirmed its support of Russia. And two days later, France issued "standby" mobilization orders.

The tangled web of intrigue and alliances was now widening by the hour. And the hands on the clock moved relentlessly forward. Events took on their own tragic momentum.

On 28 July, a month to the day after the Archduke's assassination, Austria declared war on Serbia.

On 30 July, the Russian Tsar, Nicholas II, after some vacillation, ordered general mobilization, upping the ante from "preparatory measures." The next day, Germany, alarmed by Russia's move, gave it a 12-hour ultimatum to demobilize, and at the same time asked France what its intentions were.

On the same day, a worried British government warned Germany to honor Belgium's neutrality as guaranteed by the treaty of 1839, which both Germany and England had signed.

France ambiguously answered Germany's question on the first day of August, saying merely that France would be guided by its own best interests. But France's actions were to prove far more forceful than its ambivalent words. Mobilization was ordered at 3:55 the same afternoon. Only minutes later, Germany did likewise. Three hours later, when its ultimatum to Russia expired, Germany issued a formal declaration of war.

The next day, 2 August, German troops crossed into Luxembourg, and the German Ambassador to Belgium demanded passage through Belgium. Belgian King Albert replied that his country was "firmly resolved to repel by all means in its power every attack upon its rights." He immediately turned to the British and French for assistance.

On Monday, 3 August, Germany declared war on France. And now the war clouds over Europe cast worldwide shadows. Four of the five European powers were at war. Only England held back.

In faraway Canada, it was a civic holiday, a day usually reserved for picnics and parades. But this day was different as crowds gathered around newspaper offices to read the latest alarming bulletins.

On the morning of 4 August, a shocked world heard that German troops had crossed the border onto Belgian soil, which Berlin justified by saying "necessity knows no law." Britain's Foreign Secretary, Sir Edward Grey, sent Germany an ultimatum giving it until midnight to withdraw its troops. Germany balked, chiding Britain for risking friendship and war over a "scrap of paper" — the 1839 treaty that guaranteed Belgian neutrality, signed by five major powers, England, France, Russia, Prussia, and Austria.

Midnight came. The ultimatum expired. Great Britain was at war with Germany. Britain's Secretary for War, Lord Horatio H. Kitchener, feared a long conflict. Said Sir Edward Grey on 3 August 1914, "The lights are going out all over Europe; we shall not see them lit again in our lifetime."[11]

As part of the British Commonwealth, Canada, too, was at war. (News of the outbreak of war had reached Ottawa at 8:45 p.m. on 4 August, and was published in the *Canadian Gazette* (*Extra Edition*) the next day.)

The North Sea Cables

Before sunrise the next morning, 5 August, a ship plied the dark waters of the North Sea, apparently fishing just off the coast near the German/Holland border. But it was not a fishing trawler. It was the British cable ship *Telconia*, systematically dropping grappling irons into the deep, then scooping up and severing communication cables. The work was thorough. The *Telconia* located and cut all five of the German lines that ran through the English Channel to France, Spain, North Africa, and the United States.

Though not immediately obvious, the *Telconia*'s mission would have profound consequences. Germany would now have to rely on its powerful wireless station at Nauen, near Berlin, for communication with the Americas. Because wireless communication could be intercepted by the enemy, Germany would have to develop complicated ciphers and codes for security. Could they?

Only time would tell. England immediately began to set up hundreds of new listening posts all along her coastline.

NOTES

1. Newfoundland was not yet a Canadian province, but a colony of Britain. Its regiment, on the small steamer SS *Florizel*, would meet and sail with the Canadian convoy as well as another ship carrying the (British) 2nd Battalion of the Lincolnshire Regiment. Still another ship, the *Manhattan*, carrying miscellaneous "leftover" cargo including 90 motor vehicles and 863 horses, would sail independently on 5 October.

2. Countless books are available for further insights into the causes of the First World War. Among them are Winston Churchill, *The World Crisis*, vol. 1 (London: Thornton Butterworth, 1928); S. S. McClure, *Obstacles to Peace* (Houghton Mifflin Co., 1917); Barbara Tuchman, *The Guns of August* (New York: Ballantine Books, 1962), and *The Proud Tower: A Portrait of the World Before the War 1890-1914* (New York: The MacMillan Co., 1966); A. J. P. Taylor, *The First World War: An Illustrated History* (Harmondsworth, England: Penguin Books, Ltd.,1963). Causes frequently cited include the population explosion, new doctrines, new technology and industrialization, more sophisticated weaponry, class antagonism, rising nationalism and militarism, and, of course, extraordinary miscalculations on the part of many. Taylor is among those who claim that statesmen miscalculated, and "great armies, accumulated to provide security and preserve the peace, carried the nations to war by their own weight" (p. 16).

3. John Laffin, *Jackboot: A History of the German Soldier 1713-1945* (New York: Barnes & Noble Books, 1964), 101.

4. *Ibid.*,100.

5. *Ibid.*, 107.

6. *Ibid.*, 113.

7. General Friedrich von Bernhardi, *Germany and the Next War* (London: E. Arnold, 1914).

8. Quoted in McClure, *Obstacles to Peace*, 298.

9. S. L. A. Marshall further notes that by the age of 33, he had shot his thousandth stag, and by age 46, five thousand. He, indeed, was not a moderate man. *World War I* (Boston: Houghton Mifflin Co., 1992), 8.

10. In one of the countless tragic ironies of the war, the German Kaiser wrote in the margin of the Serbian response "every reason for war drops away . . . . On the strength of this I should never have ordered mobilization." The bitter irony is that his words remained secret until after the war. Austria went to war with Serbia about an hour after the Kaiser had written these words. B. H. Liddell Hart, *History of the First World War* (London: Macmillan Publishers, 1997), 20; originally published as *The Real War, 1914-1918* (Boston: Little, Brown and Co., 1930).

11. Sir Edward Grey spoke these words as he stood at the window of his room in the London Foreign Office, as lamplighters were turning on the lights in St. James Park.

They can be completely ignored so far as concerns any European theatre of war.
— Friedrich von Bernhardi,
speaking of Canadians in 1911

Chapter 2

Canada's Military Preparedness

THE OUTBREAK OF hostilities in far-off lands, and growing outrage at Germany's violation of neutral Belgian territory provoked a wave of loyal demonstrations from British Columbia in the west to the island province of Prince Edward Island in the east.[1] (Though not yet a province of Canada, Newfoundland would respond with equal ardor and loyalty.) In Toronto, Vancouver, and Winnipeg, people took to the streets to wave flags and demonstrate unanimity of purpose. In Montreal, Quebec, people sang "La Marseillaise" and "Rule Britannia." Canada seemed of one mind and heart.

But what could the youthful nation of fewer than eight million people contribute to the cause? Though geographically a large nation — second only to Russia in land mass — Canada had little, it seemed, to offer the mother country.

She had no air force; indeed air power was still in its infancy in all nations.

She did have a navy of sorts, if one can call two old training cruisers, and 393 officers and ratings a navy. On the west coast sat the 3,600-ton HMCS *Rainbow* (commissioned in 1891) which had not raised steam since March 1913. About 4,000 miles away on the east coast was the HMCS *Niobe*, of 1897 vintage. *Niobe* had been stranded on Cape Sable in July 1911, and had not been to sea since. However, in an interesting turn of events and rare burst of speed, between 29 July and 5 August, Canada purchased two submarines, with the imaginative names *C.C.1* and *C.C.2*, for their resemblance to the Royal Navy's "C" class of submarines. The subs had actually been built in Seattle, Washington, for Chile, but now would be based at Esquimalt, British Columbia, for patrol duty on the Pacific coast. Such was the Canadian navy.

And did Canada have an army?

Canada, never a military nation, had a very small Permanent Force. Though 5,000 troops had been authorized by Parliament in the Spring of 1914, the country had a force of only 3,110 (including all ranks) and 684 horses. However, she had a Non-Permanent Active Militia (NPAM), consisting of 77,323 citizen soldiers (and 17,410 horses) who trained part-time for military service should the need arise. But the militia had been badly criticized as "unsatisfactory in the extreme." Nor were significant armaments on hand.

All in all, therefore, Canada's army was not a force to be feared. Even Germany scoffed. Canadians, predicted Prussian General Friedrich von Bernhardi in his 1911 book, *Germany and the Next War*, "can be completely ignored so far as concerns any European theatre of war."

But Canada did have someone who was ready, willing, and able — at least in his own view — to pull the army together and whip it into shape: the irascible, bombastic, often insensitive, Colonel Sam Hughes. There were some who thought him eccentric, if not mad. To others, he was "a charming braggart, with just a hint of mental imbalance."[2] Whatever the case, Colonel Sam's ego was simply monumental. In his own mind, he was incapable of making an error. (In one instance, Hughes addressed a Lieutenant as Captain. When the error was pointed out, Hughes promoted the Lieutenant on the spot, rather than appear wrong.[3])

To his credit, however, Sam Hughes accomplished what probably few others could. In spite of his infuriating cockiness, it was nonetheless he who had had the foresight in 1912 to push for the acquisition of several thousand acres of land at Valcartier, Quebec. The site had considerable value because it was located less than 20 miles northwest of the St. Lawrence River port of Quebec City. Valcartier would serve as an ideal training ground.

Colonel Sam was in his glory as he personally oversaw the transformation of the swamp and bush land into a humming military training camp of more than 12,000 acres. By 10 August, only six days after Canada went to war, firing ranges and waterworks were being constructed. Hughes later reported that by the 20th of the month, 1,500 targets were in place and 12 miles of water mains had been laid. Additionally,

> Army Service Corps and Ordnance buildings were constructed, railway sidings laid in, fences removed, crops harvested, ground cleared, streets made, upwards of 200 baths for the men put in, water chlorinated, electric lights and telephones installed . . . and 35,000 men got under canvas in less than three weeks from the acceptance of the call.[4]

Thanks to Colonel Sam's contempt for bureaucracy, and his insistence on doing things his own way, initial recruitment and mobilization instructions were frequently confusing, cumbersome, and sometimes contradictory. Ultimately, however, most volunteers joined through existing militia units in the manner prescribed before the war.

While troops of the first contingent (authorized at a strength of 25,000 men) were being recruited, Britain accepted an offer of four more from various parts of Canada, though at a strength of 1,000 men each. However, three of the proposed forces (from New Brunswick, Manitoba, and Calgary) found themselves financially unable to comply. Yet one offer held. Captain A. Hamilton Gault, a Montreal millionaire, harking back to earlier times when wealthy patriots sometimes rallied to the cause by funding regiments, offered $100,000 toward the cost of raising a battalion. The remarkable battalion, the Princess Patricia's Canadian Light Infantry (PPCLI), was ready to sail within three weeks of its date of authorization. (It actually crossed the Atlantic with the First Contingent in October, landed in France in December 1914, and entered the line on the night of 6-7 January 1915.)

Though Canada was destined to play a significant role in the faraway conflict, one would not have predicted it from the ways things began during the first chaotic weeks of mobilization. Perhaps the confusion was not surprising given the youthful state of the nation, the character and culture of the young volunteers pouring off troop trains into Quebec, and the speed with which the Canadian Expeditionary Force (CEF) had to be clothed, trained, and equipped.

Unlike Germany, which was also a young nation (and which, it will be recalled, had a standing army of more than 800,000 men by August 1914), Canada was fairly unsophisticated, unmilitaristic, and without imperialistic ambitions. Its economy in the summer of 1914 was ailing, following the worldwide depression of the previous year. Unemployment was high. And, unlike Germany, Canada hadn't been preparing for war for years. Who would train the soldiers? (Because Canada had only 12 Staff College-trained officers at war's outbreak in 1914, it even had to import several from the United Kingdom to serve as Divisional Staff Officers.) Where would matériel come from on such short notice? Though in the peacetime militia, men had to provide their own boots, shirts, and under-clothing,[5] the immediate equipping of thousands of troops for war was unprecedented and could be a staggering undertaking.

And staggering it was. Nothing seemed to go well in the early days.

One of the most critical decisions to be made concerned the choice of the all-important rifle. The decision, heavily influenced by the opinionated Colonel Sam, was soon made. Canadian soldiers would shoulder the heavy Ross rifle to England and then into battle in France. It was a fateful choice that would haunt the common soldier later.

How did it happen?

Until 1900, Canada had purchased what few rifles she needed from England. However, when England couldn't produce 15,000 of the popular .303-inch Lee-Enfield rifles in 1900, the Canadian government decided to manufacture its own.

The excellent Lee-Enfield could have been produced in Canada, but politics — and craftiness — intervened. In an effort to determine the best rifle for Canadian troops, tests in dusty field conditions were arranged in 1901 to compare the Lee-Enfield with the cheaper, lighter .303-caliber Ross rifle, the latter a creation of Sir Charles Ross, a Scottish aristocrat. The Ross rifle was excellent as a target weapon, but its dependability in less than ideal conditions was questionable. Incredibly, during the tests, Ross was observed dabbing oil into the competitor's rifle, to gum it up and give his own creation the edge. In spite of his deceitful action, the Lee-Enfield outperformed the Ross, which misfired and jammed repeatedly.

Ross argued persuasively, however, making various excuses for his rifle. Incredibly, his rifle was chosen. Politics had won the day, and Ross then proceeded to build a factory, which opened in 1903 in Quebec City.[6]

Complaints followed soon after, first in 1906 by the Royal North West Mounted Police using the Mark I version of the Ross rifle, and subsequently by the Militia trying to use the Mark I and the later redesigned Mark II version. The latter eventually incorporated more than 80 design changes before it was replaced — by the Mark III. Ironically, the new Mark III was heavier, longer, and more expensive, than the Lee-Enfield, though its original lighter weight, shorter length, and cheaper cost had been major factors in its selection over its competitor.

Worse yet, the Mark III still had the same tragic flaws! It jammed and misfired so much that jokes circulated saying it killed or harmed as many behind it as in front of it. But Colonel Sam still stubbornly endorsed it, saying that it was "the most perfect military rifle . . . in the world today." On 10 August 1914, 30,000 Mark IIIs were ordered for Canada's soldiers. The wretched Ross rifle was merely one of many military equipment difficulties that followed with frustrating frequency.

In addition to rifles, more than 8,000 horses had to be purchased, and somehow they were found locally at an average cost of $172.45. At least 480, however, were deemed unsuitable or unfit and sold in Quebec for little more than $50 each.

Then came the wagon issue. When nearly 1,000 farm wagons and other horse-drawn vehicles were needed — and needed quickly — eight different kinds or makes were purchased. But the lack of standardization would generate countless parts, maintenance, and repair problems later. Similarly, motor trucks were of several different makes, hampering serviceability.

Poor equipment decisions abounded. One Hughes favorite was the "MacAdam" shovel, 25,000 of which were purchased from the United States at $1.35 each. No ordinary shovel this! It was also an entrenching and defensive (*i.e.*, shielding) tool. With its thick blade, it was said to be capable of stopping a bullet at 300 yards when stuck into the ground by its folding handle. But it, too, was a flop! Though taken to England and later to France, the shovels were found almost useless and were sold as scrap metal for $1,400.

Nor did equipment problems end there. The boots supplied to the new recruits were of inferior quality and couldn't stand up to the harsh conditions of rain and mud. Even their stitches rotted. The footwear had to be replaced.

Inferior weapons, unstandardized equipment, and poor quality supplies were to burden the new, inexperienced soldiers and haunt them in the months ahead in the battlefields of Flanders. But that was yet to come. For now, by the thousands, from every corner of the Dominion, the young volunteers full of enthusiasm and faith in their cause, poured into Valcartier on troop train after troop train.

NOTES

1. For a delightful insight into life on the home front during the First World War, see L. M. Montgomery, *Rilla of Ingleside* (Toronto: Seal Books, 1992).
2. Desmond Morton and J. L. Granatstein, *Marching to Armageddon: Canadians and the Great War 1918-1919* (Toronto: Lester and Orpen Dennys, 1989), 8.
3. Recounted in Pierre Berton, *Vimy* (Markham, Ontario: Penguin Books Canada Ltd., 1987), 40.
4. From Hughes's report in the House of Commons debates of 23 January 1916. Colonel G. W. L. Nicholson, C.D., *Canadian Expeditionary Force 1914-1919: Official History of the Canadian Army in the First World War* (Ottawa: Queen's Printer, 1964) 21.
5. *Ibid.*, 25.
6. Ross had at least one characteristic in common with Archduke Ferdinand. He bragged that he shot his first stag at the age of 12, and that he once bagged 25 in one morning in 1910.

*Canada would send across the ocean
"an army greater than Napoleon ever
commanded on any battlefield."*
— Francis Whiting Halsey, *The Literary
Digest History of the World War*, Vol. 3

Chapter 3

Chaos in Quebec

*R*OBERT JAMES KENNEDY of Orleans, Ontario, was one of the thousands of young farm boys who found themselves in the strange new world of Valcartier on the east bank of the Jacques Cartier River in the hot, humid days of August 1914. At age 22, and already in the Reserves with the Governor General's Foot Guards (GGFG), he was not quite sure that he wanted to follow his father's example and make farming his life work. He was, in fact, taking courses in telegraphy in nearby Ottawa, when he, like thousands others, became increasingly concerned about events in faraway Europe. Should he volunteer?

It didn't take long to make a decision. On Saturday, 8 August, just four days after Canada joined the war against Germany, while working in the fields with his younger brother Thurlow, Robert stuck his pitchfork into the ground and declared, "I'm going to war." He soberly shook hands with his brother, (who would follow him to France not long after), then cycled ten miles into Ottawa to enlist. He

18

DISTANT THUNDER

was signed up on the spot, then sent back home to await further orders. Shortly after, he wrote (a postcard, with a one-cent stamp bearing the likeness of King George V) to his sweetheart, Eva Farmer, who was visiting family friends in Haileybury, Ontario:

> **10 August 1914**
> **Keep a brave heart for my sake. I wanted to ask you if I should go, but felt that it was a question I had to decide for myself. It was the thought of you that made it difficult, but mother has other children to comfort her if anything should happen to me.**
>
> **I have just come back from the drill hall. The 43rds are to leave on Wednesday, and we (the GGFG) will not leave until Saturday at least. Don't be discouraged. From what I've been told, the Canadians will be used as garrisons and there will be little danger. Please look on the bright side.**

Two weeks later, on 22 August, the orders came at 1:40 in the afternoon. Kennedy was to be in Ottawa at 3:00 p.m! He had already done a good day's work, having milked the cows, separated the milk, and finished up a host of farm chores. Unfortunately, he would not have a chance to say goodbye to his sweetheart, Eva. But everybody said that the war would be short, and he would surely see her by Christmas. Four months or so should not be too catastrophic.

In Ottawa, he turned in his tunic, belt, and bearskin of the Reserve Militia, received a haversack and water bottle, and marched with other Ottawa Valley boys to the Grand Trunk Station. His father caught up to him there, handed him a lunch, then watched with a mixture of pride and concern until the train pulled away for Valcartier at 5:15.

Army life began immediately. He was put on picket (guard) duty on the train from 6:00 p.m. until 9:00 p.m., after which he found a vacant coach seat for the night. The next morning at 7:40, the train huffed its way into Valcartier under cloudy skies. The new soldiers were immediately marched to the sprawling military camp, reaching it by 8:15. As rain fell, in a foretaste of things to come, the men were appointed to tents — 14 men to each. Blankets and oilcloths were issued. With a little lump in his stomach, Kennedy wrote two letters: one to his parents whom he had left just the day before, and one, of course, to Eva. Thus ended his first day in boot camp.

Routine was established quickly. On 24 August, soldiers were routed at 5:30 a.m. and assigned a 25-minute drill in a strong northwest wind before breakfast. After breakfast there was parade duty and more drill until dinner at 1:00 p.m. Then it was more drill until 5:00 p.m.

One day followed another in predictable order — a 25-minute exercise before breakfast, parades to inspection, and picking up supplies. Finally, in the late evening or on Sundays, there was time to write home or update one's diary.

Although not a prolific writer, Kennedy recorded his thoughts faithfully.

> **August 25: Up at 5:15 and helped pioneers[1] clean up. Bright and clear with west wind. Had a 25-minute drill, breakfast at 6:30. Got towel, soap and candle, and fell in at 7:45 for fatigue[2] party to put up tents. Worked until 11:30 a.m. and marched in for dinner at 12. Fell in at 1 p.m., and put up tents until 4 p.m. then marched back and dismissed. Got caps and trousers, overcoat and boots. Tea at 5 p.m. Gathered up camp outfit and fell in at 6 and marched to new tents.**

An excerpt from a letter Kennedy wrote from Valcartier, Quebec, 28 August 1914 reads:

> **We don't get much time for writing letters here. When we're not drilling, we are generally lined up getting some part of our uniforms. When we are served with all our clothes and boots it's quite a large undertaking and can't be done in an hour or so, especially when one has to go back several times to change things that don't fit.**
>
> **Every man has to wash his own knife and fork and mess tin, and it isn't very easy especially when we are served meat (which makes the tins greasy). We have to scour them thoroughly with sand, and then wash them with water. I don't mind it in the least, and have never felt better.**
>
> **Most of the fellows are from offices and are not used to the hot sun. They are terribly sunburnt now.**

We had a heavy frost on Tuesday night. Yesterday afternoon all of 1st Battalion were marched to the river to swim. The water was pretty cold, but I was glad for the dip.

Last night there was a woman arrested in camp in an officer's uniform. I have no idea what she was doing, or what became of her. I know I could have arrested her (I had the opportunity) but I simply couldn't arrest a lady. (I have too much respect for a woman to do anything that would place her in an embarrassing position.) She was arrested shortly afterwards.

Kennedy's entry for 30 August noted that the Protestant church parade was canceled because of rain, and that he cleaned his rifle, before trying to look up friends and relatives in nearby batteries. But it was in his letters to his beloved Eva that he was most expressive. From one dated 30 August 1914:

I'm quite sure this war will not last long, but still I'm sure I will be in Europe inside two months, and then we'll be further apart than ever! But a few miles between us won't separate our hearts. . . .

And so you think it's funny that I enlisted! Somehow I couldn't do anything else. I didn't have to do it, but to me it seemed to be my duty. If I had to do it over again, I would do the same thing.

I got my rifle yesterday, a Mark III Ross rifle. We were told when we were given them, to get married to the numbers (every rifle has a number stamped on it) — meaning that they were ours to keep during the war. You can be sure I'll take good care of it.

We were at the ranges yesterday afternoon even though it was raining. I did pretty well, but should have done better.

By September, the troops were being vaccinated. But drill and rifle practice dominated every day. Some days began as early as 4:30 a.m., and lasted until 9:30 at night, though most were a bit shorter. On 3 September, the young Kennedy was transferred to the 2nd Battalion, but routine was strikingly similar: Drill. Eat. Fall in. Battalion drill. Fatigue party to dig ditches. Drill. Fatigue party to water horses. Supper. Rifle practice.

Even the weekends provided no relief. There was more rifle practice at the ranges, cleaning up the lines, more marching, and parade reviews.

From a 6 September 1914 letter to Eva:

> **It's after 9 p.m., and all the rest of the lads in this tent are asleep. I wonder what you have been doing this Sabbath Day your first Sunday at home for nearly four months. I suppose you will again be the dear organist of St. Mark's Church.**
>
> **We had service at 9 this morning, and this afternoon the Duke of Connaught was down to inspect the troops. I suppose you will read about it in the newspaper. [*The Duke of Connaught was Prince Arthur, the youngest son of Queen Victoria, who was serving as Governor General of Canada.*] Must close now as the light must go out in a few minutes.**

Conditions sometimes seemed to border on the primitive. In his diary of 7-9 September 1914 Kennedy wrote:

> **Had two hours' drill and got some dry wood out of a barn, and dried my serge. We had battalion drill for a while, but with a thunder shower coming up, we beat it back to camp. Captain De Ville tipped the cook and we had some good hot soup. He is very good to us.**
>
> **September 8: Threatened to rain so we had no parade. Washed and mended some clothes. Got two weeks' pay — $14.00. After dinner we had more drill and then were marched to a shed near railroad where we exchanged our rifles.**
>
> **September 9: Fell in at 6:45 and went to rifle ranges. Made 30 out of 50, and 14 out of 25 at rapid firing. We fell in again at 2:45 and drilled till 4:30. Col. Sam Hughes was down to see us. Razors were issued tonight. Got a pretty good one, I think.**

From a letter to Eva of September 13:

> **We get pretty good board here — no pies or cakes, but the meat is always fresh and the bread good. One of the GGFGs came around the other evening collecting a small fee (25 cents) from each soldier to buy extra rations, so I believe we are to have pudding and pies at dinner today.**

Then, in a somewhat prophetic note, he wrote to Eva two days later:

> **The allies seem to be doing well lately but will have a hard nut to crack if the Germans entrench themselves.**

Life at Valcartier for the rest of September took on a new urgency as preparations increased for the move overseas. Kennedy's diary, at first maintained regularly, was now sometimes neglected for days, and then reconstructed later. Because there was no calendar immediately available to the troops, it was particularly difficult to figure out the date. On one page of his notebook, he had written consecutive Mondays, September 14th, 21st, 28th, and October 1st to keep track.

Young Kennedy also had concerns other than the daily drill routines and rifle practice. On Sunday, 20 September, he learned that, because his company had 160 men when only 125 were needed, he might be transferred to a Reserve unit and left behind. Upset, he went to the Ammunition Column of the 1st Artillery Brigade to see if there were any vacancies. Yes, they could use him — but there was a glitch. Someone had neglected to give him the necessary transfer papers. On Monday, he was still on his old company's strength. "Nothing doing," he thought. Showing some determination he didn't know he had, he insisted on having a transfer and on the same day, 21 September, officially became a member of the 1st Brigade's Ammunition Column. He would not be left behind!

Kennedy had reason to be concerned about his future service. The authorized strength of the CEF was 25,000. However, more than 32,000 had volunteered for service and reached Valcartier. About 6,000 were, at this point, likely to be sent back home. Eventually, 619,636 men and women would serve in the Canadian forces in the war, of whom 66,655 would perish, and another 172,950 would be wounded.

Kennedy's elation was heightened when he heard that they would be leaving for Quebec City the next day. He and his friends spent half the night feverishly emptying the ammunition wagons. But there was far too much to be done and word soon spread among the troops that there would be at least a 24-hour delay. Personal belongings had to be packed. Medical exams, part of the attestation process, had to be completed prior to embarkation. With the delay came a reversal of duties. Now they had to load the ammunition wagons and take the ammunition to the storehouse. At least with the delay, he could return to his old "C" Company and pick up his mail and pay. But alas, there was nothing for him, so with disappointment in his step he returned to his tent and went to bed.

Urgency filled the air the next day. First, Kennedy was given a team of horses. Then came a final physical examination to ensure that he was "fit for the Canadian Over-Seas Expeditionary Force." Young Kennedy couldn't know that the young doctor who checked him over would later become immortalized by his poem "In Flanders Fields" — Major John McCrae of Guelph, Ontario. Major McCrae "found no causes for rejection" in young Kennedy and signed the Certificate of Medical Examination.

Finally, on 23 September came the long-awaited order, though not until the end of the day. At 9 p.m., the soldiers were told to harness the horses. But as luck would have it, only part of the column moved off for Quebec. The remainder, including Kennedy, were held. Off came the harnesses, and once again the troops began the waiting game. But not for long. At about three o'clock the next morning, he was awakened and assigned to picket duty. Surely it meant that they would soon be leaving for Europe. The hours dragged by. Finally at 2:30 in the afternoon, troops were told once more to prepare for departure.

In spite of a heavy downpour, the troops hitched up and at 5 p.m. set out for Quebec City, some 16 miles distant. They plodded all night in the driving rain, but finally rode into Quebec City 14 hours later, on Friday, 25 September, at 7 a.m. They were thoroughly drenched and had no dry clothes to put on. And in some inevitable mixup, no provisions had been made either for supper or breakfast. They went without.

The men had little time to worry about such things, however, as they immediately were to board the RMS *Saxonia* with their horses. With other soldiers, Kennedy took his baggage and horses onto the ship. But now there seemed to be another problem. Apparently there were 47 horses too many on board! Some had to be taken off. And as if that weren't bad enough, young Kennedy had been unable to get a card for Eva's 20th birthday that day. He had had a pass to go to Quebec City from Valcartier, but had not been allowed to use it, because of the rush to leave.

Would anything go right for him?

Things settled down a bit on the ship the next day, but the overcrowding problem wouldn't go away, and by Sunday, the 27th, a number of troops, including Kennedy, and the excess 47 horses, were assigned to another ship.[3] Trying to hide their disappointment, they disembarked, watched the *Saxonia* pull out without them, and trudged to the *Manitou*, which they boarded with their horses. Confusion was evident there too, but finally on Monday the *Manitou* pulled away from the wharf and anchored out in the river. They weren't moving very fast, but at least they were on their way.

Kennedy explained in a 28 September letter to Eva:

> **Fatigue parties are loading the boats now, as quickly as they can. They start at about 5:30 in the morning and work until about 11 at night. The *Saxonia* pulled out from the wharf yesterday at noon, and is out in the middle of the river now awaiting the rest of the ships. I'm one of a party that was picked to go on a different ship with horses that couldn't get on the *Saxonia*. I would like to have stayed on the *Saxonia* since the Farmer boys, Tom Melvin, Martin Burns and George Muggleton are all on that boat. We were then told we would sail on the *Mount Royal*, but then were told yesterday to put our horses on the *Manitou*. We had just got them on for about an hour when we were told to take them off again. There is a great deal of bungling.**

Above and below: Postcards Robert Kennedy sent home to his sweetheart, Eva Farmer, in Ontario, Canada, in September and October 1914, from Valcartier.

The confusion young Kennedy experienced was widespread. And there was good reason for it, dating back to a decision that had been made in Valcartier in early September. At that time the Prime Minister and other members of the Cabinet decided to send *all* 31,200 eligible men overseas, an increase of more than 6,000 over the original offer of 25,000. That meant the immediate locating and leasing (and painting) of several more ships in addition to the 25 already chartered.

Then in the haste to load vessels quickly, confusion piled on confusion. Some vessels had non-military freight already on board, such as a large gift shipment of flour from Canada to England. In some cases, men hauled gun carriages and limbers (a two-wheeled, horse-drawn vehicle used to tow a field gun) onto the ships, but overlooked taking off the wheels to conserve precious space. More often than not, men were separated not only from their own baggage, but also from their horses and vehicles. Some ships departed without a full load and had to take on water ballast.

Another serious problem arose when it was discovered that motor trucks for the Supply Column and Ammunition Parks would not fit through the hatchways of the ships. Another vessel, the *Manhattan,* had to be chartered from New York.

Nonetheless, in spite of the chaos, 30 loaded transport ships had moved out into the St. Lawrence River by nightfall on the first of October. Only the *Manhattan* remained, still taking on what couldn't be accommodated on the other ships, including 90 motor vehicles and 863 horses.

By 2 October, the *Manitou* was one of 30 vessels in Gaspé Bay. On board were more than 31,000 Canadians — among them, Robert James Kennedy.

The convoy, with infantry, cavalry, signalers, engineers, medical officers, ammunition columns, and wagons, among other things, finally sailed at 3 p.m. on Saturday, the third day of October, exactly two months to the day after Germany had declared war on France.

Almost overlooked because of the rapidity of events in Europe was a small footnote in Canadian history. In 1914 there were serious concerns regarding the German Secret Service in Canada. Military historian A. Fortescue Duguid notes that the German Secret Service tried to terrify Canadians so that most of the Expeditionary Force would be retained in Canada for defense purposes. Thus, there were rumors of raids through Maine and Vermont into eastern Canada, and a plan to invade British Columbia with German cruisers in 1914. Some attempts at disruption were, indeed, made.

On 8 August 1914, agents tried to destroy the Montreal Light, Heat, and Power works. A German agent was caught trying to blow up the central span of the Canadian Pacific Railway bridge at Vanceboro, Maine. Another German agent, later caught, tried to blow up armories at Windsor. Yet another agent who said he planned to invade Canada with 150,000 German reservists, was arrested on other charges in the United States.

Perhaps the most telling indication of German intentions regarding the United States and Canada was revealed in a document from none other than General Helmuth von Moltke himself, Chief of the General Staff of the Field Army, to the Foreign Office on 5 August 1914. It reads in part:

> The feeling in America is friendly to Germany. American public opinion is indignant at the shameful manner in which we have been treated. Every effort must be made to take advantage of this feeling. Important personalities in the German colony must be urged to influence the press still more in our favor. **Perhaps the United States can be persuaded to undertake a naval war against England, in return for which Canada beckons to them as the prize of victory.**[4] [*Emphasis added.*]

NOTES

1. Pioneer comes from the French *pionnier,* or foot soldier, a member of a miliary unit (usually of construction engineers) who precedes the Regular troops to prepare roads, bridges, etc.
2. Fatigue duty is a soldier's non-military duty such as barrack cleaning. In the largely unmechanized era of World War I, considerable manual labor was necessary for digging, carrying, and other drudgery.
3. Nicholson notes that part of the unnecessary congestion was caused by the failure of the 1st and 2nd Artillery Brigades to wait as instructed at the Exhibition Grounds until vessel space was available for them. Kennedy's 1st Brigade was part of the problem! Colonel G. W. L. Nicholson, C.D., *Canadian Expeditionary Force 1914-1919: Official History of the Canadian Army in the First World War* (Ottawa: Queen's Printer, 1964) 329-330.
4. Colonel A. Fortescue Duguid, *Official History of the Canadian Forces in the Great War 1914-1918*, Vol. 1 (Ottawa: Minister of National Defence, 1938).

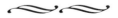

*We have lost the war. It will go on for a
long time but lost it is already.*
— Germany's Crown Prince
after the Battle of the Marne, 1914

Chapter 4

The Western Front

WHILE THOUSANDS OF citizen soldiers from all corners of Canada were tumbling off trains at Valcartier to begin their military training, hundreds of thousands of troops were already at war on the other side of the Atlantic. Well-trained soldiers were carrying out well-laid plans.

Prince Otto von Bismarck, of course, was gone from the scene in Germany, and whereas he had cautioned against further expansion of the country's geographical borders, others had not been of the same mind. One such person who left a far-reaching legacy was Alfred von Schlieffen, Chief of the German General Staff from 1891 to 1905. In a master plan that bore his name, he envisioned a massive German assault that would sweep southwards through Belgium and Holland (though Holland was later dropped) into the north of France, and then curve eastward, like a fish hook, into Paris.[1] Paris, he rationalized, and indeed France, could be taken within six weeks — a mere 42 days! The invasion would have to go through Belgium because the most obvious choice — the French-German border —

was too heavily defended by powerful and well-sited fortifications. A quick victory there was improbable!

Why was such speed necessary? By conquering France quickly, Germany could avoid the deadly horror of conducting a war on two opposite fronts — France on the west, and Russia, with her countless troops and extraordinary land mass, on the east. France would have to be annihilated quickly.

Von Schlieffen largely discounted England. Not only was her monarch related to Germany's, but she had no continental army. Furthermore, Germany's navy was reaching parity with England's.

On paper and in cold theory, his plan seemed flawless. Would it work in the heat of reality?

The aging von Schlieffen had been completely confident. After all, a similar plan had worked beautifully for the great Hannibal at the Battle of Cannae in 216 B.C. Despite being vastly outnumbered by the Romans, Hannibal cunningly allowed his center to be pushed back, like a fist pushed into and swallowed up by a pillow. However, he then outflanked the Romans, attacking them from the sides and rear, losing fewer than 6,000 men to the Roman loss of 50,000.

Von Schlieffen would replicate Hannibal's glorious victory. Doting on this battle, he warned only that the right wing of the southward thrust be kept strong to make the "double envelopment" plan work. It would be another Cannae![2]

Von Schlieffen, however, died in 1913, before the war began. His successor, General Helmuth von Moltke (the Younger) took up the mantle, and the plan — or most of it.[3] And therein lay a decision that is argued about to this day. Von Schlieffen had planned to use more than seven-eighths of the entire German army on the destruction of the French. But he was dead, and his successors cut back on his plans, moving some of the troops from the western frontier to the east. Would it make a difference?

In the early days of August 1914, the great southward sweep into France got underway with the powerful armed fist of five well-trained armies, three-quarters of the entire German strength. The mobilization was extraordinary in detail and precision.[4] And, as Germany had hoped, indeed anticipated, France's General (later Marshal) Joseph Joffre (following the precepts of his country's Plan XVII, which called for a massive offensive along the French/German border) fell right into German plans.

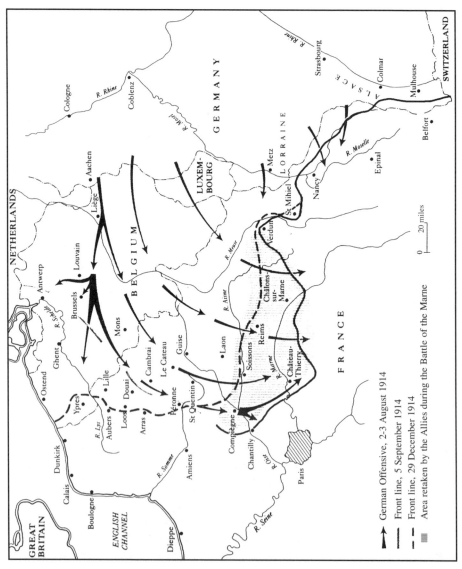

The Western Front, 1914. Adapted from Colonel G. W. L. Nicholson, C.D., *Canadian Expeditionary Force 1914-1919: Official History of the Canadian Army in the First World War* (Ottawa: Queen's Printer, 1964).

He sent troops eastward, toward the lost provinces of Alsace and Lorraine.[5] Perhaps von Moltke was right!

The German invasion of Belgium was a masterpiece of mobilization planning. Once the mobilization order had been issued, "the whole vast machinery for calling up, equipping, and transporting two million men began turning automatically." Men from every walk of life had reported to their appropriate units and "according to prepared railway timetables" moved to the frontier, "where they would be formed into divisions, divisions into corps, and corps into armies ready to advance and fight." All was precision; "everything was to move at fixed times according to a schedule precise down to the number of train axles that would pass over a given bridge within a given time."[6]

With more than a million men now assembled along the Belgian and French borders, it should be a pushover. With the German cavalry in the vanguard, their 12-foot lances glinting in the sun, the well-trained soldiers crossed the Belgium border. The Schlieffen Plan was now in motion, and once begun, plunged ahead almost automatically like a bus whose driver who had died at the wheel but still had his foot on the gas pedal.

As some invading troops rushed ahead to tear down Belgian flags and lay telephone wires, others ran to key points to keep defenders from blowing up bridges or railway tunnels. German trains, loaded with troops, rolled in with split-second regularity.

The German plan to sweep into France via Belgium had, however, one significant roadblock in the way — the city of Liége surrounded by its ring of 12 independent fortresses.

The Germans, with an army ten times the size of Belgium's, anticipated little resistance; its Second Army marched confidently toward Liége. True to their expectations, on the first day several small villages were taken. But an unwelcome surprise awaited the invaders. They were astonished to find that ordinary citizens had already cut telephone and telegraph lines. Bridges to the city had been destroyed. The feisty Belgians, led by King Albert himself as the Commander-in-Chief of the Belgium army, were resisting! Some of the snipers were civilians, of all things!

And so the atrocities began. Germans warned that ten civilians would die for every German soldier killed. Civilians — men, women, and children — were shot. Houses and barns were sacked and villages burned. And in one frightful act of barbarism, German soldiers heavily shelled the medieval town of Louvain and deliberately, proudly, sacked its university's library and, for good measure, torched irreplaceable ancient manuscripts. The civilized world was stunned by the callousness. Still the Belgians fought. They would not be cowed!

But the Germans had a new weapon to try out, and by 12 August, the first glimpses of the new monster were seen. It was the 42cm Krupp howitzer, more commonly known as "Big Bertha" (named after Krupp's wife). The gun was so heavy that 36 horses were needed to pull it, and so huge that to be moved elsewhere, it had to be dismantled and then reassembled by crane. On 12 August, the howitzer's first shell weighing 1,800 pounds was fired at 6:30 p.m. upon Fort Pontisse; the fort fell the next day. One by one, the other forts collapsed.

By 16 August, 11 of the 12 fortresses around Liége had fallen, and Germany took the city. On the same day, Germany's First Army on the extreme right entered Brussels, and began the relentless push southwards toward France. On the outer (and therefore longest) edge of the German arc, soldiers would have to cover more than 20 miles a day. No matter — they were on the way to a quick and glorious victory. Liége and the small Belgian army had bravely held up the German army only briefly. To the rest of the world, however, they had set an extraordinary example. On August 7, the French government, recognizing Belgium's heroic stand, conferred the Grand Cross of the Legion of Honor upon Liége, and the Military Medal upon King Albert.

Meanwhile in England, the War Council in London decided on 5 August to send an expeditionary force of four divisions, plus cavalry, to support France in its hour of need. Remarkably, by the next day, nearly 100,000 troops and 30,000 horses were beginning to assemble at Southampton and Portsmouth. By 9 August, embarkation got underway with transport vessels leaving the docks every ten minutes for the nighttime crossing to France. Security was so complete that when the British landed in France, the Germans were totally unaware of it.

Britain's forces of 100,000 men were dwarfed by Germany's two million soldiers, and France's one million men. But it was just the beginning.

War was raging in places other than the Western Front, of course. In what is now Grunwald, Poland, Russian General Alexander Samsonov's

Second Army attacked East Prussia on 17 August, but Germany's Field Marshal Paul von Hindenberg was waiting. With 100,000 troops, the Germans surrounded and destroyed the poorly trained, poorly equipped, half-starved Russian infantry, taking approximately 90,000 prisoners (including 13 Generals) and 500 guns. Only 60,000 weary troops managed to return to Russia. The Battle of Tannenberg (26-30 August 1914) was one of the greatest German victories of the war. The defeated Samsonov later walked into the woods and shot himself.

The Battle of Mons

The brief Battle of Mons (23-24 August) in Belgium does not rate much space in most history books. Relatively small by later standards (160,000 German troops versus 35,000 British troops), Mons was hardly decisive in terms of long-range results, though the British and French both had to retreat. But it was noteworthy in that British troops were engaged in a battle in Europe for the first time since Waterloo in 1815 — and it was at Mons that German General Alexander von Kluck would finally realize that the British had arrived.

Von Kluck with his First Army, that all-important force on the right wing, had been charging southwards with gusto, but troops were now tiring after having marched about 150 miles in 11 days. They were approaching the city of Mons just a bit north of the French border. Unknown to von Kluck, the British were nearby.

The British had reached Mons on the night of 22 August, not quite sure where the Germans were. They weren't long in finding out, however. The next day British troops spotted men in field gray uniforms emerging from some nearby woods. They opened fire and the Battle of Mons had begun.

Unlike the exhausted Germans, the British were in relatively good shape. Though its army was small, it was a professional army, with many of the men expert shooters. (Their rapid-fire rifle skills were so extraordinary, in fact, that the Germans thought they were facing machine-gun fire.) Furthermore, in this particular battle, they would have French forces on both their left and right flanks. Perhaps they could outflank and stop the German advance.

But the French troops — supposedly on the British left — never arrived, leaving that flank exposed. Then, the French Fifth Army under

General Charles Lanrezac (who had called on the British for aid in the Mons area) retreated, leaving the British right side also exposed. To complicate matters, communications were poor, and the British General, Horace Smith-Dorrien, still thinking that the French would return, ordered his troops to fight on.

However, with French troops non-existent on either side, and heavily outnumbered by enemy troops, the British were unable to prevent the Germans from breaking through. By midnight of 24 August, the outcome was obvious, and, like the French, the British began to retreat. They had suffered 1,600 casualties.

In the following days, British and French troops continued to retreat southward into France. Bad news mounted, with the fall of Namur, Belgium, once thought impregnable, and the capture of 5,000 French prisoners. The British troops reached Le Cateau in a thunderstorm just after midnight on 26-27 August and, exhausted, made a bivouac in the town. But German troops, again outnumbering the British, were hard on their heels and arrived just after dawn. Though the British fought gamely and inflicted about 9,000 casualties on von Kluck's army, they lost 8,000 of their own. Ultimately they were outgunned and outfought, and were forced to retreat southward toward the Marne River. It was not an auspicious beginning for the island nation.[7]

The Miracle of the Marne

Although the British and French were retreating, they were at least doing so in an orderly manner, no mean feat in a military endeavor, due to the logistical problems involved. On the other hand, the pursuing Germans were almost in disarray. They had just marched for days. Troops were exhausted, some with their uniforms almost in tatters. Some had "nails sticking through the soles of their boots, which were as thin as paper. Some had inflamed heels, soles, and toes, with whole patches of skin rubbed off to the raw flesh."[8] Their 84,000 horses were also tiring and, whether fatigued or robust, needed to be fed, requiring 130 tons of fodder a day. Some dropped in their tracks from sheer exhaustion.[9]

But the Germans were not the only ones to suffer. French soldiers also paid a price in retreat, as did their horses.

> Dead and dying horses that had dropped in their tracks from fatigue, lay in great numbers by the side of the roads. Worse still, horses dying but not yet dead, sometimes struggling a little, a strange appeal in their eyes, looked at the passing columns whose dust covered them, caking their thirsty lips and nostrils.[10]

Additionally, von Kluck's all-important communications were also dangerously disrupted. Von Kluck, caught in a Catch-22 situation of chasing the enemy south so quickly that his army was outrunning its supplies and heavy artillery (with railheads now nearly 100 miles to the rear), decided to stop a mere 25 miles from Paris to rethink his situation. He suspected that the British forces were heading west to the English Channel, and escaping his reach. In a stunning turn of events, he turned east to bypass Paris, instead of trying to capture it.

The British, however, were not heading west, but still retreating southward, reaching the Marne River on 2 September, crossing it the next day.

On 3 September, the old Military Governor of Paris and Commander of the Army in Paris, General Joseph Simon Gallieni (who had been pulled out of retirement less than two weeks before), issued a proclamation noting that the government had left Paris. It was now his mandate to defend the city, and he promised it was a duty "I shall carry out to the end."

On the same day, in boiling heat, von Kluck's exhausted troops reached the Marne, their faces covered with dust. They were in poor shape. Historian B. H. Liddell Hart, quoting a German regimental history, notes that field kitchens had been left behind in the rapid advance. By the time they reached the Marne, they were "dead-beat, when a man went forty-eight hours on one piece of bread — one cup of soup — one cup of coffee — unripe fruit and a raw turnip."[11] But "dead-beat" or not, they had pushed the British and French into retreat.

The German troops may have been weary, but not too weary to leave wanton destruction behind them, defiling everything seen and unseen as they went — "villages were burned, civilians shot, homes looted and torn, horses ridden through rooms, artillery wagons dragged across gardens, latrines dug in the family burial plot of the Poincares at Nubecourt."[12]

By 4 September, one month to the day after the Germans had invaded Belgium, there was triumph in the air. Back in Germany, the Kaiser was euphoric, boastfully noting it was the 35th successful day of the 42 days needed to defeat France. It would indeed be a short war.

But it was not over yet. Joffre, the French Commander, wondered whether to retreat farther, or halt and fight. In an emotional do-or-die appeal, he asked British Commander Sir John French for help. Sir John said he would do all he could. They would hold the line and retreat no farther.

The Allies began their counterattack on 5 September. More than 2 million men (1,275,000 Germans, 1 million Frenchmen, and 125,000 British) began bitter fighting in what became known as the Battle of the Marne. The Germans, still exhausted and disorganized because they had outrun their supply and communication lines, began to retreat. Old Gallieni, who had sworn to carry on to the end, showed inspired leadership. On 6 September, looking for every available soldier and anything with four wheels, he commandeered taxicabs right off the streets of Paris to transport French troops the 60 kilometers (36 miles) to the line. About 600 taxicabs, many making the round trip twice, carried 6,000 men to battle sites.

By 9 September, the tide had turned, and British and French troops (the latter in their spectacular blue coats, red trousers, and red kepi)[13] began to move northwards again — this time pursuing instead of being pursued. Both sides suffered appalling losses. But Paris was saved (and would not be threatened by German troops again until 1940 in another World War).

To this day, some refer to the battle as the "Miracle on the Marne." One historian calls it one of the most decisive battles in history (though it took several years to recognize its significance) because it sealed the fate of the Central Powers.[14] Another historian claims it was an operational defeat of the first magnitude for the Germans because the Schlieffen Plan was the "only recipe for victory." There was no alternate or back-up plan. "The German campaign of 1914 was predicated on a swift and decisive victory in the west by the 40th day of mobilization; when it did not materialize, the great gamble had failed."[15]

Perhaps Winston Churchill gives the best perspective. Churchill thought that the Marne on the whole was "the greatest battle ever fought in the world" and that it decided the fate of the war. Although he pointed out later crises where the tide of war could have changed, it was the Marne that made the initial difference; ". . . never after the Marne had Germany a chance of absolute triumph."[16]

Germany was no longer seen as invincible. Even the formerly confident Kaiser Wilhelm was shaken and depressed over the setback, saying it was "the great turning point" in his life.[17]

There are those, of course, who say the Battle of the Marne was an inconclusive tactical victory. (B. H. Liddell Hart describes it as a psychological rather than physical victory.[18]) But whatever the case, the Germans were halted in their advance southward, and the British and the French began to move northward again. The Schlieffen Plan lay in ruins, and Germany would have to fight on two fronts, the very situation she had planned against for decades.

Although few realized it at the time, the Battle of the Marne also meant that the war would not be over by Christmas, as so many had predicted. The war would not be brief. It — and the mindless, endless slaughter — had only just begun. The war of movement was about to end. Trench warfare was about to begin.

And, incredibly, four years and hundreds of thousands of lives later, in 1918, there would be — in the same place — the Second Battle of the Marne.

NOTES

1. Author Barbara Tuchman notes that at an earlier time, Germany thought it could buy off Belgium's neutrality for two million pounds sterling, possibly paid from France's coffers. Remembering the legacy of Belgium's avaricious Leopold II, they badly underestimated that nation and, even more so, its courageous King Albert. Barbara Tuchman, *The Guns of August* (New York: Ballatine Books, 1962), 24.

2. Military historian John Keegan goes so far as to say that von Schlieffen "nurtured an obsession with the Roman defeat at Cannae that helped to precipitate the First World War," in *The Face of Battle* (New York: Penguin Books, 1976), 63.

3. Von Moltke (the Younger) would never attain the stature of his uncle, Field Marshal Helmuth von Moltke. John Laffin writes that he "was as incompetent as his uncle had been efficient. He owed his appointment solely to his name, for the Kaiser thought it would instill fear into Germany's opponents." Tuchman

notes that he was sometimes considered "soft," given his interest in anthroposophism and other cults, and his awkward habit of falling off his horse. *Jackboot: A History of the German Soldier 1713-1945* (New York: Barnes and Noble Books, 1964), 111. Tuchman, *The Guns of August*, 78.

4. Moyer describes the German mobilization as a masterpiece of logistics. Having commandeered the entire railway system, "the army transported more than two-million men to precisely the correct location at the Front, 400,000 tons of materials to precisely the right place. In the early days, one troop train passed through Cologne's railway station every ten minutes." Laurence V. Moyer, *Victory Must Be Ours: Germany in the Great War 1914-1918* (New York: Hippocrene Books, 1995), 76.

5. Tuchman notes that French military Intelligence had learned of the Schlieffen Plan in 1904 and that the Germans were calling up Reserves in 1913, but ignored both warning signs. It would not be the last time that the Allies ignored vital warnings. *The Guns of August*, 41.

6. *Ibid.*, 74-75.

7. Alan Clark notes that historians generally agree that Smith-Dorrien's decision to stand and fight at Le Cateau (in spite of British Expeditionary Force Commander Sir John French's orders to retreat and General Sir Douglas Haig's withdrawal of his I Corps) had saved the day for the British Expeditionary Force. However, it did not endear him to the two men and ultimately helped lead to his downfall. Alan Clark, *The Donkeys* (London: Pimlico, 1961), 48.

8. Correlli Barnett, *The Swordbearers: Supreme Command in the First World War* (New York: William Morrow and Co., 1964), 72.

9. Holger H. Herwig, *The First World War: Germany and Austria-Hungary 1914-1918* (London: Arnold, 1997), 100.

10. Martin Gilbert, *The First World War: A Complete History*, 2nd ed. (New York: Henry Holt and Co., 1994), 64-65.

11. B. H. Liddell Hart, *History of the First World War* (London: Macmillan Publishers, 1997), 57; originally published as The Real War (Boston: Little, Brown and Co., 1930).

12. Tuchman, *The Guns of August*, 401.

13. The French uniform was far too colorful for trench warfare and would disappear at the end of 1914. It would be replaced by a less conspicuous gray-blue uniform. British soldiers wore a khaki-colored uniform, and the Germans a field gray uniform.

14. Jere Clemens King, ed., *The First World War* (New York: Walker and Co., 1972), 22.

15. Herwig, *The First World War*, 105.

16. Winston S. Churchill, *The World Crisis*, Vol. 1 (London: Thornton Butterworth, 1928), 284.

17. Herwig, *The First World War*, 105.

18. Liddell Hart, *History of the First World War*, 82.

Hell cannot be so terrible.
 — Alfred Joubaire,
 a French infantry officer

Chapter 5

Digging In

B Y THE SECOND WEEK of September 1914, Germany's well-laid plans to crush France in just 42 days had begun to unravel. Instead of celebrating a glorious victory against their old nemesis, weary German soldiers now had to retreat northward toward Belgium. By mid-September, they were forced back across the Aisne River where they began to scratch grave-like holes in the ground for protection and set up machine-gun posts.

By now, Kaiser Wilhelm II, thoroughly displeased with the German withdrawal at the Marne, sacked von Motlke, his Chief of the General Staff, and on 14 September, entrusted the command to General Erich von Falkenhayn, an arrogant creature who, it is said, claimed ancestry back to the Teutonic knights. Von Falkenhayn immediately moved his headquarters closer to the Front (from Luxembourg to Charleville) and soon realized that his right flank — the same one that von Schlieffen had warned to keep strong — was in danger of being outflanked. Now it was his turn to call an end to retreat. But where would they fight?

At the same time, there began a so-called "race to the sea" in which the Allies and Central Powers tried to swing around (or outflank) the other. (Most historians agree that it was not the sea the troops were trying to reach, but rather open country in which to gain an advantage.) Gradually the center of gravity of warfare shifted northward with both the British and Germans moving troops to the Flanders area.

Ironically, though von Schlieffen was gone from the scene, his prediction, based on the Battle of Cannae, was coming to pass. He had written that "the principles of strategy remain unchanged. The enemy's front is not the objective. The essential thing is to crush the enemy's flanks . . . and complete the extermination by attack upon its rear."[1]

Meanwhile, in Belgium, King Albert and his little army (with the help of British reinforcements) had been hanging on tenaciously at Antwerp. They were clearly outmatched by the German army, and on 9 October, after being bombarded by one-ton projectiles from 17-inch Austrian howitzers, had to abandon the city and retreat to the seacoast. But the youthful soldier-king was far from defeated. Some say, in fact, that it was Albert who fired the last shot at the invading Germans. Whatever the case, as his battered forces struggled to hold onto a remnant (about a 10- by 25-mile area) of their beloved Belgium soil, he ordered (on 25 October) that the sluice gates at Nieuport be opened, thus letting seawater flood part of the countryside near the coast. His strategy worked. The two-mile wide, chest-high water forced the Germans back behind the Yser River — and the Belgian army held on.[2]

And thus evolved the answer to von Falkenhayn's question regarding the location of the next major battlefield. It would be in the Ypres area where von Falkenhayn would tackle the British in his effort to push through to the North Sea and the English Channel. For one thing, it was a communications hub. For another, his troops held the high ground, and could observe nearly all the enemy movement below. Furthermore, the higher ground meant that his troops would not be plagued by the high water table in the trenches. There was still another reason: King Albert's opening of the sluice gates had forced von Falkenhayn back from the flooded coastal area. So Ypres it was!

Ypres (Ieper), which in the 13th century boasted a population of 40,000 and was once one of Belgium's jewels, had become by 1914 just a small town of about 22,000 people. Just north of the French-Belgian border, it was known for its two impressive Gothic structures, St. Martin's

Cathedral and the Cloth Hall. But it would soon become recognized more for horror than glory. More than a million men would die there, in Flanders Fields.

The First Battle of Ypres

The Germans began their attempt to drive the British out of the Ypres Salient on 22 October. The Germans had actually taken Ypres on 3 October, only to lose it to the British two weeks later on 18 October. Both sides fought bitterly, sometimes in hand-to-hand combat. Friend and enemy sometimes fell side by side or on top of each other in death. British troops (including the Irish Guards and the Indian Corps) were dazed by the concussion of German high explosives that detonated all around them. Even Sir John French, the British Commander-in-Chief, was at times demoralized after seeing some of his wounded troops retreating from the spiked-helmeted [*Pikelhaube*] Germans. Kaiser Wilhelm, on the other hand, was a bit more satisfied with his army's progress, and visited his troops to encourage them further.

But German hopes of breaking through the Ypres Salient to reach the Channel were, once again, premature.

Troops on both sides began to dig in, the Germans to the north, east, and south of Ypres, and the British and French holding a salient, similar to a man's profile, jutting about four miles out of the town of Ypres itself, into the German lines.

Thus, the war of rapid forward movement ended.[3] More and more soldiers on both sides dug more and more trenches trying to avoid infantry and artillery fire. By the third week of November, when fighting petered out in a blizzard, the First Battle of Ypres was over, and Ypres had become the burial place of four-fifths of the British Expeditionary Force (BEF). Each side had lost about 150,000 men. For that price, the Germans gained the strategic Messines Ridge overlooking the British lines. The British, however, still held the Ypres Salient, which though valuable, was by its very nature vulnerable on three sides.

The landscape was covered with manmade desolation and carnage — with the bodies of young soldiers; with confused, wandering, unmilked cattle; and with dead and dying horses. Over them all hung a sorrowful, symbolic pall of smoke from smoldering ruins.

And trench warfare took on a life of its own.

Trench Development

Trench warfare, which was to become synonymous with the First World War, began in late 1914, about four months after the fighting began. In the early part of the conflict, most thought the war, like those of the previous century would be short — and mobile. One who thought otherwise was Ivan Bloch, a Polish railway magnate and banker who looked at war through an economic lens. He predicted that, with new weapons and improved industrial resources, the fighting could go on indefinitely in a stalemate until attrition dictated otherwise. (With uncanny foresight, he also predicted the spade would be as important as the gun.) For the most part, however, few leaders (political or military) foresaw a long battle of trench warfare as a defining feature of the war where movement would be measured in yards, not miles. (Trench warfare was not new, however. It had occurred in both the American Civil War in 1861-1865, and in the Russo-Japanese conflict of 1904-1905.)

It is difficult for later generations to comprehend the utter baseness and horror of trench warfare and its many faces of vileness. It is little wonder that trench survivors spoke little of their ungodly "hell on earth." Most war books, understandably, devote more space to colorful battles where major breakthroughs or spectacular victories occurred. Trench life and warfare, on the other hand, were far from glorious or glamorous.

This phase of the war seems almost to have happened by accident, when troops (particularly the fleeing Germans after the Battle of the Marne) desperately scratched and dug shallow excavations in the ground to protect themselves from enemy fire and bombs. They found that one machine gun, protected by a mound of earth, could hold off scores of attackers. The first haphazard holes or pits were usually unconnected, though roughly parallel to those of the enemy in opposing trenches. (Two American inventions — the machine gun invented by Hiram Maxim, and barbed wire, though designed for a very different use in the American West — contributed to the prolonged trench warfare.)

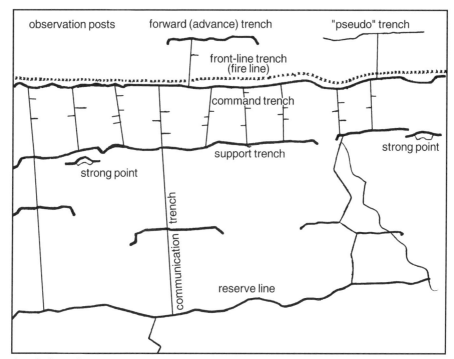

A typical trench system.

To grasp the extent of the incredible length of the trench system, one must imagine two roughly parallel lines (one German, the other Allied) of connected ditches about 475 miles long, roughly the distance between San Francisco and Los Angeles, or between Ottawa and Windsor. Those ditches would be carved out of every conceivable kind of soil from the waterlogged marshes and swamps of western Flanders, through mining areas and slagheaps, and forests, all the way to the Alps. And they would be dug by hand, not machines! Historian Holger H. Herwig estimates that by 1916 the trenches dug by the French (6,250 miles), the British (6,000 miles), and the Central Powers (nearly 12,000 miles) were enough to circle the globe.[4]

Both Allied and German trenches were to a degree similar, although the German trenches were usually more sophisticated and, therefore, more comfortable. Both consisted of three (or more) parallel lines, each with specialized functions.

The British "front" line, as its name implies, was closest to the enemy

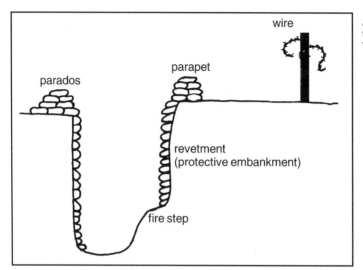

A side view of a typical World War I fire trench.

and faced "No Man's Land," the area between the two opposing lines. The British trench layout often had two parallel trench lines, the front one for actual firing at the enemy and hence called the "fire" line, and, a bit to the rear, a second one, the command trench, which had deep dugouts and off-shoots for latrines. At the front of the fire trench was the parapet, a pile or wall of sandbags (or dirt) forming a protective embankment about ten feet high. A similar bank — pile of protective sandbags — at the rear of the trench was called the parados. Troops usually had to revet or retain the walls of a trench with wire or pieces of wood planks to keep them from falling in, particularly in wet weather or after shelling.

The trench itself was from four to ten feet deep, and wide enough for troops to pass in opposite directions, with priority for passage given to ammunition bearers, reinforcements, and the wounded, in that order. Because of the waterlogged ground in the Flanders area and the inevitable water on the trench floors, strips of wood called "duckboards" were laid parallel to each other on the muddy floor.[5] However, they often proved more hazardous than helpful. Sometimes they floated away. Sometimes they disappeared in the mud. Sometimes they tripped heavily-laden or wounded soldiers. And sometimes when a soldier stepped on one end, the other end flew up and clobbered him.

To enable the soldier to fire over the top of the sandbags, a ledge or "fire step" was built two or three feet off the trench floor, on the side of the trench facing the enemy. Ideally, when a soldier stood on the fire step,[6] the rifle on his shoulder would be roughly level with the top of the parapet.

The front line had several distinct features. First and foremost, it was far from straight but was dug in a zigzag or dog-toothed fashion with fire-bays and traverses. The firebay was a straight section of trench about ten yards long, where infantrymen stood when on duty or alert. The traverse was a kink or jag in the trench line, deliberately designed to prevent sweeping or enfilading fire.

Another feature was the all-important "sap," actually a trench or tunnel, usually covered, that was carved 20 or 30 yards out toward the enemy position. It was, in fact, a listening post, where two or three soldiers or sentries would quietly crouch and try to overhear enemy names, discussions, or plans. It could take on surrealistic dimensions in the blackness of night in the best of times. It could give birth to sheer horror even in broad daylight when, after battle, soldiers could hear the moaning of comrades dying in agony in the blazing sun.

Yet another part of the trench was the "dugout," an excavation on the side of a trench line that was large enough to allow two or three exhausted men (usually officers), to grab a few minutes of sleep in relative security. More often than not, however, another soldier moving up or down the trenches would trip over their legs or feet and jar them awake. Other ranks, often merely wrapped in groundsheets, found a crude corner to slump in, or stole what sleep they could leaning against the trench wall.

In his book on trench warfare, *Eye Deep in Hell*, John Ellis notes that front-line trench dugouts were usually less deep than those at the rear, because the enemy was reluctant to use heavy artillery on front-line areas lest the shells fall short and undermine their own. Thus, with big guns aimed at the reserve and rear areas, the front-line dugouts didn't need as much depth. As the war wore on, dugouts, particularly those of the Germans, became much larger.[7]

Just beyond the front line were belts upon belts of barbed wire, sometimes ten yards wide and three or four feet high. The tangled barbs defied those who dared approach through No Man's Land, that ugly, bomb-battered, blood-soaked hell of suffering and death that lay between the German and Allied front lines.

The second major line, about 70 to 100 yards behind the first, was the support trench that usually had a number of deep dugouts — holes large enough to accommodate a number of troops, or medical officer, or company headquarters. Some had small kitchens, latrines, and stores.

Still farther back, about 400 to 600 yards behind the support line, was the reserve line. Surprisingly, reserve lines had to be dug deeply because the enemy's guns were often aimed at them for maximum disruption of the supply line.

There had to be, of course, a way to get from one line to another without being picked off by enemy fire. This was accomplished through communication trenches that zigzagged between the other three lines.

The German Trenches

General von Falkenhayn played a major part in establishing the German trench system[8] which would ultimately involve the excavation of 60 million cubic yards of earth by the Germans alone. It was he who ordered, in November 1914, the construction of several parallel lines about 100 to 200 yards from the Anglo-French lines, in order to prevent the loss of a single square foot of captured land. His reasoning was sound because by now, Germany held nearly one-tenth of France, including the important industrial area of Lille, Roubaix, and Tourcoing, eight-tenths of her coal, and nine-tenths of her iron resources, not to mention some rich agricultural areas. The German decision not to give up an inch of conquered territory impelled them to dig superior trenches to be held indefinitely. And thus evolved the malevolent trench lines from Nieuport on the English Channel to Bec de Canard on the Swiss border, some 475 miles distant. Trench warfare was nonetheless hated by the Generals, because it flew in the face of tactical initiative.[9]

The German trench line also consisted of three separate trench lines, each with its own purpose. The front line, heavily protected by rolls of barbed wire, was (like the Allied line) dug in a dogtooth pattern to prevent enfilade fire — the gun fire that sweeps along a line of men. Likewise, on the side facing the enemy, a fire step was built two or three feet off the trench floor, which enabled soldiers to peer over the ground level and fire or hurl grenades. Saps were dug out into No Man's Land to serve as listening posts or advance-warning posts.

Unlike the Allies, however, the German front line was heavily garrisoned. With her advanced planning and superior numbers, Germany had time to fortify her front trenches with machine guns in concrete strong-points. These were to give a profound advantage in the weeks and months to come.

The second German line, between 2,000 to 3,000 yards behind the first, was the support line. It featured large dugouts, room-size holes in the sides of trenches that could accommodate support troops.

The third line, another 2,000 yards to the rear, was the reserve line. Some trenches were up to 30 and 40 feet deep, and some had timbered walls and ceilings, electric lights, excellent ventilation, water tanks, and even furniture. Some were so sophisticated that they had a narrow-gauge railway to bring in food, ammunition, and other amenities.

Trench Routine

Trench life was full of extremes. In the summertime, soldiers sweltered in the blazing sun. But other seasons were worse. During the long winter nights, some men froze to death where they sat or lay. In periods of rain, men could trip and fall off duckboards and drown in the mud and slime. There was little to take comfort in, except the comradeship of equally suffering fellow soldiers, and counting the hours until your turn came to go back behind the lines in reserve.

The daily routine began with "stand-to" (a shortened form of "stand-to-arms") a half hour before dawn in case the enemy should attack. Soldiers would stand on the fire step (with their rifles) for personal inspection, while the orderly officer would check the condition of trenches and stores. At dawn, they would be "stood down" (with sentries posted, of course) for breakfast, which was usually cooked on coke fires. Rifles would then be cleaned for inspection.

Daytime brought a variety of chores including trench repair, sentry duty (on a rotating basis), uniform mending, personal hygiene (including shaving), housekeeping tasks, delousing, letter writing, and sometimes even boredom. There was always discomfort. Because of the constant danger from crack enemy snipers, very little military work could be done in daylight hours.

Night was an entirely different matter. Sometimes as long as 16 hours in the winter, the night brought not only increased activity and troop movement, but far more dangerous operations.

As in the morning routine, there would first be a "stand to" at dusk for inspection. The troops would have their evening meal, hot if they were lucky, often brought up under the cover of darkness from the field kitchens. The troops would then be divided roughly into three groups. In a system of rotation, about one-third would pull sentry duty, one-third would head rearward through the narrow communication trenches for rations and stores, and the remaining third might either be given a rest period or be assigned to fatigue duty. Fatigue duty was every soldier's lot with frustrating frequency. There were always sandbags to be filled, or trench walls to be revetted. New saps or latrines had to be dug. (However, some soldiers with special skills or duties, such as stretcher bearers, snipers, and bombers, were usually excused from fatigue duty.)

Sentry duty was usually nerve tingling. Was the muted cough or whisper heard from friend or foe? Was that distant dark shadow a tree stump, or was it a concrete column made to look like one, providing innocent-looking cover for a sniper? Some men would volunteer to crawl into No Man's Land to rescue the wounded, check enemy movement, or lay or repair barbed wire. There was never a time to let down one's defenses. The tension never ended. Violence could erupt at any time. Sniper fire was always a deadly, lurking possibility. Sleep was elusive.

Troops were relieved at night. It was not a simple process, though it sometimes was lightened by the exchange of remarks between troops. Those coming in to relieve often struggled up through the communications trenches with 70 pounds of equipment (rifle and bayonet, ammunition, shovels, sandbags, water, and rations) weighing them down. Sometimes they had marched several miles just to reach the communication trenches, and had to rest before continuing the rest of the way. "Then they peeled off in single file into the pitch-black trenches, struggling to keep up, tripping on a broken duckboard, or catching on overhead wires."[10]

Fortunately, in the space of a month, a soldier would likely spend only a week in the two front (fire and support) lines, and another week in the reserve line. He would then be sent back behind the lines before being recalled for his next stint.

One of the most thoroughly chronicled events of the war was the weather, and few books on World War I fail to mention its critical significance. Water-soaked trenches were all but inevitable in the high water table Flanders area, where water could be found at a depth of two or three feet. Relentless rains added to the discomfort and disease. And rain it did. It has been recorded that in the winter weeks between 25 October 1914 and 10 March 1915, only 18 days were without rain or sleet.

Consequently, men had to stand for days in mud, usually ankle-deep, but sometimes knee-deep. There were times when the mud reached their armpits. Very often dirty water (or mud) covered or washed away the fire step. One officer on the Ypres Salient took three hours to slog 400 yards in a communication trench where the freezing water turned the trench floor to thick, clinging mud.[11] A French soldier described the communication trenches as "no more than cess-pools filled with a mixture of water and urine."[12] Many soldiers described their surroundings graphically as "liquid shit."

Keeping dry was impossible. Men slept in their wet muddy uniform, hoping it would dry out on their bodies. Their greatcoats, once a source of warm comfort, became useless stinking sponges soaking up 20 or more pounds of additional mud and water, fit only to be discarded. The extra weight, along with the 40 to 60 pounds of equipment carried by each man, sometimes caused an overburdened soldier to slip into the slimy water and disappear forever. In one instance, 15 men from one British Guards battalion drowned in the heavy mud in the winter of 1914-1915.

One soldier said he went for 42 days in 1915 without taking off his tunic or boots.[13] Very often soldiers would return to the trenches in the same dirty, damp uniforms that they had left them. Naturally, illness and disease followed. Trench foot, one of the side effects of continuously wet feet, became such a problem that officers were severely reprimanded if they didn't see that their men changed socks frequently. And there were other serious problems. One writer notes that in January 1915 there were about 4,500 sick reports a day, chiefly from pneumonia and blood-poisoning.[14]

Men suffered through the bitter cold nights. "Hot tea froze in minutes and bully (corned) beef became chunks of red ice. Bread acquired a sour taste and boots froze solid in seconds if they were taken off."[15]

The wet and the frigid weather were not the only curses in the trenches. Particularly loathsome was the pervasive stench. Although lime and other disinfectants were used generously, nothing could cover the smell of wet uniforms, unbathed men, unsanitary latrines, and the decomposing bodies of men and animals. The foul air was inescapable.

Only rats, lice, and flies thrived in the trenches, and flourish they did. The rats became increasingly repulsive enemies that seemed not only to multiply in astonishing numbers, but to grow in girth and boldness. Exhausted men trying to steal a moment's sleep would be awakened by a rat scurrying over their faces or burrowing under their blanket for food. Some men would be physically sickened when they saw the loathsome, bloated rats feasting on corpses.

Lice, too, which could spread trench fever, were an ever-present problem, though soldiers seemed to be able to cope in their ongoing battle to delouse themselves. And with thousands of horses producing tons of manure daily, the flies soon followed. Though not as repulsive as the rats and lice, their spreading of serious disease was always a concern.

And, like the rats, the lice, and the flies, the rain was an incessant enemy. Even in the summer, it was not so much a gentle rain from heaven but rather a ruthless, relentless adversary, almost an ally of the enemy who was less adversely affected because he held higher ground.

Yet all of heaven's rain could not disguise the grotesqueness of the putrid trenches or cleanse the stench of decomposing bodies on blood-soaked fields.[16]

NOTES

1. Barbara Tuchman, *The Guns of August* (New York: Ballantine Books, 1962), 20.
2. Historians rate King Albert highly. Barbara Tuchman calls him one of the few real heroes of the war. Winston S. Churchill termed the Belgian King and Queen "magnificent," saying that the calm, grave King's "unconquerable majesty" in the time of tragedy would never pass from his mind. The King, who became Commander-in-Chief of the Belgian army on the outbreak of war, set up his headquarters at La Panne (below Ostend on the Belgian coast) and stayed with his troops throughout the war.
3. Years before (1902), in the *Swiss Military Review*, Emile Mayer had written a prophetic description of the nature of events now unfolding. "The next war will put face to face two human walls, almost in contact, only separated by the depth of danger, and this double wall will remain almost inert, in spite of the will of

either party to advance. Unable to succeed in front, one of these lines will try to out swing the other. The latter in turn, will prolong its front, and it will be a competition to see who will be able to reach farthest. There will be no reason for the war to stop. Exterior circumstances will bring the end of the purely defensive war of the future."

4. Holger H. Herwig, *The First World War: Germany and Austria Hungary, 1914-1918* (London: Arnold, 1997), 244.

5. For the sake of accuracy, it should be pointed out that duckboards were not yet in use in the early part of 1915, making trench conditions even more primitive. Alan Clark notes that striking water at 18 inches or less, troops had to deal with waist-high water, fire-steps that crumbled away, and sheer horror when the wounded "who collapsed into the slime would often drown, unnoticed in the heat of some local engagement, and lie concealed for days until their bodies, porous from decomposition, would rise once again to the surface." Alan Clark, *The Donkeys* (London: Pimlico, 1961), 40.

6. Obviously, fire steps always faced the enemy. Thus, when soldiers seized an enemy trench, the fire steps faced the wrong direction, and they had to make new ones quickly (usually of sandbags).

7. John Ellis, *Eye-Deep in Hell: Trench Warfare in World War I* (Baltimore: The John Hopkins University Press, 1976).

8. Herwig, *The First World War*, 118, 244.

9. Martin Middlebrook, *The First Day on the Somme* (New York: W. W. Norton and Co., 1972), 30.

10. Desmond Morton, *When Your Number's Up: The Canadian Soldier in the First World War* (Toronto: Random House of Canada, 1993), 123.

11. Ellis, *Eye Deep in Hell*, 44.

12. *Ibid.*, 47.

13. Denis Winter, *Death's Men — Soldiers of the Great War* (London: Penguin Books, 1978), 83.

14. Clark, *The Donkeys*, 40.

15. Winter, *Death's Men*, 95.

16. A number of excellent books offer further insights in the ugliness and "physical and spiritual desert" of trench life, including John Ellis, *Eye Deep in Hell*, and Denis Winter, *Death's Men*.

Canada sends her aid at a timely moment.

— Winston Churchill,
First Lord of the Admiralty, in a
cable, to the government in Ottawa

Chapter 6

The Atlantic Crossing

O N THE SLATE-GRAY ships bobbing about in Gaspé Bay, tension mounted as troops waited impatiently for some sign of movement. Little appeared to happen on 2 October, though Sam Hughes rather characteristically wove in and out between the troopships in a small cruiser distributing bundles of his pamphlet, "Where Duty Leads." Not everyone was overjoyed to see him.

Though Hughes was proud of his soldiers, he was less than impressed with the four aging British warships — HMS *Eclipse*, HMS *Diana*, HMS *Talbot*, and HMS *Charybdis* — that were assigned to escort the First Contingent across the Atlantic. He called them (among other things) "altogether inadequate."

He wasn't the only one with concerns. Colonel J. A. Currie, Commanding Officer of the 48th Highlanders, on the HMS *Megantic*, noted the "obsolete small cruisers of slow speed" and looked upon them "with a good deal of apprehension."[1]

Worse yet, the Commander of the whole escort, Rear Admiral Sir Rosslyn Wemyss, on the flagship *Charybdis*, was a bit apprehensive.

The name of his ship was something of an irony. Like Odysseus, he was poised for a long journey, beset not by mythical monsters Scylla and Charybdis, but by concern that the convoy provided far too large a target for the enemy. He worried that his "old tubs" couldn't provide adequate protection.

The situation was not as bleak as it seemed, however. The British Admiralty had promised that two battleships, HMS *Glory* and HMS *Majestic* would join the convoy shortly. And unknown to the Canadians and even to Admiral Wemyss himself, another great ship would provide additional protection for the Canadian Contingent. For security reasons, they were not told that HMS *Princess Royal* would join them in mid-Atlantic.

Finally, in preparation for sailing, the ships were lined up in three columns, designated X, Y, and Z, with one British cruiser leading each column, and the fourth (HMS *Talbot*) bringing up the rear.

Z	Y	X
HMS *Eclipse*	HMS *Diana*	HMS *Charybdis*
Megantic	*Caribbean*	*Scotian*
Ruthenia	*Athenia*	*Arcadian*
Bermudian	*Royal Edward*	*Zeeland*
Alaunia	*Franconia*	*Corinthian*
Ivernia	*Canada*	*Virginian*
Scandinavian	*Monmouth*	*Andania*
Sicilian	*Manitou* (Kennedy's)	*Saxonia*
Montezuma	*Tryolia*	*Grampian*
Lapland	*Tunisian*	*Laconia*
Cassandra	*Laurentic*	*Montreal*
		Royal George
	HMS *Talbot*	

Finally, at 2:30 on Saturday afternoon, 3 October, the long-anticipated moment came, and the flagship *Charybdis* signaled all transports:

> Have cables hove short. All ships in Column Z will raise anchors at 3:00 p.m. and proceed, keeping column formation, steaming at 9 knots following leading cruiser *Eclipse*.[2]

Precisely at 3:00 p.m., the HMS *Eclipse* began to lead the port (left) Column Z, through the narrow exit from Gaspé Bay into the Gulf of St. Lawrence. Once it had cleared the exit, HMS *Diana* followed suit, leading the middle column through the passage. Column X, led by HMS *Charybdis*, then followed, with HMS *Talbot* bringing up the rear.

It was an extraordinary sight for those who watched from the shores, or waved from little fishing boats. All in all, it took 3½ hours for the 21½-mile line of gray troopships to pass though the entrance, as they began their 2,500-mile journey to distant shores.

The convoy, once out to sea, regrouped in its original three columns. At the slow speed of ten knots set by the plodding HMS *Monmouth*, it carried its more than 31,000 Canadian troops to an uncertain fate.

Even while the First Contingent was at sea, Canada's Governor General, Prince Arthur, Duke of Connaught, sent a telegram to the British Government:

> Ottawa, 6th October 1914
>
> The Dominion Government offers to place and maintain in the field a second over-sea contingent of twenty thousand men. If the offer be accepted, what form should that contingent take? Having parted with nearly all our 18-pounder guns, we cannot offer a complete division but besides infantry, we could furnish mounted rifles and units fighting or administrative required for special purposes.   Arthur[3]

The offer, though not accepted initially, would ultimately be accepted with gratitude.

The cost of the 31 ships for transportation of the First Contingent to England was given (in discussions in the House of Commons on 10 April 1916) as $3,363,240.42. The ships were chartered from eight different lines. The cost was increased, of course, due to a number of factors such as demurrage while other ships loaded and unloaded, and having the ships travel at the rate of the slowest ship — the *Monmouth* — in the convoy.

The 12-day crossing itself was smooth and largely uneventful — but not without duties. The day's routine began with reveille at 6:30 a.m. when men climbed out of their hammocks to prepare for physical drill. Meals provided a welcome break from inspections, lectures, drill, physical training, signaling practices, and, for some, duty caring for the many horses. (At one point, Robert Kennedy noted in his diary that his ship, the *Manitou*, was following the slow *Monmouth*, and very nearly ran into her twice on one night alone.)

But it was not all work. One officer wrote: "The men were the recipients of many treats, including several barrels of choice apples which were distributed en route."[4] Another diversion for the men was the frequent posting of wireless bulletins with the latest news on the war situation. And some precautions were taken. At night, for example, portholes were covered.

The HMS *Princes Royal* joined the convoy on 12 October, and troops cheered emotionally as the band on the *Royal* saluted them with "O Canada" and "The Maple Leaf Forever." Troops had ample time to write home, and many, including Kennedy, indicated that they had no idea where they would land. Even the Commander was not sure. In fact, almost at the last minute, because of reports of German submarines — U-boats — in the English Channel, the destination was changed from Southampton to Plymouth. It was there that the first transports arrived early in the morning of 14 October.

The people of Plymouth warmly welcomed the soldiers, though for security reasons a formal public reception for them was vetoed by Lord Kitchener.[5]

The Canadians had landed overseas, only two months after the war had begun.

NOTES

1. Colonel J. A. Currie, M.P., *"The Red Watch" with the First Canadian Division in Flanders* (London: Constable and Co., Ltd., 1916), 50. (Note: This was not Lieutenant General Arthur W. Currie, who later commanded the Canadian Corps.)
2. Colonel A. Fortescue Duguid, *Official History of the Canadian Forces in the Great War 1914-1918,* Vol. 1 (Ottawa: Minister of National Defence, 1938), 105.
3. *Ibid.*, Appendix 154, 127.

4. Percy L. Climo, *Let Us Remember: Lively Letters from World War One* (Coberg, Ontario: Haynes Printing Co., 1990), 144.
5. There was good cause for all the security measures. Just two months later, around 2 a.m. on New Year's morning 1915, a German U-boat would fire on the British battleship HMS *Formidable* in the Channel. In two and a half hours, the ship and more than 500 officers and men would perish in the moonlit waters.

They will go back in thirty row boats.
— Kaiser Wilhelm II, referring to the
arrival of 30 Canadian troopships in England

Chapter 7

On Salisbury Plain — Winter 1915

THERE WAS ONCE again some confusion when troops began to disembark at Plymouth on 14 October 1914. Most of the logistical problems that occurred in Quebec simply followed the troops to Plymouth. Additionally, the rail facilities at Plymouth were not as well equipped or as extensive as those at Southampton. The *Manitou* and several other ships had to wait several days in Plymouth Harbor for their turn to disembark. Though the soldiers were intrigued to see the *Birmingham* being repaired after having rammed and sunk a German U-boat, they were more excited about the prospect of standing on dry land again.

The troops finally disembarked on Saturday afternoon, 17 October, and walked two miles to the train station. There they entrained for an all-night journey of about 100 miles to Amesbury Station in the famous Salisbury Plain area, steeped in legend and history. It was there, just north of Amesbury, that the British War Office had a broad, 90-square-mile military training ground with extensive artillery and rifle ranges. The Canadians would be distributed in four camps in the lovely countryside area, with divisional headquarters at "Ye Olde Bustard." (The camps were Bustard Camp, West Down South Camp, West Down North Camp, and Pond Farm Camp. Robert Kennedy was stationed at Bustard Camp.)

Early Sunday morning, 18 October, the troops detrained, then marched more than ten miles to the military camp and then to individual training areas. There were several trips back to Amesbury Station, however, to retrieve equipment and goods.

Kennedy to Eva, 27 October 1914:

> **I was away from camp (at Amesbury Station) three days last week guarding and loading transport wagons. It has been quite a task to get the horses mated — they drive three teams (tandem) on the wagons and the men ride on the left-hand horse. There are a number of horses that are of no use with other horses, and then there are teamsters that don't know how to handle the horses. But things are in better shape now.**

Many men spoke gratefully of the warm reception (and gifts of food and cigarettes) that the English people gave them, though there were instances when brash young Canadians were amused by the remarks they heard. In one instance, on learning the lads were from Canada, one woman remarked in astonishment, "Why they look just like us!"

The Canadian troops were now under the command of British General E. A. H. Alderson (since Canadian Generals had no war experience) and were distributed among four camps over a five-mile area. Thousands of bell tents, plus circus-sized marquees and kitchen shelters, had already mushroomed on the chalky plain, courtesy of the British Territorial Army Reserves — the equivalent of the U.S. National Guard — with the help of some New Zealanders. Things were looking up.

But not for long.

Even before the last troops reached Salisbury Plain, the weather changed. On 21 October, a quarter of an inch of rain fell on the less than sturdy tents. Over the next five days, the heavens dumped another full inch. As various historians point out, this marked the onset of a period of "abnormally heavy precipitation," during which rain fell on 89 out of 123 days. Cruel, capricious winds sometimes tore the light fabric of the tents (which some described as "so thin you could count the stars through them"), and on several occasions, blew them down completely, scattering everything inside into mud and oblivion. "Rain-taut guy ropes dragged tent poles from the sodden soil, collapsing tents upon the slumbering occupants."[1]

The foul weather played havoc with training schedules, but the infantry still had to continue with its progressively longer marches and endless entrenching drills; the artillery still had to practice at the firing ranges; and the engineers still had to work on construction projects. With no way to dry uniforms that were thoroughly soaked by the never-ending rain, men often had to sleep in their clothes and let them dry on their backs, much like the poor unfortunates in the trenches of France.

The misery did not go unnoticed. The Australian and New Zealand contingents en route to Salisbury Plain were so alarmed by the conditions in southern England that officials diverted their troops to Egypt for training.

Attempts were made to build huts for the troops, but while some were completed for the 2nd and 3rd Infantry Brigades, by Christmas 11,000 troops were still under canvas, many of the tents leaky. Adding to the misery were serious cases of the flu, and later an outbreak of meningitis, which would ultimately claim the lives of 28 men before they even got to war.

And still it rained. Yet, there was little grumbling.

The weather had an even more devastating effect on the horses, some of which had already deteriorated from the long voyage across the ocean. Many had become so debilitated that they couldn't pull the guns. Many died.[2] On numerous occasions, seeing the horses standing for days in mud up to their hocks, and their sodden blankets rendered useless on their backs, soldiers expressed more concern for their animals than for themselves. Gradually, where possible, horses were put under cover. In one instance, in late November, Major A. G. L. McNaughton, pitying the suffering creatures, had some "small spruce boughs cut and placed under the horses' bellies to keep them from sinking deeper in the mud."[3]

Morale remained high, however, and troops continued to train, come hell or high water. They had generous portions of both.

One might wonder why the soldiers were subjected so incessantly to the rigors of marching and drill. The reasons were manifold, including tradition, pride, and *esprit de corps*. Military theory held that through rigid training and drill, a soldier would gain self-confidence and respect for others in his unit. But the real reasons ran deeper. Precision marching on command indoctrinated the soldier, teaching him to obey his officers instantly, even in terrifying situations. Discipline was the key. A soldier was to obey without question, almost as a robot. This was critical in the heat and confusion of battle. There was no time for questions or indecision. As author John Laffin puts it, drill is "indispensable" to an army. A soldier "must have obedience drilled into him, so that his natural instincts can be curbed by the spiritual compulsion of his Commander, even in the most awful moments."[4]

There were other reasons for marching of course. For example, it increased the soldier's physical fitness. While marching "in step" can probably be traced back to the Greeks, the Prussians developed the marching pace, 72 steps a minute, to coincide with the human heartbeat. (Laffin claims that a half hour of the "goosestep" practiced by the Germans "did as much for the muscles of the legs and abdomen as a half-day route march."[5])

And so the marching continued, often in the never-ending rain. But sometimes the rain provided time for letter writing. Kennedy wrote to Eva on 11 December:

> **We have been loading ammunition all fore noon, and now (2 p.m.) we are in our tents as it is pouring again. I hope we won't have to go out this afternoon in the wetness.**
>
> **It's hard to realize that we can't spend this Christmas together. I wish this war were over, and back I'd go to the girl I left behind me. But duty lies before me and duty will not let me go, even if I were free to go back to Canada. God's will be done. Bob.**

The rain temporarily let up on 4 November, however, when the Contingent was inspected by King George V, Queen Mary, Lord Kitchener, and other officials. Another famous personage, Rudyard Kipling, visited the 3rd Brigade on 19 November.

And so, Christmas 1914 came and went on Salisbury Plain. Letters and parcels from home brightened the dreary weather, and all troops on a

Candians in training on Salisbury Plain, England, 1915. *National Archives of Canada, PA 0022704*

rotating basis were given six-day leaves with a free rail ticket to any city in the United Kingdom.

Kennedy wrote to Eva 22 January 1915:

> **I hope to get your photo soon as we expect to go to the front in a couple of weeks. God grant that the war will be over before 1915 passes away.**
>
> **I wrote to my father last night and sent a little money home. I often wish we had been married before I left Canada. I would have sent you all my wages.**
>
> **I was kicked by a horse a few days ago. I got both heels in my ribs on my right side. Nothing was broken, but I was laid up for a few days. I'm fine now.**

By late January 1915, there were indications that the move to France and the Front was imminent. The 18-pounder artillery brigade was reorganized into four four-gun batteries. Much to the chagrin of Sam Hughes, some of the poor Canadian equipment — boots and tunics, trucks and wagons, and the useless shovels — was being replaced by better-made British equipment. Unfortunately, however, the Canadian soldier would carry the Ross rifle to the Front.

Then the most telling sign of all warned the First Contingent that they would soon be heading for France. On 2 February came the announcement that King George V would visit the troops on Thursday the 4th. For once the weather cooperated as the Canadians, in an alignment that stretched for more than two miles, were inspected by their King, who, with Lord Kitchener, walked the entire length. The King appeared to be impressed by "the fine contingent from the Dominion of Canada" and admired the cheerful spirit of the soldiers in spite of "overwhelming difficulties."[6] He was speaking, of course, of the inclement weather.

And so it was that on Sunday, 7 February, once again in driving rain, the soldiers prepared to leave for France. (Actually, some advance and billeting parties had already left. And some Canadian newspapers had mistakenly reported that Canadian troops had already landed in France. The stories may have been planted by the War Office to deceive the Germans.)

Just as concern over German U-boats had necessitated a change in ports for their arrival in England, so now did a similar concern about unrestricted submarine warfare bring about another change. Instead of taking the obvious, more direct, Southampton-to-Le Havre route, the troops would leave from Avonmouth, on the Bristol Channel, and disembark at St. Nazaire in the Bay of Biscay. It would be longer, but safer.

After the troop train ride to Avonmouth, the soldiers were loaded, almost like cattle, in the holds of small cargo vessels, for what should have been a 36-hour crossing to France. However, disastrous weather patterns not only continued, but worsened, deteriorating steadily until the storm reached gale proportions. Some soldiers spent five desperate days in the dark, rank holds of the vessels.

Many officers and men wrote of the terrible conditions. Colonel J. A. Currie noted that, on 13 February, he was awakened by the rattling of dishes and banging of furniture on his ship, the *Mount Temple*. Currie wrote, "The ship was going like a pendulum, swinging nearly forty-five degrees every jump." Noting that the storm, which turned the sea into

The route the Canadian troops took from Salisbury Plain overland to Avonmouth on the Bristol Channel, to St. Nazaire, France.

pyramids, might get them if the submarines didn't, Currie expressed real concern over the gun lashings, fearing if one got loose it would punch a hole right through the side of the ship, which was at best making about half a knot an hour, if anything.[7]

While the men suffered terribly by the rolling and pitching (with one fatality), the horses once again were even worse off, being thrown in all directions, in terror and confusion. Many were badly injured:

> Many of the horses were on the exposed steel decks, which were swept by gigantic waves. Fully harnessed, some were so exhausted from being repeatedly knocked down that they had to be shot and cast overboard.[8]

Kennedy was too sick to write. He managed only a couple of lines in his diary:

Traveling SW. A rough boat, *Pancras*, 4,000 tons rolling badly. Seasick.

By 16 February, the last of the transport ships had reached St. Nazaire, and the beleaguered troops, many in soiled uniforms, reached the shores of France. Most were too weary to care that they had arrived merely six short months after the outbreak of war.

But they were not at the battle stations yet. Next on the agenda was a two-day, 500-mile rail journey to the Front itself, this time in miserable boxcars designed for cattle and horses (labeled "*Hommes* 40, *Chevaux* 8"). Fortunately, the affectionate greetings from French civilians helped to lift their spirits.

NOTES

1. Colonel G. W. L. Nicholson, C.D., *The Gunners of Canada: The History of the Royal Regiment of the Canadian Artillery, 1534-1919,* Vol. 1 (Toronto: McClelland and Stewart Limited, 1976), 202.
2. Mabel Agar, who visited her husband at Salisbury, wrote that the horses were dying at the rate of 30 every day. Sandra Gwyn, *Tapestry of War: A Private View of Canadians in the Great War* (Toronto: Harper Collins Publishers Ltd., 1992), 115.

3. Nicholson, *The Gunners of Canada*, 203.

4. John Laffin, *Jackboot: A History of the German Soldier 1713-1945* (New York: Barnes and Noble Books, 1964), 113.

5. *Ibid.,* 14.

6. Daniel G. Dancocks, *Welcome to Flanders Fields* (Toronto: McClelland & Stewart, Inc., 1989), 109.

7. Colonel J. A. Currie, M.P., *"The Red Watch" with the First Canadian Division in Flanders* (London: Constable and Co. Ltd., 1916), 107-108.

8. Nicholson, *The Gunners of Canada*, 206.

The machine gun and the spade had changed the course of European history.
— A. J. P. Taylor,
The First World War: An Illustrated History

Chapter 8

To the Front

HE 500-MILE TRIP from St. Nazaire to the Front was a foretaste of things to come. The railway cars, in addition to being dirty, were so crowded that troops couldn't lie down to sleep. But the excitement of nearing the battle kept spirits reasonably high, and toward the end of the second day on the train, the distant thunder of guns could be heard. After the miserable ride, the men were more than happy to be billeted in nearby farms and villages. The clean straw on barn floors or lofts was far superior to the train accommodations. More important, though the men were not quite sure where they were, they were finally near the fighting!

But if Canadian troops thought they were now ready to face the enemy, they were wrong.

Before their baptism by fire, there would be still more training. First, they would be attached for a full week to British units that held the line in front of Armentières. Every soldier — officer and man alike — was required to spend a full 48 hours with his exact counterpart in the British army for last-minute indoctrination. It was only when this additional training was completed that the Canadian troops were deemed ready to take over 6,400 yards (about 3½ miles) of the line facing Armentières.

General E. A. H. Alderson, the British General in charge of the Canadian Division, immediately visited many of the troops, offering encouragement and almost fatherly advice, and cautioning them not to expose themselves unnecessarily to enemy fire. The Canadians liked and responded well to the General, but it was not long before Alderson fell from favor with the headstrong Sam Hughes. Alderson had diminishing respect for the Ross Rifle, the MacAdam shovel, and the shoddy army boots, all Hughes's favorites. Worse yet, Alderson was given Lieutenant Colonel Garnet Hughes (Colonel Sam's son), as an assistant. It did not bode well for Alderson.

And so it was that on Monday, 1 March 1915, the main force of the Canadians finally took their place in the front line. They followed in the footsteps of the Princess Patricia's Canadian Light Infantry (PPCLI), a skirmishing force that had sailed with the other Canadians in October 1914 but had entered the line on 7 January 1915, as part of the British 27th Division. By Tuesday, 2 March, the first guns of the Canadian army's 1st Brigade thundered into life.

The three and a half mile Canadian sector was divided into three parts, each held by one infantry brigade and its attendant field artillery brigade. (The fourth brigade was being absorbed into the others as reinforcements.) At any one time, each brigade usually had two of its battalions in the front line, while the other two remained in the rear. As a rule, the battalions would, at least at the beginning of the war, spend four days in the front lines before being relieved. Major General Malcolm S. Mercer (a Toronto lawyer), Lieutenant General (later Sir) Arthur W. Currie (a Vancouver real estate investor), and Major General R. E. W. Turner (a wholesale merchant from Quebec City) commanded the three brigades.

During the first few days, the Canadian sector saw no significant warfare, save for periodic shelling and ever-present snipers' bullets. Alderson stressed bold patrolling and accurate shooting, hoping to convince the Germans that the Canadians were superior fighters. But even the relative quietness of the first week brought 4 fatalities and 20 wounded.

One officer was struck by the surroundings:

Hardly a farm house where we were billeted that did not have the graves of the peaceful occupants in the gardens close by. Men, women, and children were destroyed by shell and other implements of war.[1]

Kennedy wrote to his sweetheart:

It's such a lovely day here — the first day of Spring. We are making the best of it, sitting on the south side of a house, and sunning ourselves. We have little to do today as it is Sunday. Sundays are so different here. Won't I be glad to reach dear old Cumberland again which I hope to do by August?

The old farmer here is much amused. A hen started to cackle and one of the fellows started to look for the egg. While he was looking, the old lad came along and got it, as he knew right where the nest was. I don't think he gets many. There are too many of us looking for them. They are a real treat to us.

We can get many things, such as apples, oranges, chocolate, etc., in the villages around here, but we have to pay about three times what they're worth.

I wish my letters weren't censored. I would write a different letter. Wish I were with you during the maple sugar season.

Although Kennedy wrote faithfully to his sweetheart, his diary entries were becoming briefer, less detailed. He briefly noted attending an open-air service on 4 April, Easter Sunday, and then stood guard duty in the evening, again on 5 April, and the next day, after reveille at 4:30 a.m., moving off (with the 1st and 2nd Artillery Brigades) through Steenvoorde to billets near Cassel. So far, the action was relatively uneventful.

April 9: Reveille starts at 5:30 until further notice. Exercise ride before breakfast. Enjoyed it very much. Inspection of total kit by General Morrison at 2:30 p.m.

Saturday, April 10: Exercise ride. Reduced to 2 blankets each. I turned in our kit bags at 2 p.m.

Sunday, April 11: Reveille at 6 a.m. After breakfast fell in for Church Parade at 9:30. Major McCrae spoke to us.[2] Went on guard in the evening.

April 12: Reveille at 5:30 as usual. Half an hour exercise ride. Cleaned up and fell in for inspection by General Smith Dorrien. Saw old chums of 2nd Bat., 1st Infantry Bd., Stoddart, Boulter, Andrews etc.

In a letter to Eva, 20 April, 4:45 a.m.:

It is now daylight. I have been on guard and just came off duty at 4:30 after two hours of sentry. George M. gave me this envelope so I'll make good use of it.

I'm not sorry I enlisted, and now that the rough weather is over, we will have to put up with chilly weather. From now on we will be living entirely in the open-air, except on wet nights when we will sleep in barns.

I can't tell you where we are, but we've moved twice in the last two weeks. Perhaps you can see what's on the outside of the envelope.

(There was nothing to indicate the location of the troops, of course. The gray/green military envelope merely said "Field Post Office.")

The quiet was not to last. The French forces (under General Joffre), were heavily committed in the Champagne area farther south and had asked for more help in the Flanders area. The British Expeditionary Force Commander, Sir John French, agreed to send troops to relieve several French units in the Ypres area. He assigned the task to General (later Field Marshal) Sir Douglas Haig and his British First Army.

Thus came the Battle of Neuve Chapelle, the first real attempt by British forces to seize part of the heavily defended German trench system.

Neuve Chapelle

The battle began on Wednesday, 10 March, at 7:30 in the morning when 342 British guns rumbled into life with a deafening 35-minute barrage on the German line.[3] Just 36 minutes later, the infantrymen of the British First Army climbed from their trenches and advanced onto No Man's Land. Less than an hour later, they took Neuve Chapelle. It appeared to be wonderfully successful.

Unfortunately, however, the battle was not over. With telephone lines severed, messengers had to run back and forth with orders and instructions, some of which were confused or conflicting. Because of the disastrous breakdown in communications, the British Commanders halted where they were, waiting for more instructions. Their wait stretched into five hours, during which Germans rushed in reinforcements and retook much of the ground they had just ceded.

Just two days later, 12 March, most British gains had evaporated, and lines were almost where they had been originally. About 13,000 men on each side had died for a few yards of relatively unimportant frontage.

Though anxious to "get on with it," Canadians had not been summoned to fight in this battle, although they provided backup artillery support to distract the enemy. To their chagrin, they were still receiving further training. When the Canadians had come to France, they had been preceded by

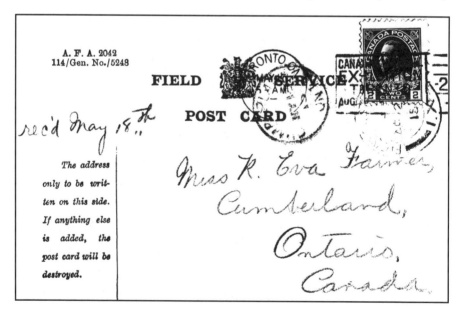

NOTHING is to be written on this side except the date and signature of the sender. Sentences not required may be erased. If anything else is added the post card will be destroyed.

I am quite well.

~~I have been admitted into hospital~~

~~{ sick }~~ ~~and am going on well.~~
~~{ wounded }~~ ~~and hope to be discharged soon.~~

~~I am being sent down to the base.~~

I have received your { letter dated *March 15*.
~~telegram~~ ,, ─────
~~parcel~~ ,, ─────

Letter follows at first opportunity.

I have received no letter from you

~~{ lately.~~
{ *for a long time.*

Signature } *Bob*
only. }

Date *April 26 / 15.*

[Postage must be prepaid on any letter or post card addressed to the sender of this card.]

(3023) Wt. W 13084-411. 1,300m. 3/15. C. & S.

Robert Kennedy sent this "Whizbang" (the nickname for the Canadian Field Service standardized postcard) to Eva, on March 15, 1915. It was received by her on May 18th. Note that he made his "selections" from the various options listed on the Whizbang.

rumors that questioned their drill and discipline. They were anxious to prove otherwise.

Insight into the non-battle routine can be found in a "Memorandum on Training" from Colonel C. F. Romer to the 1st, 2nd, and 3rd Canadian Infantry Brigades on 26 March 1915. He noted that while brigades would be called on for various working parties, the Commanding Officers should pay attention to further training, such as "charging in marching order over cultivated ground" (which required extreme physical fitness) and rapid entrenching both by day and by night. Battalions, including "bombers" (men trained in the use of hand grenades and explosives), wire cutters, plank or bridge carriers, should be trained to assault hostile trenches.

"Officers and men must be trained to lay out a line of trenches at night over unreconnoitered ground."[4]

A change finally occurred on the first day of April. Sir John French decided to transfer the Canadians to the British Second Army, commanded by General Horace Smith-Dorrien, in the Ypres Salient. They would come under the immediate command of General Sir Herbert C. O. Plumer of Second Army 5th Corps. By 5 April, the Canadian troops were heading northward to the Cassel area, less than 20 miles west of Ypres. From there they continued to march over torn-up ground, past bombed houses, and to and through the battered town of Ypres on the Yser Canal at the southern margin of the Flanders plain. There was little time to contemplate the once-stunning Cloth Hall or the historical St. Martin's Cathedral.

The men were excited. Their turn had finally come.

The Ypres Salient, it will be recalled, was that embattled profile-like area that projected about six miles north and eastward from the town of Ypres into the German line. The ancient moated town and the Salient had remained a volatile area since the first battle of Ypres the previous Fall, when Germany's Fourth Army had attempted — but failed — to drive the British from the Salient as part of a wider endeavor to break through to the Channel. The curving perimeter of the Salient line itself was about 17 miles long, stretching from Steenstraat on the north to St. Eloi on the south.

In a way, the Salient was not really of strategic importance. Better, higher ground lay elsewhere. Furthermore, jutting out as it did, it was vulnerable from three sides. But Ypres was the only significant town left unconquered in Belgium, and the British, like the French before them, were determined to hold it at all costs. Now the Canadians, in relieving some of the French troops, would also play a part in holding the infamous Ypres Salient.

When the Canadian troops took over the French trenches, however, they were in for a rude awakening. The field fortifications left much to be desired. The French troops had seen their trenches as temporary arrangements only — something that would be abandoned shortly as they forged ahead. Thus, parapets were poorly constructed, if at all, and in many instances, not bulletproof. In some cases there were no parados to protect troops from the rear. There were no gun pits for the artillery. For concealment, gun muzzles had to be poked through a hedge or bush, or covered by a few branches. Trenches were not always connected. There were few

A road close to the 2nd Infantry Brigade HQ (Fortuin) at the Second Battle of Ypres, April and May 1915.   *National Archives of Canada, PA 004643*

or no kinks in the line (traverses) to prevent enfilading fire. Sanitary conditions were generally appalling; more often than not, men would simply relieve themselves in the nearest shell hole or crater.

One report on the condition of the trenches was written on 21 April 1915, by Captain T. C. Irving of the 2nd Field Company. He noted 15 isolated portions of trenches in Section 1, some with no parados, some with water level two feet below the surface of the ground, some with plugged drains. "In front of these sections are numerous dead bodies in a decomposed state lying on the surface of the ground, also in the trench itself." The report continued, "There is also human excreta littered all over the place."[5]

The Canadian troops immediately began to connect the trenches, shore up the parapets, build gun emplacements, construct dugouts and traverses, and revet and thicken the parapets, adding sandbags in the process to make them bulletproof. Hindering the process was the shock and stench of trying to work amid decaying bodies and human excreta. Disinfectant had to be applied liberally.

While the troops were working feverishly to bring the trenches up to British standards, far more ominous events were surfacing elsewhere.

On 30 March, a bulletin of the French Tenth Army noted that the German army in the Salient area was making rather peculiar preparations for something or other. A fortnight later, 15 April, there was more disturbing news. The 5th Corps reported that a German deserter (August Jaeger, captured near Langemarck on 13 April) had revealed plans by the Germans to release an asphyxiating gas through pipes in the forward trenches.

But the Allies didn't pay much attention to the reports, even after a Belgian spy stated that the Germans would attack the Ypres area on the night of 15-16 April. Nothing happened. Obviously the reports and rumors were wrong. (The spy was actually correct with regard to the day; however, the winds didn't cooperate and the Germans delayed the attack.) Besides, the Allies were fairly confident that the Germans would never violate the rules of international warfare. After all, the use of asphyxiating gas had been banned by the International Declaration at the Hague in July 1899. Germany had signed it.

Still the rumors and reports persisted, and on 16 April, a Belgium army bulletin reported that the Germans were buying 20,000 respirators or mouth protectors for their own troops. Again, no one paid much attention. General Joffre's French Headquarters scoffed: "All this gas business need not be taken seriously." The British, too, turned a deaf ear.[6] And life labored on in the trenches.

As scheduled, the Canadian troops relieved the French (11th Division) between 14 and 17 April, with General Alderson assuming command on the 17th. With responsibility for a two and a half mile (4,500 yard) sector, Alderson sent the 2nd and 3rd Brigades to the front line. He moved the 1st Brigade into reserve, west of Ypres at Vlamertinghe, to be on call if needed at a place called Hill 60.

Hill 60, just 4,000 yards southeast of Ypres itself, was really not much of a hill in the ordinary sense of the word. It was a mound of earth — actually an artificial pile of dirt thrown up by excavations for a railway — just

60 meters high (hence its name) currently held by the Germans, who had captured it in December 1914. Its value lay in its location at the edge of the Salient, and in its height, which gave the Germans an overview of Ypres and the Salient. Naturally, the British wanted it badly, and to this end had dug several mines under the hill, filling the excavations with five tons of explosives. On the evening of 17 April, they detonated the explosives, killing most of the 150 defenders.[7] British troops (13th Brigade) rushed up the now cratered hill and took the German trenches. However, the Germans immediately counterattacked in a desperate attempt to hold the hill. For three days, vicious fighting continued. On 20 April, the Germans began a relentless bombardment of Ypres, with many of the shells weighing a ton or more. The battle for Hill 60 was escalating.

The following day, Major General Mercer, Commander of Canada's 1st Brigade, received new orders. The British needed help. Mercer was to be prepared to advance to Hill 60 at an hour's notice. The Canadians immediately prepared to move off quickly.

But they would not go to Hill 60. Fate — and Germany — intervened.

NOTES

1. Colonel J. A. Currie, M.P., *"The Red Watch" with the First Canadian Division in Flanders* (London: Constable and Co., 1916), 146.
2. This was Major (later Lieutenant Colonel) John McCrae, the army physician who had signed Kennedy's military papers in Quebec, and who would, in just a few days, write one of the best-known poems of the war, "In Flanders Fields."
3. Historian Martin Gilbert notes the remarkable transformation of the nature of war in just 15 years, in that more shells were fired in that 35-minute barrage than in the whole 1899-1901 Boer War. *The First World War, A Complete History*, 2nd ed. (New York: Henry Holt and Co., 1994), 132.
4. Colonel A. Fortescue Duguid, *Official History of the Canadian Forces in the Great War 1914-1918*, Vol. 1 (Ottawa: Minister of National Defence, 1938), Appendix, 306.
5. *Ibid.*, Appendix, 334.
6. Colonel G. W. L. in Nicholson, C.D., *Canadian Expeditionary Force 1914-1919: Official History of the Canadian Army in the First World War* (Ottawa: Queen's Printer, 1964), 61.
7. Underground tunnels, loaded with explosive charges were deadly. Often dug by volunteers who had been miners in peacetime, their explosions would confuse, concuss, or kill the defenders. Martin recounts the time British entered a dugout

that they had exploded and found "four German officers comfortably seated and outwardly unhurt. They were dead from concussion." Gilbert, *The First World War*, 131.

The English and Scotch troops say that the Canadians are the bravest they ever heard tell of, but add that they are also the most headstrong, and that is the reason why so many Canucks get killed.
— Norman McIntosh, in a letter to his father, June 1915 (Percy L. Climo, *Let Us Remember*)

Chapter 9

Gas — And the Second Battle of Ypres

THE FACT THAT THE Allies had held the Ypres Salient in Belgium since the first battle of Ypres months before was unsettling to the Germans, particularly to their Fourth Army just north of Ypres, commanded by Duke Albrecht of Württemberg. But because many German troops had been shifted eastward to prepare for the big push against the Russians, no large-scale offensive could be undertaken at the Western Front. However, that didn't rule out nettlesome activities on a lesser scale — and the German High Command therefore sanctioned smaller offensives in the Ypres area partly to draw attention from its eastward movements.

But there was also another, more sinister, reason for these small offensives. Because of the favorable wind directions, Ypres could provide a marvelous opportunity to experiment with a new, secret weapon — gas![1] Accordingly, General von Falkenhayn and Duke Albrecht decided to launch a gas attack against the French lines (specifically the 87th Territorial and 45th Algerian Divisions) north

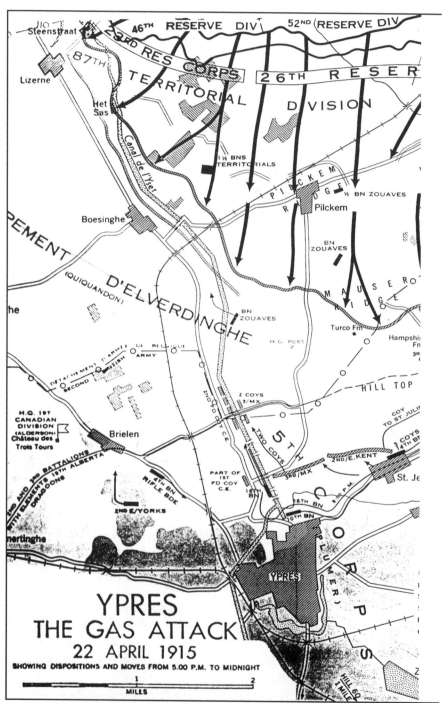

Adapted from Colonel G. W. L. Nicholson, C.D., *Canadian Expeditionary Force 1914-1919: Official History of the Canadian Army in the First World War* (Ottawa: Queen's Printer, 1964).

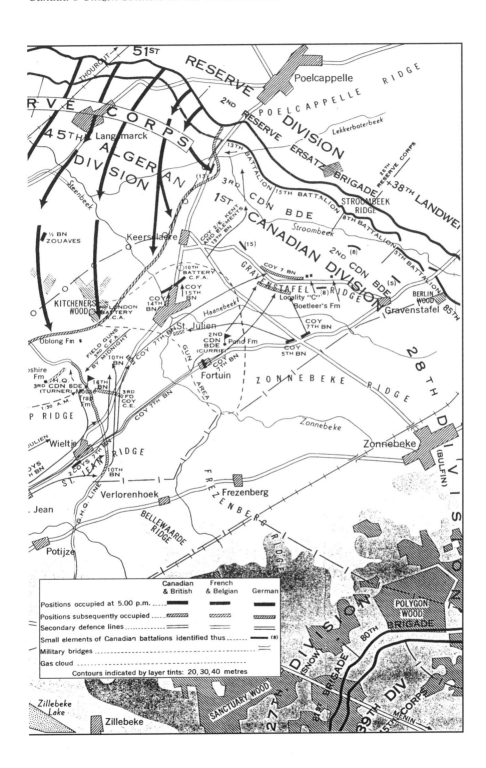

of Ypres in the area of Pilckem Ridge and Mauser Ridge. They set the time for the early morning hours, 5:30 a.m., of 22 April.

And so dawned the fateful day — another glorious Spring day too lovely for warfare. Though there was a bit of morning mist, it soon dissipated in the growing warmth of the sunshine. Even the larks and thrushes were singing. But there was hardly any breeze. And that for the Germans was a serious problem. They would have to delay the attack and, with the delay, risk discovery!

At the same time, on the Canadian side of the front line, and just to the right of the Algerians, troops of the 3rd and 2nd Brigades of the First Division (commanded by Major General Turner and Lieutenant General Currie, respectively) were somewhat subdued, having spent much of the previous night repairing and fortifying the trenches and repairing wire. They were tired. The 1st Brigade, still in reserve but on alert as it waited for its summons to Hill 60, continued training. (Robert Kennedy, however, with his Ammunition Column, had already moved to a farm near St. Julien, just behind the Algerian-Canadian front line.) Only the continual bombardment of Ypres distracted the troops.

As the morning wore on, Germans continued to devastate Ypres with shells from heavy guns and howitzers, blowing up roads and bridges. One five-foot, one-ton (42cm) shell landed in the Grand Place, killing about 40 soldiers and civilians in one blast. People streamed out of Ypres, "old men sweating between the shafts of handcarts piled high with household treasures . . . aged women or wagons stacked with bedding or in wheelbarrows trundled by the family in turn."[2]

Kennedy found snatches of time to scribble disjointed notes in his diary in the early part of the day:

Thursday April 22: Eight months today since I left Ottawa. Looked after the horses and made dugouts to stay in. . . . Rapid firing in trenches and shells dropping near batteries. Terrible hail of shells. Jack Johnsons[3] in front and behind.

Gas Attack

North of the Ypres Salient, German soldiers hunched in their front-line trenches sweltering in the heat. They couldn't release the gas. There was no wind. They waited. Noon came and went. Still, no wind! But finally, in late afternoon, the wind stirred, and some light breezes began to blow southward. The attack could go on! German artillery immediately began to bombard the French lines. Then they opened the valves of the gas cylinders, and the deadly vapors began to drift southward over No Man's Land and onto the unsuspecting French and Algerian troops.

Those receiving the brunt of the attack (the French Territorials, Moroccans, and Algerians) began to flee backwards, sometimes falling, fainting, and vomiting. Many, frothing at the mouth or blinded, could not rise again and lay where they fell, writhing in agony. Some, terrorized and grasping their throats, jumped into trenches or shell holes, the worst possible places to take shelter because the chlorine, being heavier than air, settled in the lower spots. Those who could, ran southward in terror, trying to outrun the noxious suffocating, yellowish-green gas. Because the cloud was drifting south at five or six miles an hour, however, they could not.

Soldiers of 13th (Royal Highlanders of Montreal) Battalion, some of the same troops who had been repairing trenches the night before, were among the first Canadians to notice the peculiar phenomenon — "a cloud of green vapor several hundred yards in length" — over to their left near the French trenches, and drifting slowly southward. They were not sure what to make of it. They weren't long in finding out.

Fortunately for the Canadian troops, two medical officers, Lieutenant Colonel George Nasmith of Toronto and Captain F. A. C. Scrimger, a surgeon from the Royal Victoria Hospital of Montreal, were both near Ypres and quickly assessed the situation. Nasmith immediately began working on a chemical solution to the gas problem. Scrimger had a more immediate solution. He told men to urinate on their handkerchiefs or puttees (a long strip of cloth wound spirally around the leg for protection and support) and tie them over their nose and mouth. The action would save many.

Many men would later pen their thoughts of those first frightful hours. Lieutenant Colonel Edward W. B. Morrison, a former editor of the *Ottawa Citizen*, now Commander of the 1st Artillery Brigade, Canadian Field Artillery (CFA), wrote to his Mother on 1 May of the demoralized French troops, of artillery horses being unhooked from guns and limbers ("horses with men on them but no guns behind them") for quick transportation, and civilians fleeing in terror. The artillery had been in almost continuous action for ten days, and as he wrote, he was still in the trenches under heavy fire. (Morrison's letter was reprinted in the Ottawa newspaper.)

Then came the saddest sight of all, the miserable inhabitants of Ypres, chiefly women and children and very old men, streaming along the road, many of them wounded, many more too young or too old to hobble along.

With these came wounded soldiers, partially asphyxiated soldiers, auto ambulances, traction motors, staff officers in racing motors trying to get us to the front; behind all the town of Ypres beginning to blaze in the thickening gloom under a hell of shell fire.

. . . Of the men actually engaged with the guns I have already lost more than fifty killed and wounded and about the same number of horses killed, though the latter are a mile in the rear. My men are standing the gaff splendidly. Whatever may happen, I think Canada can depend we will finish in style.

Morrison also noted that Lieutenant Alexis Helmer, son of Lieutenant Colonel R. A. Helmer of Ottawa, had been instantly killed and was buried in rear of the trenches, with Major John McCrae of the 1st CFA, reading the burial service. McCrae, the sensitive gunner/physician from Guelph, Ontario, was profoundly moved by all the casualties. The world would hear more of him.

One soldier of the Canadian Scottish (16th) Battalion, Private Nathaniel Nicholson, recalled seeing people running wildly every which way. "As a matter of fact, I saw one woman carrying a baby and the baby's head was gone, and it was quite devastating."[4]

Later, on 12 July 1915, Kennedy wrote to Walter Farmer of Cumberland about the fateful day.

I will never forget the night of the 22nd of April. We, part of the ammunition column, had moved up to a farm near St. Julien on the night of the 21st, and spent the next day digging dugouts to sleep in. In the afternoon, when I had almost finished mine, we heard rapid fire and in a few minutes could see a haze of greenish yellow smoke rising up where we knew the trenches were. This was the gas which you have read so much about, but we didn't know it at the time. Soon the shells started coming over, searching for batteries near us — big shells and little ones, filling the air with smoke, and making one continual roar. Finally the

gas reached us, but we were too far back for it to do any harm, though it made our eyes sore and caused the horses to cough.

We saw the Algerians coming back, but we didn't understand what was really happening. Just as we finished supper we got orders to harness up and hook on.

We did so, and waited. The rifle bullets started to whistle over our heads and a messenger came running up and told our captain to beat it. We did so immediately, but found the road crowded with French people, trying to escape with their household goods from the Germans. The German shells were, by this time, passing over our heads, and as they increased their range, were falling on Ypres.

In trying to pass a French wagon, I lost mine (a transport wagon). We were told to pull across a little ditch and then catch up to the rest of the column, which was ahead of us. I didn't think we could cross the ditch but my wheel driver and I couldn't very well do anything else so we tried. The front wheels stuck and the reach broke, but with a mighty pull, our horses pulled the front wheels out of the ditch and out of the wagon too.

We could see the Germans coming over the ridge on our right, and we had to travel along a road parallel to them for quite a while. They saw us and fired at us with their rifles, but no one was injured. In the engagement, we lost two wagons and had one horse killed. We got the wagons back several days later, however.

For days and days we worked like slaves, sleeping when we could grab a minute, always with our clothes on. I found the first days the hardest. Afterwards, I got used to it.[5]

In a letter to his Mother, John McCrae wrote:

The general impression in my mind is of a nightmare. We have been in the most bitter of fights. For seventeen days and seventeen nights none of us have had our clothes off, nor our boots even, except occasionally. In all that time while I was awake, gunfire and rifle fire never ceased for sixty seconds. . . . And behind it all was the constant background of the sights of the dead, the wounded, the maimed, and a terrible anxiety lest the line should give away.[6]

Gunner J. A. Butler, of the 2nd Battery, 1st Brigade, wrote to his mother in Ottawa on 28 June:

> . . . the war is certainly claiming dead every day. It has been fierce here since the hot weather set in. I helped bury some of the Canadians and I tell you it was some job. . . . The smell on the roads would knock you down, caused by so many horses being killed and not buried.
>
> We have moved quite a bit around the firing line. There is not a position on the line that the Canadians have not been in. We have been in some pretty hot engagements and although our casualties were many, we are still going strong.
>
> I was in a barn one day, with another chap, just about half a mile behind our infantry trenches, and we started to go back to our guns. But the Germans were shelling the roads, so it was impossible for us to get there. We stayed in the barn where there were six cows. The other fellow started to milk the cows nearest the wall at one end of the barn. I left him there and went to the other end of the barn where there were some hens. I got quite a few eggs and was going back to ask if we would bring any of the hens back with us. When I was about fifteen yards away from him, a shell came right through the wall and killed him and the cow he was milking and the next cow too. I certainly got splattered and went into the house to wash myself. You may not believe me, but I was washing myself in a basin that was on a table and a shell came through the wall and took basin and table.[7]

The letters from the Front told only part of the story.

In the late afternoon hours of 22 April, the devastating effects of 168 tons of chlorine gas on front-line troops resulted in a critical gap in the Allied line, though no one seemed to know at the time exactly how great the gap was. The confusion was understandable. With telephone lines disrupted by heavy shelling (wireless radio was not yet in use), initial reports were conflicting. Some indicated that the French had lost all their guns (they had indeed lost 57[8]) and had been driven backwards. Several messages around 7 p.m. indicated that the Canadian line had also broken and been forced back as far as St. Julien, northeast of Ypres. There were reports of a gap of 8,000 yards threatening the loss not only of Ypres itself, but all Allied troops still holding the Salient.

There were many questions. How great, in fact, was the gap? Was a major rout in the offing? Had the Germans broken through the Canadian line as well? Was the whole Ypres Salient in jeopardy?

The answers would take hours to determine. Whatever the case, however, one answer was obvious. The French had suffered a serious setback.

To be sure, there was confusion at Mouse Trap Farm, headquarters of Major General Turner and his 3rd Brigade. Although not lacking in personal courage (he had won the Victoria Cross in the South African War and now concealed broken ribs to be in the thick of battle), Turner was unable to grasp the overall situation, and sent several erroneous messages to the 2nd Brigade and to Division headquarters. To be fair, however, it should be noted that his headquarters were now almost in the front line, and in the midst of shelling and disruption.

Though few knew it, the Canadian line had not broken. Unknown to many on either side of No Man's Land, troops of the 13th (Royal Highlanders of Canada) Battalion were still holding their part of the front line north of St. Julien, immediately to the right of the gassed Algerian Division. At 5 p.m., at the first hint of trouble, their Commanding Officer, Lieutenant Colonel Frederick Loomis had ordered his men to stand to arms, and take battle positions. They would hold their ground as long as humanly possible, though, with the Algerians having been routed, their left side was now exposed.

Their trenches, however, were now pulverized, almost non-existent. Some men had only 12 to 18 inches of earth for protection. (It will be recalled that the Canadians had inherited very poor trenches from the French troops, some with neither parados nor parapets.) Just to their rear (about 600 yards) two of their platoons, headed by Major Edward Norsworthy, second in command of the 13th Battalion, tried desperately to hold back Germans sweeping in from the left side. But the little group was no match for the superior numbers of the enemy. Norsworthy, in fact, had been tricked into thinking that French reinforcements were arriving when he saw men approaching in French uniforms and carrying a French flag. He held his fire until he realized, too late, he was surrounded by Germans. As darkness fell, all men in the platoons were killed or captured. Norsworthy himself, "disabled by a bullet wound in the neck, was bayoneted and killed while rallying his men with easy cheerfulness."[9] Also killed at the same time was Captain Guy Drummond. There were many people back in Canada who believed that the talented young French Canadian from a prominent Montreal family would someday be Prime Minister of Canada. It was not to be.

As word spread about the gas, troops everywhere sprang into action. Several batteries of the Canadian Field Artillery opened fire on the German trenches. About two miles behind the 13th Battalion, the 10th Battery under Major William B. M. King was holding an orchard just 500 yards above St. Julien with four 18-pounder field guns. At about 7 p.m., King peered over a hedge and spotted the helmets of a large group of advancing German soldiers. They had already broken through the line formerly held by the fleeing Algerians just to the left (west) of the 13th Battalion. Worse yet, they could now easily swing in behind the Montreal Highlanders and cut them off. (Some already had, in fact, in wiping out Norsworthy's men.) King's men opened fire, but the Germans quickly dug in. Realizing that only a few isolated pockets of Canadians and Algerians were holding off the enemy, King called for backup support.

King stubbornly continued to blast away, slowing the German advance. He was detaining them, but knew it was only a matter of time until his battery, too, would be overwhelmed. And every time horses hauled up ammunition wagons, they were immediately cut down by enemy fire, stranding the wagons. Work parties then tried to bring up some ammunition by hand.

Finally, some help arrived in the form of 60 more troops, including a 19-year-old machine gunner, Lance Corporal Frederick Fisher of the 13th (Royal Highlanders of Canada) Battalion. Fisher and his four-man volunteer crew hurriedly set up their Colt machine gun, and time and time again drove back the advancing Germans. As Fisher's men were picked off one by one, others rushed in to take their place. Finally, however, he alone was left. Instead of retreating, he stubbornly lugged his gun forward, firing incessantly. His defiance in the face of death brought him the Victoria Cross, the first Canadian in the war to receive the highest of all British military honors. Fisher, however, didn't live to receive it; he was killed the next day.[10] But his heroic actions gave King enough time to pull his guns back to some surviving horses where the men were able to hitch up and retreat into the darkness.

By 9 p.m., less than four hours after the gas had been released, the whole Ypres Salient (including the 50,000 British troops and their 150 guns), was in jeopardy.[11] Then came reports that the Germans had taken St. Julien and Mouse Trap Farm (Headquarters of the 3rd Brigade). By 10:00 p.m., another report indicated that the Germans had moved even closer, taking Wieltje.

Both reports, however, were erroneous. The 3rd Brigade was still holding its front-line trenches, though its situation was becoming increasingly precarious. In fact, the whole Canadian line still held, even though its four and a half battalions were badly outnumbered by two German brigades. But their initial 4,000-yard front now had another 4,000 yards of unprotected front line, which had been left vulnerable when the French and Algerians fled.

The Deadly Counterattacks

While Norsworthy, King, Fisher, and others were delaying enemy advances on the road to St. Julien, dramatic events began to unfold elsewhere. The battle had only just begun. Reinforcements had to be found immediately. General Alderson, the Commander of the First Canadian Division was immediately given (by General Smith-Dorrien) the 2nd (Eastern Ontario) and 3rd (Toronto) Battalions, which had been on standby status for action at Hill 60. The 1st (Western Ontario), and 4th (Central Ontario) would be turned over to him the same evening. At the same time, General Plumer transferred the 2nd East Yorkshire Battalion to Alderson. (The Yorkshire battalion was the first of 33 that the British would transfer to Alderson during the second battle of Ypres.)

Late that evening, at the Canadian Divisional Headquarters, General Alderson learned that the French army was planning a counterattack by its 45th Division at nearby Pilckem, and had asked for Canadian help.[12] Alderson agreed to aid the French, and decided to bring forward two more battalions to help at Kitcheners Wood.[13]

One battalion was the 10th (Canadians), from Calgary and Winnipeg, commanded by 34-year-old Lieutenant Colonel Russell Boyle, an Alberta rancher. Though the men of the 10th had been in reserve, they had already been in the thick of battle, having been heavily hit by some of the long-range shells falling mercilessly in and around Ypres. Boyle's troops immediately headed out. Carrying 58 pounds of ammunition, rations, and personal belongings, they marched toward Mouse Trap Farm en route to Kitcheners Wood, nonchalantly singing "O Canada."

The second battalion was the kilted 16th (Canadian Scottish), which had also been in reserve. It was commanded by a former mining engineer from Vancouver, Lieutenant Colonel R. G. E. Leckie. After hearing encouraging words ("A great day for Canada, boys!") from their padre, Major (later Lieutenant Colonel) Canon F. G. Scott, the Canadian Scottish began their move toward Mouse Trap Farm and their colleagues at 8:00 p.m. They soon ran into difficulties. Artillery traffic, civilians, and ambulances all blocked the roadway. And now, for the first time, they could smell and taste the aftermath of the earlier gas attack. Some troops, plodding slowly with their heavy packs dumped their cumbersome greatcoats. (They would never recover them; the Germans mistook them for troops the next day and blew them to smithereens.) By 10:00 p.m., however, they reached Mouse Trap Farm and joined the 10th Battalion to wait for further instructions.

The orders for what would be Canada's first major attack of the war (and the first Canadian attack on an enemy since the Boer War in South Africa), soon come through. They were to retake Kitcheners Wood and retrieve lost guns. They would attack about midnight (22-23 April), in the bitter cold, with the 10th Battalion in the lead, in "six waves of men marching shoulder to shoulder on a two-company front."[14] Watches were synchronized.

Private W. J. McKenna expressed the danger: "We were told that our efforts were regarded as practically hopeless and that our work was to be in the nature of a sacrifice charge."[15]

Just before midnight, the 1,500 troops from the two battalions were fully assembled in perfect formation immediately east of Mouse Trap Farm. Then in column, they began to march stealthily northward, shoulder to shoulder, toward Kitcheners Wood. Behind them, 100 bombers and back-up artillery waited in support. Onward they moved, quietly, expectantly — just 1,000 yards to go, hoping to take the enemy by surprise.

But it was not to be. More than halfway there in the dark night, the Canadians bumped into a large beech hedge that was interlaced with barbed wire. The 10th Battalion, in front, with entrenching tools and wire cutters, finally cut and wiggled through the barrier and reformed on the other side. But they couldn't avoid considerable noise in the process. Suddenly, a German flare lit up the sky, fully revealing below it the two Canadian battalions. Though the exposed troops quickly dropped to the ground, many were picked off like sitting ducks by the Germans now ensconced in Kitcheners Wood. The slaughter was enormous. Still, some continued to fight on in the terrible confusion, many engaging in hand-to-hand conflict, bayonets flashing in the light of the Very flares. Captain John Geddes of the 16th Battalion, as he lay dying, urged his troops to continue. Though many officers fell dead, the soldiers fought on.

But now there was rampant confusion in the dark woods as troops, separated by hand-to-hand skirmishes, tried to sort themselves out. There were, of course, far fewer to sort. It soon became evident that they, too, would need help, and need it quickly. By two o'clock in the morning, Colonel Leckie (16th Battalion) was calling for assistance.

For its part, the 10th Battalion was now under its third Commander within an hour when Major Dan Ormond, formerly a lawyer from Manitoba had to take over. The first Commander, Colonel Boyle (the Alberta rancher), had been felled by a German machine gunner as he tried to read his map by flashlight, and, though not yet dead, was mortally wounded. His replacement, Major Joseph MacLaren, a former schoolteacher, had been sent to the rear for treatment of a wound, ironically to be killed almost immediately in his ambulance by a shellburst in the streets of Ypres. Now Ormond was Commander of the 10th Battalion, and half of his troops had already been wounded or killed. And he and his few men were surrounded.

Help was on the way, however. By now the two fresh battalions, the 2nd (Eastern Ontario) and 3rd (Toronto) were en route to the area. Both had begun to move quietly through the darkness, though the fields were lit here and there by burning farm buildings. The Toronto battalion was headed for a spot facing north behind the General Headquarters line. The Eastern Ontario troops were groping their way to Kitcheners Wood to help in the counterattack. But a number of setbacks, caused by trying to negotiate narrow roads in the darkness and unfamiliar territory, tragically delayed them until daylight.

Just "as dawn rolled away night's sheltering curtain" the Eastern Ontario battalion's "A" Company ran into heavy German machine-gun and rifle fire, as well as tear gas. In less than two minutes the attack was over. "The slope was littered with lifeless or writhing bodies. No one reached the redoubt and only a dozen managed to join the men of Ormond's decimated 10th battalion."[16]

British troops (the chaps of the 13th Brigade who had been battling tooth and nail for Hill 60) were now "loaned" to the Canadians, though it was their own General (Smith-Dorien) who determined their location. He told Alderson to use them in an attack between Kitcheners Wood and the Canal de l'Yser.

In the chaos of war, Canada's 1st and 4th Battalions, though they themselves were pinned down on Mauser Ridge, were then told to back up the British troops. Lieutenant Colonel Arthur P. Birchall, Commander of the 4th Battalion, was still looking for French support, believing them to be nearby and merely hidden behind hedges. Assuming they would attack in concert with his troops, Birchall forged ahead. But his battalion was by itself. The French didn't materialize. They couldn't. Their 45th Division, its troops in disarray and suffering from the effects of the gas, and its artillery lost, was almost non-existent. The 87 Territorial Division was equally shattered.

As Birchall and his men advanced toward the crest of Hill Top Ridge in the early morning hours (about 5:30 on 23 April), the Germans held their fire, but only until the advancing Canadians were in perfect range. Then, rifle and machine guns decimated the 4th Battalion. By 7:30 a.m., many of Birchall's troops lay dead or dying in the fields. Birchall desperately appealed for help.

The survivors of the 1st Battalion with "The Diehards" of the British 3rd Brigade (Middlesex Regiment) immediately pushed forward another 100 yards to try to help, but then had to pull back in bitter frustration. By 8:00 a.m., they looked back over the "Field of Manure Piles" where they had fought. The extent of the carnage was all too visible in the daylight hours. Hundreds of bodies, some in khaki and some in the bright blue, white, and red of the 45th Algerian Division lay on the field — men who had fled through the field in the opposite direction the day before. A few survivors were still clutching their throats from the effects of the suffocating gas.

And now they were joined in death by hundreds of Canadians, lying where they fell, some easily identifiable by the kilts they were wearing. Of the 10th Battalion whose 816 young men had charged out at 11:45 the night before nonchalantly singing "O Canada," only five officers and 188 other ranks survived.[17] The 16th was equally decimated. They counted off 5 officers and 263 other ranks. The flesh of the advancing troops had been no match for the machine gun. Even the surviving troops were shaken. Sargeant Charlie Stevenson of Calgary, Alberta, described the scene:

> I looked back across the field we had crossed the previous night, and I could see what havoc had been wrought on our boys, for all around were the dead bodies of men who, a few hours before, had been singing Canada's national song. They died with it on their lips, but their memory will live for many a day and year to come. For they made a name for the Dominion that will live in history.[18]

The fighting continued, though it was hastily planned and based in part on erroneous information. During the day on 23 April, the Canadians repulsed four attacks on St. Julien, but casualties mounted fiercely. The 13th (Montreal's Royal Highlanders) and 15th (Highlanders of Canada) Battalions were hit by tear gas shells. Ontario's 1st and 4th, sometimes with only manure piles to protect them, were now suffering not only from shell fire but hunger and thirst. They had each lost more than 400 men. Colonel Birchall, a cane in one hand and a revolver in the other, was killed as he led a charge on a German trench. Meanwhile, the besieged Major Ormond and what remained of his 10th Battalion watched in horror as more than 2,000 British Regulars were scythed down in a matter of moments on their way to help the Canadians. Only 10 or 15 men reached the troops they had come to help.

Personal heartbreak was a frequent visitor everywhere on the bloodied battlefield. Lieutenant Arthur Ryerson of Toronto was hauling ammunition to his guns across the fields replete with bodies when he came across the body of his own brother George. His malignant luck was to follow him. He was later wounded and sent to England to recuperate. His mother and little sister, their hearts set on visiting him, would take the great liner, the HMS *Lusitania* in May to see him, compounding the tragedy.[19]

The situation seemed hopeless. Colonel Leckie (of the 16th Canadian Scottish), seeing the human wreckage, ordered the two battalions to withdraw. They could not hold Kitcheners Wood. The plucky but inexperienced young Canadians had to retreat.

By the end of the day, there were extraordinary Canadian and British losses. There had been no gains.

The night brought scant relief. Soldiers in sweaty uniforms now found themselves in poor, water-logged trenches or ditches, or behind manure piles. The temperature fell below freezing. Kennedy noted that the night was cold, and they had "nothing but saddle blankets" to keep warm. Some had not eaten for more than a day. But as flames shot skyward from the terrible fires in Ypres, the two shattered Ontario battalions (1st and 4th) were sent to the rear for rest, and replaced by British battalions.

Left behind, at least temporarily, were heart-breaking scenes. "There was one horse out there between us and the Germans. For three days after the attack he went around with just the lower part of a man's body in the saddle. From the waist up there was nothing. A good-sized shell had hit him."[20]

The Battle Continues

Meanwhile, on the German side of the front, Duke Albrecht, originally elated by German advances, was now less than happy. His troops still had not taken the Salient. Perhaps he should try gas once again in the hopes of taking St. Julien. And so he ordered a second gas attack — this time on the stubborn Canadians where they held the apex of the Salient.

The next day, 24 April, at four o'clock in the morning, the Germans opened their bombardment on the Canadians and released chlorine gas in front of the 8th (90th Rifles) and 15th (48th Highlanders of Canada) Battalions. Swarming in behind the gas cloud came the German infantry, the favorable wind at their back.

But the "Little Black Devils" of the 8th Battalion (as they were called) weren't quite ready to collapse and flee, though their bandoliers and hand-kerchiefs, dampened by water or urine, were next to useless against the gas. Many fell like flies. At one point, Sergeant Major F. W. Hall dodged bullets to drag two wounded men back into the relative safety of the trench. But he couldn't bear to hear the anguished groans of another victim still in the open, so crawled back out to the wounded man. Sticking his head up to find the way back, he was shot and killed. (He received the Victoria Cross posthumously.)

Meanwhile, those who could, fired their Ross rifles repeatedly until they jammed. Desperate soldiers, some of them cursing their rifles, tried to unjam the bolts with their entrenching tools or the heels of their boots, often to no avail. But still they fought, killing many of the approaching Germans in their tracks, some of whom were a bit too confident in the potential of the gas. And backing up the Little Black Devils, the 2nd Field Artillery Brigade shot off shrapnel at the rate of half a ton a minute.

In the heat of battle, confusion returned. At 7:15 a.m., about three hours after the new gas had been released, the 15th Battalion (48th Highlanders of Canada) was told to hold the front line and not retreat. By that time, however, the kilted fighters had lost 671 men and had been largely anni-hilated by the Germans. There were few left to hold.

The Germans had halted briefly in the face of such unexpected resis-tance, but soon resumed their assault, and the Canadian and British forces had to pull back. Once more the beleaguered 13th Battalion was vulner-able, and it, too, had to abandon its trenches.

There were numerous acts of bravery as the carnage continued. Lieu-tenant Edward Bellew, formerly with the Royal Irish Regiment and now a machine-gun officer of the 7th Battalion, though completely cut off from his battery, fired relentlessly at the enemy till he ran out of ammunition. Then, wounded, he fought hand-to-hand with fixed bayonet until he was captured and taken prisoner. Like Hall, Bellew received the Victoria Cross for valor.[21]

By 11 a.m., seven hours after the gas was released, and in the face of overwhelming odds, the Commanders of the 15th and 7th Battalions (Lieutenant Colonel J. A. Currie[22] and Brigadier General Victor Odlum) decided to withdraw 300 yards.

The fighting continued all afternoon, however, and British troops (two Yorkshire battalions) were moved in to help the besieged Canadians. But still the German forces, far superior in numbers, surged southward.

Again, individual acts of heroism graced the battlefield. Captain F. A. C. Scrimger, who just days before had urged men to urinate on their hand-kerchiefs to ward off the effects of gas, once more found himself in a desperate situation as enemy fire hit the headquarters of the 3rd Brigade at Mouse Trap Farm. He immediately dashed into the burning building to retrieve wounded men. Most were rescued, but one man, Captain Harold MacDonald, remained. Scrimger returned for him, dressed his wounds on the spot, then carried him out on his back. At one point, under shellfire, he put MacDonald on the ground and sheltered him from gun fire with his own body until help arrived.[23] Scrimger was the fourth Canadian in the second battle of Ypres to win the rare and precious Victoria Cross.

As evening turned to darkness, there was more confusion in the Allied lines. The reader today might wonder why, but in 1915 there was little in the way of aerial observation or photography, as well as poor telephone communications and large-scale deficiencies in signal communications. Most messages were delivered by runners who, as often as not, were killed trying to get through. And so conflicting reports begat confusion among the Commanders. Nonetheless, another counterattack by Allied forces was ordered for the early morning hours of 25 April, even though the remaining troops were by now terribly exhausted.[24]

When the British troops moved forward, they were hit by rifle and machine-gun fire, and were cut down in droves, with "the dead and wounded lying in long rows."[25] By 9:15 a.m., though the battalions had fought magnificently, the attack was deemed a failure. And by now the 10th Battalion had yet another Commander. A former politician in New Brunswick, Major Percy Guthrie, had come from England on a legal matter, and hearing of the plight of the 10th, volunteered on the spot to serve with them as a junior officer. Now, as the senior surviving officer, he was their fifth Commander in three and a half days. Such was the slaughter.

By the following day, 26 April, the Germans held the ridge west from Gravenstafel and St. Julien. General Smith-Dorrien, sickened by so many casualties and the prospect of losing still more, suggested in a letter to his superior, British Commander Sir John French, that they fall back. Sir John was not amused, and promptly replaced Smith-Dorrien with Lieutenant General Sir Plumer. (Actually, Smith-Dorrien had already fallen from Sir John's favor because he, engaging in battle *against* Sir John's directions, had averted a major defeat at Le Cateau.) It would be a strange twist of fate later, when Sir John would allow Plumer to pull back for exactly the same reason advocated by Smith-Dorrien.

On the 27th of April, the British tried to recapture ground taken by the Germans during the previous five days. But in spite of spirited fighting and individual acts of valor, no gains were forthcoming. And that evening, the exhausted Canadians, who had held the line in the first gas attack of the war, were ordered into reserve. After their first 12 days at the Front and 6 days of desperate fighting, the citizen soldiers had proved themselves second to none on the battlefield. By now, aghast at the slaughter, Sir John was prepared to abandon the whole Ypres Salient. He was concerned about the French rout, and he worried about the possibility of yet another deadly gas attack — though he had earlier dismissed Smith-Dorrien for the same prudent thought.

And so Sir John French drove that morning to meet with France's General Ferdinand Foch, at the hilltop town of Cassel. Was the ruined city of Ypres worth defending at such a high cost, he asked Foch. At each turn, Foch out-argued him, and in addition promised a large number of French reinforcements who would mount a renewed assault to retake the original line and trenches. Sir John reluctantly changed his mind and agreed to fight on. He issued orders for a second counterattack almost immediately.

But Foch had not been forthright. His French troop support would actually be in short supply. (Foch later admitted to General Joffre that he had deliberately misrepresented the support he could give. Foch also later confessed to Joffre that far from sending more reinforcements *to* Ypres, he was, rather, calling for troops to be pulled *from* Ypres to strengthen the coming offensive near Arras.[26])

On 30 April, a worried Sir John French visited Sir Douglas Haig warning that British troops should commence to withdraw that night unless the French Divisions "succeeded in advancing their line." Haig tended to agree, and Plumer was allowed to begin to pull back in the darkness with weary soldiers manhandling "tools, rations, boxes of ammunition, and the manifold equipment that sustained a battalion in the line"[27] over the devastated ground.

Some fighting continued, of course, but on a smaller scale. Once again, on 2 May, the Germans used gas, but its effects were so scattered by the wind that most Allied guns, including all Canadian field batteries, were able to drive back the German infantry.

Duke Albrecht still stubbornly lusted for the Salient, however, and continued with his gas attacks. After three such attacks on 5 May, Albrecht's Corps finally recaptured Hill 60 at the edge of the Salient.

By now, troops of the Princess Patricia's Canadian Light Infantry held the British trenches from Menin Road to Frezenberg. So heavy were their casualties on 8 May alone that their Commander, Major Hamilton Gault (who had personally contributed $100,000 to raise the regiment), had to pull in pioneers, orderlies, and batmen (message carriers) to take the place of their fallen comrades. When Major Gault was wounded, Lieutenant H. W. Niven took over (other senior officers having been killed or wounded) and he refused to retreat. But he immediately faced a sad dilemma. He had no stretcher bearers for the wounded, yet was reluctant to let them to die alone. By the time the Patricias were relieved that night, their one-day casualties numbered 392. Their strength was down to 4 officers and 150 men. Though not subjected to poison gas, they had faced "the most overwhelming superiority of artillery fire ever concentrated upon British trenches."[28]

The artillery had suffered as well, having fired and been fired upon, day and night, since 23 April. The 1st Field Artillery Brigade (of which Kennedy was a part, though he worked on 4.5- inch howitzers), had gone into action with 16 18-pounder guns. Now it had only seven, and they were loose on their carriages. They had lost "nearly a hundred officers and men killed or wounded [and] 125 horses."[29]

Lieutenant Colonel Morrison had great praise for his men.

> The gunners were cool even under the heaviest fire and the showing of the batteries was excellent. The dash and skill with which the Drivers brought up ammunition to the batteries under the heaviest shellfire elicited general admiration.[30]

Both sides paid a heavy price in the second battle of Ypres. The BEF had, between 22 April and 31 May, lost 59,275 men. Canadian losses in their first major engagement of the war, between 15 April and 3 May, were 6,036, not including 678 casualties in the PPCLI.[31] The First Division had lost half of its infantrymen. The French and Germans had also lost great numbers, about 10,000 and 35,000 respectively.

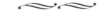

In Flanders Fields

It was in the midst of the havoc and horror of the second battle of Ypres, that Major John McCrae wistfully contemplated the wild poppies blowing in the fields that were now being hallowed by the graves of countless young soldiers, including his friend Alexis Helmer. During a brief lull in the fighting, the Commander of the 1st Artillery Brigade (CFA), Lieutenant Colonel Morrison, watched McCrae scribble a few lines as he looked sadly over the graves. Morrison asked what he was writing. McCrae, thinking his lines worthless, crumpled the paper and threw it in a waste basket. Morrison retrieved it.[32] Who could have foreseen that his poignant lines would be remembered by so many for so long?

> In Flanders Fields
>
> In Flanders fields the poppies blow
> Between the crosses, row on row,
> That mark our place; and in the sky
> The larks, still bravely singing, fly
> Scarce heard amid the guns below.
>
> We are the dead. Short days ago
> We lived, felt dawn, saw sunset glow,
> Loved, and were loved, and now we lie
> In Flanders fields.
>
> Take up our quarrel with the foe:
> To you from failing hands we throw
> The torch: be yours to hold it high.
> If ye break faith with us who die
> We shall not sleep, though poppies grow
> In Flanders fields.

In Retrospect

Although McCrae was deeply saddened by the ungodly loss of life at Flanders, his comrades had indeed caught and held high the torch of valor. Though the Canadians had lost some ground, the reverses were minimal — and more important, the retreat was over! The Germans with far superior numbers and artillery had made a dent in the front line, but they had been denied a breakthrough. They now held Kitcheners Wood and St. Julien, but they had not broken through to Ypres. The Channel ports had been denied to them. The British forces had not been cut off. The Allies still held the Ypres Salient.

Why hadn't the German forces taken the Salient with their advantage of numbers, the element of surprise, and the new weapon of gas? There were a number of factors. Although they were tired (having spent most of the day sweating in the trenches), fatigue was not really a factor. For some reason, some of the gas was not discharged on the west side of the attack. But that, too, was not a defining factor. The Germans, though wearing respirators, had deliberately advanced slowly and cautiously to test the gas. After taking 2,000 prisoners and 51 guns, they halted, at least temporarily, giving the Allies time to regroup. Why did they halt? They halted because they had limited infantry (with some troops already pulled eastward against the Russians), and they had limited objectives. Their primary objective was not a breakthrough, but the experiment with gas. According to the German *Reichsarchiv*:

> The battles of Ypres which began on the 22nd April had their origin on the German side solely in the desire to try the new weapon, gas, thoroughly at the front.[33]

And there was another reason. The assault on the Canadian sector had been a remarkable stroke of luck for the Allies. In spite of all the gaps in the Allied line, the Germans just happened to pick the only place where defenders were still fairly well organized. They had to encounter stiff pockets of resistance from stubborn defenders like Norsworthy, Fisher, and King, and several gallant battalions.

As military historian Colonel A. Fortescue put it:

> . . . The steadfast holding of the line by the 13th Battalion, the irresistible midnight attack of the 10th and 16th [battalions] on

Kitcheners Wood and the vigorous advance of the 1st and 4th [battalions] at daybreak combined to delay and derange formation and execution of Germany offensive plans on the 23rd.[34]

Again, on the 24th of April, the line was held by the 8th and 15th Battalions, in spite of several gas attacks.

Later battle evaluation would show that of Canada's three brigade Commanders, Currie (of the 2nd Brigade) showed the most extraordinary leadership, even when going for days without sleep. He responded immediately to German advances and kept control of his troops. Turner, (3rd Brigade) though personally courageous (he picked up his revolver and vowed to fight to the end), did not appear to have a good grasp of military strategy, and never seemed sure of his position in the front line.[35] Mercer, whose 1st Brigade was originally in reserve, didn't have many opportunities for great leadership. In fairness to all three however, it must be remembered that the much-pledged promises of help from the French never materialized, reconnaissance was far from adequate, and some of the counterattacks were almost suicidal. Nor was there adequate backup artillery support. There was much to learn.

The inexperienced young citizen soldiers in the Canadian army, still equipped with its inferior Ross rifle, had not been found wanting. And their efforts did not go unnoticed. British General Alderson, who commanded the Canadian forces, said he had never been so proud of anything in his life as "this armlet with 'Canada' on it . . . ." Sir John French claimed the Canadians had averted a disaster. French Marshal Ferdinand Foch (who would later became Allied Supreme Commander) called the Canadian counterattack "the finest act in the war." A captured German officer said to the Canadians, "You fellows fight like hell."[36]

Even the King of Great Britain himself cabled the Governor General of Canada:

> Congratulate you most warmly on the splendid and gallant way in which the Canadian Division fought during the last two days north of Ypres. Sir John French says that their conduct was magnificent throughout. The Dominion will be justly proud.
> GEORGE

NOTES

1. For a full account of the Canadian battle at Ypres in 1915, see Daniel G. Dancocks, *Welcome to Flanders Fields: The First Canadian Battle of the Great War, Ypres, 1915* (Toronto: McClelland & Stewart, Inc., 1989); James L. McWilliams and R. James Steel, *Gas! The Battle for Ypres, 1915* (St. Catherines, Ontario: Vanwell Publishing Limited, 1915); George Cassar, *Beyond Courage: The Canadians at the Second Battle of Ypres* (Ottawa: Oberon Press, 1985); or Sandra Gwyn, *Tapestry of War: A Private View of Canadians in the Great War* (Toronto: Harper Collins Publishers, Ltd., 1992).

2. Colonel A. Fortescue Duguid, *Official History of the Canadian Forces in the Great War 1914-1918*, Vol. 1 (Ottawa: Minister of National Defence, 1938), 228.

3. Various names were given by the British troops to bullets, shells, and explosives, among them "Whizzbangs," "Moaning Millies," "Jack Johnsons," "Rum Jars," and "Coal Boxes." The "Jack Johnsons" were large 15-cm high-explosive German shells that left a trail of black smoke and packed a powerful punch, and thus named after the famous American world heavyweight champion boxer, from 1908-1915.

4. In Dancocks, *Welcome to Flanders Fields*, 162-163, and Cassar, *Beyond Coverage*, 71.

5. Kennedy's letter was reprinted in an Ottawa newspaper (date unknown) under the heading "An Ammunition Driver's Story."

6. Quoted in a Canadian Government Veterans Affairs publication.

7. From a letter to Mrs. A. Butler, 168 Murray Street, Ottawa, dated 28 June 1915, and reprinted in an Ottawa newspaper (date unknown) under the heading "Just Missed Two Shells."

8. Duguid, *Official History*, 238.

9. A. B. Tucker, *The Battle Glory of Canada* (London: Cassell, 1915), 110.

10. Duguid, *Official History*, 236.

11. The loss of guns bodes ill for any army. As Stokesbury points out: "Every soldier knows that battles, even victorious ones, cost casualties, but to lose guns is a sure sign that the enemy has won and dominates the field." James L. Stokesbury, *A Short History of World War I* (New York: William Morrow and Co., 1981), 47.

12. Colonel G. W. L. Nicholson, C.D., *Canadian Expeditionary Force 1914-1919: Official History of the Canadian Army in the First World War* (Ottawa: Queen's Printer, 1964), 66.

13. This was not named after the British General Kitchener but came from *Bois des Cuisiniers*. It was located about a mile west of St. Julien.

14. Nicholson, *Canadian Expeditionary Force*, 66. McWilliams and Steel say the battalions advanced in eight waves, but the difference seems unimportant. They describe the odds of surviving the assault, noting that the two battalions advanced "in eight waves on a narrow front only two companies wide. A bullet missing its intended target in the front rank could hardly fail to claim a victim

in one of the seven succeeding waves." The order for the formation, suitable perhaps for a war in an earlier century, came from Lieutenant Colonel Garnet Hughes, son of Colonel Sir Sam Hughes.

15. In Lyn Macdonald, *1915: The Death of Innocence* (London: Penguin Books, 1993), 203.
16. McWilliams and Steel, *Gas!*, 77.
17. *Ibid.*, 77.
18. In Dancocks, *Welcome to Flanders Field*s, 187.
19. Recounted in Tucker, *The Battle Glory of Canada*, 139-140, and Dancocks, *Welcome to Flanders Fields*, 208-209.
20. McWilliams and Steel, *Gas!*, 97-98.
21. Nicholson, *Canadian Expeditionary Force*, 75.
22. No relation to General Arthur W. Currie.
23. Recounted in McWilliams and Steel, *Gas!*, 169.
24. They were also depleted. Norm Christie notes that 7 of the 12 Canadian battalions engaged in the battle had been decimated. "Fifteen hundred Canadians were prisoners (the largest number of Canadian prisoners taken in the war." In *For King and Empire: The Canadians at Ypres* (Winnipeg: Bunker to Bunker Books, 1996), 22.
25. Nicholson, *Canadian Expeditionary Force*, 81.
26. B. H. Liddell Hart, *History of the First World War* (London: Macmillan Publishers, 1997), 191.
27. Macdonald, *1915*, 268.
28. Gywn, *Tapestry of War*, 149, quoting the official regimental history.
29. Dancocks, *Welcome to Flanders Fields*, 314-315.
30. Nicholson, *Canadian Expeditionary Force*, 230, also notes an innovation developed on the Ypres Salient. Previously, artillery brigades had been assigned to support a specific (usually its own) infantry brigade. At Ypres, however, in the confusion of attacks and counterattacks, some Canadian batteries became separated from their parent brigade and "furnished artillery support to whatever troops happened to be holding the particular sector which their guns were in position to cover."
31. Nicholson, *Canadian Expeditionary Force*, 92.
32. Cassar, *Beyond Courage*, 194.
33. *Reischarchiv. Der Weltkreig, 1914-1918*. Berlin, 1932.
34. Duguid, *Official History*, 410.
35. One military writer, Denis Winter, is far more critical, calling the gas attack a military embarrassment because of the ignored warnings. He also claims that the 3rd Brigade's war diary later "was burnt so that a re-write would exonerate the Commanding Officer." In *Haig's Command: A Reassessment* (London: Penguin Books, 1978), 307.
36. In Dancocks, *Welcome to Flanders Fields*, 188.

Chapter 10

The HMS *Lusitania*

*O*N THE VERY DAY that the world was shaken by the first use of gas in the war at Ypres in April 1915, the pride of the Cunard line, the *Lusitania*, was preparing to make her 202nd crossing of the Atlantic. Ads in New York papers announced her scheduled departure for England.

But there was also another ad — this one, a black-bordered ominous warning.

In spite of the warning, there were few cancellations. And on the first day of May 1915, about two hours behind schedule, the sleek 785-foot liner, with its four funnels painted black for wartime crossings, her engines throbbing, slowly edged away from her berth in New York City, bound for Liverpool. Among her passengers was a Mrs. G. Sterling Ryerson of Toronto, wife of the president of the Red Cross Society. Having lost one son (Captain George Ryerson) in the war at Ypres, she was on her way to England, to visit another son (Lieutenant Arthur Ryerson) who had been severely wounded.[1] (It will be recalled that it was Arthur who came across the body of his

---

NOTICE!

Travelers intending to
embark on the Atlantic voyage
are reminded that a state of
war exists between Germany
and her allies and Great Britain
and her allies; that the zone of
war includes the waters adja-
cent to the British Isles; that,
in accordance with formal notice given by the Imperial German Government, vessels flying the flag of Great Britain,
or any of her allies, are liable to
destruction in those waters and
that travelers sailing in the war
zone on ships of Great Britain
or her allies do so at their own
risk.
IMPERIAL GERMAN EMBASSY

Washington, D.C. April 22, 1915

---

brother in the devastated fields after the first gas attacks in the second battle of Ypres.) No German warning would stop the grieving mother.

Six days later, in the late morning of 7 May, Lieutenant Colonel Walther Schwieger, Commander of the German submarine *U-20*, munched on his lunch as his submerged vessel patrolled just off Old Head of Kinsale, off the south coast of Ireland. It was time for his vessel to surface to recharge its batteries. Up top, he was impressed by the calmness of the water.

At around 1:30 in the afternoon as he scanned the horizon, he saw smoke in the distance. Then he discerned something rather unusual — a four-funneled steamer, about ten miles distant. Only large, important ships had four funnels. Was it the *Mauretania* or the *Lusitania*? More important, could he catch it? He quickly gave orders to submerge and pursue.

The rest is history.[2] Shortly after, two great torpedoes ripped into the *Lusitania*'s side.

The great liner almost immediately listed to starboard and in less than 20 terrifying minutes sank into the deep. Of the nearly 2,000 passengers on board, 1,198 drowned,[3] including 128 Americans. One of the Canadians who perished was Mrs. Ryerson of Toronto.

Although Germany was elated by the kill (and struck a medal to commemorate the feat), the Allies were stunned. Anti-German riots broke out in Canada.

Americans, too, were incensed. President Woodrow Wilson protested to Berlin in the name of humanity (noting previous German attacks on the British passenger steamer *Falaba*, and the American vessels *Cushing* and *Gulflight*). Former President Theodore Roosevelt argued that the American government should denounce "such wrong" and urged the United States to abandon its role as a neutral mediator between the warring sides.

America, however, was not quite ready to join the war. But the stakes were rising. And the European war clouds cast even heavier shadows over the shores of the Americas.

NOTES

1. Recounted in A. B. Tucker, *The Battle Glory of Canada* (London: Cassell, 1915), 139-140, and Daniel G. Dancocks, *Welcome to Flanders Fields: The First Canadian Battle of the Great War, Ypres, 1915* (Toronto: McClelland and Stewart, Limited, 1989), 208.
2. For fascinating new insights into the mysteries of the great tragedy, see Robert D. Ballard, *Exploring the Lusitania* (Toronto: Madison Press Books, 1995).
3. Many were later buried at nearby Queenstown (now Cobh), in Ireland, where their graves can still be found.

A hospital alone shows what war is.
                    — Erich Marie Remarque,
           All Quiet on the Western Front

Chapter 11

Festubert and Givenchy

THE CANADIAN TROOPS, now in reserve after having lost half of their infantry in the slaughter at Ypres, were not going to get much chance to recuperate. There were too many battles in the offing.

French General Joffre wanted more help and continued to needle the British, for some reason claiming they were not pulling their weight. Matters worsened as French forces tried to take Vimy Ridge, the strategic hill that rose 61 meters above the Douai Plain and held by the Germans since October 1914. Because it was key to the German defense system (and because they had commandeered vital French mines and factories in the area), they had added significant fortifications to its natural dominance. On 9 May 1915, the French attacked Vimy Ridge, hoping to retake it, only to suffer more than 100,000 casualties without gaining the ridge of the hill.

The British, too, had met with little success. They had tried to take Aubers Ridge, south of Ypres just outside the Salient line, and met with sheer disaster when German riflemen and machine gunners mowed down more than 11,000 men in 12 hours. No ground was gained. Once again, massed manpower was no match for machine-gun fire.

General Haig, Commander of the First Army, stubborn and undeterred, resolved to continue the assault. But he would need the Canadians to help.

And so, merely two weeks after their ordeal in Ypres, the still-recovering 2nd and 3rd Brigades were summoned to support the British Divisions. At 7:45 on the evening of 20 May, the two brigades were to begin an assault at two different points, about a mile and a half apart. The 2nd Brigade was to seize "K.5," and the 3rd Brigade was to capture "M.10," part of the enemy's new front line, and an adjoining building. (On trench maps, topographical features and tactical objectives were characterized by letters and numbers. The letters delineated narrow sectors of the front in alphabetical order. The numbers represented consecutive sectors from the British front line into enemy territory.)

And so, for the obscure letters and numbers K.5 and M.10, the Canadians again went into battle — and into the unremitting slaughter of machine-gun bullets.

The 2nd Infantry Brigade seemed doomed to disaster. Its Commander, the methodical Brigadier General Arthur Currie, who had performed so well under fire two weeks before at Ypres, had been unable to identify the ultimate objective, K.5, shown as it was as only a small dot on a military map. The map itself was replete with inaccuracies, with errors of as much as 450 yards in some positions. To make matters worse, it was printed upside down, with the north at the bottom of the page.[1] That, and the fact that the assembly trenches were badly breached and under fire, led Currie to ask, understandably, for a postponement. He was refused.

One of Currie's battalions — the 10th (that had fought so well at Ypres) — charged and cleared 100 yards of the enemy's communication trench, but had to halt the suicidal advance when its leaders were shot down, one after the other.

Over on their left, the now-seasoned 16th Battalion (Canadian Scottish) also ran into machine-gun fire. They reached and cleared the orchard, only to find that the house they were to take was heavily garrisoned and protected by barbed wire. So while they, too, had gained ground, they were forced to stop and revamp.

The attack was resumed at 8:30 the next evening, 21 May, after supporting artillery bombarded the enemy, but it was too little, too late. The Allied field guns, firing mainly shrapnel, couldn't inflict much damage on the German strong points. As the Canadians (10th Battalion and a 1st Brigade grenade company carrying 500 bombs) advanced over open ground toward K.5, they were cut to shreds by machine-gun fire.

By noon the next day, 22 May, Currie withdrew his men from all but 100 yards of the newly occupied line. His 10th Battalion alone had lost 18 officers and 250 men.

While Currie was pulling back his men, General Haig visited General Alderson to express his displeasure with the Canadian efforts and their lack of success. To drive his point home, he ordered the Canadian Division *directly* under the command of the First Army. Further, the Canadians would simply have to go back and take K.5, albeit after additional reconnaissance of the enemy's position.

So, in the early morning hours of 24 May, at 2:30 a.m., two companies of the 5th (Western Cavalry) Battalion, led by 30 bombers with the cry of *"Lusitania"* on their lips, scampered across 12 footbridges over a 10-foot wide, water-filled ditch, and assaulted and took the German redoubt at K.5. But they suffered another 250 casualties in the process.

That evening, Canadian troops resumed their attack on the left, and the fortified house at M.10. But once again German machine guns were insurmountable, and but a few men reached the German trenches, only to be captured.

By now, however, the First Division's ranks were so decimated that it needed reinforcements desperately. Filling the bill were volunteers from the Canadian Cavalry Brigade. Though they had no experience in trench warfare, they left their horses in England and crossed to France on 4 May to shore up the battered battalions.

Nonetheless, another battle was over. Unfortunately, however, while gains had been made, they were hardly substantial. Once again, superior German artillery had dictated the outcome. Once again, there were many casualties, this time 2,468 losses — for about 600 yards of German trench area across a 1-mile front. Once again, letters of condolence began their way from foreign fields to Canadian homes. And, once again, black-bordered notices of war casualties dominated pages of newspapers all across Canada.

In the early days of June, the Canadians enjoyed a brief break from battlefield horrors. Their new assignment, under General Haig's reorganization plans, placed them north of the La Bassée Canal, with responsibility for a reduced area (1,000 yards) in the front line. While one brigade held the front, the other two could be spelled off along the banks of the canal in the Bethune area. Moreover, the trenches were on higher ground and were dry for a change. That alone would make life more tolerable.

Robert Kennedy's diary entries, meanwhile, were becoming briefer, more sporadic. On 17 May, he had merely noted:

> **Moved off at 6 a.m. Arrived at destination near Bethune at 3 p.m.**

In several instances he noted that he was "registering" guns, aligning or positioning them for range accuracy on the targets. On 26 May, he was hospitalized for five days for enteritis and influenza at No. 1 Canadian Field Ambulance, but after being released, rejoined his battery building gun emplacements and, as always, registering guns. On 10 June, he saw Givenchy for the first time, "all in ruins and deserted save for a few troops." But in spite of the devastation of war, Kennedy found several beautiful gardens, and the farm boy from the pastoral Ottawa Valley delighted in the beautiful flowers, carnations, seven kinds of roses, plums, apples, peaches, pears, and cherries that he found.

But the beauty and quietness were short-lived.

The French were planning a new offensive on 15 June 1915, in coordination with the British, and the Canadians would be needed to render assistance. This time, the 1st Brigade was to assault two strong points — H.2, opposite Duck's Bill, and H.3, a point another 150 yards farther north.

Surely the battle would go a bit better this time. For one reason, there was some time for preparation. And knowing from bitter experience that the enemy's machine guns simply had to be silenced for the assault to be effective, Brigadier General H. E. Burstall, Commander of the Canadian Divisional Artillery, brought in more guns, including three 18-pounders. Silencing the wheels by installing rubber tires on them, the troops rolled two of the field artillery pieces almost to Duck's Bill, just 75 yards from the German trenches, and the other one to an abandoned farmhouse near H.3.

And there was yet another factor to help the Ontario lads. They had just received the British Lee-Enfield rifle in place of the jamming, oft-misfiring Ross rifle. This assault should be a vast improvement over previous ones.

The attack was set for 6 p.m.

At 5:45, the camouflage was removed from the big guns, and two of the three shuddered into life, blasting the German parapets. But the third, its gunners not wanting to hit their own advancing troops, held fire. It failed, therefore, to take out the machine gunners in H.3. Though the other two 18-pounders near Duck's Bill knocked out several machine guns, they themselves were subsequently knocked out of action.

Just before 6 p.m., British engineers and tunnelers blew up a mine close to H.2. In a tragic turn of events, however, the explosion not only failed to destroy the German strongpoint, but inflicted numerous casualties on the bombing parties of the 1st Battalion.

The enemy still held H.3.

At one point, Lieutenant F. W. Campbell, the 1st Battalion's machine-gun officer had propped his gun on the back of Private H. Vincent because the gun's tripod was broken. Campbell and Vincent scrambled forward, with Campbell firing until he fell, mortally wounded. Vincent crawled back to the Canadian lines, dragging the machine gun behind him. (Campbell received the Victoria Cross, Vincent the Distinguished Conduct Medal.)

The fighting continued all though the night and into the next morning with seesaw thrusts and retreats, but by late afternoon of 16 June, the Germans still held off the Allied troops. Later that evening, Sir John French decided that since the French offensive in Artois had ended, the British and Canadians would make no further attempt for the moment.

Thus on 24 June, the First Canadian Division began to move to Ploegsteert (usually called "Plug Street" by the soldiers) just north of Armentières. The now-experienced troops, though vastly reduced in number, would finally be assigned to a quieter area of the Front. There would be plenty of entrenching, sandbagging, digging, wiring, and building to do.

But there would also be a few days of relative peace — and time to write letters home. From Norman McIntosh's letter:

> They have killed thousands by that awful gas (Chlorine) but they are going one better now. They pile their dead . . . in front

of the trenches and just barely cover them with earth, and when our big guns fire on their trenches, the dead and decayed bodies are all stirred up. You can imagine the result.[2]

Kennedy also wrote to Eva on 24 July 1915:

> One day is much like another, I'm on phone duty and we take turns going into the first line trench and to the observing station. The observation post is the place they use for observing the effects of the gun fire and watching for anything the enemy might be doing. I've been at the observation place for the last two days but returned to the battery last night. There was a dandy telescope there and we could see behind the German trenches for several miles. One can't see the men in the trenches but I saw where some of them had been working, shoveling the earth out of the trench. Away behind the trenches I saw, occasionally, men moving past open spaces.
>
> On Wednesday, R. L. Borden [Canada's Prime Minister] visited us and we fired about 20 shells in his honor. I hope you'll read about his visit in the Ottawa papers.
>
> It is about ten p.m. and we have just witnessed a very pretty sight, and "whack." There's an answer in the shape of a German shell. Our 2nd Batt. guns were silent but guns all around us were bombarding a town in the German lines for ten or fifteen minutes and we could see the flashes of the guns. It was pretty, but we knew we were liable to get an answer.

NOTES

1. Colonel G. W. L. Nicholson, C.D., *Canadian Expeditionary Force 1914-1919: Official History of the Canadian Army in the First World War* (Ottawa: Queen's Printer, 1964), 100.
2. Reprinted in the *Coburg World* and quoted in Percy L. Climo, *Let Us Remember: Lively Letters from World War One* (Coburg, Ontario: Haynes Printing Co., 1990), 177.

*Ludendorff: "The English soldiers fight
like lions."*
*Hoffman: "True. But don't we know that
they are lions led by donkeys."*
— General Erich von Falkenhayn

Chapter 12

The Gathering War Clouds

*W*HILE CANADIAN TROOPS were maturing quickly in the fields of France and Belgium, the thunder of war continued to echo around the world with increasing turbulence and urgency. As thousands of young men fell daily on various fronts of the war, it was clear that countless more would be needed to fill the decimated ranks. Thus, even before Canada's First Contingent had reached the shores of England (in fact, merely three days after it had sailed), Canada had offered a Second Contingent of 20,000 men. It wouldn't be a complete contingent, however, since Canada had already sent most of her army's 18-pounder guns.

Once more volunteers headed for recruiting stations all over Canada, from British Columbia on the Pacific to Prince Edward Island on the Atlantic, to become part of the Second Division.

In Canada, as in England, stories abounded regarding the "too old" or "too young" volunteers who changed their ages capriciously to get by the all-too-accommodating recruiting sergeant. On more than one occasion a recruiting officer turned down a 16- or 17-year-old, saying "come back tomorrow when you're 18." As often as not, the underage youth would return the next day, miraculously aged 18.

Some men were over the age limit. Once when General Smith-Dorrien was inspecting the Canadian troops in Europe, he asked a man how old he was.

> "Thirty-seven years, sir."
> "How many years have you served?"
> "Forty-one, sir."
> "How do you make that out?" asked the General.
> "Well, sir, actually I am fifty-seven years of age, but I was allowed . . . to enlist as at thirty-seven years. I have four sons now at the front."[1]

Fortunately, military officials had learned from the trials and tribulations of the First Contingent. This time, the route to England and France would follow a different plan and course. For one thing, with Winter just around the corner and no cold-weather facilities available for an entire contingent, new recruits would be given preliminary training in their own military districts. In addition, the British War Office, concerned for lack of accommodations and equipment in England, asked that the Second Division wait until early May to arrive, well after the First Division had left for France. Furthermore, this group would not cross in one mighty convoy, but rather in stages, in groups of about 5,000. Each would have a cruiser escort.

Finally, on 18 April 1915, the first part of the contingent (largely engineers, medical and service corps) set sail from Halifax. Ultimately, however, due to a shortage of transport ships, 17 vessels, shrouded in secrecy, were dispatched singly without escort in May and June.[2] The Second Division, though late, had arrived in England.

Nor did the Second Division go to Salisbury Plains. The Canadians had no desire to experience a repeat performance of the miserable conditions there, so the new volunteers were sent to Shorncliffe Camp near Folkestone, where they were accommodated in tents, huts, and barracks. The Militia Department had offered canvas, but in typical bureaucratic fashion, the offer was late being made, and later still in being accepted. (By the time the tents finally arrived, the troops had left for France.)

The training of the new division was much improved. For one thing, the weather was more conducive to training. But more than that, experienced British and Canadian officers were brought in to explain and demonstrate the construction and siting of trenches and the methods of defending them. All troops were instructed in trench routine. Some of the senior officers were even sent to France to see, firsthand, the units of the First Division.

But some things didn't change. When King George V, accompanied by Lord Kitchener, visited the troops on 2 September, they knew that the move to the Front was imminent.

On the nights between 13 and 17 September, under the cover of darkness, the Second Division crossed the Channel to Boulogne, France, then continued by rail to St. Omer, Cassel, or nearby stations, from whence they marched, heavily laden, to Hazebrouck.

The crossing still had had moments of concern. At one point, troops of the 18th (Western Ontario) Battalion were knocked off their feet when their paddle-wheeler steamer was rammed amidships. Troops were given lifebelts, expecting to abandon ship, but the steamer didn't sink. It had to be towed the rest of the way, however.

Even before the Second Division reached France, there were growing suggestions that it should be teamed with the First Division to create the Canadian Corps. The Canadians desperately wanted to serve together. And the British seemed anxious to oblige, so General Alderson, Commander of the First Division, became Corps Commander, and thus overall Commander of both divisions. Taking over his old position as General Officer Commanding (GOC) of the First Division was Lieutenant General Arthur W. Currie who had led the Second Brigade so well at Ypres. Major General S. B. Steele was made GOC of the new Second Canadian Division.

There was not much to celebrate in the summer of 1915. Allied fortunes had suffered terribly on the Eastern Front. Closer to home, the British and French disagreed as to the policy to pursue on the Western Front. At a Franco-British conference in June, the British argued for a delay in offensives at the Western Front because of a critical shortage of heavy guns, howitzers, and shells. General Sir Douglas Haig, Commander of the British First Army, argued against any offensive until the shortage was rectified. The French General Joffre, an eternal optimist, wanted to press on. He envisioned two great, widely-separated thrusts, the main one in the Artois (Arras-Lens) and the other in the Champagne (Reims-the Argonne) areas. If successful, he said, they "would compel the Germans to retreat beyond the Meuse [*River*] and possibly end the war."

By August, Joffre was able to prevail over British objections, partly as a result of the depressing Allied setbacks in the April 1915 Gallipoli Campaign in Turkey and on the Russian Front. And this time, Joffre emphasized, the French would have 53 divisions in the offensive, not 15 as in the Artois Offensive; this time they would have 2,000 heavy guns and 3,000 field guns, not the 300 heavy guns as at Artois! And they would use chlorine gas as well. Lord Kitchener ultimately agreed "to do our utmost to help France in this offensive" and committed the British forces to the assault. Canadian forces would stage a phony gas attack in an attempt to draw German artillery fire and expose their positions.

Accordingly, on 21 September, the British and French mounted the joint offensive.[3] The British would attack between La Bassée Canal and Lens, near Loos, as planned. But the French forces had revised their plan. They would attack (with 17 divisions) northward from Arras and include the area around Vimy Ridge (still held by the Germans). But their larger thrust (27 divisions) would be in the Champagne area, not the Artois as originally intended, because of fewer obstacles there. And so the two offensives began.[4]

But once more, the dreams and plans of Generals were just that. Although great advances were made the first day by both French (two and a half miles in the north) and British forces (who gained a small salient), most advances sputtered and fizzled like a damp match in the rain. The French were driven back in Champagne as the battle went on, and ultimately lost 120,000 killed or taken prisoner, and another 260,000 wounded.The British lost 8,000 men in the first hour. Even the Germans were overwhelmed by the losses and, with compassion, ceased firing at the sight of so much bloodshed on the "field of corpses."[5]

The British hopes of taking the French mining towns Loos and Lens (and possibly Lille) were shattered when the battalions of the "Kitchener armies," some fighting for the first time, ran into steel and concrete pillboxes and shelters. Even the British use of gas was undermined when the feeble winds changed direction and blew the gas back into the British lines. It was futile.

One of those who perished at Loos was a young lieutenant in the 2nd Battalion of the Irish Guards. He probably shouldn't have been there because he had abysmally poor eyesight, but his famous father had used his influence to get him a commission in the Guards. When the 1st Battalion was largely wiped out on 27 September, the 2nd Battalion was sent in. Though no one knows exactly what happened next, it seems that the young man had been badly wounded in the face. Part of his jaw had been shot away. His legs, however, were not hurt, and wounded men, if ambulatory, were expected to find their own way back to a dressing station. He had lost his eyeglasses, of course, was nearly blind with pain.

He started back for medical help. But he got only a mile or so, wandering through badly cratered ground that was littered with dead and dying men and horses. Then he collapsed, taking refuge in a shell hole. He probably bled to death, alone.

The young man was Lieutenant John Kipling, son of the famous Rudyard Kipling.[6]

By 4 November 1915, the offensive was called off. In a little over a month (25 September to 4 November) thousands more young men had fallen. The French lost 200,000, the British 60,000, and the Germans 150,000.[7]

In spite of all the sacrifices, little of the Front had changed except that the land claimed more casualties. And, since failure always demanded a scapegoat, real or imagined, Sir John French, who was criticized for his decision-making in the offensive, was deemed a worthy candidate, and was transferred back to Britain. In his stead on 19 December 1915, as overall Commander-in-Chief of the British (and Canadian) forces came a man around whom controversy would swirl for generations and, in fact, continues to this day.

His name was Sir Douglas Haig.[8]

Trench Raids

As the waning year's days grew shorter and colder in 1915, offensives petered out on the Western Front. The French were somewhat content to "sit out" the quiet Winter period. Not so the British. The high command directed that the Winter months be used constructively in continued training, reinforcing trenches, surprise bombardments and sniping, and generally harassing enemy troops. The hierarchy, particularly Haig, also encouraged trench raids.

Whether or not the Canadians "invented" the trench raid is subject to dispute, but no one questions the fact that Canadian troops perfected the practice. The enemy objectives would be photographed and studied, and timetables worked out. Knives and bayonets would be sharpened. Then, with faces blackened or masked, troops would remove all identifying insignia, fill their haversacks with bombs, and set out on their hazardous journey. Trench raids could be suicidal. Casualties were usually high. But they sometimes — not always, but sometimes — gleaned critical information for subsequent battles.

Although troops from the PPCLI had staged a trench raid months before in February, the practice had been temporarily set aside. But in November 1915, plans once more got underway for a joint effort astride the Douve River. The raid, if successful, could accomplish three things: yield German prisoners (useful for Intelligence); prompt the Germans into bringing up reserves; and taunt and demoralize the enemy. The dangerous assignment was given to volunteer parties from the 5th (Western Cavalry) and 7th (1st British Columbia) Battalions, involving 5 officers and 85 volunteers from each. To hone their skills, they were excused from all other duties for more than a week to practice exclusively on ground somewhat resembling their objective.

Finally, at 9:00 a.m. on 16 November, booming 18-pounders of the 1st Canadian Field Artillery Brigade and British howitzers, assisted by 13-pounders of the Royal Canadian Horse Artillery (RCHA), blasted the enemy positions to demolish the defensive wire. In the afternoon, a trench mortar battery blasted the German-held Petite Douve Farm. And when darkness came that night, cutting parties ventured out to cut any wire the bombs had missed.

In the dark morning hours of 17 November, at 2:30 a.m., the almost full moon having already set, the two groups crept stealthily toward the German objectives. The 5th Battalion immediately ran into complications when it found barbed wire in the water-filled moat. The men had to withdraw, but suffered no casualties in spite of rifle fire.

The Vancouver party fared better. Because rain had begun to fall, the German sentries had taken shelter, and in so doing were taken completely by surprise. The trench raiders killed or wounded about 30 defenders, took 12 prisoners, and, to the delight of Canadian Intelligence officers, brought back some new rubber gas masks. They had only two casualties, one killed and one wounded.

The trench raid was deemed a great success, and word of it spread to the highest echelons.

Trench raids would continue, of course, amid growing controversy. Sometimes the casualties were hard to justify. Though different figures are given for losses associated with the raids, the costs were always high. Denis Winter writes that between 19 December 1915 and 30 June 1916, for example, 5,845 men died and some 119,296 were wounded.[9] Desmond Morton, quoting Tony Ashworth, claims that between December 1915 and May 1916, in a period of no significant battles, "the BEF lost 83,000 men, most of them in actions associated with raids."[10]

Life in the Trenches

As Christmas of 1915 approached, the troops had little to look forward to. The initial excitement of "going into battle" had long since been replaced by the grim realities of war. Men suffered from a variety of diseases, including influenza and pneumonia, brought on by the deplorable conditions and poor diet. Some lost feet not just from bombs and shrapnel, but from trench foot and gangrene, after standing for days on end knee-deep in foul mud and water. Bloated rats and loathsome lice were constant companions.

And there was always the rain.

> There was no escape from it. The trenches, which were nothing more than sandbagged breastworks, simply dissolved. The earth within the sandbags liquefied and oozed out. Everything collapsed. Every indentation of the ground filled with water, and to make things worse, the enemy, being on higher ground, delighted in draining his trenches across No Man's Land into those occupied by the Canadians.[11]

Meals were often unpredictable. While officers usually had food brought to them (though sometimes getting cold en route) soldiers had to cook their own over a coke or charcoal brazier, a makeshift stove that was often nothing more than an old drum with holes poked in it. Men at the Front were supposedly entitled to receive 14 ounces of beef a day (including bone, fat, and gristle) or a 12-ounce container of bully beef — canned or pickled beef. A loaf of bread was to be shared by three men. There was sometimes a tin of jam of questionable origins.

Lieutenant Earl Croft wrote in a letter to the *Coburg World*:

> For a wash dish we use a square oil can with one side cut out. Our lamps are tin cans with one side cut out, then by placing a candle inside, we have a reflector and lamp too. Our stove is of the same invention.[12]

If there was one reliable gratification, it was the mail which, come fire or flood, seemed miraculously to get through most of the time. Unfortunately, soldiers had to destroy all letters immediately after reading them once or twice. Because their outgoing letters were heavily censored, there was little mention of names or places.

Robert Kennedy's life in the trenches that summer of 1915 was probably fairly typical of a soldier in an artillery column. In late May, he was hospitalized for several days with influenza, and after returning to his unit went back to digging dugouts, registering guns, wire cutting, and working in the horse lines and on guard duty. He noted on several occasions being on duty with the Forward Observation Officer (FOO).

His diary entries now were often brief, possibly because the duties of one day were often repeated the next. In June and July, he spent still more time on guard duty, gathering in wire, building gun emplacements, registering guns.

June 15: We attack in the evening, gain three trenches, but evacuate them later. On duty and phone from 11 p.m. till 3 a.m.

In a 17 June 1915, letter to Eva:

I have discovered some paper but haven't been able to find an envelope yet. Perhaps you will be able to get a newspaper saying

something about us Canadians. I wonder if there will be anything about the evenings of June 15 and 16.

I'm not driving now; I got tired of grooming horses so asked them to make me a gunner about a month ago, as they were short of gunners they did as I requested. We were given training in gun laying and fuse setting.

Tues. 29: On duty with Wilks at 6 p.m. at F.O.O.

Sat: Went with Haley to F.O.O. in trench. Quiet. Spent all day there and Sunday too.

Mon: In trench. Saw Capt. Varett and some of the fellows I knew in 2nd Batt. Came back to guns on Monday night.

From a 6 July 1915 letter to Eva:

I don't know whether this is Tuesday or Wednesday, but it makes little difference. Some of the boys are speaking of taking leave to see their relatives in England, but I'm not so lucky — all mine are back in dear old Canada.

On July 21, he noted that Canadian Prime Minister Borden visited. On 27 July, Kennedy went into the First-line trenches, returning to his battery two days later.

July 31: Saturday: Attended Communion service in dugout at battery.

Sometimes his letters told a little of trench life, but more often than not, they spoke of home.

To Eva, 17 August 1915:

Hotel De Buzz

Hotel de Buzz is our telephone station down in the trenches. Quite an appropriate name isn't it? We use a phone or buzzer as some call them, and you can send a message by speaking, or by Morse, by buzzing it. I came back from the trenches last evening

(11pm) and it was very dark when we got in. Though it rained heavily at noon, it's a lovely day now, and everything looks fresh. I love the country and roses, and you. I love flowers. I wish I could press them decently and send you some. I used to pick all mother's best geraniums and give them to you; she knew very well what I wanted them for. I hope the day will soon come when I'll be able to gather flowers to put in your beautiful hair, but am afraid, now, it won't be for another year. Then, please God, we'll live together forever.

I'm glad Dad got a new set of driving harnesses. I saw a piece in the Citizen saying that private subscriptions had amounted to enough to buy one thousand machine guns for Canadians, and that would mean that every Canadian battalion would have twenty along with what the government gives them (eight), making twenty-eight to each battalion. Formerly the government gave them just four, and it is only a few days since they decided to increase the number to eight. It just what was wanted and I'm so glad the Canadians are responding so well to the call of the Empire. Of all the weapons the Germans use, the machine gun is the one I hate most, as they have taken the lives of so many of our brave troops. Now with twenty-eight guns to each battalion, our lads will be able to repulse any attack the Germans might make.

3 September 1915 from another letter to Eva:

I'm up in the trenches in our dugout with the phone on my ear, and thought I would write a few lines to you. I have been reading, and making a ring out of aluminum off a German shell I found yesterday, but after spending some time on the ring, I found a flaw in it, so will have to melt it over again when I go back to the battery tomorrow night.

It rained during the night but we should worry; we have a roof over our heads though it does leak in a couple of places. We can keep dry by avoiding the wet places and crowding into the dry corners. We have stopped up the worst places. I don't care if it rains all night, if only it lets up so we can cook our supper. We have to do our own cooking while in the trenches.

This morning I went out and got some dry wood in a

communication trench. We had lamb steaks or mutton chops for breakfast. I don't know which is the proper name. Anyhow I had to cook them without any fat and I didn't burn them. They were delicious.

I'm going to send to London for an oil stove soon. We can buy oil in a nearby village and you may be sure we'll be trying all sorts of experiments. . . .

Cooking outside can be a difficult undertaking — and needless to say, a wet one, so we tried a new scheme. I went out and got a tin box about 4 or 5 inches deep and 6 inches square, that was punched full of holes. This box I placed on three bricks on the floor of the dugout in the doorway. There's no fireplace in our dugout, and of course, no chimney, so it was our choice to be either smothered or drowned, and we preferred the lesser of two evils, and took chances on being smothered. We had wood and water inside so it was plain sailing. A few blows with a trenching tool and we had sufficient wood! I then lit the fire, and puff — the place was full of smoke in two minutes. But you know it makes a terrible smoke at first, and when it is going well, practically none at all. Most of the smoke went out the doorway, but it was far from pleasant inside.

We had some onions too, and tears were streaming down our faces from the combined effects of smoke and onions. We did enjoy them inasmuch as we had eaten practically all our forty-eight hour ration of bread today.

P.S. It's now September 7. It's been four days since I wrote this and I haven't been able to obtain one of those green envelopes, but I'll find a way out of it.

This particular letter was in a gray-green envelope marked "On Active Service." It also noted:

Correspondence in this envelope need not be censored Regimentally. The contents are liable to examination at the Base. The following certificate must be signed by the writer: *"I certify on my honour that the contents of this envelope refer to nothing but private and family matters."*

In a letter to Eva, 2 October 1915, Kennedy reminisced:

One year ago we sailed from Gaspé Bay across the sea which now rolls between us. I hope this war won't last another year.

I saw a walnut tree yesterday, and found two or three dandy nuts on the ground. I threw sticks at the branches and the nuts came down in showers. Soon there were a dozen fellows there.

Last Wednesday evening, about 10 P.M., I was on my way to the trenches with rations. It had been raining and was very dark when I saw a pretty sight. I was up on a hill and could see — across a valley — the flares (shells that are sent up to light up the land between the trenches) — four or five at a time. There were also several signal rockets of different colors, and I could see the red flashes of bursting shells and the white puffs of shell smoke drifting off. It lasted only a few moments.

Enclosed are some pansies I picked near our observing place.

When conditions of war were so abysmal, what kept the soldiers from sharing some of the more degrading news in their letters home? There were no doubt countless reasons. Some wanted to spare their families from the knowledge of the wretched circumstances. Some didn't wish to complain in the face of adversity. Some, as Pierre Berton points out in *Vimy*, couldn't bear to tell parents or loved ones of the casualties and callousness of the war scene. "But perhaps the overriding reason" was that "conditions truly *were* unspeakable." And perhaps there was another reason. Perhaps when soldiers saw their comrades shot through the head or blown apart, the mud and filth were of lesser importance.[13]

NOTES
1. Recounted in A. B. Tucker, *The Battle Glory of Canada* (London: Cassell, 1915), 83.
2. Colonel G. W. L. Nicholson, C.D., *Canadian Expeditionary Force 1914-1919: Official History of the Canandian Army in the First World War* (Ottawa: Queen's Printer, 1964), 111.

3. For a fuller account of the Anglo-French offensive, see B. H. Liddell Hart, *History of the First World War* (London: Macmillan Publishers, 1997), or Alan Clark, *The Donkeys* (London: Pimlico, 1961).

4. At the same time, another drama was unfolding in German-occupied Brussels. British nurse Edith Cavell was on trial for (and found guilty of) helping British and French prisoners of war escape to neutral Holland. In spite of protests by American diplomats (who represented the British) she was executed on 12 October 1915.

5. Denis Winter, *Haig's Command: A Reassessment* (London: Penguin Books, 1991), 41. Alan Clark puts the losses in perspective. He writes: "In the first two hours of the Battle of Loos more British soldiers died than the total number of casualties in all three services on both sides on D-Day in 1944." *The Donkeys*, 11.

6. Kipling and his American wife Caroline searched in vain for the rest of their lives for their son's grave. Kipling continued to write poetry ("Have you news of my boy Jack?") and letters regarding the war. In 1916, he wrote to former President Teddy Roosevelt: "If it be found when the battle clears, Their death has set me free, Then how shall I live with myself through the years Which they have bought for me?" Young Kipling's grave was eventually discovered in 1992 by Norman Christie, an Ottawa Valley man who has since written several books on Canadian efforts in the First War. Kipling's grave is in Row D, Plot 7, at St. Mary's Advanced Dressing Station Cemetery near Loos, France.

7. Nicholson, *Canadian Expeditionary Force*, 121.

8. Volumes have been written on the controversial General Sir Douglas Haig who, when he assumed command of the British forces, took charge of more than one million soldiers (including Canadians and ANZACs) on the Western Front. While he has both admirers and detractors, most seem to agree that he had shortcomings. He was often described as courteous, but cold and inarticulate, frequently twiddling with his moustache. It is also generally acknowledged that he was a stubborn man. (His stubbornness was evident not just in his reluctance to call off hopeless battles, but even to admit that horses could be stopped by bullets and machine guns.) With his undistinguished record at Sandhurst and Camberley Staff College (he failed his staff college entry examination but applied a second time and under the auspices of the Duke of Cambridge, had his entrance exam waived), one might wonder how he rose to such a high position. Patronage by people in high places is part of the answer. Winter, in *Haig's Command*, puts it bluntly: Haig's rise, he writes: "had always owed more to intrigue and patronage than to any evidence of talent as a soldier" (41). Winter also claims that Haig "systematically falsified the record of his military career," rewriting parts of his diary after the fact (3).

9. Winter, *Haig's Command,* 92.

10. Desmond Morton, *When Your Number's Up: The Canadian Soldier in the First World War* (Toronto: Random House of Canada, 1993), 127.

11. Colonel W. W. Murray, *The History of the 2nd Canadian Battalion (Eastern Ontario Regiment) in the Great War, 1914-1919* (Ottawa: Mortimer Ltd., 1947), 75.
12. Reprinted in Perry L. Climo, *Let Us Remember: Lively Letters from World War One* (Coburg, Ontario: Haynes Printing Co., 1990), 273.
13. Pierre Berton, *Vimy* (Markham, Ontario: Penguin Books Canada Ltd., 1987), 55-56.

Ils ne passeront pas! — They shall not pass!
— General Robert Georges Nivelle

Chapter 13

The Battle of Verdun — 1916

*N*O BOOK ON THE Western Front can be written without reference to the battle of Verdun, so massive was its undertaking, so incalculable its losses, so extraordinary its outcome. Though it did not directly involve Canadians, it pulled French support from the Somme and Flanders areas where the British and Canadians fought.[1]

About 160 miles east of Paris, sitting astride the River Meuse, is the ancient city of Verdun. Its population of about 20,000 in 1916, though subjected to occasional German shelling (being only about ten miles from the German lines), still could claim to be one of the quieter zones of the Western Front. True, Germans had cut the railway line between Verdun and Nancy in 1914, but they had been unable to do much damage beyond that.

There was good reason for their lack of success. Verdun was

reputed to be one of the most effective fortifications on earth. It had always been a garrison city, and now was defended by two separate rings of forts — 18 outer strongholds and 18 redoubts (enclosures) and batteries (artillery-equipped units) girdling every height around the town. So sophisticated were the forts' defenses that their guns could pick off any enemy ascending the slopes (*glacis*) of neighboring forts. Verdun's two principal bastions were Fort Douaumont (said to be impregnable) and Fort Vaux. If they held, Verdun could not be taken. But reputation and fact may not be synonymous, and the forts, and Verdun itself, were not nearly as formidable as they seemed. They had been largely disarmed.

It all happened after the Germans shelled and shattered the forts in Liége, Belgium, and Maubeuge, France, in the early part of the war. Seeing the terrible wreckage, the French High Command took a second look at the forts around Verdun and decided that their guns and men could be better used elsewhere. After all, some said, Verdun was not of strategic importance. The forts were little more than death traps, some critics argued. There were others, however, who expressed deep concern about the dismantlement of the guns and general neglect of the forts, among them General Coutanceau, the Governor of Verdun (who was sacked for his impertinence), and Colonel Emile Driant, whose warning so infuriated General Joffre that he might have been court-martialed had he not soon thereafter died a heroic death.

Also terribly concerned was General Joseph Simon Gallieni, the Minister of Defense, the savior of Paris who had mobilized the taxis to move troops to the Marne in 1914. He was sufficiently alarmed to alert Joffre in December of 1915 to the lack of organization and defense at Verdun. But Joffre was still not concerned. "Nothing justifies the fears expressed," he told Gallieni. Besides, as he and others insisted, the Germans were not aware of the disarmed status of Verdun.

The guns continued to be dismantled.

But Joffre was wrong. And there were many indications that something ominous was afoot. For one thing, aerial observers reported highly increased German troop movement on rail lines in the area north of Verdun. Some reported sightings of massive guns being lugged closer and closer to Verdun on caterpillar tractors. Others heard rumors of new tunnels being built and, worse, of the preparation of secret "Stollens" — the enormous shell-proof bunkers that could hold a half-battalion of men. There were rumors of German hospitals being established near the front lines. Some letters taken from captured prisoners referred to some kind of review that the Kaiser himself would hold at Verdun!

But still Joffre was confident that Verdun was not the target. He was convinced the Germans would attack Russia, not Verdun. In fairness to the French, it should be noted that their Intelligence (spy network) had been penetrated and disabled by the Germans, so that information was sketchy and unreliable. And the forts fell into further neglect.

Besides, why would Germany attack Verdun? Joffre, apparently, failed to comprehend the German motives.

One motivation was that the Kaiser's own son, the Crown Prince, led the German Fifth Army facing Verdun, and victory there would have important political and psychological ramifications. Then too, there were rich iron fields in the nearby Briey basin, and whoever held Verdun could claim them as well. But there was another far craftier reason. General von Falkenhayn thought that Verdun, the symbolic heart of France, was so important to the French that they would spend *every last soldier* on its defense. He would let them. He would *literally* bleed them white.[2] That would be victory indeed!

And so it was that the quietness of the clear Winter morning on 21 February 1916 was shattered by a colossal shell from a Krupp 15-inch gun 20 miles away.[3] While nobody was watching, Germany had quietly lugged to Verdun some of the very guns that had pulverized the Belgium forts so successfully in August 1914. Though the shell may have been aimed at a fort or bridge, it landed in Verdun itself, hitting the cathedral. A relentless nine-hour bombardment followed, and incredible numbers of French soldiers were buried alive in their collapsing trenches. And that was just the beginning.

The next day, 22 February, the Germans again used their new weapon of destruction, the flamethrower (*Flammenwerfer*), which had been introduced in the Battle of Hooge on 30 July 1915. The long tongues of fire hissed and spewed and struck, snakelike, at the defending French soldiers. With 96 of the evil devices scorching the way, the Germans quickly advanced two full miles, taking 3,000 prisoners in the process. Some French soldiers were burned to their death.

But though the Germans advanced quickly, they paid a price for their success. Their losses for the day were 2,350, not extraordinarily high by battle standards, but they included some of Germany's best — the elite, highly trained Storm Troopers.

And just ahead lay the "impregnable" Fort Douaumont.

Fort Douaumont, on the highest hill above Verdun, had been called (by Marshal Henri-Philippe Pétain and others) the cornerstone in the defense of Verdun. The polygon-shaped fort was protected from attackers by, among other things, two fields of barbed wire 30 yards across, an 8-foot high line of spiked railing, and a 24-foot-deep dry moat. For protection from shelling and bombardment, the fort's superstructure was shielded by nearly eight feet of reinforced concrete. The concrete in turn was protected by several feet of earth.

But Douaumont lacked many protectors! Although it had a permanent garrison of about 500 infantrymen in 1914, most had been deployed elsewhere. And now it was up to the few remaining to defend the fort.

For three days the Germans assaulted Fort Douaumont. Never before had history seen such fire or deafening explosions of bursting shells. The French front lines were obliterated, as well as some portions of the support lines. Trees were turned to stumps, and stumps to splinters. Malignant projectiles flew in every direction. With deadly precision, the Germans had pinpointed the French lines and strong points, and they bombarded them mercilessly from three, largely camouflaged sides.

And after the guns and bombardment came the bayonets as men fought in hand-to-hand battles. Most of the wounded lay untended on the torn earth. Many bled to death.

> It took twelve hours to remove only five casualties from the inferno. Everywhere roads had become impassable. Motor ambulances became stuck in shell holes; horses frenzied by the shell fire overturned their drays, scattering the badly wounded along the road. [4]

Suffering and death, instant and prolonged, covered the fields. Some soldiers, caught in the barbed wire, lay screaming for hours until the overworked medics could reach them.

> Horses especially suffered . . . easy prey for both artillery and snipers. Many combatants retained images of horses with belly wounds still kicking their legs in deep shell holes 5 and 6 days after being shot.[5]

Losses weren't limited to the forts themselves. At one little village, Samogneux, the French were holding valiantly in spite of crippling losses, including most runners and all their horses. Catastrophe piled on disaster. With communications shattered, the French Colonel Herr believed that the Germans had taken the town, and ordered a heavy barrage. Unknown to Herr, French troops still held the town, and the "friendly fire" only succeeded in killing their own, thus ironically helping the Germans take the town.

By the evening of 23 February 1916, the Germans had taken 10,000 French prisoners, 65 heavy guns, and 75 machine guns. On 24 February, Verdun's second line fell. Some nearby villages simply disappeared from the face of the earth. French morale was plummeting.

And still the German 8- and 12-inch guns pounded Fort Douaumont mercilessly. Douaumont had to be taken because it was the key to Verdun, and Verdun was the key to greater glory and victory. German plans called for entrance to Verdun on 2 March.

Like a fatally wounded horse, Fort Douaumont continued to struggle, but its fate was sealed. Even Kaiser Wilhelm II came in for the kill and, from a safe distance, watched the death struggle through a periscope for six hours.

On 25 February, Fort Douaumont finally fell. Germany was triumphant. Church bells in the Fatherland rang out in victorious celebration. The battle of Verdun was, for all intents and purposes, over.

Almost.

By now, Joffre realized the significance of Verdun, and at the urging of several of his Generals, agreed to move his Second Army, currently in reserve, to Verdun. Its Commander, General Pétain, was finally found in Paris, and the next day, through cold rain and snow, headed to Verdun. Pétain was moved to tears when he first saw some of the survivors.

In spite of falling ill the next day with pneumonia, Pétain plunged into battle details, immediately beginning to reestablish the artillery and organize transportation in and out of Verdun. Sensing that the city itself could hold out indefinitely, he called for 190,000 reinforcements and 23,000 tons of ammunition. Because the narrow-gauge railway lines connecting Verdun to supply depots were totally inadequate, every conceivable kind of truck was rounded up, and pioneer troops were summoned to shore up the roads to help establish a lifeline of supplies along the *Voie Sacree.*[6]

The bombardment continued in and around Verdun. Deadly shells would pulverize the ground, sometimes disinterring bodies and ravaging them further, denying the fallen soldiers peace in death. Shells seemed almost to "play with them as a cat plays with a mouse."[7]

The German soldiers suffered, too, of course. Some iron-disciplined German troops sprang from rear trenches to take the place of their fallen comrades, as "upheaved corpses formed a continuous embankment, each additional dead man giving greater protection to his comrades."[8]

Heavy-laden soldiers, trying to climb up the slippery sides of water-filled shell holes, would slither back down into the putrid mud and drown. In one instance, a chaplain saw a horse, still strapped to its wagon, struggling in the mud of a crater hole: "He had been there for two nights, sinking deeper and deeper, but the troops, obsessed by their own suffering, passed by without so much as casting a glance at the wretched beast."[9]

There were many unsung heroes. Cooks sometimes had to dodge flying shrapnel and dead bodies as they brought food to the men. Stretcher bearers risked death every time they tried to rescue a fallen comrade. Runners took extraordinary risks, trying to take messages to the front or rear.

> The battered ground bore nothing but groaning wounded who couldn't be helped, distended bodies that our foot sank into, among broken guns, punctured helmets, scattered equipment.[10]

As the battle went on, Pétain was prepared to yield ground if Germany paid a steep enough price for it. He deeply sympathized with "the youths of twenty going into the furnace of Verdun" and didn't want to leave them in battle too long. He would pull back divisions after a few days and send in fresh troops. Ironically, Joffre, who months before refused to consider a German attack on Verdun, now wanted a strong offensive battle, not Pétain's defensive mode. To rid himself of the popular Pétain, he promoted him, replacing him with General Robert Georges Nivelle.

By now, the eyes of the world were on the titanic struggle. France had to hold on, for its honor was at stake. Germany had to take Verdun because it had already made an enormous down payment on it. After all, its troops had already taken Fort Douaumont.

The next step would be Fort Vaux.

Defending Fort Vaux was Major S. E. Raynal, who although already wounded, had taken over the fort on 24 May. With him were about 600 troops, including some who were wounded, and four carrier pigeons.

By the second day of June 1916, Germans were attacking Fort Vaux's strong points, and the next day assault troops crossed the moat to reach the fort itself. Climbing up onto the roof, they penetrated through slits in the fort's galleries. Desperate struggles took place in underground corridors amid fumes, decomposing bodies, and often in pitch blackness. With all communications cut, Reynal began to send his pigeons out to ask for help.

By 4 June, German soldiers brought in the flamethrowers to smoke and burn out the defenders. The situation was now critical. Desperate, Raynal decided to send his last pigeon, which itself was badly gassed, with a message asking for relief. Somewhat disoriented, the poor bird fluttered around until finally "coaxed" on its mission.

> It reached Verdun, was delivered of its message, then — like Pheidippides at marathon — fell dead. (The only one of its species to be "decorated" with the Legion d' Honneur, the noble emissary was stuffed and sits to this day in a Paris museum.)[11]

Though the pigeon had done its noble work, Fort Vaux was encircled. Inside, the exhausted troops were going mad with thirst. By 5 June, the Germans blew a breach in one wall and soldiers with flamethrowers advanced again. This time fate intervened. French artillery in turn pounded the Germans, and some of their flamethrowers, twisting and turning as they were hit, actually spewed flames on their own men.

Inside, Raynal gave his troops the last of the water. Some resorted to drinking their own urine. There was still no relief.

On 7 June, Fort Vaux surrendered. The captured French soldiers crawled out on their hands and knees begging for water, and seeking even the dank, fetid water in the shell holes.

To take the fort, the Germans had sacrificed 2,678 men and 64 officers. They had bombarded it with everything they had, including Big Berthas, gas, and flamethrowers. Though the French had held them off for days, they couldn't survive another day without water.

After the fall of Fort Vaux, German forces still had to advance more than six miles over tormented earth, every inch of which would be stubbornly defended by French troops. Still more troops on both sides would have to be fed into the human meat grinder.

Though with the capture of the second major fort the Germans had scored another victory, there seemed always yet another fort or strongpoint to take, one more corner to turn. One of the corners, actually a crossroads of sorts, was the Thiaumont Works (*Ouvrage de Thiaumont*), important for its geographical prominence. Neither a fort nor a village, it was a labyrinth of trenches, hidden gun emplacements, underground shelters, and, of course, the inevitable barbed wire. Whichever side held it would hold the approaches to Souville.

The Germans finally took the Works on 8 June, only to lose it again soon after. Neither side could possibly know that it would change hands more than a dozen times that summer, with casualties mounting daily. Germany would sacrifice three divisions — 36,000 men — trying to take and hold the site that was to become one of the bloodiest in the war. (During the war, many towns were lost and retaken time and time again. The town of Fleury, for example, changed hands 16 times between 23 June and 17 July.)

By 21 June, the battle that von Falkenhayn thought would be over in weeks was now four months old, and the capture of Verdun was still elusive.

But von Falkenhayn was still hopeful! There was really only one more significant barrier to Verdun — Fort Souville. And on the evening of 22 June, the Germans attacked it with a new kind of gas. Phosgene was a colorless, odorless heavier-than-air gas, so deadly that it could even pene-trate gas masks. Men fell, gasping, clutching their throats. Horses, froth-ing at the mouth, lay twitching and contorted in dying agony.

Once again water became a problem, this time for soldiers on both sides, as men, horses, wagons, buckets, and barrels were more often than not blown to bits when attempts were made to bring water to the hot and thirsty soldiers. By 23 June, the Germans had inflicted 13,000 casualties on the French (including taking some 4,000 prisoners[12]). Still, the Ger-mans could not take Fort Souville and break through to Verdun. In words that would become famous, General Nivelle defiantly shouted, "*Ils ne passeront pas*," ["*They shall not pass!*"], and exhorted his troops to fight on.[13] And that day, June 23, marked a turning point at Verdun.

As June turned to July, and July to August — and the second anniver-sary of the beginning of the war — the change became more obvious. Ger-many, having to pull three divisions from the town to cope with the major British thrust on the Somme River, was now on the defensive. Verdun, although in ruins and uninhabitable, was still unconquered.

Kaiser Wilhelm II, who had come to Verdun months before for the kill, was now impatient with von Falkenhayn. Just as he had been upset by General von Kluck for his retreat at the Marne and replaced him with General von Falkenhayn, he was now irritable with von Falkenhayn, and replaced him with Field Marshal von Hindenberg. But the change in command was not the answer.

Now it was France's turn. With Britain taking the brunt of the fight on the Somme, France began to pull to Verdun several mighty guns, includ-ing two new, well-camouflaged 400-millimeter railway guns. On 19 Octo-ber, the blasting and bombardment began, and on 24 October, with Nivelle's creeping barrage providing strong coverage for his troops, Fort Douaumont was back in French hands. In several days, the French retook most of the ground that the Germans had spent four and a half months capturing.

On the second day of November, Fort Vaux, too, was recaptured by the French.

By December 1916, the longest pitched battle in history was over. In ten months, France had lost more than 348,000 men, and nearly three-quarters of her soldiers had spent some tormented time there. Germany had sacri-ficed an equal amount. Some said total casualties reached one million. In the first five weeks alone, "German soldiers were killed at the astounding rate of one every forty-five seconds. French deaths were even higher."[14] As Winston Churchill said, *"Victory was to be bought so dear as to be almost indistinguishable from defeat."*

Yet the two adversaries were only a few kilometers from where they had started. Verdun was in ruins, but it was still French. German General von Falkenhayn had lost his command, and the French were becoming disillusioned with Joffre, at least in part for neglecting the forts.

Elsewhere, Britain had taken over from France the responsibility for the Somme. And thousands of miles away, across the Atlantic, the United States was watching the titanic struggle.

But not until 12 September 1918 would Verdun's final relief be accomplished, by the American First Army.

NOTES

1. Much of the material in this chapter is based on the insightful book by Alistair Horne, *The Price of Glory, Verdun, 1916* (London: Penguin Books, 1962).
2. Holger H. Herwig notes that von Falkenhayn by now had informed Wilhelm II that France was weakened to the point of exhaustion, and that Great Britain was the archenemy. But the German navy couldn't risk a decisive battle at sea, and the island empire couldn't be readily reached by German troops. The German U-boats could strike in unrestricted warfare and rob England of her essential supplies. The United States could not intervene in time, so France could be bled white on the Western Front at symbolic Verdun. Von Falkenhayn, coldly predicting the loss of five French soldiers for every two Germans, would annihilate France. *The First World War: Germany and Austria Hungary 1914-1918* (London: Arnold, 1997), 181-184.
3. The day chosen for the attack was actually 12 February, but on that day it snowed, and snowed hard. German gunners couldn't see their targets. The assault was delayed, first for one day, then another and another, as snow, rain, and fog took turns obliterating the whole Front.
4. Horne, *The Price of Glory*, 103.
5. Herwig, *The First World War*, 189.
6. Horne, *The Price of Glory*, 148.
7. *Ibid.,*176.
8. Francis Whiting Halsey, *The Literary Digest History of the World War*, Vol. 3 (New York: Funk & Wagnalls Co., 1919), 100.
9. Horne, *The Price of Glory*, 186.

10. George A. Panichas, ed., *Promise of Greatness: The War of 1914-1918* (New York: The John Day Co., 1968), 60.

11. Horne, *The Price of Glory*, 259.

12. *Ibid.*, 292.

13. Some authors (for example, Martin Gilbert) ascribe the famous exhortation "They shall not pass!" to General Pétain. Martin Gilbert, *The First World War: A Complete History*, 2nd ed. (New York: Henry Holt and Co., 1994), 232. Horne, *The Price of Glory*, claims the remark was Nivelle's (231).

14. Gilbert, *The First World War*, 232.

War is the realm of uncertainty; three quarters of the factors on which action in war is based are wrapped in a fog of greater or lesser uncertainty.
— Karl von Clausewitz, *On War* (1833)

Chapter 14

Outgunned and Outfought in the Mud of St. Eloi

FOR THE CANADIANS, Christmas of 1915 had come and gone uneventfully. Units lucky enough to be in reserve could enjoy a holiday dinner in their billets, but troops in the front lines had to be content with rations brought to them. Though there was no repeat of the informal front-line truce of the previous year (and Allied troops still smarted from the surprise gas attack at Ypres), there were few shots exchanged. And on Christmas Day came news of the authorization of yet another Canadian Division — the Third. Taking over its reins as General Officer Commanding would be the former Commander of the Eastern Ontario Brigade, Major General Malcolm S. Mercer, the former Toronto lawyer. (Early in 1916, the Princess Patricia's Canadian Light Infantry, the first Canadian regiment to land in Europe and which had fought brilliantly while attached to a British Division, was transferred to the Third Division.)

As 1916 dawned, the unparalleled war continued to grind on with mounting losses but no significant signs of ultimate victory for either side. The overall situation for the Allies, however, ranged from disturbing to dismal. In spite of two bitter battles at Ypres, the Allies now held only part of the Salient. Large parts of both France and Belgium were in German hands. On the Eastern Front, Austro-German forces had repelled the Russians. Even the Gallipoli Campaign had failed. There was little room for optimism.

The Allies to this point, though united in determination to defeat the Central Powers, were far from united insofar as a comprehensive, coordinated effort was concerned. The need for simultaneous offenses had been discussed at conferences the previous year (July and November 1915), but it was not until December that agreement was reached that major offensives, simultaneous if possible, were absolutely essential on the Russian, Franco-British, and Italian Fronts.

Meanwhile, Canada was sending over about 5,000 reinforcements monthly,[1] and front-line troops continued with their harassment of the enemy by sniping, surprise artillery shoots, and, of course, trench raids.

On the night of 2 January, the 25th (Nova Scotia Rifles) Battalion gave the enemy a surprise New Years's gift by crawling into No Man's Land to cut the barbed wire by hand, rather than rely on the hit-and-miss results of artillery fire. The success was short-lived, however. The Germans soon introduced new tempered steel wire to discourage the practice.

Not to be outdone, specially trained volunteers from the 28th (Northwest) and 29th (Vancouver) Battalions staged two separate successful raids in the early morning hours of the last day of January, capturing a number of German prisoners, destroying dugouts, and gaining new Intelligence. With a loss of only two killed and ten wounded, the well-rehearsed, successful raids gained attention — and admiration — along the British Front.

February and March brought new challenges. The Germans, in diversionary tactics (to draw attention away from Verdun), initiated a series of attacks against British and French positions. In one area, the Canadian Corps was called in (on 17 February) to relieve the British 5th Corps of some 700 yards of the Front, thus extending the Canadian sector to the ruins of St. Eloi.

The Canadians tried a few diversionary tactics of their own, too. Lord Beaverbrook (Sir Max Aitken) recounts the story of Captain Costigan of the 10th Battalion, who, in an ingenious attempt to distract the enemy, decided to float a raft loaded with explosives down the Douve River and explode it when it reached enemy lines. Fearing that the raft would become entangled with overhanging branches or caught in obstacles on the way, he jumped into the water, and steered it downstream until it reached the enemy's barbed wire strung across the river. Undeterred, he waited in the cold water for the signal (flare) to light the fuse. His efforts were rewarded. The enemy responded with machine-gun fire, revealing previously hidden positions.[2]

Trench life continued to be grim. Troops were exposed not only to the incessant, blistering fury of enemy attacks, but filthy, waterlogged, collapsing trenches. To add insult to injury, they had to contend with driving rain, bitterly cold winds, and disease. Casualties mounted. In the first three months of the new year, 546 were killed, 1,543 wounded, 3 more were gassed, and 1 was taken prisoner.[3]

A New Assignment

Sometimes, in a large unfamiliar city, in broad daylight and with street signs on every corner, a tourist — even with map in hand — will get lost. In a mutilated landscape, pockmarked with crater holes, strewn with barbed wire and the bodies of dead and dying men and animals, with bullets and shrapnel flying about, sleet and snow limiting visibility, it was almost inevitable that soldiers would become disoriented or lost.

Such would be the scene for the Canadian Corps in its next battle in April 1916. This time, the Second Division would have its standard tested.

By April, the French, fighting for their lives and honor at Verdun, were appealing to the British for more help. (The United Kingdoms's war committee had already determined that France would constitute the major theater of the war, and therefore increased efforts to expand the BEF, which, of course, included colonial troops. Sir Douglas Haig's command was growing from 3 armies (and 38 infantry divisions) to 4 armies (and 49 divisions), with 5 cavalry divisions.)

At the western end of the St. Eloi Salient was a nondescript clay bank called "The Mound." Once 30 feet or so in height, it was now much reduced in size by shelling, but was still worthwhile for the observation advantage it afforded. As usual, both sides wanted the Mound, and had fought throughout most of 1915 to seize it.

British tunnelers proposed a new way to capture the objective and, with the 3rd Canadian Tunneling Company, had been quietly digging under it for months, from shafts well out of sight to the rear. So quiet and deep (50 to 60 feet) was their work that the enemy had no idea that the tunnelers were, by March, right under them.

The British Third Division originally had been detailed to make the assault. However, its ranks by now had been seriously depleted, and the surviving troops were close to exhaustion. The grim weather had further exacerbated their weariness. As a result, General Alderson proposed that the recently arrived Second Canadian Division make the assault instead. This presented a dilemma, however. The new Canadian troops hadn't yet had time to practice over a simulated enemy course. To take time to train them might risk German discovery of the secret mines and the undoing of weeks of work.

Furthermore, the exchange of one corps by another, even at the best of times, represents an extraordinary undertaking. Lord Beaverbrook describes it as a wave of immigration and emigration and "nothing less than the gradual interchange of all the population of two countrysides and all the means of feeding and clothing them"[4] — all with a minimum of disturbance, of course. Furthermore, the trenches were clogged in places by debris and shells, and by the dead and wounded of both sides.

To solve the dilemma, a compromise was worked out whereby the Third British Division would, as originally planned, provide the striking force, but then turn the area over to the Canadians as soon as the objectives had been reached and the area stabilized. The date for the assault was set for late March.

The deafening thunder from the salvos of 41 guns and howitzers erupted at 4:15 on the morning of 27 March 1916, followed by the massive explosions of the 6 mines, each one timed to detonate a few seconds after another. The volcanic eruptions demolished landmarks, collapsed trenches, formed massive holes and craters (one as large as 50 feet deep and 180 feet wide), and vastly altered the landscape. Some German frontline companies (such as the 18th Reserve Jager Battalion) were simply obliterated.[5] Men of the 9th British Brigade, who had spent most of the miserable night lying in the mud, quickly drove forward, stumbling through the debris to capture new ground.

But once again, what looked plausible in the planning process, was far less so under deplorable fighting conditions. Massive confusion entered the murky picture. With the landscape altered beyond recognition, and with enemy machine-gun fire holding them back, the British troops groped and fought and struggled their way through wind-whipped sheets of rain, over the battered ground. They finally were successful in taking Craters 6 and 7, though they thought they were in Craters 4 and 5. (Unknown to them at the time, Craters 4 and 5 were still held by neither side. Crater 7 was actually the result of an earlier explosion.) But by the end of the month, the British troops successfully established a machine-gun post in Crater 4. By the third day of April, the British took the real Crater 5.

Day after day the fighting and shelling continued, and there was no let-up in the appalling weather. Troops often stood knee-deep and sometimes waist-deep in muddy ditches and shell holes, surrounded by the dead and wounded of both sides. Their supply of food, water, and ammunition had been sporadic at best. By now, the troops were close to collapsing from complete exhaustion.

It was under these circumstances that the 27th (City of Winnipeg) Battalion and 31st (Alberta) Battalion of the 6th Canadian Brigade, some wearing new steel helmets for the first time, came in to relieve the British troops in the middle of the night of April 3-4. The 3rd Divisional Artillery remained behind, since it was difficult to register new guns in the middle of a battle. Canada's young citizen soldiers who had come from scattered parts of the Dominion to make up the Second Division would now have their own opportunity to play their part in foreign fields.

Their inheritance was shabby indeed. Some trenches, their drainage systems blown and pulverized, were filled with two and three feet of water. Some were nothing more than shallow drainage ditches. Near Craters 4 and 5 they found only 4 machine guns in posts that should have had 12. To make matters worse, enemy forces still held the Wytschaete Ridge and had the advantage of the sun at their backs.

Major General Turner, Commander of the Second Division, found the situation dismal. Though men tried to dig more trenches, the troops were struggling against incessant enemy fire, deplorable ground conditions, and wet weather. There was no communication between the newly captured line and the rear, except around the flank of the gaping craters, and the four central craters created an almost insurmountable obstacle. Although the 2nd Canadian Pioneer Battalion (assisted by the 4th and 5th Brigades) worked feverishly for two nights to improve the defense system (pumping water out of trenches, evacuating British wounded, and burying or removing British and German bodies — all under heavy bombardment), conditions deteriorated further.

By 5 April, both the 27th (Winnipeg) and 31st (Alberta) Battalions had been bombed almost incessantly for two days, and men scrambled to dig even shallow depressions in the mud for cover. Some trenches were completely obliterated by exploding shells, leaving the men defenseless.[6] It had been a baptism of earth, fire, and water. Some had only two or three hours of sleep in a 48-hour period. But now the 29th (Vancouver) Battalion would come in to relieve the Winnipeg troops. And though it did not seem possible, battle conditions and the weather deteriorated further.

The mechanics of relieving exhausted troops by fresh men in the battle was even more complex than had been anticipated. Troops had to be moved up and down the communication trenches at night to avoid the murderous fire. The relief progress was therefore awkward and heartbreakingly slow. Pioneer working parties could barely pass each other in the crumbling soggy trenches as they met outgoing, heavily-laden troops and incoming stretcher bearers and the walking wounded. The exchange of troops was so slow, in fact, that all were caught in the middle of the night (actually 3:30 in the morning of the 6th) in a renewed and concentrated German assault.

By the early morning hours of 6 April, the Winnipegers (27th Battalion) had been under fire for 60 hours, most of the time without food or rest. Try as they might, they found it almost impossible to keep the splattering mud from their rifles and guns. And it was then that they saw in the cold gray dawn the figures of German troops advancing confidently toward them up the St. Eloi-Wytschaete Road. The Canadian Westerners sprung into action, but the inevitable happened. Many of their Ross rifles jammed. (Unlike the First Division, they had not yet received Lee-Enfields.) Cursing both mud and guns, they grabbed weapons of fallen comrades until these guns failed also.

Under such circumstances, there could be little resistance by the Canadians, and by the end of the day the Germans took Craters 2 and 3, and then 4 and 5, essentially regaining all the ground they had lost to the British between 27 March and 3 April.

But the Canadians would not leave without a fight. They would counterattack on the night of 8-9 April and try to regain the wretched craters. The 6th Brigade's plan called for bombing parties from the 27th (Winnipeg) and 29th (Vancouver) Battalions to attack Craters 2 and 3, while their counterparts from the 28th (Northwest) and 31st (Alberta) would attack Craters 4 and 5.

But they were doomed to failure. Though the men of the 27th and 29th struggled through the clinging mud toward their objective, none could get anywhere near the craters with their grenades before being caught in enemy fire. The 31st Battalion (with a detachment of the 28th) didn't fare much better. It became disoriented in the unfamiliar surroundings, and, in a pitiful repetition of the mistake made by their British counterparts ten days before, occupied Craters 6 and 7, thinking they were in Craters 4 and 5. To the mud-caked, struggling soldier, one mud hole, with no distinguishing characteristics and landmarks, looked pretty much like another.

Although the 21st (Kingston and Eastern Ontario) Battalion[7] also sent out bombing parties to try to regain some of the lost ground, the men lost their way in the driving rain and darkness, and succeeded only in capturing several small German patrols. They had not accomplished their objectives, nor had they even been able to identify where they were. Additional attacks by other Ontario battalions (18th and 20th) also were repulsed by enemy gun fire. In some cases, troops who went forward to relieve other parties found that everything had been wiped out. Sometimes only one or two survivors crawled back. Some parties, like those of the 25th (Nova Scotia Rifles) and 26th (New Brunswick) were simply never seen again.[8]

By the dawn of 7 April 1916, the 6th Brigade, now exhausted, had lost 617 officers and men. But they still held Craters 6 and 7 as the 4th (Central Ontario) Brigade came in to relieve them.

On the night of 8 April, the fresh troops launched counterattacks, but in spite of extraordinary acts of bravery by night bombing parties[9] and heavy losses, they too met with little success. The brigade encountered heartbreaking setbacks time and time again. Enemy barrage from higher positions, foul weather, darkness-disfigured ground, obliterated landmarks, and omnipresent mud, all seemed to conspire against them. Canadian gunners, fearful of hitting their own countrymen in what they thought were captured craters, held their fire. More trenches collapsed. Communication lines were shattered, and runners risked their lives darting like rabbits from shell hole to shell hole, trying to deliver messages. Newly introduced carrier pigeons dropped dead from shell bursts. Stretcher bearers died in the attempt to bring in the wounded. Guns jammed as splattering mud, flying in all directions, clogged the breeches and firing mechanisms.

Unfortunately, the soldiers' disorientation was reflected and magnified at higher levels. For several more days there was deadly confusion with regard to the craters — which was which, and who occupied what. In fairness to the Commanders, however, bad weather had prevented aerial observations for days on end (from 8 April to 16 April). And it was only on 16 April when the weather finally cleared that an aerial photograph showed that Craters 2, 3, 4, and 5 were all in German hands. On 19 April, the Germans finally took Craters 6 and 7. All craters were lost.

The cost was high. Canadian casualties between 4 and 16 April were 1,373. One garrison of the 29th Battalion, consisting of 80 men, had *one* man survive unwounded.[10] British losses in the 6th Brigade in the four days before being relieved by the Canadians were 617. German losses were 483.[11]

The Canadian loss of the territory previously gained by the British did not set well with the higher command, in spite of the appalling conditions under which the battles had been fought. Questions were raised. Why the initial delay in capturing some critical points? Why were not aerial photographs interpreted more accurately? Why was Intelligence so faulty? Were the Commanders incompetent?

The men of the Second Division, though not demoralized nor dispirited, were far from content. In spite of bitter fighting and countless individual acts of bravery, their first major operation had resulted in the loss of trenches previously captured at great cost by the British. Though they had fought with commitment and valor, just as their brothers in the First Division had fought in the gas attack a few miles to the north at Ypres, their efforts in the mud of St. Eloi had met with failure and frustration. It was a bitter pill.

The Spring of 1916 saw battles and skirmishes on a smaller scale, though in May alone, the Canadians suffered more than 2,000 casualties, mainly from German artillery bombardment. May also brought two other significant developments. The Canadian Corps began to use wireless communication to control artillery fire — and they received a new Commander. For reasons long disputed, General Alderson, the man who had welcomed the Canadians to England, had overseen their training on Salisbury Plain, had commanded them at Ypres, and had commended them for their valor, was transferred to England — to become a somewhat redundant Inspector General of the Canadian Forces in England.

Alderson attributed his removal to his ongoing differences with Sam Hughes, the stubborn, half-mad Canadian Minister of Militia, over the controversial Ross rifle. Others said the change resulted from the St. Eloi debacle and the conflict between Alderson and one of his Generals (Turner). Lord Beaverbrook, the Canadian whose influence was growing with the British, wrote that Alderson was "incapable of holding the Canadian Divisions together."

And so he was replaced by Lieutenant General Sir Julian H. Byng, who would later become Governor General of Canada and be immortalized in hockey circles for the "Byng Trophy" awarded annually to the most gentlemanly player in the National Hockey League.

At home, anti-German feeling swept over Canada. In Regina, Saskatchewan, crowds set fire to buildings believed to be owned by Germans. In Berlin, Ontario, where there were many citizens of German heritage, angry patriots threw a statue of Kaiser Wilhelm II into a lake. By May 1916, the city fathers had renamed the town after Lord Kitchener.

Canadian fortunes continued on a downward spiral in June of 1916. But now there were three divisions fighting side by side in the battlefields of France — the third and newest, comprising the 7th and 8th Brigades, having come into being in January.

NOTES

1. Colonel G. W. L. Nicholson, C.D., *Canadian Expeditionary Force 1914-1919: Official History of the Canadian Army in the First World War* (Ottawa: Queen's Printer, 1964), 133.
2. Sir Max Aitken (Lord Beaverbrook), *Canada in Flanders*, Vol. 1 (London: Hodder and Stoughton, 1916), 81.

3. Nicholson, *Canadian Expeditionary Force*, 137.

4. Aitken, *Canada in Flanders*, 83.

5. Nicholson, *Canadian Expeditionary Force*, 139, notes that German losses in a three-day period were said to have been 921, with 300 killed or buried by the mine explosions.

6. Nicholson, *Canadian Expeditionary Force*, relates that by noon on 4 April, every second man in one of the forward companies of the 27th Battalion had been hit.

7. Nicholson, *Canadian Expeditionary Force*, 144.

8. Aitken, *Canada in Flanders*, 115.

9. *Ibid.,* 135-142.

10. *Ibid.,*163.

11. Nicholson, *Canadian Expeditionary Force*, 143-144.

*We see men living with their skulls blown
open; we see soldiers run with their two
feet cut off; they stagger on their splin-
tered stumps into the next shell-hole; . . .
we see men without mouths, without jaws,
without faces*   — Erich Marie Remarque,
All Quiet on the Western Front

Chapter 15

Vindication and Victory at Mount Sorrel and Observatory Ridge

As the summer days of 1916 grew longer with the advent of June, Canada had three divisions on the battle-fields of France and Belgium. The Second Division was still in front of St. Eloi, where it had suffered the loss of the mined craters. Farther north, the First and Third Divisions were in the Ypres area, holding ground purchased with the blood of thousands of their comrades.

The Third Division held a barren piece of higher ground aptly called "Observatory Ridge," located between Sanctuary Wood and Mount Sorrel. The ridge was critical — the only ridge (or portion of ridge) in the Ypres area that remained in Allied hands. From it, the Canadians could spot the enemy movement without having to rely on planes and balloons. Moreover, troops on higher ground were not quite so susceptible to enemy fire. As some military writers have pointed out, having the high-ground advantage is almost akin to hav-ing sight where your enemy is blind.

The Third Division, as well as the First Division on their right, had been heavily shelled for days — so much so that they were becoming suspicious of the German antics. They had good reason. The Germans had driven "T" saps (regular trenches with an extension out on each side, thus looking like the letter "T") and connected them to form a new trench line. Although poor weather prevented consistent observation behind enemy lines, some Royal Flying Corps observers reported seeing German trenches that oddly resembled Canadian trenches. And they were correct. The Germans had replicated Canadian trenches for practice purposes. In addition, there were reports of the arrival of large-caliber trench mortars in the German lines.

On the night of 1-2 June, the heavy shelling ceased for seven hours. Unknown to the Canadians, the Germans were sending out wiring parties and didn't wish to hit their own men. But then the onslaught began again.

It was under these circumstances that GOC Major General Mercer, of the relatively new Third Canadian Division, set out at 6 o'clock on the second morning of June to tour the trenches. With him was Brigadier General V. A. S. Williams, Commander of the 8th Brigade, which was defending Observatory Ridge. By 8 o'clock, they had reached the battalion headquarters of the 4th Canadian Mounted Rifles. A few minutes later, they reached the front trench line.

At 8:30 that morning, the inferno struck. High explosives, almost unbearable in their power and intensity, created almost tornado-like devastation. Men were knocked to the ground, some killed outright by the concussion of the explosions, some killed or maimed by hot steel fragments screaming through the morning air. Headless trees and woods were uprooted and hurtled skyward. Lines of trenches caved in. Some soldiers were buried alive. The tortured earth was littered with broken and bleeding bodies, dazed men, and pulverized sandbags. Even the dead could not escape the fury. Some bodies were disinterred and reburied by the exploding earth.

One of the first shells wounded Brigadier General Williams (who was subsequently taken prisoner) and stunned Major General Mercer who, nonetheless, sent an urgent message to the rear asking for howitzer support. But shortly after, GOC Mercer fell, his eardrums shattered by shellfire, and his leg broken by a bullet. While he lay on the ground, just after entering his first major action in his new command, he was killed by a burst of shrapnel. Canada had lost her first General.

But the now leaderless troops fought on.

Some trenches simply collapsed from the bomb blasts and disappeared completely. Among them were those of the 4th Canadian Mounted Rifles, along with 89 percent of the men in the unit. Their casualties numbered 637, including their Chaplain, Captain A. G. Wilken, who had been guiding stretcher-bearers back to the rear, then carrying ammunition up to the front on his return trip.

The enemy shellfire raged all morning, and succeeded in killing all Forward Observation Officers. Each artillery battery's FOO actually worked up ahead (forward) with the infantry, spotting targets, recording where his own battery's shells fell, and signaling corrections back to his battery by field telephone. It was an extremely dangerous position.

All telephone lines were crushed or wrecked. And there was more to come. At 1 p.m., the Germans exploded four mines near the Canadian trenches on Mt. Sorrel. Immediately after, a line of gray-coated German soldiers — carrying fixed bayonets, hand grenades, and wire cutters — began to advance toward the Canadian lines with an air of confidence that indicated they thought their opponents had been wiped out. They were followed by a second, third, and fourth line carrying entrenching tools, floorboards, and sandbags. They had come, apparently, to stay.

The Canadians offered what resistance they could, sometimes in hand-to-hand fighting. But they were powerless against flamethrowers. Though machine guns of the PPCLI and 5th (Western Cavalry) Battalion tried to throw back the advancing Germans, they were unable to stop them.

The Germans pressed on, capturing three strongpoints on Observatory Ridge, and then surged over the 5th Battery of the Canadian Field Artillery, killing or wounding every last gunner. The gunners however, went down fighting. A German regimental historian later wrote that "here too the Canadians did not surrender, but at their guns defended themselves with revolvers to the last man."[1]

Still the Germans punched forward, seizing most of Maple Copse and most of Sanctuary Wood, though the PPCLI suffered more than 400 casualties, including their Commanding Officer Lieutenant Colonel H. C. Buller, trying to hold them back.

The second day of June was proving to be a deadly, long day, and it still was not over. That evening, Lieutenant General Sir Julien Byng, the new GOC of the entire Canadian Corps, ordered that "all ground lost today will be retaken tonight."

The ground wasn't retaken that night, however, for a host of reasons, including ever-present communication difficulties, difficult distances to be covered, continuing enemy fire, and the misfiring of some signal rockets. Moreover, many Canadian attacking units had been significantly weakened by casualties. Nonetheless, the Canadians fought on and advanced about 1,000 yards, eventually closing a 600-yard gap on Observatory Ridge.

And finally, they were about to get some formidable help. Though Ypres was important to the Higher Command, few infantry troops could be pulled away from the Somme area farther south. But the artillery could help! The Canadians, who had suffered enormous losses from the German guns at St. Eloi, could soon return the favor and give the Germans a dose of their own medicine.

Thus came Brigadier General H. E. Burstall and his powerful array of 218 guns, including 116 18-pounders, representing several Canadian, Lahore, British, and South African artillery groups and batteries.

For several days there were attacks and counterattacks by both sides, but a new Canadian assault by the First Division was planned for 13 June, under the direction of Lieutenant General Arthur Currie of Ypres fame. The artillery began daily bombardments of only 20 to 30 minutes for each of the four days leading up to the assault, hoping the enemy would anticipate an immediate attack, then be lulled into complacency by the false alarms. But on 12 June, Burstall and his artillery blasted the German positions between Hill 60 and Sanctuary Wood for not 20 or 30 minutes but for 12 solid hours. At 8:30, in heavy evening rain, the Canadians attacked behind a smoke screen.

This time the attack was a success. The Germans could not hold their gains of 2 June. The 3rd (Toronto) Battalion retook Mt. Sorrel; the 16th (Canadian Scottish) retook the north part of Armagh Wood; the 13th (Royal Highlanders) cleared Observatory Ridge; and the 58th (Central Ontario) recovered many of the trenches in Sanctuary Wood. The Canadians had also taken nearly 200 German prisoners.

Robert Kennedy merely noted in his diary that on the 17th of June the Germans

bombarded us at 12, 1 a.m. and again at 2:30. We retaliated.

By now, Kennedy had become almost blasé about the bombardment. He had noted briefly, on 16 March, that he returned from the Observation Post to the guns, and his battery had been shelled. The shelling got as much space in his diary as the entry on 22 March:

Went for a bath today.

He noted heavy bombardment of St. Eloi on 27 March; mentioned being awakened at 1:00 a.m., on 5 April to haul ammunition for the guns, arriving at the wagon lines at 5:30 in the morning; and wrote of colleagues being wounded and killed. He also noted, on 28 May, that his unit had been firing on the infamous Hill 60 as the Germans were sending over rifle grenades.

What had started out as a defensive battle on 2 June had become a small but clear victory for the Canadians. And the soldiers had something else to cheer about! By 12 June, they were able to replace their Ross rifle with the British-made Lee-Enfield.

As usual, however, the fighting had not come without cost. By mid-June, the Canadian Corps counted approximately 8,000 casualties, including Major General Mercer. In the same period and theater of war, the Germans listed 5,765 casualties.

The figures would mount for months and months to come.

NOTES

1. Quoted in Colonel G. W. L. Nicholson, C.D., *Canadian Expeditionary Force 1914-1919: Official History of the Canadian Army in the First World War* (Ottawa: Queen's Printer, 1964), 150. Nicholson also notes that this was the only occasion in the war when guns of the Canadian Corps were captured by the Germans. Fortunately, the two 18-pounder guns were later recovered.

A sunlit picture of Hell.
    — Siegfried Sassoon

Chapter 16

Slaughter on the Somme

THE SOMME IS A slow-moving, weed-choked river in Northern France. About 150 miles in length, and in some places 500 yards wide, it meanders monotonously from St. Quentin through Picardy on its way to the English Channel, as if in no rush to get there. Its west-by-northwest route more or less bisects the department[1] Somme which, like the river, seems as unhurried now as it was in Roman times, when Julius Caesar and his legions camped on its banks. (Some of the Roman-built roads are still there.) North of the river are chalk-based hills. To the south are dense woods and copses, and flatter fields for wheat and sugar-beet farming.

During the first part of the war, in 1914 and 1915, the Somme area was relatively quiet with both the Germans and French regarding it as a "live and let live" sector. It was so quiet, in fact, that the Germans north of the river left much of the 18-mile front in the hands of reserve divisions. But the troops were not inactive. On the contrary. They took advantage of the lull to build elaborate trenches and timbered dugouts, some of them 30 and 40 feet deep in the chalky soil. Some were relatively comfortable, even to the extent of having barracks, kitchens, electricity, forced-air ventilation, laundry facilities, and repair shops. More important, the trenches had protection, partly from their catacomb-like depth, and especially from their watchdog machine guns and hefty rolls of barbed wire that faced No Man's Land.[2]

But the serenity on the Somme was to change profoundly. Fate and politics would intervene to spawn a tragic battle of epic proportions.[3]

Why the Somme?

The year 1915 had been unkind to the Allies, with unsuccessful French attacks in Artois and Champagne and heavy British casualties at Neuve Chapelle, Festubert, and Loos. It is estimated that during that year on the Western Front, the British had lost nearly 300,000 men and the French more than one million. (The Germans had lost nearly 700,000.) The French, at one point, had seemed almost on the verge of collapse. The Dardanelles expedition had failed. The Russians were suffering catastrophic setbacks and losses.

To make matters worse, there was a general impasse on the Western Front. Slight gains in seizing new trenches were purchased with heavy casualties one day, only to be lost — again with more casualties — the next. Murmurings were growing of the need for a Franco-British offensive somewhere in the Western Front during the summer of 1916. Perhaps a big push would end the terrible stalemate. It would be primarily French, the thought went, but Britain would provide preliminary attacks to grind down the enemy. Something had to happen somewhere.

The first concrete suggestion for a Franco-British offense on the Somme had actually come from France's General Joffre in late December 1915. He had suggested in a letter to the British Commander-in-Chief General Haig that the "French offensive would be greatly aided by a simultaneous offensive of the British forces between Somme and Arras." Three weeks later, Joffre again suggested to Haig that the British could wear down the enemy in attacks north of the Somme.

Haig was initially disinclined to take up the suggestion. For one thing, he feared the cost in lives. Most of the old Regular Army had been wiped out, and his new troops, many of them fresh volunteers in the New Army, were not yet well trained. Nor was there any strategic prize to be gained, nor any great city or fort to be captured. Furthermore, the Germans occupied all the high spots in the Somme, thereby having an extraordinary advantage both in sighting the French and British troops, and in firing down on them. To Haig, offensives in the Flanders area farther north would make more sense in that they would help deny Germany access to the Belgian ports of Ostend and Zeebrugge.

On the other hand, Lord Kitchener had told Haig to cooperate with the French. On being appointed Commander-in-Chief, Haig was told that "the closest cooperation between the French and British as a united army must be the governing policy." True, the Somme would offer a unique advantage; it was the *only* place where the French and British troops could fight side by side. So Haig changed his mind. He even became convinced that the Somme might offer the spectacular breakthrough that could change the whole direction of the war, perhaps even speeding up its conclusion.

And so the big push would be at the Somme, with the French leading the way. But, as we know, Fate again intervened.

This time, Fate was the battle for Verdun, which would consume not only France's heart and soul for almost a year, but also her finest young men. As February turned into March, and March into April, more and more young French soldiers were called to the mortal struggle at Verdun. France, understandably, turned increasingly to England for help. And thus, because of the enormity of the French attrition at Verdun, it would be the British, not the French, who would have to provide the brunt of the attack on the Somme.

But when? Joffre visited Haig in May after the French had lost more than 100,000 men at Verdun. Haig suggested that August would be a good time. But Joffre objected. As Haig later wrote:

> The moment I mentioned August 15th, Joffre at once got very excited and shouted that "The French Army would cease to exist if we did nothing till then."[4]

They settled for late June.

And so the planning for the Battle of the Somme began.

Spearheading the operation would be the newly formed British Fourth Army led by Lieutenant General Sir Henry Rawlinson. His 13 divisions would attack over a 15-mile-wide front north of the River Somme. On their left, General Sir Edmund Allenby's Third Army with three divisions would hit the Gommecourt area in a diversionary attack. A Reserve Army under General Sir Hubert Gough would stand in waiting. On Rawlinson's right, the French Sixth Army would attack over an eight-mile area where German defenses were less developed. France's original responsibility was for a 25-mile front, with 40 divisions. However, due to the carnage at Verdun, the number of divisions had dwindled to 16, and then to 5.

The massive undertaking would dwarf the largest previous effort at Loos, by three times or more. It would be largely a United Kingdom operation, though there would be, from far across the Atlantic, a Newfoundland battalion serving with the 29th Division, and some men from Bermuda who were with the 1st Lincolns.

The overall plan was deceptively simple. The British would inflict a massive preliminary bombardment of the German lines lasting four or five days to destroy the barbed-wire entanglements, pulverize the enemy, and leave virtually nothing alive. Rawlinson wanted the enemy to have no sleep, and live in a constant state of doubt, terror, and confusion. Then, the British and French could almost walk over the enemy's first lines. After troops had captured the confused Germans, the British barrage would lift and pound the second line into submission. The three German lines would successively be reduced to nothing, then rushed and taken, so that the cavalry could pour through all the way to Bapaume and ultimately Arras. It was all so incredibly simple.

The original bombardment was scheduled from the 24th to the 28th of June, with a final bombardment on 29 June, the first day of the actual Somme assault. Britain wanted to attack at 5:00 a.m., when Allied lines would be protected by semidarkness. The French, however, wanted to wait until 9 o'clock when their artillery could assess the results of the Allied bombardment. They compromised and chose 7.30 a.m. Thus, in an exact and inflexible schedule, the multiple-day bombardment of the first German line would cease precisely at 7:30 to allow Allied troops to move forward to it; the bombardment would then be lifted and redirected to the enemy's second line.

The plan was rigid. With an exact, fixed timetable there was no room for last-minute, *ad hoc* field decisions. Thus, local Commanders could not switch guns or targets as local circumstances dictated. The plan was thorough — and final. Rawlinson was confident. Said he, "Nothing could exist at the conclusion of the bombardment in the area covered by it."

As they prepared for the assault, news of two significant events reached the troops. In early June they learned about the Battle of Jutland, of 31 May, in which the British lost 14 warships, but nonetheless chased the Germans back to their own bases. Several days later, they learned that Lord Kitchener had drowned en route to Russia when the cruiser *Hampshire* hit a mine and sank.

But with plans now in place, extraordinary preparations moved apace. Troops began to arrive in droves. Ceaseless sounds of movement could be heard day and night as 400,000 men and 100,000 horses moved in behind the British line. Food and fodder were brought in for the horses. Stables and hutments were built. Rail lines with both standard and narrow gauges were constructed. Bridges were repaired and in some cases widened. Wells were dug. Pipes were laid and pumps installed. Miles of telephone cables were laid. Field guns, heavy guns, and howitzers were readied. Artillery and emplacements in orchards and copses were camouflaged by coloring and netting. Ammunition was brought forward to the dumps. Enclosures were constructed for soon-to-be-captured German prisoners. Casualty Clearing Stations were constructed. And inevitably, mass graves were dug.

And the Germans observed the increased activity.

The preparatory "softening up" bombardment began as scheduled on 24 June, with the primary task of demolishing the barbed-wire entanglements immediately in front of the German trenches. But a slight crinkle developed when the weather began to deteriorate. Allied observers had difficulty seeing how much damage had been inflicted on the wire. Scouts returning from night patrol brought back conflicting reports. In some places, such as Beaumont Hammel and Serre, they said, the German wire seemed not to have been cut at all. Even in some places where it had been cut in the daytime bombing, the Germans merely went out and repaired it at night. Could this be so after such heavy pounding?

And raids had provided critical Intelligence from prisoners, but they were terribly costly, as when Captain H. Price of British Columbia, in charge of a raiding party, had courageously returned to No Man's Land to look for missing men. He was shot dead, and was later buried in Albert, France.

The weather continued to worsen, with storms breaking out on 26 and 27 June. Late the next morning, 28 June, the ground was deemed too wet to attack, so the assault was postponed to the first day of July at 7:30 a.m. But the bombardment continued. As battalions marched to the trenches on 30 June, they passed through their own artillery lines where they "could see the gunners stripped to the waist and sweating over their work, their eyes blood-shot and some bleeding from the ears after six days of serving their guns."[5]

Meanwhile, the soldiers heard a number of rousing, confident speeches, all assuring success.

> *You will be able to go over the top with a walking stick, you will not need rifles. When you get to Thiepval, you will find the Germans all dead, not even a rat will have survived.*[6]

Yelled one divisional General,

> *Good luck men. There is not a German left in their trenches, our guns have blown them all to Hell.*[7]

On the other side of the line, German troops in their trenches suffered enormously through the bombardment. Some of their dugout entrances fell in and were blocked by earth. Some electric cables were smashed. Water pipes were broken and thirsty troops ran short of water. Men in the front line sometimes could not evacuate the wounded or bury the dead. While some soldiers were safe in the deep trenches, others almost went mad with the clamor and mounting tension. And still the bombardment continued. It was hell on earth. Nonetheless, those who could, watched the movement in and beyond No Man's Land by mirrors fastened on the end of long sticks.

More than a million and a half shells fell on the German trenches during the bombardment. Some explosions could be heard across the English Channel as far as London. But new problems emerged for the British. The quality of the shells, from both England and America, was poor. Almost one-third of them were defective, either detonating prematurely, or failing to explode at all.

Finally, however, by the last day of June, all was in readiness.

Seldom has a battle been approached with more confidence in victory — and with some justification. What enemy could withstand such massive bombardment and shelling? So confident was Haig that he told three cavalry divisions to ride on to Bapaume, which was ten miles beyond the Front. (Five months later, they still hadn't arrived.)

> The men are in splendid spirits. Several have said that they have never before been so instructed and informed of the nature of the operation before them. The wire has never been so well cut, nor the artillery preparation so thorough.[8]

Men waited tensely in the trenches on the eve of the battle. Some trenches were so crowded that soldiers had to prop themselves against the sides or against other soldiers. Not everyone was lucky enough to get a meal on the eve of the battle.

And somewhere that night, a message from Lieutenant General Rawlinson to the Front was sent by a junior officer over telephone lines, telling of the battle the next morning. The Germans overheard it. Moreover, "with their advantage of higher ground, Germans knew to the meter the position of every British trench."[9]

The Battle Begins

The next morning, the first day of July 1916, the British barrage ceased precisely at 7:30 a.m., according to plan. The pause was brief, again according to plan. The barrage then lifted and concentrated on the next line of German defenses. The battle was joined!

The men from Lieutenant General Rawlinson's 13 British divisions, heavily loaded with 66 pounds of equipment, surged forward, uniformly, toward No Man's Land, for the anticipated walkover.

Some believe that Rawlinson was so certain there would be no German resistance that he ordered his troops to advance in slow, uniform lines, or parade formation. Others say Haig made that decision because his recruits were inexperienced and he feared massive confusion if they charged across pulverized, cratered ground.

But walkover, it was not to be. For one thing, much of the German wire had not been cut. Worse yet, all along the 19-mile front the Germans quickly emerged from their dugouts to man their machine guns. They couldn't believe their eyes! They had masses and masses of perfect targets — British soldiers walking right into their gunsights.

Wave after wave of men fell. Whole companies were cut down where they stood; others were hung up, trapped in and on the uncut wire. Some never got beyond their own wire. Sometimes barbed wire, tangled, twisted, and buried in the churned-up ground, caught the legs of unsuspecting men and stopped them in their tracks. Some lay writhing and dying in agony in No Man's Land. Some would slowly bleed to death in the hot July sun. (Fellow soldiers had been instructed not to stop to attend to the wounded but to leave them where they fell. But they were to stick the wounded man's rifle in the ground, bayonet down, to mark the spot for the Royal Army Medical Corps.)

Martin Middlebrook describes the slaughter in his *The First Day on the Somme*:

> Desperately, men struggled to get through the wire but only got more enmeshed; their equipment caught on the long barbs and made them helpless. They were picked off at leisure by the German riflemen, bodies jerking in their death throes, in the writhing, twanging wire.[10]

Those who died instantly were fortunate. Thousands who were wounded in the early part of the day had to lie in No Man's Land all day, some for up to 14 hours, in the hot sun.[11] Their thirst was indescribable. (As Middlebrook notes, many waited even longer, because even under the cover of darkness, it would take two stretcher-bearers more than an hour to carry one wounded man to a Dressing Station, and many had become casualties themselves. From the Dressing Stations, the wounded were shuttled by motor ambulances sometimes up to ten miles to the Casualty Clearing Stations. Sometimes the ambulances were also blown up.)

Later, in one part of the bloody battle, Brigadier General H. Gordon was

German soldiers in trenches demolished by Allied artillery shelling, July 1916.
National Archives of Canada, PA 000128

urged by his divisional Commander to send in yet another battalion to attack. *"You seem to forget, sir, that there is now no 70th Brigade,"* he replied.[12]

Equally poignant was the marker placed at the grave site (actually a trench) where brave Devonshire lads were mowed down en masse by a single German machine gun: *"The Devonshires held this trench. The Devonshires hold it still."*

The stricken animals suffered fiercely, too.

> Dead and dying horses, split by shellfire, with bursting entrails and torn limbs, lay astride the road that led to battle. Their fallen riders stared into the weeping skies.[13]

The battle continued all day. That evening, Rawlinson estimated, in his diary, that he had suffered 16,000 casualties. He badly underestimated. His Fourth Army alone had more than 50,000 losses! So great and so pitiful

Emplacement of two forward guns in Sanctuary Wood, captured by Germans and recaptured by Canadians, July 1916.
National Archives of Canada, PA 000094

The distinctive Caribou Memorial at Beaumont-Hamel, France, dedicated to the Royal New-foundland Regiment.   *Mac Johnston*

was the slaughter that even German stretcher-bearers came out under white flags to pick up some of the wounded British soldiers.[14]

The Lads from Newfoundland

Although the British bore the brunt of the battle and suffered devastating losses (her one- day casualties exceeded those of the Crimean War, Boer War, and Korean War combined), a notable regiment from one of her colonies also deserves mention — the Newfoundland Regiment, assigned to the 29th British Division. Newfoundland, still a British colony at the time, had a population in 1914, at the outbreak of war, of only 250,000; but by the end of the war, 6,241 men had served in the Newfoundland Regiment, most of them volunteers. Still others served with the Canadian Expeditionary and British Forces. (Newfoundland became Canada's tenth province in 1949.)

Like their British comrades, the 790 young men from farms, fishing villages, and lumber towns of the faraway colony had watched eagerly as the blazing summer sun rose and burned off the morning mist. It was to be a day like no other for them. They were waiting in reserve trenches known as St. John's Road, opposite Beaumont Hamel, where they listened in anticipation as the pre-attack bombardment shelled the German trenches. Their turn would come later. They had heard the explosion at the Hawthorn Redoubt mine on the Hawthorne Ridge. They knew that by now, the first waves of British troops would be climbing from their trenches on the way to the German front line.

But some things were puzzling. Why was there such heavy machine-gun fire from the German trenches? They were supposed to have been obliterated. Had our first wave taken the first line? Something seemed amiss.

Gradually, word filtered back that few, in fact, had crossed the enemy line. How could this be?

There was little time to wonder. At 8:45, orders crackled over the phone lines ordering the Newfoundland Regiment to move forward immediately from the rear trenches. The 1st Essex Regiment would attack with them, but independently, on their right.

It would not be easy. Like others, the men would carry heavy loads — most had about 66 pounds, including rifle and bayonet, entrenching tool, water, haversack, 220 rounds of ammunition, two empty sandbags, and two grenades or bombs. Some also carried telephones or carrier pigeons. Some carried a pick or shovel, or poles to serve as markers for artillery. The weight was a problem — but they had been trained for this. They could cope.

But an unanticipated problem emerged. There was no time to scramble through the relatively safe communication trenches to get to their own front line because they had become too congested. The troops would, instead, have to go up top, over *open* ground. Thus, they would need to advance 300 yards (the length of three football fields) over churned-up, unprotected ground, just to get to their own (British) front line. Then they'd need to survive another 300 yards across the deadly No Man's Land to reach the German trenches. But it should still be okay. Hadn't Rawlinson said that nothing could survive the bombardment?

So out of the trenches they struggled. But again, something went terribly wrong. Some of the gaps in their *own* wire were not wide enough to get through. They had to cluster in and around the narrow gaps to wiggle through. And they, too, found Germans were neither dead nor disabled. The young Newfoundlanders were trapped in raging machine-gun and artillery fire, even as they searched frantically for the gaps in front of their own trenches. The Germans picked them off like fish in a barrel.

It was madness. Where was their own supporting artillery fire? And where was the Essex Regiment? (The Essex Regiment had been ordered to advance to the front lines via the safer but slower communication trenches because the area between St. John' s Road and the front was under deadly fire. It would take them two hours. By then, most of the Newfoundlanders were dead.)

Those who made it through their own barbed-wire gaps staggered on. Only a few ever reached the German line to hurl a grenade into the enemy trenches. Most were cut down in a hail of bullets long before they got within striking distance.

In less that 30 minutes it was all over. Of the 790 Newfoundlanders who went into battle, only 68 were able to answer the roll call the next day. The regiment was virtually annihilated. One divisional Commander, informing the Newfoundland Prime Minister of the outcome, said that the assault failed to succeed "because dead men can advance no further."[15]

The Newfoundland Regiment was bestowed with the prefix "Royal," in 1918, by King George V in recognition of its valor at the Somme and its

The remains of the tower of St. Martin's Cathedral at Ypres, Belgian, bombed out in 1915. This photo was taken in July 1916, as the Battle of the Somme was raging.
National Archives of Canada, PA 000329

"magnificent bravery and resolute determination" at Ypres and Cambrai. The small loyal colony had suffered more losses proportionally than any other part of the Empire, including Britain.

By the end of the first day of battle that hot first day of July 1916, near-ly 60,000 soldiers of Britain and her Empire had fallen. Half of them were cut down in the first hour of battle. They had gained about 20 acres of pul-verized ground.

The losses have been lamented ever since. As historian James L. Stokesbury notes: "Britain lost three times as many men on the first day of the Somme as she had lost in combat during the entire twenty-two years with France and Napoleon."[16] Lloyd George wrote " . . . for the disastrous loss of the finest manhood of the United Kingdom and Ireland there was only a small gain of ground to show . . . ."[17] Some were even more critical.

The interior of the Cathedral at Ypres, July 1916.   *National Archives of Canada, PA 000303*

The devastation of a battlefield at the Ypres Salient, July 1916, showing what appears to be sandbagged dugouts.
National Archives of Canada, PA 000086

Denis Winter argues that no other battlefield in the war witnessed more killing per square yard. He notes the grim testament to the losses as evidenced by a Routine Order of the British army (a month after the fighting began), to the effect that

> all burials were to be in trenches rather than individual graves. The first layer of corpses was to be buried four feet down, with quicklime separating it from the next layer.[18]

No number of soldiers or grave diggers could keep up with the carnage.

As the skirmishes continued and losses mounted, the two adversaries seemed deadlocked in a mortal struggle. Nonetheless, a small chink in the German armor appeared. General von Falkenhayn was becoming more and more fretful, so much so that he decided on 11 July to pull back from the Verdun battlefield. At last, the British offensive was diverting some of the German attack from the besieged city and its forts.

Nor was British General Haig through with his Somme offensive. It would continue for another four months. Now he planned another assault on the Somme, this one for mid-September.

But this time he would have a surprise in store for the Germans. He would launch a new, secret weapon!

NOTES

1. A department in France is a municipal division, somewhat equivalent to a county in Canada or the United States.
2. Holger H. Herwig, (*The First World War: Germany and Austria Hungary 1914-1918* (London: Arnold, 1997), 244, notes that by July 1916, Germany was shipping 7,000 tons of barbed wire to the Front every week.
3. Extraordinary books have been written on the historic Battle of the Somme, among them Martin Middlebrook, *The First Day on the Somme* (New York: W. W. Norton and Co., 1972), on which much of this chapter is based; John Keegan, *The Face of Battle* (New York: Penguin Books, 1976); and Malcolm Brown, *The Imperial War Museum Book of the Somme* (London: Pan Books, 1997).
4. Robert Blake, ed., *The Private Papers of Douglas Haig, 1914-1997* (N.P., 1952), 145.
5. Middlebrook, *The First Day on the Somme*, 89.

6. From a speech to the Newcastle Commercials, as quoted in Middlebrook, *The First Day on the Somme*, 78.

7. *Ibid.*, 88.

8. Blake, *The Private Papers of Douglas Haig*, 151.

9. Middlebrook, *The First Day on the Somme*, 83.

10. *Ibid.*, 112.

11. Sunset on 1 July was at 9:02 p.m. by the newly introduced British Summer Time.

12. Middlebrook, *The First Day on the Somme*, 182.

13. Martin Gilbert, quoting Hugh Boustead in *the First World War, A Complete History*, 2nd ed. (New York: Henry Holt and Co., 1994), 262.

14. John Ellis, *Eye Deep in Hell: Trench Warfare in World War I* (Baltimore, MD: The John Hopkins University Press, 1976), 171.

15. Gilbert, *The First World War*, 262.

16. James L. Stokesbury, *A Short History of World War I* (New York: William Morrow and Co., Inc., 1981), 260.

17. David Lloyd George, *War Memoirs of David Lloyd George, 1915-1916* (Boston: Little Brown, 1933), 9-10.

18. Denis Winter, *Haig's Command: A Reassessment* (London: Penguin Books, 1991), 46.

*Dante would never have condemned lost
souls to wander in so terrible a purgatory.
Here a shattered wagon, there a gun mired to
the muzzle in mud which grips like glue, even
the birds and rats have forsaken so unnatural
a spot.*
— Robin Prior and Trevor Wilson, *Passchendaele*

Chapter 17

The Battle
of the Somme Continues —
August-November 1916

Pozières Ridge

*N*ORTH OF THE Somme River is Pozières Ridge, an eight-
mile long crest of limestone that stretches from Thiepval
to Ginchy and Morval. Though low lying (only 500 feet above sea
level), its height nonetheless once more gave the well-entrenched
Germans the advantage over the Allies. Britain's General Haig, who
was coming under heavy criticism for having nothing to show after
the massacre on the Somme, badly wanted the ridge and the village
of Courcelette beyond it.

With his British troops decimated at the Somme, Haig now turned
to the Australians to take the ridge and capture the village of
Pozières. He assigned the task to General Hubert Gough, GOC of the
British Reserve Army, under whom the Australian Imperial Force
(AIF) served.

Australians of the First Division fought with valor in numerous
assaults throughout July, eventually taking Pozières (24-25 July),
though it was now little more than rubble and debris. They lost more

than 5,000 men in the process. Gough then brought in the 2nd Australian Division to Pozières Ridge, where they were shelled mercilessly for 12 consecutive days — the losses were 6,848 officers and men, and most of 5 battalions.[1]

In pitiful repetition, one Australian Division replaced another, some returning for a second siege of slaughter in August. While some ground was taken, the cost was appalling. The Australian Divisions had sustained 23,000 casualties.[2]

The Australians, like the British, were spent — but the wretched ridge remained in German hands. So General Haig next called for the Canadians (also part of Gough's recently constituted "Reserve Army"), and on 30 August, the Canadian Corps began to relieve the Australian & New Zealand Army Corps (the ANZAC) around Pozières. (It was at this time that the Canadian Divisions first wore their identifying rectangular insignia on their shoulders — Red for the First Division, Blue for the Second, Gray for the Third, and, later, Green for the Fourth.)

Even before the troop exchange was completed, on 5 August, Canadians launched assaults. Some German trenches were taken. One NCO, Corporal Leo Clarke, like a one-man demolition machine in spite of a bayonet wound in the leg, cleared part of a trench himself after most of his comrades were killed. (He won the Victoria Cross for his valor but was killed before the award was announced.)

Robert Kennedy, whose diary entries were now becoming infrequent, merely noted duties at various sites (such as Trench 44 or at the Forward Observation Officer). His unit had not yet moved south to the Somme. After maneuvers, his group left Arques (three kilometers southeast of St. Omer), on the edge of Flanders, by train on 26 August. His battery reached the Thiepval area at 8:00 a.m. on 27 August, and went into action the next day.

Kennedy made few diary entries for the next three months, and most were terse. When he wasn't on duty in battery action, he was laying telephone lines, erecting telephone boxes, or on guard duty. The days were long and often full of risk.

Laying or repairing telephone lines might appear a routine undertaking. It was not, for those who worked on these lines were extremely vulnerable to enemy fire. Historian John Keegan describes the complexities of the communication network, which relied on both "land lines" and "air lines." The above-ground air lines would run from major headquarters well behind the front lines (by some 15 miles or so) to the Corps and Division headquarters. But closer to the front lines, from brigade and battalion headquarters, land lines were strung along trench walls or under duck-boards — the boards laid across the wet, muddy ground. The lines were then buried deeper, even up to six feet, as they neared the front-line trenches.[3] Because enemy fire frequently demolished the lines, other methods of communication were pressed into service. They included lamps, flags, pigeons, and of course, runners, to hand-carry messages.[4]

Sergeant R. B. Gibson told of the perils of being a lineman:

> My job is to see that telephone communication is kept up between the front line and brigade headquarters — a job that sounds easier than it really is. I remember one day in particular we had a stretch of line that was rather worse than usual. We had forty three breaks in that small 300 yards in a day, and when anybody went out to fix same it was the last we expected to see of him. Linemen work practically sixteen hours a day and are under the most intense shell-fire during that period. But telephone communication has got to be kept up, for on it rests the success and co-operation of the whole attack.[5]

The New Weapon

The small-scale, *ad hoc* attacks of late July and August, though costly, were not sufficient for Generals Haig and Gough, so they planned a new, coordinated assault for 15 September. And this time, Haig would have a couple of surprises in store for the Germans. This time he would employ a creeping barrage just in front of the attacking Canadians to wipe out the defenders. And realizing, finally, that artillery couldn't pulverize all oppo-sition, Haig would introduce the *coup de grâce* — the new weapon of war — the armored, caterpillar-tracked, land battleship with the odd name — the still-secret "tank."

The tank, or "land battleship," was conceived by many, including Leonardo da Vinci, but brought into practical usage by Winston Churchill and Colonel Ernest D. Swinton. Because of its enormous size, the British were having difficulty keeping the new weapon a secret, even under can-vas, as it was being moved about. Someone suggested that because it was large and mobile, the British could say it had been developed to carry water in the desert — it then could be called a "water tank." And thus

Canadian troops in a communication trench at Ypres, September 1916.
National Archives of Canada, CO 707

came the name of the new land vehicle, the "tank." Its crews were largely made up of wealthy young men — experienced drivers — who had been able to afford cars before the war.

Not everyone wanted to use the untested tank at this time. Furthermore, only 49 were available. Churchill was shocked to learn of the piecemeal introduction of the tank, and was bitterly opposed to the idea of exposing "this tremendous secret to the enemy upon such a petty scale." He appealed in vain to Prime Minister Lloyd George to postpone introduction of the tanks until they could be used in more profitable numbers. Colonel Swinton also urged the High Command to wait for increased production. In order for the still-secret tank to have maximum effectiveness, he warned, several precautions should be taken. He then spelled out several important requisites, such as a carefully chosen sectors (since the tanks might have to fit under tunnels, for example), special approach routes, and wireless sets in the tanks.

But Haig could not be persuaded to wait for all the prerequisites. And on the appointed day, 15 September, the 49 existing tanks began to roll forward. (Only 32 machines, however, had reached the assembly area at zero hour.)

Seven tanks were allotted to the Canadians (all going to Major General Turner and the Second Division), and following the deafening roar of the artillery at 6:20 that morning, the tanks churned their way toward the German front line of trenches where the Canadian artillery had already blasted the defenders.

The tanks were spectacular in appearance. As anticipated, the sight of them terrified some Germans, at least initially.

> One stared and stared as if one had lost the power of one's limbs. The monsters approached slowly, hobbling, rolling and rocking, but they approached. Nothing impeded them: a supernatural force seemed to impel them on.[6]

However, the new machines weren't exactly impressive in their accomplishments. All six tanks in the Canadian attack (the seventh was in reserve) either broke down, bogged down in the mud, or were put out of action by shellfire. (The other 32 being used by the Fourth Army suffered a similar inglorious initiation, with only 10 reaching their objectives. Many of Swinton's thoughtful conditions had been disregarded.) Haig,

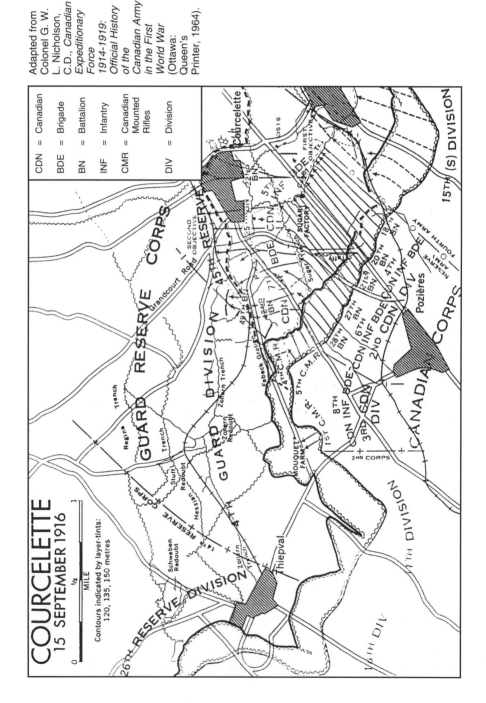

COURCELETTE
15 SEPTEMBER 1916

Adapted from Colonel G. W. L. Nicholson, C.D., *Canadian Expeditionary Force 1914-1919: Official History of the Canadian Army in the First World War* (Ottawa: Queen's Printer, 1964).

CDN	=	Canadian
BDE	=	Brigade
BN	=	Battalion
INF	=	Infantry
CMR	=	Canadian Mounted Rifles
DIV	=	Division

Contours indicated by layer-tints:
120, 135, 150 metres

nonetheless, was pleased with the tanks, and ordered another thousand. Churchill, however, was far from happy, writing: "This priceless conception was revealed to the Germans for the mere petty purpose of taking a few ruined villages."[7] Prime Minister Lloyd George later complained as well, saying the "great secret was sold for the battered ruin of a little hamlet."

Courcelette

The Allied attacks ground on, with Lieutenant General Byng, General Officer Commanding of the Canadian Corps, ordering an early evening attack (it was still 15 September) on the German-held village of Courcelette. At 6:00 p.m., in what was still daylight, the 22nd (French Canadian), 25th (Nova Scotia Rifles), and 26th (New Brunswick) Battalions engaged in hand-to-hand bayonet fighting as unscathed Germans rushed out of cellars and tunnels. It took the Canadians two days to take the village.

Nearby, battalions of the Third Division also struggled forward with some units (including the Royal Highlanders of Canada) winning a piece of trench line, and others struggling to find their way through the mangled countryside, now devoid of landmarks. The PPCLI, the 4th Canadian Mounted Rifles, and the 49th Edmonton Regiment all endured heavy shelling and enfilade fire long enough to seize sections of the German trench lines.[8] But it was slow going. British troops on either side of the Canadians were likewise making slow progress.

The rains began again, with sickening monotony, but that didn't prevent the Germans from trying to retake Courcelette. The Canadians drove them back, even winning the praise of General Haig in the process.

But still the main objective was elusive. Though the Allies had taken three small villages, the Germans held much — and both ends — of Pozières Ridge. The Germans would simply have to be driven from the entire crest line!

The Canadians were assigned (along with the British 2nd Corps on their left) a 6,000-yard front between Courcelette and Thiepval. There were three "successive" objectives, or, in other words, three successive lines of trenches. The Canadians were to take the first *Zollern Graben* line, then the second "Hessian" line, and finally the Regina Trench line, with its branch, the "Kenora" line. For good measure, they would also have to take the short but deep and deadly "Subway" line, running off at a right angle from the *Zollern* Trench. It was a tall order.

The artillery shelled the German lines for three days, and on 26 September at midday, waves of infantry hauled themselves out of the trenches and over the parapets.

On the right, the Second Division troops of the 29th (Vancouver) Battalion quickly reached and occupied the first enemy trenches, though the 31st (Alberta) Battalion had less success. The 28th (Northwest) was to attack with the two tanks allotted to the Canadian Corps for this endeavor. But one tank broke down and the other burst into flames when hit by a German shell. They were trapped in their trenches.

On their left, troops of the First Division were being hit repeatedly by machine gunners ensconced in hidden nests. Nonetheless, the 14th Royal Montreal Regiment jumped the deep Sudbury Trench, took 40 prisoners and, flushed with success, headed for the Kenora Trench. Unfortunately, however, the Highlanders and Albertans couldn't keep up with the Montrealers, who now found themselves with undefended flanks and exposed to heavy machine-gun fire from three sides. In the bitter fighting, the Kenora Trench changed hands twice on 27 September, before the badly depleted Montreal Regiment had to retreat toward Sudbury Trench. Other Canadian troops on their left, principally the 5th, 8th, and 10th (Western Cavalry, 90th Rifles, and "Canadian") Battalions were also pushing toward the first objective in spite of heavy shelling.

But still the enemy held the commanding positions of the ridge. Byng, however, was determined to reach the third objective, the Regina Trench.

Regina Trench

In the middle of the night, at 2:00 a.m., 28 September, the 14th Royal Montreal Regiment was given another opportunity to attack. With them were some weary survivors of the 28th Northwest Battalion — only about 75, many having been killed or wounded in the previous 40 hours of fighting. Together they struggled through the mud and rain, but just as they approached the Kenora Trench, German flares lit up the skies. The attack had to be called off. The 14th alone had now lost 370 men, including 10 officers.

The junction of the Regina and Kenora trenches at the Battle of the Somme, September-October 1916. *National Archives of Canada, C-014151*

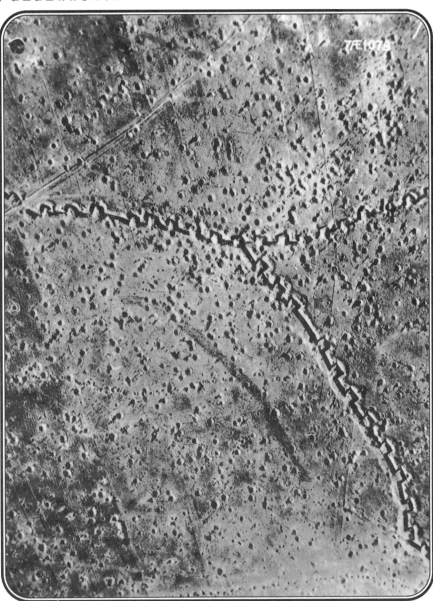

By the end of September, the blood-soaked, rain-drenched ridge was still not taken. The Regina Trench was still an objective.

The next attempt was not long in coming. It was set for 3:15 p.m., on the first day of October. Troops waited in the rain, soaked to the skin, while the Allied artillery blasted the enemy trenches. Some shells fell short, hitting the Canadian troops. It got worse. Two battalions of the Canadian Mounted Rifles (CMR) immediately met a hail of machine-gun fire as they climbed out of their trenches. Then, because much of the German wire had not been cut successfully by the artillery, whole groups of men were cut down in No Man's Land. One company somehow reached the German line, only to be killed to the last man. One company of the 5th CMR actually reached and took a section of the Regina Trench, but they were driven out the next morning.

The grisly scenes were repeated elsewhere. Troops in the 5th Brigade were decimated. Some men of the 22nd (French Canadians), managed to survive an intense artillery barrage only to run into undamaged wire entanglements. They soon realized that their attack was doomed to failure. Though some reached the Regina Trench through desperate bayonet fighting, the survivors ultimately had to withdraw. Their friends in the 25th (Nova Scotia Rifles) Battalions were equally hard hit. About 30 of them reached the Regina Trench, but they, too, under relentless machine-gun fire, had to retreat to the Kenora Trench, half of their numbers now dead, missing, or wounded.

The 24th (Victoria Rifles of Canada) had also reached the Regina Trench, just where it branched with Kenora, and took a 50-yard section. But they too had lost heavily in the process.

By 2 October, the 5th Brigade had only 773 men. They had gone into the line on 27 September with 1,717.[9]

And still the Regina Trench was not taken. But they would try again!

After nearly a week of preparations, still in dark, dismal weather, a new Canadian assault was launched on 8 October, just before 5 a.m. Again, with incredible consistency, it rained.

This time the 4th (Central Ontario) and 3rd (Toronto) Battalions reached the Regina Trench. Further west, the 16th (Canadian Scottish) were caught in the wire, like fish in gill nets, and struggled desperately to

The ruined village of Courcelette, October 1916. *National Archives of Canada, PA 000771*

extricate themselves to get through. It seemed hopeless. But suddenly, the plaintiff, soul-stirring skirl of the bagpipes filled the damp morning air as 18-year-old Piper James Richardson defied the bullets and piped his way up and down in front of the wire entanglements. With renewed determination, a hundred of the Canadian Scottish stormed the impenetrable wire. A few even broke through and reached the Regina Trench. But once again they, like the small group of survivors of the 13th Royal Highlanders, were driven back from the heavily defended trench.

Some attacking Canadians, having used some of their grenades to break through the wire, soon ran out of them. German marines, who now held parts of the trench, were relatively secure behind the wire.

By nightfall on the miserable rainy October day, the survivors of the weary battalions of the First and Third Divisions were just about back where they started out at 4:50 that morning. The Canadians had lost 1,364 men for little or no gain.[10]

Among them was Piper James Richardson.

Why had the attack failed? For one thing, the artillery's shrapnel simply couldn't cut the wire. For another, heavy shells were considered undesirable because they created new, almost impassable craters and water-filled death holes. Further, the artillery, having been allotted a limited number of shells, hadn't been able to demolish the Regina Trench. The assault of 8 October was deemed a "fiasco" — but if nothing else, they would learn from it!

Robert Kennedy's diary noted some of the casualties close to him:

Oct 11: Sgt. Kerry wounded. Bdr. Chapman, Bdr. Fernie, Gunners Gibson, Day and Hanley wounded.

He took more time to write to Eva that same day:

I just got back last night from the trenches after having spent three days there. The time is passing quickly. We're looking forward to more real work and better news. Last Autumn, Great Britain had very few trained soldiers and her munition factories weren't organized, but now after having held the enemy at bay for a whole year while she trained her troops and organized her munition factories, she is able to more than merely hold the enemy. Bombardments are going on, on our right and keep us on the alert. After dinner I thought I would like some blackberries so started up along a hedge nearby where I knew I could find some. I didn't pick many for suddenly there was a "whizz" and two shells burst in the air about fifty yards from me. Fortunately they burst away from me, and not towards me.

On the 25th, in another letter to Eva:

I wrote to you a few days ago but you may not receive the letter. Our officers' billet was burned to the ground the same night and there was quite a bit of outgoing mail in it. It's chilly today with a cold east wind and rain, but what else can one expect just two months from Christmas? I just got my rubber boots in time.

> **I'm going to the trenches tonight for three days — hope I will be able to get a shot at the Germans. I've often watched for them to put their heads above the parapet but they won't. The trenches are a long distance apart here, and it is hard to see them. The crows and starlings have returned with the cool weather. They were here when we came over from England last winter, but went away in the spring.**

On 17 October, the three Canadian Divisions began to move to a quiet sector between Arras and Lens. But new Canadians were now on the scene. The Fourth Division had arrived to relieve its colleagues, and the fresh troops took over part of the line just as the first indications of a severe winter made its appearance. (The Fourth had arrived in France in mid-August, and entered the line on 25 August. Most of the division had remained in the north of France while the other three divisions had moved to the Somme.) The new troops found that the so-called trenches on Pozières Ridge were not much more than ditches filled with detritus and muddy water. Was this awful wasteland really all that important?

It was, apparently, to General Haig. He would not give up his goal to take the Regina Trench.

And so, on 21 October, fresh troops of the 11th Brigade — principally the 87th (Canadian Grenadier Guards) and 102nd (North British Columbians) Battalions — stormed into and took a section of the Regina Trench after a systematic bombardment. Another assault to their right was planned for 24 October, but a 24-hour deluge of rain half-filled the jumping-off trenches with mud and water. The 44th (Manitoba) Battalion, whose turn it now was, had to wait, rain-soaked, another day before attacking.

But 25 October brought disaster. The Canadian artillery barrage was ineffective, and the defending German riflemen and machine gunners were untouched. They simply mowed down the attacking Manitobans. Not one soldier reached the Regina Trench. No one had apparently listened to the Canadian artillery officers who had warned that they wouldn't have time to get all their guns in position, and that "most of them that could fire would not be registered."[11]

The battlefield at the Somme after a Canadian charge, October 1916.
National Archives of Canada, PA 000868

The Manitobans had suffered nearly 200 casualties. And still a large part of the elusive Regina Trench was in German hands.

In what was beginning to sound like a broken record, the Fourth Division would try again. But again, with incessant cold rain (at one period it rained on 16 out of 21 days), and "indescribable" trenches, the attacks were postponed several times.

The troops themselves suffered dreadfully in the wretched weather. The official history of the Canadian army notes that toward the end of the Canadians' tour of the Somme, infantry battalions had as much as eight miles to march to the trenches from their billets in Albert and "men's clothing became so coated with mud, great coat, trousers, puttees and boots sometimes weighing 120 pounds, that many could not carry out relief."[12]

A regimental historian wrote another graphic description of the nightly horror:

> Men toil through the darkness under heavy loads, flounder, at times, waist-deep in water; climbing wearily over slimy sandbags, stumbling across dismembered corpses — tired, dazed and shaken by the incessant bombardments; clothes soaked and equipment clogged with mud; faces grey from want of sleep.[13]

Nonetheless, the men of the Fourth Division, who not long before were civilians back in the cities, towns, villages, mountains, prairies, and forests of Canada had not been found wanting. They had learned to cope in the wet and cold trenches sometimes with only the help of a rubber groundsheet for protection from the elements.

Finally, on 9 and 10 November, in bitterly cold weather, the Canadian gunners had two successive days of good weather for bombardment — which they said they *must* have to be effective. This time the barrage was almost perfect. At midnight of 10-11 November, under a full moon, the Canadians attacked again. The 46th (South Saskatchewan) and 47th (British Columbia) Battalions hit the right side of the Regina Trench, and the 102nd (North British Columbians) the left — all of them supported by full divisional artillery. (The 11th Brigade was supported by the First Division's four field artillery brigades, which had stayed at the Somme. The 10th Brigade was backed up by the artillery of the Third Division.)

By 2:20 on the cold morning of 11 November 1916 (two years to the day before the war's end), the Regina Trench, or what was left of it, was finally taken by the Canadians. It was now not much more than a muddy, mutilated depression in the chalky soil, in many places filled with dead bodies of young soldiers.[14]

But it was still not enough for General Gough.

The next objective for the Fourth Division was set for 18 November. They were to capture the Desire and Desire Support Trenches, which lay about 500 to 800 yards north of the newly captured Regina Trench. The Canadians were to attack on a mile and a quarter-wide front (actually 2,200 yards).

In weather conditions depressingly familiar, including the season's first snow which later turned to sleet and rain, the advance began on the night of 17-18 November. Some troops fumbled forward, trying to find their way through freezing mud and snow-covered mounds. More than once they lost their way. Some battalions, like the 54th (Kootenay), in spite of the wretched weather, enjoyed considerable success, seizing new ground and sending back dozens of German prisoners. Others were not so fortunate. The 46th (South Saskatchewan) and 50th (Calgary) Battalions were forced back to the Regina Trench under heavy machine-gun fire.

Nonetheless, the Fourth Division finally advanced almost half a mile over freezing mud. They suffered 1,250 casualties in the process.

By now the ground was a disastrous mess. Even Haig described it as a "morass" and felt it was time — finally — to halt actions on the Somme. And so, on 18 November, in the coldness of snow and sleet, the Battle of the Somme, one of the biggest slaughters in the history of mankind, was over.

On 27 November 1916, Robert Kennedy and his unit left the Somme to head north toward Camblain (where he was promoted to Corporal) near Lens.

The long battle had consumed more than one million men, and countless thousands of horses and mules. Britain and her Empire had suffered 420,000 casualties, including 24,029 Canadians.[15] The French had lost 200,000. German losses were said to be between 437,000 and 680,000.[16]

Yet, Allied troops were still three miles short of Bapaume and Serre, where they had hoped to be on the first day of the battle, more than four months before.

General Sir Douglas Haig claimed victory. His three objectives, he wrote, had been achieved — the relief of Verdun, keeping the main German forces involved at the Western Front, and wearing down the Germans. Perhaps he was right. Even the German General Erich Ludendorff wrote in his memoirs: "The [German] Army had been fought to a standstill and was now utterly worn out."[17]

Others, then and now, were not so sure. Oxford historian A. J. P. Taylor calls the battle an "unredeemed defeat" from a strategic standpoint, adding that while it eroded the German spirit it also wore down the British spirit — "Idealism perished on the Somme."[18] John Keegan writes: "Militarily, the advance had achieved nothing. Most of the bodies lay on territory British before the battle had begun."[19] Sandra Gwyn claims: "The most that was achieved was to substitute British blood for the haemorrhaging [*sic*] that the French were suffering at Verdun."[20] Winston Churchill called the battlefields of the Somme "the graveyards of Kitchener's Army."

Tragically, there would be more erosion of the spirit, more bodies, more hemorrhaging, and more graveyards before the war was over.

NOTES

1. John Laffin, *British Butchers and Bunglers of World War One* (Phoenix Mill, Great Britain: Sutton Publishing, 1989), 87.
2. *Ibid.,* 88. The South African Brigade also suffered enormous loss in taking Delville Wood.
3. John Keegan, *The Face of Battle* (New York: Penguin Books, 1976), 264.
4. One notable runner of the First World War was later to tell German General Staff members that he learned the realities of war because of his experience as a runner. His name was Adolf Hitler, of the 16th Bavarian Reserve Regiment.
5. In Bill Rawling, *Surviving Trench Warfare: Technology and the Canadian Corps, 1914-1918* (Toronto: University of Toronto Press, 1992), 80.
6. In Bryan Cooper, *The Ironclads of Cambrai* (London: The Souvenir Press, 1967).
7. Winston S. Churchill, *The World Crisis*, Vol. 1 (London: Thornton Butterworth, 1928) and Laffin, *British Butchers and Burglers*, 94.
8. To the Allied troops, the captured German trenches were sometimes stunning in their sophistication. As Francis Whiting Halsey notes, troops already knew that many trenches had electricity and some degree of comfort. Now they found a hospital with 32 beds and an operating room. Some underground quarters had steel doors, staircases, and passages, lined with food, full-length mirrors (for officers), cushioned armchairs, and pictures. Francis Whiting Halsey, *The Literary Digest of the World War,* Vol. 3 (New York: Funk & Wagnalls Co., 1919), 269-270.
9. Colonel G. W. L. Nicholson, C.D., *Canadian Expeditionary Force 1914-1919: Official History of the Canadian Army in the First World War* (Ottawa: Queen's Printer, 1964), 183, quoting from the 5th Infantry Brigade diary of October 1916.
10. The figures are from Nicholson, *Canadian Expeditionary Force*, 186.
11. *Ibid.*, 191.
12. *Ibid.*, 197, quoting General David Watson.
13. E. S. Russenholt, *Six Thousand Canadian Men: Being the History of the 44th Battalion, Canadian Infantry 1914-1919* (Winnipeg: DeMonfort Press, 1932), 46.
14. Pierre Berton relates the poignant actions of Brigadier General Archibald Cameron Macdonell, Commander of the 7th Brigade, who walked among the wounded after the attack on Regina Trench, then stopped and saluted the individual corpses of the Black Watch, saying to each one: "I salute you, my brave Highlander." Pierre Berton, *Vimy* (Markham, Ontario: Penguin Books Canada Ltd., 1987), 210.
15. Canadian figures are from Desmond Morton and J. L. Granatstein, *Marching to*

Armageddon: Canadians and the Great War 1918-1919 (Toronto: Lester and Orpen Dennys, 1989), 120, and Nicholson, *Canadian Expeditionary Force*, 198.

16. Malcolm Brown, *The Imperial War Museum Book of the Somme* (London: Pan Books, 1997), 252.

17. Nicholson, *Canadian Expeditionary Force*, 199.

18. A. J. P. Taylor, *The First World War: An Illustrated History* (Hammondsworth, England: 1963), 140.

19. Keegan, *The Face of Battle*, 249.

20. Sandra Gwyn, *Tapestry of War: A Private View of Canadians in the Great War* (Toronto: Harper Collins Publishers Ltd., 1992), 296.

The world must be made safe
for democracy.
— President Woodrow Wilson

Chapter 18

German Plans Revealed, American Neutrality Ends — 1917

*I*N THE COLD, bleak January of 1917, there was little to lift the spirits of combatants of either side. Britain had lost 60,000 at the Somme. But the war continued. France had been bled almost white at Verdun. But the war continued. Canada, Australia, New Zealand, and Newfoundland and other members of the British Empire had lost countless sons. But the war continued.

Germany's fortunes were hardly better. Kaiser Wilhelm II had predicted to his departing troops, "You will be home before the leaves have fallen from the trees." However, the anticipated short war had seen endless slaughter and still there was no end in sight. The army had reached the Marne (and almost Paris just 25 miles away) back in 1914, but had not broken through to victory. Germany had struck deep into the Russian empire, but Russia was still in the picture — though weakened and in chaos. Germany had battered France mercilessly, but France was still fighting.

~~~

The Turnip Winter

At home in Germany, people were subsisting on turnips. The harvest of 1916 had been dismal when heavy rains, an early frost, and shortage of field workers had slashed in half the usual 50-million-ton potato harvest. By December, citizens were told that their weekly ration of seven pounds of potatoes would be reduced to five, supplemented by two pounds of turnips. Though they didn't know it at the time, the ratio would soon be reversed until all the potatoes were gone. By February, the lowly, hard turnip, which before the war was strictly grown for animal consumption, became a staple in the human diet. It was used to "stretch" bread, soups, casseroles, and even marmalade. Erich Marie Remarque noted in his classic *All Quiet on the Western Front,* that new recruits spoke of turnip-bread for breakfast, turnip-stew for lunch, and turnip-cutlets and turnip-salad for supper — all of which, of course, was better than sawdust.[1]

Vehicles had to function with tireless wheels, and hospitals had to resort to bandages made of paper.[2]

The misery didn't end there. During January and February, frigid arctic air blew relentlessly over the distorted face of Europe, making it one of the coldest winters on record. Because of coal shortages, thousands of homes ran out of fuel, water pipes froze and burst, and some cities couldn't turn on streetlights. By the end of January, more than half of Berlin's elementary schools had to close for lack of heat.[3]

Conditions were equally austere in Austria-Hungary where, in an energy conserving measure, Daylight Saving Time had been introduced in May 1916. By the following winter, families were allowed to heat only one room in their home. Churches, schools, public offices, and theaters all had to forego heat. Horses that were not sent to the Front were so emaciated that they couldn't pull carts and had to be replaced by dogs.[4] Women were called on increasingly to work in factories (and paid one-third to one-half the wages of men). Some basic essentials like soap were non-existent.

But Germany's leaders had not been idle. Far from it. In November and December 1916, Admiral Henning von Holtzendorff, Chief of the German Admiralty Staff, had drawn up sophisticated plans showing how Germany could yet replace Great Britain as the strongest naval power in the world. Then Germany could "annex" the Belgian coast (and its important harbor cities of Bruges, Ostend, and Zeebrugge) as well as the Baltic coast. To do it, Germany, had to knock England out of the war. With England gone, France would surely sue for peace, and Russia couldn't possibly stand alone. But it would involve a controversial undertaking — unrestricted submarine warfare.

Von Holtzendorff had a stunning proposal. With the help of experts from the Kiel Institute for World Economy, and using countless mathematical computations, the Admiral — with the backing of Field Marshal von Hindenburg and General Ludendorff — presented his "scientific" argument to Kaiser Wilhelm II and Chancellor Theobald von Bethmann-Hollweg on 10 January 1917. Von Holtzendorff said he could prove that Germany could win the war in five months, or at the latest, well before the next harvest. They could force England into submission simply by sending 600,000 tons of British shipping to the ocean floor every month for five months. England would lose a critical 40 percent of its imports. So confident was von Holtzendorff with his charts and tables and figures that he could predict almost to the day that England would capitulate.

Chancellor von Bethmann-Hollweg was dubious. Wouldn't unrestricted submarine warfare sour world opinion and bring the United States into the war?

Von Holtzendorff had anticipated the question. He and his colleagues had, with their meticulous calculations, figured it would take five or six months for victory if they began the U-boat war on the first day of February. They were entirely confident that the United States could not possibly mobilize, train, equip, and ship troops across the Atlantic within that time frame. Said the confident von Holtzendorff, "I guarantee on my word as a naval officer that no American will set foot on the Continent."[5]

The Kaiser signed the already drafted document: "I order that unrestricted submarine warfare be launched with the utmost vigor on the first of February."

But the announcement would be kept secret initially. For maximum effect, it would not be made until the evening of 31 January 1917 — the very night before the unrestricted warfare was to begin. Even Austria-Hungary, Germany's closest ally, would not be told.

The plotting didn't end there.

The Zimmerman Telegram

Alfred Zimmerman, the German Foreign Secretary, decided to send a coded note to Heinrich von Eckhardt, the German Imperial Minister in

Mexico, to propose an alliance with Mexico and Japan. But Germany's more secure transatlantic cables no longer existed — they had been severed and scooped up by the British cable ship *Telconia* on 5 August 1914, hours after the war broke out. And so, Germany had to rely on Nauen, a powerful wireless station near Berlin, and two other routes for communication. Zimmerman decided to send the coded message in a "Most Secret" telegram over these three different routes, never dreaming that the British would intercept one message, let alone all three. Nor, apparently, did he realize that within minutes, the British would be starting to decode the bombshell message.[6]

The first efforts by the British decoders left many gaps and question marks, but certain passages in the unusually long message clearly stood out. They knew the sender was Zimmerman. They found the words "Most Secret" which, of course, merely spurred them on. Then they discerned that "unrestricted submarine warfare" was proposed for 1 February, as well as some kind of alliance with Mexico. Little by little, more words fell into place. The decoders rushed their imperfect message to Rear Admiral Sir William Reginald Hall, the Director of Naval Intelligence.

Hall found himself on the horns of a dilemma. Though elated by the significance of the message, he immediately wondered how to share the remarkable news without betraying Britain's knowledge of the code to the enemy.[7] If Germany knew its code was broken and switched to a new one, it could take years to break. Hall put the telegram in his safe to ponder how best to handle the shocking implications of the message.

The bitter January days plodded on, and as scheduled, at the end of business hours on the last day of the month, Germany advised the American government of its decision to begin unrestricted submarine warfare the next day. Americans were surprised, angered, and tense. Still, some in Germany hoped that America, with its "peace without victory" President would do nothing. Wilson, who had been reelected on an antiwar platform, still hoped to keep his country neutral and well away from the conflict.

~·~

Unrestricted Submarine Warfare

On 1 February, Germany's unrestricted U-boat war began. On 2 February, President Wilson broke off relations with Germany, though

Zimmerman argued that it really meant very little because Wilson was for peace and nothing else. But the next day, the USS *Housatonic* was sunk, and war fever rose another notch in the United States.[8] As the war entered its 31st month, the prospect of American entry into the war was gaining momentum. And other far-reaching developments were in the offing.

Two days later (5 February), a nervous and impatient Zimmerman sent a second telegraph to von Eckhardt in Mexico, advising him to "take up the alliance question" with Mexico now, even though the United States had not entered the war.

And on the same day, Rear Admiral Hall went to his safe and withdrew the Zimmerman telegram. It was time to share it.

Earl Arthur James Balfour, the Secretary of State for Foreign Affairs, was intrigued by the telegram, and anxious to leak it to the Americans. But would they believe it? Would they think it a ploy to bring them into the war?[9] But the telegram was finally sent to President Wilson on 24 February, with the strong request that its source remain secret. It was now in American hands.

～·～

Operation Alberich

On the same day, another significant event began to unfold on the other side of the Atlantic. Under a cover of heavy mist, the Germans began an extraordinary retreat (ordered by the Kaiser on 4 February) to their recently fortified Hindenburg Line.

Why a retreat? The Kaiser's reasoning was that by abandoning some of the salients and by straightening out the kinked line (notwithstanding the grim fact that the approximately 1,000 square miles he would cede had been purchased with the lives of thousands of German soldiers over a three-year period), he would be able to reduce his front line by about 25 miles, and thereby free-up several divisions for service elsewhere. Some historians, indeed, called it a "brilliant defensive move."[10] In fact, the Germans called Operation Alberich a "retreat to victory."

Not everyone agreed. Some thought it indicated nervousness or weakness on the part of Germany. *The New York Times* called the German explanation of the withdrawal from elaborate trenches and impregnable positions, "forlorn whistling in a graveyard."

Whatever the case, the retreat began in earnest on 15 March when "war material, tools, and food were removed at night by 900 trains hauling 37,100 carloads."[11]

Unfortunately, the troops would not go quietly. They left a scorched wasteland behind them. They hacked and hewed, burned, destroyed, and looted. Nothing was spared. Wells were poisoned. Libraries were wrecked. Inmates of mental asylums were turned out to wander helpless and fend for themselves. Small cottages of peasants were burned or blown up, their humble contents and family photos smashed with picks and axes. Fruit trees that weren't cut down "were so mutilated, the bark so cut, that they would perish."[12] Innocent-looking booby traps were rigged everywhere. A shovel left lying carelessly across a garden path would blow up when someone stooped to pick it up. Even the animals met grief. They were killed, eaten, or carried off. German soldiers admitted they transformed the countryside into a wasteland.

Edith Wharton who visited the scene wrote of the choked-up wells, flooded fields, orchards with felled trees, and farm utensils that had been ruined. She noted the bitter irony of a nearby neat German graveyard above which was inscribed, "I am the resurrection and the life."[13]

The systematic devastation of the area even shocked Crown Prince Rupprecht of Bavaria who protested the incredible destruction. He was overruled, however, by Ludendorff who, with others, called it a "military necessity."

In any case, the Germans gave up more than 1,000 square miles of ground, more than three times the area they had lost at the Somme over an eight-month period.

Then on 26 February, another liner, Cunard's *Laconia*, was torpedoed without warning. Two Americans went down with the ship. And in the United States, American ships, unwilling to sail in the face of U-boat attacks, were now clogging American ports.

And so the brutal days of February wound down and 540,000 tons of shipping had been sunk by U-boats. The Germans were almost on their target of 600,000 tons per month. But then February was a short month. They would surely do better in March.

But the last day of February saw one more significant development in the war. President Wilson, just four days after having received it, decided to make public the Zimmerman telegram.

The headlines of the morning papers on 1 March 1917 screamed the news of Germany's effort to seek an alliance with Japan and Mexico, with sub-headings stating, *"Texas, Arizona and New Mexico to be Reconquered."* Some papers printed the entire text.

> We intend to begin unrestricted submarine warfare on the first of February. We shall endeavor in spite of this to keep the United States neutral. In the event of this not succeeding, we make Mexico a proposal of alliance on the following basis: make war together, make peace together, generous financial support, and an understanding on our part that Mexico is to reconquer the lost territory in Texas, New Mexico, and Arizona. The settlement in detail is left to you.
>
> You will inform the president (of Mexico) of the above most secretly as soon as the outbreak of war with the United States is certain and add the suggestion that he should, on his own ini-tiative, invite Japan to immediate adherence and at the same time mediate between Japan and ourselves.
>
> Please call the President's attention to the fact that the unre-stricted employment of our submarines now offers the prospect of compelling England to make peace within a few months. Acknowledge receipt.   Zimmerman[14]

Some Americans were incredulous. Some immediately wondered if — and how — the telegram could be verified. The Mexicans and Japanese immediately denied it. So did von Eckhardt, to whom the message had been sent. Zimmerman himself asked the U.S. to prove its authenticity.

But the next morning, in one of the puzzling twists of history, Zimmer-man himself admitted, "It is true."

American hostility to Germany, now rising daily, was sharply boosted on 18 March, when three American ships were sunk by U-boats, again without warning.

Two days later, 20 March, President Wilson met with the Cabinet, which was now pressing hard for a declaration of war. Though he would not commit himself on the spot, the next day Wilson ordered Congress to reconvene on 2 April, two weeks earlier than scheduled.

By the end of March, another 600,000 tons of shipping had been sunk by U-boats. The Germans were right on schedule. They would claim another 900,000 tons in April 1917, sinking nearly 12 ships a day.

The United States Enters the War

And on 2 April 1917, President Wilson addressed a joint session of Congress, finally uttering the words that the exhausted Allies had longed to hear. Neutrality was no longer possible. "The world must be made safe for democracy."

The United States of America would join the fight.

NOTES

1. Erich Marie Remarque, *All Quiet on the Western Front* (Boston: Little Brown and Co., 1929; New York: A Fawcett Columbine Book, Ballantine Books, 1996).
2. Alistair Horne, *The Price of Glory, Verdun, 1916* (London: Penguin Books, 1962), 191.
3. Laurence Moyer, *Victory Must Be Ours: Germany in the Great War 1914-1918* (New York: Hippocrene Books, 1995), 175.
4. Holger H. Herwig, *The First World War: Germany and Austria Hungary 1914-1918* (London: Arnold, 1997), 277.
5. Tuchman, Barbara, *The Zimmerman Telegram* (New York: The Viking Press, 1958), 141.
6. For a gripping overview of this episode in the war, see Tuchman, *The Zimmerman Telegram*.
7. Winston S. Churchill would face the same dilemma regarding the bombing of Coventry during the Second World War.
8. Also on 3 February 1917, the Portuguese Expeditionary Force arrived in France, but did not see action for the first time in Flanders until 17 June.
9. The British fears were well founded. According to Tuchman, *The Zimmerman Telegram*, Edward Bell of the American Embassy was "the first of a long line of Americans whose immediate reaction was to pronounce the thing a fraud," 163.
10. Martin Gilbert, *The First World War: A Complete History*, 2nd ed. (New York: Henry Holt and Co., 1994), 308.
11. Herwig, *The First World War*, 251.

12. Francis Whiting Halsey, *The Literary Digest History of the World War*, Vol. 3 (New York: Funk & Wagnalls Co., 1919), 236.
13. *Ibid.*, 340.
14. Tuchman, *The Zimmerman Telegram*, 146.

*No matter what the constitutional histo-
rians may say, it was on Easter Monday,
April 9, 1917, and not on any other date,
that Canada became a nation.*
— D. J. Goodspeed, *The Road Past Vimy*

Chapter 19

The Ill-Omened Vimy Ridge, and the Birth of a Nation

*R*ISING OUT OF THE western edge of the Douai Plain in France, roughly halfway between the devastated fields of Flanders and the equally mangled Somme battlefields, was Vimy Ridge.[1] It was a lozenge-shaped barrier or escarpment, about eight miles in length, overlooking Lens to the north, Douai to the east, and Arras to the south. Like the other battlefields, it, too, had a muddy surface that was pitted, pockmarked, and pulverized by two years of bombardment.

The Germans had captured Vimy Ridge relatively early in the war, in October 1914, and with it they controlled the French industrial area of Lille, along with the Lens coalfields. In 1915, the French had tried mightily to re-capture the ridge and its strategic 360-degree view, only to lose more than 100,000 men in the attempt. The British would try too, and although their tunneling companies would force the Germans to abandon their mining operations, the ridge still "belonged" to German forces in early 1917, as Colonel G. W. L. Nicholson notes in his official history. In fact, with the massive

Operation Alberich withdrawal between Arras and Soissons to the Hindenberg Line in late March, the ridge was more important than ever — the keystone or anchor point for the Germans' new defense system linking the Hindenberg Line to the main German lines north from Hill 70 all the way to the Belgian coast.[2] Vimy Ridge was probably the strongest German position in all of France.

The Allies badly needed a breakthrough in 1917. The previous year, like the year before, had been more of a stalemate than a success. On the Western Front, the French had held Verdun, but at a terrible price. Anglo-French forces had pushed forward, slightly, on the Somme, but also only after suffering incredible losses. Elsewhere, the Central Powers had overwhelmed the Italians at Caporetto. And now, Russia was tottering, its armies unruly and fragmenting under the weak Tsar Nicholas II. (The incredible sagas of the Russian Revolution, the rise of the Bolsheviks, the fall of the Romanov dynasty, and the mad monk Rasputin are all stories unto themselves.) On the high seas, U-boats were rapidly gaining strength, sinking thousands of tons of Allied shipping every month.

French General Joffre had wanted a new offensive in mid-January, but now he was gone. (His neglect of Verdun was neither forgotten nor forgiven. He had been promoted to another post.) In his place had come the charming General Robert Georges Nivelle, the so-called "savior of Verdun." Nivelle promised that he had the secret to winning the war, though he didn't yet reveal it. It wasn't such an extraordinary secret, in fact. It really just amounted to a theory that he could break through the German lines "with violence, brutality, and rapidity" in less than 48 hours, if the British first mounted a large diversionary attack in the north.

After some arguments, Nivelle's plan was accepted with the General directing the French forces and Field Marshal Haig the British forces. (Haig had been promoted to Field Marshal as of the 17th of January.) Nivelle would mount a massive French assault on the Chemin des Dames Ridge southwest of Arras — which had been fought over since the days of Julius Caesar — after the British mounted the important diversionary battle at Arras. It was that simple.[3]

The British Third Army (under General Sir Edmund Allenby) would attack south of Vimy Ridge on an eight-mile front astride the Scarpe River. The task of launching an offensive simultaneously along an adjoining four-mile (7,400-yard) front — including the taking of Vimy Ridge — was given to the First Army, which included the Canadian Corps. General Sir Henry Horne, Commander of the First Army, turned to the Canadians.

British Lieutenant General Sir Julian Byng and his four Canadian Divisions, operating together for the first time as a unit, were to take the crest of Vimy Ridge, including the two highest points, Hill 135 north of Thélus, and Hill 145 — the very keystone of the German defense — two miles farther northwest. Although Byng would also have use of the Fifth British Division, and would be backed up by Canadian and British heavy artillery, it was still a tall order. Incredibly, he and his men were to do in one day what the British and French couldn't accomplish in more than two years.

The Germans had had more than two years to strengthen their defenses on Vimy Ridge. They had used the time well. They had three main defensive lines — the first having its own three lines of trenches, concrete machine-gun emplacements, and masses of barbed wire, with some rolls "as high as a house with five inch barbs."[4] The second line, also protected by belts of barbed wire, had massive dugouts, some large enough to shelter an entire battalion. The third line, in some places as much as five miles behind the first, was also well protected.

All in all, the ridge — with its maze of trenches, its fortified underground chambers, its concrete machine-gun emplacements with barbed wire defending them for good measure — would not be easy to take. The ridge seemed invincible.

Sir Douglas Haig, though increasingly impressed by the Canadians, wasn't sure they could take the ridge. General Nivelle was even more skeptical and predicted that the Canadian operation would result in disaster. Even the Germans scoffed.

The Canadians had other ideas.

Plans and Preparations
By early February 1917, rumors about a new Allied offensive had begun to surface, and increased activity gave currency to them.

> Casualty Clearing Stations were established in conspicuous places; ammunition dumps, sand-bagged like so many huge mole-hills, cluttered the roadsides, steam tractors dragging

heavy howitzers rumbled ceaseless over the pavé; wagon lines sprang up in almost every field.[5]

There were also, of course, "long and unbroken columns of transport limbers, motor lorries, engineer wagons, ambulances, guns, tractors and troops"[6] that clogged the roadways. Even the lowliest troops knew something significant was afoot.

Lieutenant General Byng was in charge of the overall plan of attack by the Canadian Corps. Training and preparation were critical.

In late March, Byng directed the officers of the Canadian Corps:

> Make sure every man knows his task. Explain it to him again and again; encourage him to ask you questions. Remember, also, that no matter what sort of a fix you get into, you mustn't just sit down and hope that things will work themselves out. You must *do* something. In a crisis the man who does something may occasionally be wrong; but the man who does nothing is *always* wrong.[7]

Much of the actual training for the attack devolved on Major General Arthur Currie, the former Victoria realtor who now commanded the Canadian First Division. Currie couldn't stomach the needless loss of a single man, and didn't want to repeat the mistakes of previous battles where "entire brigades had advanced blindly in neat waves to vague spots on the map."[8] Like Byng, he would neglect nothing in his preparations. In fact, it has been said that no Allied operation on the Western Front was ever more thoroughly planned.

Byng had sent Currie to Verdun to learn what he could from the French regarding reconnaissance and Intelligence. His time was well spent. Historian Bill Rawling notes:

> Every man saw the ground over which he would have to attack;
> his objective was pointed out to him as well as the places where
> he might expect resistance and check.[9]

Like a realtor's philosophy, which claims the three most important elements in buying a home are "location, location, and location," Currie's three military precepts were "training, training, and training." There

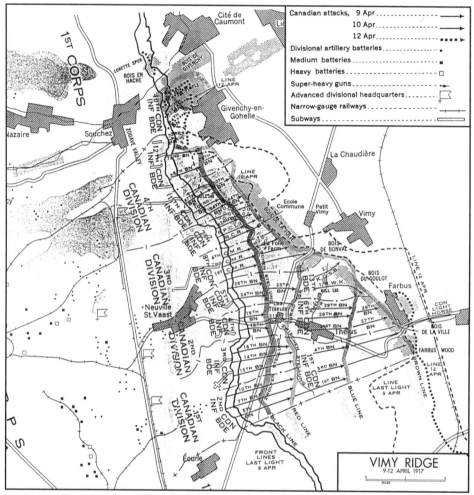

Adapted from Colonel G. W. L. Nicholson, C.D., *Canadian Expeditionary Force 1914-1919: Official History of the Canadian Army in the First World War* (Ottawa: Queen's Printer, 1964).

would also be thoroughness, discipline, attention to the smallest detail, rehearsals, and split-second timing. Nothing would be left to chance. *Nothing!*

The overall plan (the "Scheme of Operations" prepared by Lieutenant General Byng) called for assaults that would be carried out in four stages, marked by colored lines on a map[10]:

1st Objective: Black Line — German forward defense zone and about 750 yards from the Canadian front trenches.

2nd Objective: Red Line — including La Folie Farm and Hill 145.

3rd Objective: Blue Line — including Thèlus, Hill 135 and woods overlooking Vimy.

4th Objective: Brown Line — including the German Second Line, Farbus Wood, Bois de la Ville.

The timing would be critical, measured not to the minute but to the second.[11] If troops pressed forward too quickly, they would be hit by the "friendly fire" of their own creeping barrage. If on the other hand, they fell behind, the Germans would have time to come out of their deep dugouts and slaughter them with machine-gun fire. Split-second timing was critical.

Preparations, at least to some soldiers, seemed endless, and not at all pleasant, especially as they tried to endure the coldest winter of the war. But the preparations and training went on. Moreover, unlike the usual practice in previous battles, every soldier, not just the senior officers, had to know exactly what to expect, exactly what the German-held territory was like, exactly where every trench, every mound, every fortification was located. Even section leaders were given maps.

In fact, the Canadian Corps "distributed forty thousand . . . maps to men newly trained to act when necessary on their own initiative rather than follow orders blindly."[12] Only the date of the attack was kept secret.

As battle preparations continued, so did the trench raids — oftentimes costly, but nonetheless invaluable in picking up enemy Intelligence. The first trench raids, it will be recalled, had been carried out as early as February 1915 by the PPCLI. They had never ceased, and Canadians were now considered experts in the technique.

Some credit Brigadier General Victor Odlum, former Commander of the 7th (British Columbia Regiment) Battalion, and now Commander of the 11th Brigade, with perfecting the trench raid.[13] Odlum, the bookish (he tried to read a book a day), much-decorated officer, personally led some of the raids and knew firsthand both their potential benefits and deadly costs.

In the Spring of 1917, Canadian raids had grown in frequency and size. Whereas the first raids involved only a few men, more than a thousand troops might participate later. In spite of the casualties, the raids were deemed indispensable. German dugouts were destroyed, machine-gun emplacements bombed, supply dumps blown up, and prisoners taken. Perhaps more important, newly gained military Intelligence gave the Allies more accurate figures on German army strength, fortifications, movements, and plans. The Intelligence was vital in planning the Vimy Ridge assault.

There was a cost, of course. In the two weeks preceding the Battle of Vimy Ridge, the Canadians lost 1,653 men, including 71 officers.[14]

But the officers and men apparently scoffed at the cost. Lieutenant A. A. McDougall, of the PPCLI, described his wounds:

> . . . My left leg is off, my right leg is shattered below the knee, my left arm is broken, I have some shrapnel in my hip, but otherwise I am jake.[15]

One significant and far-reaching trench raid took place on the first day of March, the largest ever conducted by the Canadians, involving 1,700 men of the new Fourth Division. Ominously, there were telltale signs of trouble even before the raid began. First, the weather didn't cooperate, and the attack had to be delayed for several days while the troops waited, tensely, in the cold and mud. Then, some of the gas cylinders leaked, sickening many. This was Canada's first use of the new horror weapon. Then, the wind changed directions, blowing back toward the Canadian lines.

Some thought the attack should be called off — but neither Brigadier General Odlum nor Major General David Watson, General Officer Commanding of the Fourth Division, agreed. The preparations had been set in motion. The trench raid would go on. And almost in a microcosm of the entire war itself, the attack took on a momentum of its own. Like the *Titanic* steaming toward an iceberg, once moving along rapidly, the movement was hard to slow or turn around.

What was worse, the Germans knew all about the raid. They had machine guns, ready and waiting, for the unsuspecting Canadians.

The slaughter was all too predictable. The Canadians were mowed down in droves. Some who ducked into shell holes to escape the fire died grievously of the gas they had planned for the enemy. Of the 1,700 Canadian attackers, 687 became casualties, including two battalion Commanders.

So great was the carnage that the Germans offered a truce, allowing the Canadians to bury their dead lying out in No Man's Land. In broad daylight and under a Red Cross flag, the Germans and Canadians met in the middle of the desolate, corpse-strewn area to return the Canadian bodies. One was that of Lieutenant Colonel A. H. G. Kemball, Commanding Officer of the 54th (Kootenay) Battalion. Ironically, he had argued against the attack because of the adverse wind conditions. He had been overruled.

The raid was a disastrous failure, and seriously weakened not only the 54th Battalion but the entire Fourth Division, just weeks before the great Vimy assault.

Although considerable Intelligence was gained by the trench raids, the artillery would need far more information in order to be effective against enemy wire and trench fortifications. Some of this critical information was gleaned from wireless interceptions and captured documents, among other things. Aerial observations and photographs also played an important part. Observation balloons, floating at 4,000 or 5,000 feet, enabled their occupants using strong field glasses to get an overview of enemy positions and activities. But the balloons, tethered to the ground, were sitting ducks for German guns.

Still more enemy information was needed in preparation for the Vimy Ridge attack. Fortunately, the Canadians had several new devices — and some remarkable individuals — that filled the bill.

Major Andy McNaughton, 29, the Counter Battery Staff Officer who had commanded the 11th Brigade, Canadian Field Artillery, at the Somme (and the chap who had mercy on the suffering horses back on Salisbury Plain), had been frustrated by the disheartening task of trying to cut barbed wire with field-gun shrapnel. It simply didn't work! He had resolved to do something about it — and as a result became one of the best artillery officers in the British Empire. It was his responsibility to see that the German batteries were knocked out.

Described as "more scientist than soldier,"[16] McNaughton had been educated at McGill University in Montreal, and had studied under physicist Ernest Rutherford, who would later win a Nobel Prize.[17] McNaughton also had long been fascinated by the deleterious effects of wear on the gun barrel, and continued his analysis in France, where he worked with another McGill graduate, Harold Hemming, on "flash spotting." Flash spotting was a method of more accurately locating enemy guns by triangulation of their muzzle flashes. McNaughton studied both.

Pierre Berton describes the critical importance of studying gun-barrel wear:

As a gun barrel wears from constant use, its muzzle velocity
drops and shells start falling short.[18]

For an 18-pounder (which the Canadians were relying on), firing at a
range of 8,000 yards could translate into a loss of 300 yards during a gun's
life — "enough to kill all the troops moving behind the curtain of shells."[19]
Knowing this, McNaughton, painstakingly measured the muzzle velocity
of every single weapon. As a result, every key gun in the Vimy battle
would be individually calibrated. (A falling barometer could also make a
difference of 300 yards on a 5,000-yard target.)

McNaughton himself sometimes went up in the balloons to study
enemy positions. On one occasion, at 4,000 feet, he was nearly shot down
by enemy fire. His on-the-spot analysis of the shelling, however, enabled
him to guide his ground gunners to the German position, probably saving
his life.[20]

McNaughton also consulted with several British scientists, chiefly Laurence Bragg, Charles Galton Darwin, and Lucien Bull. All three had interesting credentials. The Australian-born Bragg had won (with his father) a
Nobel Prize in physics in 1915, and developed with Colonel A. G. Haig
(not to be confused with Field Marshal Sir Douglas Haig) instruments that
could determine the location of enemy guns by the placement of micro-
phones along the front lines.[21] Darwin was the grandson of Charles Darwin; and Bull had invented the first sound-ranging recorder. All three
were, in Berton's words, "ignored as dangerous radicals" by the British
army.[22] McNaughton, however, welcomed them — and their theories —
and used them to develop more accurate pinpointing of enemy gun positions.

Yet another new theory and method of firepower was to be tried at
Vimy, though not immediately appreciated nor sanctioned by the Commanders. It was called "indirect fire" and promoted by a former Reserve
officer in the French army, Brigadier General Raymond Brutinel, who
now commanded the 1st Canadian Motor Machine Gun Brigade. Indirect machine-gun fire was not aimed directly at the enemy, but over
the heads of the assaulting troops to support and thicken the barrage of
larger guns and hit the gaps left by artillery fire. Properly used, it would
disrupt road traffic and prevent the enemy from bringing in new
troops and supplies. Although it couldn't cut or destroy the barbed-wire
entanglements, it would prevent the Germans from repairing them.[23]

Brutinel would take great pains to see that the German wire remained cut.

Meanwhile, the soldiers plodded on.

Driver George Teasdale wrote in a letter home:

> I have slept out doors, in old ruins, barns, cellars, root houses, in fact any place that I could crawl for a rest, often I have slept under a tree, with my clothes all on and my horse saddled with her lines tied to my arm in case we were called on to get out in a hurry. We are now camped in an old shell wrecked town, not a whole building standing, in the fields the mud is ankle deep.[24]

Author Pierre Berton, in *Vimy*, stresses the importance of the artillery:

> In battle the emphasis is usually on the infantry; but at Vimy it was the gunners, stripped to the waist, sweating despite the wind and the sleet, labouring hour after hour without rest or let up, who were the real victors in the battle to seize the ridge.[25]

The bitter lessons of past inadequacies of artillery bombardment guided the plans of the Canadian Corps, particularly Brigadier General E. W. B. Morrison, GOC Royal Artillery. Using information from the aerial observers, trench raids, prisoner interrogation, and wireless interceptions, Morrison and his men would begin the preliminary day and night bombardment two weeks before the assault. During the daylight hours, they would fire on enemy trenches, dugouts, machine-gun emplacements, supply dumps, road junctions, and key communication points. During the night, when the Germans would be tempted to repair wire that had been cut the previous day, the Canadians would continue to blast away, preventing any repair.

Such relentless bombing would take massive preparations. To accomplish it, 25 miles of road had to be repaired and new plank roads constructed. Twenty miles of tramway had to be reconditioned and extended. Hundreds of weary, bewildered mules (supplemented by light trains) would have to haul forward 800 tons of ammunition daily.

And there was one more exacting detail to be written indelibly in the mind of every soldier, so much so that actions and reactions in the battle itself would be second nature. Under Lieutenant General Byng's personal direction, a full-scale replica of the battle area was laid out on a field to the rear of the Canadian lines, over which the men could practice. When aerial photographs revealed changes on the German front, the changes were made on the model. The men had to know it by heart.

Using colored tapes and flags, and with mounted officers representing the rolling barrage, officers and men practiced daily, almost to the point of boredom. But they all knew where every German trench was, and what to do when they got there. Every officer and man also knew his superior's role and what to do if he were to become a casualty. Nothing was overlooked.

And the Canadians had still *another* "concealed weapon" of sorts. British tunneling companies, assisted by Canadian work parties, for some time had been digging 12 underground tunnels or "subways" that connected front and rear trenches. Some subways had electricity. Some had narrow-gauge railways. Some had ammunition stores, dressing stations, or kitchens. All of them, with a combined length of more than six miles, had critical telephone communications. But their greatest asset was the ability to conceal attacking troops until the last minute, when the tunnel mouth would be blasted open, enabling the Canadians to pour out. Such concealment should prevent a Somme-like slaughter.

On 20 March 1917, the preliminary bombardment began. Not wanting the enemy to suspect the full strength of the artillery batteries, the Canadians fired only half their guns for the first 13 days. At the same time, the Royal Marine Artillery hauled its massive 15-inch howitzers, each weighing 20 tons and capable of hurling a 1,500-pound shell, to the rear of the Canadian positions.[26] It took nine tractors, each pulling one or two trailers, to haul the various parts of the weapons to the gun pits. Crawling forward at a sluggish eight miles an hour, they tore up roads and snarled traffic behind the lines.[27]

By now, Gunner Robert Kennedy was neglecting his diary. He noted on 20 March, the day of the preliminary bombardment, that it was his 25th birthday, which he had spent establishing communications. His next entry was on 28 March:

Saw two of our planes brought down today, one, hit in the engine landed ok but the other came down in flames in German lines.

He was fascinated by the air maneuvers, however, and immediately sought out his superiors about a commission in the Royal Flying Corps (RFC). But there would be no chance to transfer to the Corps. And there would be no more diaries, for by this time, the keeping of diaries was largely forbidden lest they fall into enemy hands.

In the midst of all the artillery thunder, the trench raids continued, principally by the 10th Canadian Infantry Brigade. They paid off. With the Royal Flying Corps and other Intelligence sources, the Canadians were ultimately able to identify 83 percent of the estimated 212 enemy guns opposite their forces.[28]

It was not until the second day of April, however, that the full force of hellish fury of the Canadian bombardment fell on the German positions. The massive artillery barrage that had begun on 20 March had involved 245 heavy guns and howitzers, and more than 600 pieces of field artillery. Supporting British artillery added 132 heavy guns and 102 field pieces. The Germans, understandably, had called the period of bombardment "the week of suffering."[29] Ultimately, more than a million rounds of heavy and field ammunition, with a total weight of 50,000 tons, pounded, blasted, crushed, and tore into the German territory, devastating most of the trenches and totally destroying the occupied (and heavily fortified) villages of Thélus, Farbus, and Givenchy. The Germans would not be able to use them as hiding places for snipers or machine-gun fire.

The Germans were harassed, and to a degree, demoralized. They had been unable to sleep, eat, wash, or shave in peace. Sometimes their food didn't reach them because the Canadians were bombing not only them but their approaches and crossroads.

But suddenly on 3 April, the Canadian Corps ran into a terrible predicament. The Royal Flying Corps had spotted masses of German troops pulling out of Vimy Ridge! Had all the preparations been in vain? Captain Harry Clyne, who knew exactly where to find a gap in the enemy wire, offered to lead a small group of scouts of the 29th (Vancouver) Battalion that night to find out. Off they squirmed in deathly quietness on hands and knees out to and across No Man's Land, all the way to the German trenches. They were empty! Had the Germans discovered the Canadian plans?

Had they retreated to more fortified lines in the rear? Clyne and his men wondered if their preparations had been for nought.

Then suddenly, out of nowhere in that the dark night, was heard the sound of hurried footsteps, and in came fresh, clean German troops on the double. The trenches had not been abandoned.

But now Clyne and his men faced a new quandry. They immediately had to get word back to Corps headquarters. Somehow, in spite of the thick freezing mud, deep craters, and armed German sentries, they clawed and crawled their way back.

The assault would go on as scheduled.[30]

The 1st Canadian Field Artillery Brigade *War Diary* reflects the growing drama:

> April 6th, 1917. Today (Z-3) all preparations rushed for the coming attack by the Canadian Corps on VIMY RIDGE. Heavies up to 12" Howitzers concentrated on all towns immediately in rear of enemy's line. A standard gauge railway has been built and is now completed up to the 2nd Hows. Battery.

> April 7th, 1917. Weather fair and warm. All wire suspected is engaged, some 3800 rds. expended by our 18 Pdr. Batteries. 4.5" Hows. busy on Trench Destruction.

> April 8th 1917. Many horses died during the past few days owing to so much hauling of ammunition and cutting down of hay and straw ration. Infantry Commanders of the 5th and 17th Battalions report that there is no more wire on their zones, this confirms our report.[31]

Easter Sunday, 8 April 1917, dawned bright and clear. Canon F. G. Scott, the ubiquitous chaplain from Montreal, held an Easter service in a YMCA hut, already full of soldiers who were more interested in sleep than in church services. Scott had to keep relighting the candles which were blown out time and time again from the percussion of the heavy guns. As senior Protestant Chaplain of the First Division, Scott was much loved by the soldiers for his insistence on sharing hardships and danger with "his boys."

Meanwhile, high overhead, Major Billy Bishop was in the process of becoming one of Canada's most famous flying aces by tackling five enemy planes single-handed.

Though Canada had no air force of her own in the First World War, thousands of young Canadians served in the British air services. Of the 27 leading aces in the British forces, 10 were Canadians who accounted for the loss of 238 enemy aircraft. Bishop, who earned the Victoria Cross, had 72 victories, while another Canadian, Major Raymond Collishaw, had 60. Another warrior, Lieutenant Colonel William G. Barker of Manitoba was one of the most decorated in the war, with nine medals for gallantry and the Victoria Cross. (*The Book of Remembrance* in Canada's Peace Tower in Ottawa lists the names of 1,563 who did not survive the conflict.)

Back in the communication trenches, in strict silence, reserve troops were trudging toward the front in the subways. In the rear, troops were filling barrels of water to be used in cooling overheated guns.

In some places, men struggled through the mud, often losing their boots in the process. Some waded through sickening, waist-deep water. Some, struggling to bring rations up from the rear, were killed en route, so soldiers went without. Some shivered uncontrollably, partly from the cold and dampness, partly from fear. Some wrote a last letter home, "*just in case.*" For all too many, it would indeed be the last.

But Lieutenant General Byng had one more surprise on that Easter Sunday evening.

With all ammunition carefully stacked, shells fused, barrels full of water to cool overheated guns, and thousands upon thousands of Canadian quietly waiting for the assault, Byng tried a tactical surprise. Instead of increasing the final bombardment just before the assault, he ordered the artillery to slacken its fire, hoping to throw the enemy off balance.

Would it work?

So Loud the Silence
By four o'clock on Easter Monday morning, 9 April, all units were in position. There were 23 battalions in the forward line, 13 directly behind them, and another 9 (with 3 British battalions) in reserve — all in all,

30,000 men stretched out over four miles.[32] But just before dawn, a hitch developed when a crippling northwest wind, laden with snow and sleet, whipped over the area, forcing cancellation of a bombing sortie by the Royal Flying Corps. There was one consolation, however; at least the assaulting Canadians had the strong gusty wind at their backs.

And at 5:30 a.m., the deafening thunder of nearly a thousand guns and mortars rocked the heavens and earth. The battle for Vimy Ridge had begun.

The soldiers were heavily laden, as, of course, they had no idea where they'd be spending the next night, and had to carry their gear with them. Each soldier carried at least 40 pounds of equipment including a rifle, ammunition, two British Mills hand grenades, sandbags, rations, gas mask, round flare, water bottle, and pick or shovel. Crawling out and over the top of the wet slippery trenches was thus difficult, especially when coupled with an unwelcome load of wet mud, sometimes weighing as much as 20 pounds, that clung to their uniforms and equipment. (Some men had been known to cut the bottoms off their greatcoats to lessen the weight of the mud. However, they risked being reprimanded for destroying government property!)

Once out of the trenches, the attacking Canadians threaded their tortured way through shell holes and battered wire entanglements. The earth was a clammy, pulverized mush of mud.

The veteran First Division, commanded by Major General Currie and proudly wearing the red shoulder patch they had earned on the Somme, plunged forward on the right. In army tradition, the division would line up from right to left. Its six battalions (5th, 7th, 10th, 15th, 14th, and 16th) would attack a front more than a mile wide. Of the four Canadian Divisions, the First also had the greatest distance to cover.

Farbus Wood, which concealed deadly German guns, was more than two muddy miles away. But the Canadian troops knew where all the intervening obstacles were, and quickly reached the initial line of German defenses, where they overpowered the sentries. On and on they pushed, sometimes engaging in hand-to-hand fighting, some falling dead from machine-gun fire. But Currie's First Division reached the first objective — the Black Line — in just over 30 minutes, almost to the second, as planned. There they dug in to rest and regroup. And while the first wave of soldiers rested, the reserves slogged forward behind the perfectly-timed creeping barrage to the next objective — the Red Line.

The War of 1914-1918.

Canadian Forces.

No. 40828 Cpl. R. J. Kennedy, 2nd Bty., 1st Bde.

was mentioned in a Despatch from

Field Marshal Sir Douglas Haig, G.C.B., G.C.V.O., K.C.I.E.

dated 9th April 1917

for gallant and distinguished services in the Field.

I have it in command from the King to record His Majesty's

high appreciation of the services rendered.

Winston S. Churchill

War Office
Whitehall, S.W.
1st March 1919.

Secretary of State for War.

Life and death dramas played out in the grim mud. Men simply had to press on as they watched friends falling and sinking into the muck. They were forbidden to stop for casualties. Some displayed enormous gallantry, like Private W. J. (Bill) Milne of the 16th (Canadian Scottish) Battalion. Milne momentarily wondered why a haystack should be left standing when everything else had been obliterated. Then he realized it was a clever cover for a concrete machine-gun emplacement. He immediately charged the haystack and destroyed the machine guns, allowing his fellow troops to continue. He won the Victoria Cross for his actions, but like so many others, never knew it. He was killed the same day.[33]

In the 2nd Howitzer Battery gun pit, Robert Kennedy and his veteran chums had been firing the 4.5-inch howitzers since 5:30 a.m. And by the end of the day, Kennedy had been singled out for his gallantry under fire.[34]

The Second Division (to the left of the First Division) was also charging forward with clockwork precision, in spite of the mud and driving snow. Although the eight tanks allotted to the division had to be left behind because their treads couldn't grip the slimy mud, the soldiers were able to advance by following the grayish puffs of their own exploding artillery barrage in front of them. Again, all was in the precision timing.

Or almost all. Individual valor, seen and unseen, also carried the day.

In almost hyperbolic Hollywood fashion, Lance Sergeant E. W. Sifton spotted a hidden enemy machine gun and relentlessly charged and bayoneted every single one of its crew. When other Germans saw what happened, several charged down the trench to join the fray. Sifton still held them all off, until more Canadians arrived. He would be awarded the Victoria Cross, for his valor, but he, too, never knew of it. One of the Germans whom he had wounded was still alive and carefully took aim, killing him.

Though there were mounting Canadian casualties at Vimy Ridge, enemy casualties were likewise horrendous. Some entire battalions were annihilated. Hell could paint no worse a scene as the greenish slime in shell holes gradually turned blood-red brown.

The horror was palpable:

> Wounded men sprawled everywhere in the slime, in the shell holes, in the mine craters, some screaming to the skies, some lying silently, some begging for help, some struggling to keep from drowning in the craters, the field swarming with stretcher-bearers.[35]

By 6:15, just 45 minutes after zero hour on that snowy Easter Monday morning, both the First and Second Divisions had reached the Black Line. In fact, the First Division lads were already on their way to the next objective.

Still farther to the left, the Third Division likewise forged ahead with the split-second precision they had practiced, though in some cases eager troops rushed forward so quickly that they almost ran into their own barrage. In theory, the Third Division should have a less onerous day than its sister divisions on its right, for they had to reach and take only two objectives — the Black and Red Lines. Furthermore, La Folie Wood was just 1,200 yards away.

For once, reality conformed to theory, and the Third Division charged over the front-line German trenches like men possessed. They swept over the crest of the ridge right on time, and were "digging in" within two and a half hours, while fighting continued on either side of them. The Third Division, like the First and Second, had benefitted from the meticulous work of McNaughton and his "radical" friends who had enabled the artillery to knock out enemy batteries.

But not everything was completely as expected. Germans were raking the men of the Third with machine-gun fire from Hill 145 on their left. The Fourth Division should have been there by now.

The Fourth Division, on the extreme left of the Canadian Corps (and next to the British 1st Corps), had for its major objective the highest point of Vimy Ridge, Hill 145, with its commanding view of the whole Douai Plain and, of course, the rearward German trenches.

Although Canadian and British Intelligence had been extraordinarily thorough, it hadn't revealed how well Hill 145 was fortified. And the Germans had a few deceptions of their own. Just as the Canadians had not used all their guns in the preliminary bombardment in order to lull the Germans into false security, so too did the Germans hold back some of their machine-gun fire until the Canadian troops were almost on top of them. The result was deadly predictable.

The Fourth Division had other drawbacks to overcome as well. Its troops were the newest, most inexperienced. They also had the steepest terrain to cover. Furthermore, they had suffered severe losses, including two battalion Commanders, in the ill-fated trench raid that had gone awry just weeks earlier on 1 March.

Unfortunately, unlike the split-second timing and orderliness in the other three divisions, there was confusion within the Fourth. When the creeping barrage moved forward exactly as scheduled, the Fourth Division troops had not been able to keep pace, thereby giving the Germans time to come out of their trenches and fire on them. Telephone lines were destroyed. Runners who tried to get messages to the rear were killed before they got there. Scouts going forward with or for information were likewise picked off.

And there was yet another variable. One acting battalion Commander, Major Harry Shaw of the 87th Grenadier Guards, had asked that the

The Canadian Field Artillery bringing up the guns at Vimy Ridge, April 1917. *National Archives of Canada, PA 001073*

A captured German gun emplacement in Farbus Wood, April 1917.
National Archives of Canada, PA 000994

artillery *not* destroy one specific German trench. His reasoning seemed to make some sense. The trench in question was fairly close to the Canadian lines, and Shaw thought it could be easily — and quickly — captured, thereby affording immediate protection from enemy fire farther up the hill.

It was a devastating miscalculation.

The Grenadier Guards lost half their men in less than ten minutes. Ten of their 11 officers were wounded, 5 mortally. Worse, the critical timing of the attack was thrown asunder. Because the enemy soldiers in the undamaged trench badly slowed the attacking Canadians, they couldn't keep pace with the protective but unalterable creeping barrage in front of them. Many battalions ran into death struggles. Scores of men fell, wounded or dead, in the greasy mud. Scores simply slipped into slimy shell holes, never to surface again.

Some battalions suffered incredible losses. The lads of the 54th

German trench mortars captured by Canadians, April 1917. *National Archives of Canada, CO 1131*

(Kootenay) Battalion, whose job it was to take the infamous Hill 145, were trapped in cross-fire and pinned down from the left and above. Though relatively green,[36] they did not lack in courage. In spite of the machine-gun fire, several men stubbornly struggled upward in the blowing snow toward their objective. None returned.

As always, there were countless instances of drama and courage. Major Thane MacDowell of Lachute, Quebec, with two battalion runners, managed to bomb and destroy two machine-gun nests just over the crest of the ridge. But one German soldier got away, heading into a deep underground tunnel. MacDowell, undaunted, decided to follow him. Down and down he went into the tunnel, some 55 steps into the darkness, chasing his prey. He kept pursuing, only to round a corner and come face-to-face with about 75 soldiers of the Prussian Guard and two German officers.

MacDowell was clearly outmanned. But with remarkable coolness, he hollered orders to the troops behind him — all imaginary because he was alone — and the Germans surrendered. His monstrous bluff had worked. Still with a predicament on his hands, knowing he could be overpowered if they learned his secret, MacDowell calmly counted off prisoners in groups of 12 and sent them upwards, where they were captured. (MacDowell, who had already won the Distinguished Service Order at the Somme, was awarded the Victoria Cross.)

In spite of the hellish gun fire and blowing snow, the Fourth Division persevered. The 72nd (Seaforth Highlanders) Battalion, badly stricken with casualties, finally gained a foothold in the German third line. The 78th (Winnipeg Grenadiers) Battalion was having difficulty "leapfrogging" through the 38th Ottawa Battalion because of machine-gun fire. Nonetheless some men neared Givenchy, only to be overpowered by defending Germans.

The hours wore on. By 6:00 p.m., though much of the Ridge had been taken, Hill 145 was still not secure, and the Fourth Division brigades were still crippled by fire from "The Pimple," a heavily fortified German stronghold on a wooded knoll about a mile north of Hill 145. Knowing the

11th Brigade was too exhausted to reach its Red Line objective, Major General Watson (the GOC of the Fourth Division) called in fresh troops of the 10th Brigade, which had been waiting in reserve to attack The Pimple. He threw them at Hill 145 instead.

The carnage continued, but by mid-afternoon the next day, 10 April, Hill 145 was in Canadian hands.[37]

But the battle wasn't quite over. The Pimple to the north was still in enemy hands. And no wonder. It had every conceivable kind of defense that the German engineers could concoct. The maze of trenches on the surface was protected, of course, by barbed wire, booby traps, and mines, largely camouflaged. Then, there were the concrete pillboxes sprouting machine guns. Underneath the surface were deep dugouts and tunnels.

The Pimple had been a British objective initially, but was now given to Lieutenant General Byng's Canadian troops. It was to have been assaulted within 24 hours of the southern operation, but the weather had deteriorated into almost gale-like proportions with driving sleet and snow. The grim weather, however, didn't keep the western troops of three battalions, the 44th, 50th, and 46th (Manitoba, Calgary, and South Saskatchewan), from moving toward the enemy positions.

And at five o'clock in the early morning hours of 12 April, the western troops advanced through the freezing mud and snow as the artillery bombed the German front-line trenches.

So unexpected was the attack in the blinding snowstorm that the Manitoba and Calgary troops took the first two trenches with little fanfare. The men from South Saskatchewan encountered heavy fire (suffering 108 casualties) but forged ahead, sometimes engaging in hand-to-hand fighting.

By daybreak, the incredible happened. When the sky began to clear, the Canadians had also taken The Pimple, as well as Vimy Ridge.

The Outcome

Surprisingly, many books on the First World War (other than those written by Canadians) give short shrift to the 1917 Battle of Vimy Ridge. Perhaps that's because the wider battle of which it was a part, the Battle of Arras, was largely a failure. Perhaps it's because Vimy Ridge was later, on 16 April, overshadowed by the terrible failure of the massive French

The Canadian National Vimy Ridge Memorial, at Ypres, Belgium. In 1922, the government of France gave 91 hectares (250 acres) of former trenches and shellholes, hallowed by the blood of young soldiers, to the people of Canada "in perpetuity," on the site of Hill 145. The two towering pylons of the memorial soar majestically over the 1917 battlefield. Another 6,994 names of missing Canadians are listed on the Menin Gate at Ypes. All in all, Canada lost 66,000, including those who died after the war as a result of their wounds.   *Mac Johnston*

assault at Chemin des Dames (the Second Battle of the Aisne), which brought the downfall of yet another General who couldn't deliver on his promise — this time Robert Georges Nivelle.[38] Nor did Vimy Ridge end the war.

Nonetheless, the Canadian victory at Vimy Ridge was extraordinary — a victory where none was expected. Anglo/French forces had attempted to take the Ridge and both had failed. But the determined, disciplined Canadians had proved British General Haig, French General Nivelle, and even the Germans wrong.

As the official history summarizes:

> In six days the Canadian Corps had advanced some 4500 yards and seized 54 guns, 104 trench mortars and 124 machine-guns. It had inflicted severe losses on the enemy, capturing more than 4000 prisoners.[39]

Some 150 officers were taken prisoners, including five battalion Commanders.[40] And the Corps had advanced two and a half miles.

In the entire Battle of Arras, the *only* successful operation was the taking of Vimy Ridge by the Canadians, assisted by the British 51st Highlander unit, which was operating under Canadian command. It was the most important British victory of the war so far.

The French called it an Easter gift from Canada to France. The King, George V, sent congratulations to the Commander-in-Chief, Field Marshal Sir Douglas Haig.

Even French soldiers were impressed. Colonel G. W. L. Nicholson, in *Gunners of Canada*, recounts an incident where a young officer, of the 25th Battery of the Canadian Field Artillery overheard French officers scoffing at the news that Vimy Ridge had been taken by the Allies.[41]

"*C'est impossible!*" they claimed. Then came word that it was the Canadian Corps that took the ridge. The mood changed. Incredulity evaporated.

"*Alors, c'est possible!*" they nodded.[42]

The victory at Vimy Ridge was not without cost, of course. The Dominion suffered 10,602 casualties, all ranks, 3,598 of them fatal.[43] (The Fourth

Division was hardest hit, with 4,401 of its infantrymen becoming casualties.[44]) The British lost 380 men of the 13th Brigade, and the Royal Flying Corps also paid a price, with No.16 Squadron losing 3 of its 24 aircraft between 1 and 13 April.[45]

And there is yet another footnote — an important one — to the Battle of Vimy Ridge, where all four of the Canadian Divisions fought together for the first time and, amidst swirling snow and freezing mud, covered themselves with glory.[46] Many believe that it was on Vimy Ridge, in France, that Canada became a nation.

NOTES

1. For a thorough overview of the 1917 battle for Vimy Ridge, see Pierre Berton, *Vimy* (Markham, Ontario: Penguin Books Canada Ltd., 1987).

2. Colonel G. W. L. Nicholson, C.D., *Canadian Expeditionary Force 1914-1919: Official History of the Canadian Army in the First World War* (Ottawa: Queen's Printer, 1964), 244-245.

3. The French offensive began on 16 April, well after the Vimy Ridge assault. Though the French gained some ground, they did not break through, in spite of the loss of nearly 100,000 men in the first ten days of battle. The French government, then disappointed in Nivelle, moved him to North Africa, and he was replaced by General Pétain as French Commander-in-Chief. French forces were close to mutiny.

4. Berton, *Vimy*, 107.

5. Colonel W. W. Murray, *The History of the 2nd Canadian Battalion (Eastern Ontario Regiment) in the Great War, 1914-1919* (Ottawa: Mortimer Ltd., 1947), 155.

6. *Ibid.*, 155-156.

7. *Ibid.*, 157.

8. Berton, *Vimy*, 157.

9. Bill Rawling, *Surviving Trench Warfare: Technology and the Canadian Corps, 1914-1918* (Toronto: University of Toronto Press, 1992), 90.

10. See Nicholson, *Canadian Expeditionary Force*, 247; and Berton, *Vimy*, 216.

11. Berton notes that Currie made officers synchronize their watches constantly and warned one, whose watch was three seconds off, not to let it happen again (209).

12. Berton, *Vimy*, 104.

13. *Ibid.*, 113.

14. *Ibid.*, 123-124. There was always a cost. Martin Gilbert notes that in air struggle prior to the offensives at Arras and Vimy Ridge, 75 British aircraft were shot down, and 19 pilots killed. *The First World War: A Complete History*, 2nd ed. (New York: Henry Holt and Co., 1994), 320.

15. Berton, *Vimy*, 120.
16. *Ibid.*, 110.
17. Ernest Rutherford, a New Zealander, was ultimately to rank in fame with Sir Isaac Newton and Michael Faraday. Later in the war, he worked on submarine detection by underwater acoustics.
18. Berton, *Vimy*, 168.
19. *Ibid.*, 167.
20. *Ibid.*
21. Rawling, *Surviving Trench Warfare*, 94.
22. Berton, *Vimy*, 164.
23. Berton points out that after the Battle of Vimy Ridge, "indirect fire, scorned for so long by the brass hats, was adopted by all Allied armies," *Vimy*, 174.
24. In Perry L. Climo, *Let Us Remember: Lively Letters from World War One* (Coburg, Ontario: Haynes Printing Co., 1990), 249.
25. Berton, *Vimy*, 170.
26. *Canada in the First World War and the Road to Vimy Ridge*, Canadian Veterans Affairs Publication, 1992.
27. Berton, *Vimy*, 180.
28. Nicholson, *Canadian Expeditionary Force*, 251.
29. *Canada in the First World War.*
30. This incident is recounted by Berton, *Vimy*, 184-185.
31. *War Diary of the 1st Canadian Field Artillery Brigade* (Ottawa: National Archives of Canada).
32. *Berton.*, 209.
33. A number of military historians note that decorations were more readily won by officers than men. Martin Middlebrook writes, for example: "Leave, pay and decorations were received in direct proportion to the rank held, with the private soldier being worse off in all respects." *The First Day on the Somme* (New York: W. W. Norton and Co., Inc., 1972), 281.
34. In one of the more frustrating puzzles of the author's research in both the National Archives of Canada and the Imperial War Museum in London, she was unable to trace Kennedy's specific action. Kennedy himself never referred to his actions on Vimy Ridge. His citation was recorded in the *London Gazette*, No. 30107, dated 1 June 1917. Some records were lost forever as a result of an arsonist's fire in the Imperial War Museum.
35. Berton, *Vimy*, 235.
36. Berton recounts that one rifleman in the Fourth Division had never fired a rifle since arriving in France, and when he finally did, missed the target entirely. *Vimy*, 267.
37. Rawling, *Surviving Trench Warfare*, disputes the disastrous trench raid as a cause of the Fourth Division's difficulties, and points to the successes of several battalions including the 54th (Kootenay), 72nd (Seaforth Highlanders of Canada), 73rd (Royal Highlanders of Canada), and 75th (Mississauga), that

suffered excessive losses on 1 March. He views a decision by the 87th Battalion to leave an enemy strongpoint untouched as a major factor in the heavy losses.

38. Nicholson notes that the Canadian victory also caused the removal of the Chief of Staff of the German Sixth Army. *Canadian Expeditionary Force*, 266.

39. *Ibid.*, 265.

40. Francis Whiting Halsey, *The Literary Digest History of the World War*, Vol. 3 (New York: Funk & Wagnalls Co., 1919), 355.

41. Colonel G. W. L. Nicholson, C.D., *The Gunners of Canada: The History of the Royal Regiment of the Canadian Artillery, 1534-1919,* Vol. 1 (Toronto: McClelland and Stewart Limited, 1967), 287.

42. C. R. M. F. Crutwell writes, in *A History of the Great War 1914-1918* (Oxford: Clarendon Press, 1934; 2nd ed., 1936), 408, that the capture of Vimy Ridge was of "supreme importance in March 1918" when the German assault on Arras would have been successful had they still held Vimy Ridge. Spencer C. Tucker, in *The Great War of 1914-18* (Bloomington: Indiana University Press, 1998), 128, notes that the capture of Vimy Ridge "was one of the notable feats of arms of the entire war."

43. *Canada in the First World War*, 12.

44. Rawling, *Surviving Trench Warfare*, 131.

45. *Ibid.,* 108.

46. James L. Stokesbury writes that Vimy "holds the same hallowed place in Canadian annals as Anzac Cove in Australian, or St. Mihiel, and the Argonnne Forest in American." *A Short History of World War I* (New York: William Morrow and Co., 1981), 231-232.

Chapter 20

The Artillery Comes of Age

FTER THE REMARKABLE victory at Vimy, the first significant Allied offensive victory of the war, the Canadians began the process of strengthening their newly won positions against a counterattack. They were painfully aware that recently gained ground was subject to major counter-offensives, and all too frequently retaken by the enemy.

But the task was far from easy. It was especially onerous for the artillery field batteries who, though now going downhill on the eastern slope of the ridge, had to lug their big guns over the tortuous ground. Horses, struggling valiantly in the mud and snow, dropped pitifully from fatigue, unable to rise again.[1]

Because enemy shelling was incessant, all movement had to be carried out under the cover of darkness. Even so, enemy fire sometimes scored direct hits on gun pits, killing the gunners and destroying the guns. Sometimes it hit the dumps, blowing up the ammunition. Sometimes runners, or those bringing up rations, were hit. The 39th Battery was especially beleaguered, ultimately losing its Commander, Major A. B. Stafford, and 18 guns by direct hits. Death was indiscriminate.

Oftentimes the terrorized horses were hit and killed outright, or wounded so severely that they had to be destroyed. The dreadful plight of horses (and mules) is captured in Erich Marie Remarque's *All Quiet on the Western Front*, when two German soldiers witness the terrorized groaning horses and long to shoot them to relieve them of their misery:

> Some gallop away in the distance, fall down, and then run on farther. The belly of one is ripped open, the guts trail out. He becomes tangled in them and falls, then he stands up again.[2]

The screams of the horses continue, but the men have difficulty overtaking them because they "fly in their pain, their wide open mouths full of anguish." Finally, a shot, and one horse after another drops.

> The last one props itself on its forelegs and drags itself round in a circle like a merry-go-round; squatting, it drags round in circles on its stiffened forelegs, apparently its back is broken. The soldier runs up and shoots it. Slowly, humbly, it sinks to the ground.[3]

There was no surcease from death and suffering.

Allied Attacks Along the Scarpe River

Although the next major offensive (farther north) on the Western Front was still several months away, General Haig deemed it critical to keep pressure on the Germans with a series of ongoing attacks astride the Scarpe River. And so in late April, the Canadians were chosen to attack the Arleux Loop in the German-held Oppy-Mericourt line. On 28 April, though British armies near them met with failure, gunners of the 1st Canadian Divisional Artillery provided a barrage so effective that the 2nd Infantry Brigade was able to take Arleux, plus another 500 yards. British Official Historian J. E. Edmonds later called it "the only tangible success of the whole operation."[4]

A World War I recruitment poster.

It is estimated that more than 375,000 horses were killed in World War I. While horses are often depicted on monuments, one of the most poignant can be found at Chipilly, on the Somme River, where an artillery soldier cradles the head of his dying horse, stroking its jaw in affection and despair.

But ominous clouds were on the horizon for the artillery. The Canadian field batteries continued to suffer from enemy shelling because their new positions were so exposed. Men and horses continued to suffer direct hits. Ammunition dumps were blown sky high. Gas bombardments haunted the troops nightly. On 2 May, a direct hit on the headquarters dugout of the 5th Brigade killed its Commander, Lieutenant Colonel R. H. Britton, and Major A. Ripley, Commander of the 20th Battery.

And though the artillery was becoming more disciplined and sophisticated, it still faced one of the most basic problems — moving the guns forward to keep up with infantry advances, as historian Bill Rawling explains.

> On many occasions the guns were delayed because no one was available to build the roads they needed across no man's land; for the infantry needed engineers to build strong points on the new front line, leaving few (or none) to help the gunners. Almost anything else — ammunition, machine guns, barbed wire, and so on — could be soldier-packed if necessary, but the guns needed horses to pull them and a strong surface to prevent them from sinking into mud and earth they themselves had loosened with the creeping barrage.[5]

On 3 May, in Field Marshal Haig's continued offensive — the Third Battle of the Scarpe — the Canadians were told to take the hamlet of Fresnoy, about a mile east of Arleux, which they had just captured. With massive artillery support, the troops of the 1st Brigade stormed the German trenches in the bright moonlight, that made them easy targets. Nonetheless, they took Fresnoy and the nearby woods. Providing the artillery barrage were the 1st, 2nd, and 3rd Canadian Divisional Artilleries, the Reserve Divisional Artillery, the 26th, 28th, and 72nd Army Field Brigades, a battery of the British 5th Brigade Royal Horse Artillery, the Canadian Corps Heavy Artillery, and some British Heavy Groups.

There followed glowing praise for the gunners whose part in all successful operations was steadily increasing. The 6th Infantry Brigade's Commander, whose troops benefited from the pinpoint excellence of the barrage, wrote that in spite of intense German counter-battery fire, and in spite of many of their ammunition dumps being set on fire and blazing beside them, the gun crews were seen to stand sturdily to their guns and keep firing without a break. Their gallantry was outstanding under these circumstances, as their positions were practically in the open.[6]

Once again the Canadians distinguished themselves on the battlefield. Once again other Allied forces (the First and Third Armies) didn't quite match the Canadian achievement. And once again, the British Official Historian J. E. Edmonds complimented the Canadians, calling their achievement "the relieving feature of a day which many who witnessed it considered the blackest of the war."[7]

But, once again, the cost was high. The two assaulting Canadian brigades — the 1st and 6th — suffered more than a thousand losses. Of the 18 guns of the 4th Brigade, Canadian Field Artillery, only 8 remained in action. Three had been blown to smithereens. Nine gunners had become casualties.[8]

On 8 May, the Germans launched a strong counterattack on Fresnoy, now held by a battalion of the Fifth British Division, which had relieved the Canadians. After deadly fighting the entire day, the British battalion was "all but annihilated" and by nightfall, what had been captured by the Canadians less than a week before was back in German hands. Once again, in heartbreaking repetition, ground had been fought over, captured, and then lost, with only mounting casualties to show for it.

And so this particular offensive ground down to a less than successful conclusion. Now, operations in the Arras sector would be mainly designed to wear down the enemy in local actions, and confuse him with regard to future assaults farther north.

Messines Ridge, 7-15 June 1917

On 7 May, Field Marshal Haig told his army Commanders that after continued wearing down of the enemy, the next main blow would be once again on the Ypres front. It was there that General Sir Hubert Plumer and his Second Army had been grimly holding the war-ravaged Salient for two years. Now Haig was confident of an Allied breakthrough there, telling his senior generals, on 5 June, that the endurance of the German people was

A trench on the Canadian front showing funk holes, May 1917.
National Archives of Canada, PA 001326

"so strained as to make it possible that the breaking point may be reached this year."

The first major objective would be an assault on the Messines Ridge in early June "with the eventual object of securing the Belgium coast and connecting with the Dutch frontier."[9] The Belgium coast was becoming a matter of increasing concern, since the Germans were now threatening England with their new Gotha G IV bombers, far faster and deadlier than the Zeppelin airships they replaced. On 25 May, 23 Gothas had left German bases in occupied Belgium, flown across the English Channel, and bombed — among other places — a military camp at Shorncliffe, killing 16 Canadian soldiers, and Folkestone, killing more than 70 civilians, including 25 children. Still more were killed in early June.

The battle for the German-occupied village and ridge of Messines,

A soldier's morning's toilet on the battlefield, May 1917.   *National Archives of Canada, PA 001193*

about six miles south of Ypres, was scheduled for 7 June 1917. Preparations for it, however, had begun long before.

In an extraordinary and unprecedented mining feat, British engineers and sappers (aided by Canadian and Australian tunnelers) had, in more than six months of back-breaking, nerve-rattling, suffocating, troglodyte misery, dug 20 tunnels under German positions on the ridge. It wasn't easy. One tunnel alone was about 2,000 feet in length, and always, always, there was the gut-tightening fear of discovery. Nonetheless, they succeeded in planting in the mines a million pounds of explosives. Though one tunnel was discovered and neutralized by the Germans, the other 19 amazingly went undetected.

As scheduled, the heavy bombardment that preceded the attack by the British suddenly ceased at 2:40 a.m., on 7 June, and in the deafening quietness, some soldiers could hear the song of nightingales. But the singing of the winged creatures was obliterated precisely at 3:10 a.m., when all 19 mines were exploded as one. So loud was the blast that Prime Minister

A busy scene at an ammunition dump behind Canadian lines, May 1917. *National Archives of Canada, CO 1437*

Loos, France, July 1917.   *National Archives of Canada, PA 002031*

David Lloyd George, working in his study at 10 Downing Street, heard the distant thunder.[10] Some in southern England thought it was an earthquake.

Thousands of German soldiers were killed outright, or buried alive, in the blast. Thousands more were dazed by the massive explosions, so much so that by 10:00 a.m., the German front line was in British hands. By that afternoon, the British manned the high ground at Messines. By 14 June, when it all ended, the Battle of Messines was considered the most successful of the British Expeditionary Force operations to date.[11] Though the British sustained approximately 25,000 casualties, they had taken 7,300 prisoners, and their victory ended German control of the Ypres Salient from the south. The Germans had more than 20,000 casualties.[12]

And the stage was set for more bloodshed.

The Killing Fields of Lens, Loos, and Hill 70

A student of the First World War won't find Hill 70 listed in the index of many war books. For one thing, the battle there in August 1917 didn't change the direction of the war — nor were there the colossal numbers of men involved or lost, as at the Somme or Verdun or other major battle sites. Even the size of the hill itself was relatively insignificant, and stood out only because so much else around it was flat.

To appreciate the actions that took place on Hill 70, which had been captured, then lost by the British in the battle of Loos in 1915, one must step back and view the larger scene of war, now entering the fourth year of mounting death and destruction. It will be recalled that Field Marshal Haig wanted to continue smaller "secondary" operations farther south in the Arras area to distract the enemy from the real Ypres objective. The Canadian Corps Divisions were to make some of these secondary assaults centered in the coal-mining Lens area.

And so it was that while the British were overpowering the Germans at Messines Ridge in early June, the Canadians, about 30 miles farther south in the Arras sector, were making preparations for secondary assaults.

And they would have a new General Officer Commanding. Lieutenant General Arthur W. Currie, increasingly being seen as Canada's most talented soldier, had been given command of the Canadian Corps in June of 1917, the first time the position was not held by a British General. (His predecessor, Lieutenant General Sir Julian Byng, much respected by the Canadians, had then taken over the British Third Army. And Currie was to be honored still further; he was later knighted on Vimy Ridge by King George V.)

Currie soon received his new orders. General Haig instructed General Sir Henry Horne and his First Army (under which the Canadian Corps was a part) to capture the city of Lens in the center of the coal-mining area. The Germans had taken the city in the bloody battle of Loos in 1915, and still held the badly battered city. Horne, in turn, chose Currie and his Canadians to mount a frontal attack on the city.

But Currie, in his methodical, analytical way, wasn't sure about the soundness of the attack. With typical thoroughness, he first climbed a hill behind the Canadian lines and studied the whole area and its landmarks. He was bothered by the assignment because the city of Lens was dominated by two hills that flanked it, Sallaumines and Hill 70, the latter a treeless expanse of chalk that offered a commanding view of the Douai Plain. Obviously, the German-held hills gave the enemy a clear advantage over the Canadians on the low ground. Wouldn't it make more sense to take one of the hills, preferably Hill 70, and then, knowing the Germans would be

A Canadian officer picking flowers among barbed wire, July 1917.
National Archives of Canada, PA 001693

A Canadian Red Cross ambulance that had been hit twice within six months. The first time, the driver was killed. July 1917. *Imperial War Museum, London, CO 1661*

compelled to try to retake it, let them — rather than his troops — be in a more vulnerable position?

Currie took his proposition to General Horne, who in turn took it to General Haig. Haig, though not sure the Canadians could take Hill 70 for a number of reasons, concurred.

Although Currie would once again insist on endless preparation and training, he knew that taking Hill 70 would be a formidable challenge for a host of reasons. For one thing, the Germans were well ensconced on the hill, taking refuge in countless tunnels, trenches, cellars, and even mining cottages. As always, there would be thick belts of barbed wire to deal with. The Germans had also built carefully concealed concrete machine-gun emplacements. Besides the flamethrowers used for the first time in the February 1916 battle of Verdun, the Germans now had the deadly new "Yellow Cross" mustard gas that blistered the skin wherever it touched.

And would the weather cooperate?

There was yet another concern. The Canadian heavy guns were now badly worn, and their accuracy therefore questionable. Brigadier General E. W. B. Morrison was concerned not only about a shortage of guns — many batteries had already been moved north for the coming offensive there — but the condition of those he had.

But Currie had faith in his men, and the assault on Hill 70 was scheduled for 30 July. The First and Second Divisions would attack along a 4,000-yard front from the northern outskirts of Lens to a pit head on the northern slope of Hill 70. The Fourth Division would mount a diversionary assault in front of Lens. The Third Division would be held in reserve.

But with frustrating regularity, bad weather once more intervened, and the assault was delayed until mid-August.

The delay, however, was put to good use; Currie used it for more training. The artillery units of all four divisional artilleries (and some British batteries), which were to play a crucial role, used the time to strengthen their positions, building camouflaged gun pits and shelters, and registering their guns. For the first time, they would use Continuous Wave (CW) wireless sets, a new communication device that would vastly improve their registration of guns.

The secret Order of Battle for the artillery brigade, dated 22 July, spelled out the three-staged objectives — the Blue (first), Red (intermediate), and Green (final) lines for the infantry brigades, and the distribution of artillery. It also gave instructions regarding observation posts, whose approaches in most cases were in view of the enemy, and the quantities of artillery needed at ammunition dumps. Instructions were detailed.

Secret operational orders, drawn up in late July for "Z Day," spelled out instructions for the barrage by the 1st Brigade, and four other batteries of the CFA, with regard to the all-important wire cutting by the 4.5-inch howitzers (used by Robert Kennedy) and medium and heavy howitzers. The Secret Instructions "A" of the 1st Canadian Artillery Brigade, dated 22 July 1917 read[13]:

> Wire Cutting.
> The wire on the front line is being cut by Medium T.M.s, and if necessary, this work will be completed by 4.5" howitzers with 106 fuze and by 18 pounders. The remainder of the wire is being cut by medium and heavy howitzers.

> Concealment.
> Every endeavor will be made to keep as many 18 pounder batteries silent after registration as circumstances will permit. To ensure that these endeavors are not wasted, the most stringent orders must be issued, regarding concealment of gun pits, flash marks, dugouts, smoke from cook's fires, paths, wagon tracks, and ammunition dumps, from enemy aircraft.

> Feints.
> To mislead the enemy, a series of feint barrages and feint bombardments will be carried out extending from the Southern boundary of the proposed front of attack to the Souchez River and in the vicinity of Avion.

For Gunner Kennedy, the war seemed never-ending. In early August, his 2nd Howitzer Battery continued to cut wire on the enemy front line "with satisfactory results," as noted in the hand-written entries in the *War Diary of the 1st Canadian Field Artillery Brigade*, which seemed to become more intense, as the days went on.

A watercart stuck in mud to the axle, one wheel and one horse having gone over the edge of the brushwood track at St. Eloi, during the Battle of Ypres, 11 August 1917.
Imperial War Museum, London, Q 5943

Digging an 18-pounder field gun out of the mud near Zillebeke, during the Third Battle of Ypres, 9 August 1917. *Imperial War Museum, London, Q 6224*

A Canadian military funeral in a war cemetery at Poperinghe, Flanders, 11 August 1917.
Imperial War Museum, London, Q 5875

August 7 — Our heavies were very active all day. The 2nd Howitzer Battery expended 100 rounds on harassing fire during the hours of darkness on enemy's consolidated shell holes and tramways.

August 8 — Weather fine but dull. Visibility poor. Wire on Brigade Zone was reconnoitered, no new wire was seen. The 2nd Howitzer Battery expended 260 rounds B.X. cutting wire at N.1.a.9.4. Wire was successfully cut. Our heavies bombarded enemy back country, Cite St. Auguste and Cite du Grande Conde. The enemy retaliated very heavily on our front line for 4th Division raid on our right. Enemy aeroplanes active in the evening.

The pace of the *War Diary* picks up, with numerous notations of its own "heavies" shelling German trenches and back country, and of the hostile artillery and aircraft.

August 13 — Weather fine, visibility fair. 2nd Howitzer Battery expended 50 rounds on enemy trenches during the afternoon, and 100 rounds during the hours of darkness, on tramways and consolidated shell holes. Hostile Artillery and aircraft both very active. Enemy wire was reconnoitered, no new wire was observed. 2nd Howitzer Battery had one gun destroyed by premature. One man was wounded.

Clearly, activity was increasing on both sides.

Finally, at the break of dawn, 4:25 a.m. on 15 August, the assault began. Currie's emphasis on training and preparations soon paid dividends. Infantrymen and gunners worked as a team. Ten infantry battalions rushed into No Man's Land, following, with precise timing, the rolling barrage laid down in front of them by the gunners.

August 15: 4:25 a.m. Weather fine, visibility good. At 4:25 a.m. our Barrage opened (well synchronized and well distributed) as for Operations Order No.8 and amendments, and Barrage Map "M."

5:07 a.m. — Lieut. H. Johnson, Brigade FOO reported that 2nd

Canadian Infantry Brigade has reached the Blue Objective, and had met with little resistance.

5:35 a.m. — FOO wire was cut, communication was kept up by runner.

6:05 a.m. — Liaison Officer reported that Red Objective had been taken. Casualties slight

8:13 a.m. — Reported that 8th Canadian Infantry Battalion were held up at Red Objective by machine gun fire.

11:30 a.m. — FOO reported that he has established himself in N.2.a.45.75.

11:35 a.m. — The 2nd Howitzer Battery and 1st Battery fired on Machine Gun Emplacements in N.2.d

Noon and 12:30 p.m. — At this time 1st battery and 2nd Howitzer Battery fired in a concentration on Bois Dixhuit. Very good results reported as enemy were massing at the point.

4:25 p.m. — Firing ceased.

The hand-written diary resumes at 6:00 p.m., noting that the infantry could not advance farther "owing to exhaustion," and that the barrage resumed and "caught the enemy massing for a counter attack." At 8:35 p.m., the brigade received an SOS from the 2nd Canadian Infantry Brigade, to which all batteries answered. The final entry for the day was noted as 9:50 p.m., though it appears to have been written the next morning:

9:50 p.m. — 18 pd Batteries of this Brigade ceased firing.

Approximate expenditure of Ammunition from 4:25 a.m. on the 15 to 4:25 on the 16th was as follows —

1st Battery	3,300 rounds
2nd How. Battery	1,206 rounds
3rd Battery	3,000 rounds
4th Battery	2,350 rounds

In the early stages of the opening barrage at 4:25 a.m. the 1st Battery had one gun destroyed by premature. One man was killed and four wounded.

On the wider scene, war historians note of the battle that in spite of flamethrowers and gas, the surviving Canadians had reached their first objective within 20 minutes. By 6:00 a.m., they had crossed the summit of Hill 70, thanks in part to the effectiveness of the diversionary operations of the Fourth Division on their right flank and to the effectiveness of the artillery gun fire (and its new Continuous Wave wireless set). Gunners shot so many rounds they had to pour cold water down the barrels of the guns to cool them off. Some gunners in the artillery were hard hit.

German mustard-gas shells lobbed at the gun positions cost two artillery brigades 178 casualties after gunners had yanked off their masks to see what they were doing. Somehow, the survivors kept the batteries firing.[14]

Casualties were heavy on both sides. During the day, 1,056 Canadians were killed, 2,432 wounded, and 39 taken prisoner.[15]

Sometimes individual courage took charge of a desperate situation. On the second day of the battle, Private Harry Brown of the 10th (Canadian) Battalion was one of two runners who had to weave and bob through an intense barrage to get word back to battalion headquarters after all wires were cut. One runner was immediately killed. Brown's arm was shattered. Nonetheless, he struggled all the way back with the message, falling unconscious on the dugout steps. He later died, receiving the Victoria Cross posthumously.

The 1st Canadian Field Artillery Brigade also suffered casualties. On the 16th, the 3rd Battery had one carriage destroyed by shell fire and five casualties (two fatal). The 4th Battery had four men wounded.

The anticipated German counterattacks intensified, as Currie had predicted. On the night of 17-18 August, Germans shelled batteries of the 1st and 2nd Field Brigades with mustard gas. Some gunners, whose respirator goggles were fogged up by the gas, removed them to maintain their accurate fire. In their dedication, they then became casualties. So did

Sergeant Fred Hobson of the 20th (Central Ontario) Battalion. Not a trained Lewis gunner, he nonetheless saw a Lewis gun whose crew had been put out of action. Though wounded, he ordered a surviving gunner to man the gun while he attacked the enemy singlehandedly with his bayonet. He was shot a second time, but his actions gave others time to man the Lewis gun. He received the Victoria Cross posthumously. (By 21 August, the two artillery brigades suffered 183 casualties from this perdition alone.)

On 18 August, German soldiers carrying bombs, and backed by flamethrowers, attacked a Canadian position. Again, courage raised its noble head. One company Commander, Major O. M. Learmonth, though severely wounded, stood on the parapet leading the defense. Undaunted, he snatched in midair several enemy "bombs" — hand grenades — and threw them back with deadly effect. When he finally fell, unable to continue because of his mortal wounds, he continued to brief his junior officers in the conduct of the battle.

And thus, another Canadian had won the Victoria Cross. In all, five Victoria Crosses were won by Canadians in the capture of Hill 70.

In the final analysis, all 21 counterattacks by the Germans were repulsed by the waiting Canadians in the three-day battle. By now, the 1st, 2nd, and 3rd Batteries of the brigade were being heavily shelled with gas shells. The *War Diary* of August 18 records:

> About 15,000 gas shells of the new type were estimated to have been fired by the enemy. Gunners were firing all the time. Casualties. Evacuated gassed.

Bitter fighting continued in and around enemy strongholds in Lens in the following days. An attack was scheduled for the early morning hours of 21 August, with heavy artillery support, but for some reason the enemy anticipated it. One battalion after another ran into trouble, either from artillery fire from deep cellars or other hidden trenches, or from heavy shellfire. And in spite of the assaults by the Fourth Division on 23 and 24 August, much of the city was still in German hands.

On 24 August, the weather was fair and visibility was good. The 1st CFA Brigade was still at Elvaston Castle, Loos, taking gas precautions. In the early afternoon, men of the 1st Battery worked on registering their guns. Then the 24 August *War Diary* entry tersely, impersonally noted:

2nd Howitzer Battery were heavily shelled between 10am and 3pm and 5 pm and 6pm. About 400 rounds were fired at the position. Two gunpits were hit and two guns destroyed, also about 600 rounds of ammunition. Two men were wounded.

One of them was Gunner Robert James Kennedy.

The 1st Canadian Field Artillery Brigade would continue to hurl harassing fire on the enemy, of course, and its men would continue to serve with distinction. But Robert Kennedy's fighting days on the Front had come to an end, almost three years to the day after he had volunteered to serve. He had already been taken to No. 1 Casualty Clearing Station with a severe shrapnel wound on his left side. He didn't hear about the letter that later came from Canadian Corps Commander Lieutenant General Sir Arthur Currie, congratulating the brigade and its batteries for their excellent work in the recent operations. Kennedy had heard, however, from his sweetheart Eva, now in nursing training in New York City, that she was volunteering for service overseas with the Canadian or American Red Cross.

Before being injured, he had written:

I hope it is the Canadian [*Red Cross*] for I will have a chance of seeing you. . . .

Hill 70, where Kennedy fell, would not change hands again. Though the Canadians had suffered 9,198 casualties in 11 days, they had succeeded in wearing down the enemy, "badly mauled" five German divisions, and caused German Crown Prince Rupprecht serious reinforcement problems.

Robert Kennedy was transferred from the Casualty Clearing Station to St. Omer on 7 September, and thence to England, to a military hospital at Boscombe, Hampshire. He wrote to Eva on 16 September 1917.

The R.M.S. *Saxonia,* which brought the wounded Robert Kennedy back to Canada in October 1917. Ironically, it was the same ship he had boarded in October 1914, only to have to disembark because the ship was overloaded with men and horses. Kennedy sailed to Europe on the *Manitou* instead.

It is ages since I've heard from anyone. I hope by next Sunday I will have received some mail. I wrote to my Battery asking them to forward it. I'm in Boscombe Military Hospital and still in bed though I expect I'll be allowed to get up tomorrow. It will be good to be on one's feet once more.

The people here are awfully good, and do all they can to cheer up the wounded. They lined the streets from the station to the hospital and had a cheer — and gifts of cigarettes, apples, plums and pears and I don't know what else — for every wounded soldier that was carried in.

On 22 September, Kennedy was moved to the Canadian Convalescent Hospital at Bear Wood, Wokingham, Berkshire, until sufficiently well to be sent home to Canada. On 17 November 1917, he sailed from Liverpool on the *Saxonia,* the same ship that he had boarded with his horses in October 1914, only to have to disembark because the ship was overloaded.[16]

NOTES

1. For a thorough view of the role of artillery and technology in the First World War, see Colonel G. W. L. Nicholson, C.D., *The Gunners of Canada: The History of the Royal Regiment of the Canadian Artillery, 1534-1919*, Vol. 1 (Toronto: McClelland and Stewart Limited, 1967; and Bill Rawling, *Surviving Trench Warfare: Technology and the Canadian Corps, 1914-1918* (Toronto: University of Toronto Press, 1992).
2. Erich Marie Remarque, *All Quiet on the Western Front* (Boston: Little, Brown and Co., 1929; New York: A Fawcett Columbine Book, Ballantine Books, 1996), 63.
3. *Ibid.,* 64.
4. Nicholson, *The Gunners of Canada*, 289.
5. Rawling, *Surviving Trench Warfare*, 133-134.
6. Nicholson, *The Gunners of Canada*, 290.
7. *Ibid.*
8. Sometimes infantrymen who had to "go over the top" and face the unknown thought that men in the artillery faced a lesser danger. However, as Denis Winter points out, "aerial photography, flash spotting, and echo location made a distant gun position as vulnerable as a man moving in no-man's land." *Death's Men: Soldiers of the Great War* (London: Penguin Books, 1976), 120.
9. G. W. L. Nicholson, C.D., *Canadian Expeditionary Force 1914-1919: Official History of the Canadian Army in the First World War* (Ottawa: Queen's Printer, 1964), 279.
10. David Lloyd George had become Prime Minister of Great Britain in December 1916, succeeding Herbert Henry Asquith.
11. Not everyone agrees with this assessment. Denis Winter, in *Haig's Command: A Reassessment* (London: Penguin Books, 1991), 96, argues that the "mines laboriously dug were . . . wasted on an almost empty German position" because the Germans had pulled back significant numbers of troops, and that the "much trumpeted victory at Messines was little more than the capture of a few scattered pillboxes."
12. S. L. A. Marshall, *World War I* (Boston: Houghton Mifflin Co., 1992), 301.
13 . *War Diary of the Canadian Field Artillery Brigade*, Vol. 31 (Ottawa: National Archives of Canada).
14. Desmond Morton and J. L. Granatstein, *Marching to Armageddon: Canadians and the Great War 1918-1919* (Toronto: Lester and Orpen Dennys, 1989), 164.
15. Nicholson, *Canadian Expeditionary Force*, 29.
16. Kennedy never spoke of his war service or wounds, though his children later clearly saw the ten-inch scar on his left side when he swam with them in the Ottawa River. He carried a piece of shrapnel in his cheek until the day he died.

*Good God, did we really send men to
fight in that?*
— Lieutenant General Sir Launcelot Kiggell,
    Field Marshal Haig's Chief of Staff

Chapter 21

Gethsemane —
The Flanders Offensive —
The Third Battle of Ypres —
1917

HILE CANADIAN CORPS troops were slugging it out
with the enemy at Lens and Loos, another operation of
far greater consequence was beginning to unfold farther
north with British and ANZAC Divisions. It was the 1917 Flanders Offensive, more commonly known as the Third Battle of Ypres,
also known as Passchendaele — though the Third Battle of Ypres
was really a *campaign* involving eight battles, including Passchendaele.

Perhaps in the summer days of 1917, another major offensive
made sense. Certainly, Field Marshal Haig thought so. For one thing,
he wanted a victory, naturally, to assuage plummeting public opinion
back home. He also said that the French (and especially General
Pétain) wanted a British offensive to divert pressure from them
(though there appears to be no record of this).[1] Certainly there were
concerns about the possible collapse of the French army. Haig also

pointed to the Belgian cities of Ostend and Zeebrugge, noting that the two coastal cities had to be retaken to curtail German submarines operating therefrom. Even British Admiral Sir John R. Jellicoe, who wanted to capture the German U-boat bases in Belgium, was recruited to aid Haig's argument. Jellicoe noted that if the army could not get the Belgian ports, the navy could not hold the Channel and the war was as good as lost. Furthermore, Haig felt that this was his last chance for a single-handed victory before the Americans launched their first major offensive. Besides, he insisted, the German collapse could come at any moment.

But the Ypres area had some deadly drawbacks. Troops would again be fighting on waterlogged land that was once a swamp. It had become habitable only because it had been drained through the centuries by ditches, dikes, and canals. (Ypres itself had once been a seaport, and was an inland city now only because of the massive drainage system.) The water table was so high that one had only to dig a foot or two before hitting water. Wouldn't artillery bombardment simply liquefy the already saturated ground? More than four-million shells had already been lobbed on the enemy in a deadly foretaste of things to come.

And there was another problem, according to writer Leon Wolff:

> Everywhere by 1917 the water was contaminated, and the delivery of fresh water was a major operation. The filthy surface wash was locked in by the clay. Rivers and canals were polluted by refuse from the flooded land, and even the artesian wells became poisoned. The decay and refuse of millions of men, alive and dead, sank into the soil . . .[2]

Many warned of the diabolical hazards of the mud, including Marshal Foch, the French Commander-in-Chief, and Britain's own tank Commanders. One tank Commander called Flanders the "most unsuitable spot" between the English Channel and Switzerland.

But no one seemed to listen; the campaign would go on. And the Germans, well aware of the coming offensive, prepared accordingly. They constructed even more concrete pillboxes in a checkerboard layout near the front lines to cut down assaulting troops. They also moved up reserves. Furthermore, in Galicia, the Russian Eleventh Army had suffered an "overwhelming catastrophe," and for all intents and purposes, the war on the Eastern Front had ended. Masses of German troops were thus now available for the Western Front.

And so, the inevitable "softening up" bombardment by the Allies began on 16 July, and more than 100,000 tons of shells were hurled at the bogs and swamps of Ypres. The already tortured ground was churned once more into dark, dank, repugnant slush with a consistency that many soldiers compared to rotting porridge.

At daybreak on the last day of July 1917, the third battle of Ypres began.

The few tanks in use immediately came under heavy fire, but worse yet, couldn't achieve any speed in the gummy mud. At best, they rumbled and clanked along like giant slugs at about a mile an hour. The infantry soon outdistanced them, as one tank after another bogged down in the mud. Soon, abandoned tanks were everywhere, stranded helplessly. Crews who tried to escape from them were mowed down immediately by machine-gun fire.

In another disastrous development, the British artillery, right on schedule, lifted its rolling barrage to the second, then third objective, supposing — wrongly — that their own infantrymen were following closely behind the barrage. But telephone lines had been mangled by enemy fire, and wireless instruments were dead. With only runners and carrier pigeons available to carry messages, there was no way for the artillery to know that the infantry hadn't been able to keep up behind the creeping barrage. They were still back at the first objective, now totally bereft of their own artillery support.

Yet some progress was made by both French and British troops. By 2 August, Pilckem Ridge was captured.

Nineteen miles west of Ypres, in his railway coach that served as his headquarters, Field Marshal Haig was cheered by the modest success, even though it had cost 31,850 casualties for a gain of about 3,000 yards.[3] Back in London, newspapers hailed the victory in the Battle of Pilckem Ridge. So did the Germans!

Both sides then took time out from the madness to bury their dead, and to mercifully kill some of the horses still screaming in pain from their gaping wounds and shattered legs.

<hr />

During that first week of August of 1917, what most people had once thought would be a "short" war now entered its fourth grotesque year. But sentiment was changing, and people on all home fronts had become deeply concerned about the escalating lists of casualties. Ground gained in one day, with incalculable losses, was often lost the next. Victories announced in the media one week were often suspect the next when casualty figures began to come in. Why, in spite of all the grief and suffering, was there still no clear indication of ultimate victory? Why continue in such wretched weather? (It was the wettest August in 30 years.) And why would Field Marshal Haig want to continue in the saturated mud, which sucked the boots off the soldiers' feet and devoured men and mules and guns that slipped into shell holes?

Haig, however, insisted that Germany was weakening. Whether he was an eternal optimist, misguided, prideful, or merely stubborn, is for others to determine. Whatever the case, he continued to argue that victory was just around the next corner, the next battlefield, or just after the next offensive. After all, he insisted, the enemy was demoralized, and "tottering."

The weather cleared briefly in mid-August and dispatches from the Front had a decidedly positive spin on the progress being made. But in spite of the sanguine reports in the newspapers, General Gough's Fifth Army was becoming badly bogged down in the almost liquid mud. And by the end of August, British forces had suffered 68,000 casualties, including 3,400 officers.[4] But Germany had also paid a heavy price, using 17 divisions in the carnage, and causing General Ludendorff to say that German losses exceeded all expectations.

Meanwhile, as August bled into September, British General Herbert Plumer and his Second Army (with the stalwart help of ANZAC forces) made some progress, though the mud and rain were almost as loathsome as the enemy guns.

Teams of little donkeys hauled at the guns and wagons, their dainty hoofs slipping in the slime. Uncomprehendingly they labored in the din, ears flapping and sad of eye, and seemed to wonder (like many a soldier) what they had done to deserve their fate.[5]

Troops grimly plodded on. By 20 September, with the help of a massive artillery barrage, they succeeded in gaining about half a mile of mud in the Battle of Menin Road.

It, too, was hailed as a victory. But objectives that were to have been reached back on the opening day of the campaign, 31 July, still were not taken. Field Marshal Haig was more anxious than ever to press on.

But not everyone was convinced. Back in London, Prime Minister David Lloyd George was not terribly impressed with Haig's rationale, and their relationship grew more acrimonious daily. Lloyd George argued against continuing the offensive this late in the year. "Blood and mud," he kept repeating. "Blood and mud!"

At one point, Haig told the Prime Minister that Germany had expended all its best soldiers and was now forced to rely on old men and boys. Lloyd George, unbelieving, asked to see them. Haig immediately forewarned the compound that the Prime Minister was about to visit it, and ordered that all healthy-looking German prisoners be removed. The surreptitious effort worked.[6]

And so, the 1917 Flanders Offensive and its several battles continued into late September and early October. Finally, on 4 October, British and ANZAC troops, in spite of torrents of rain, grabbed the main ridge east of Ypres. Although the yardage gained wasn't exactly spectacular, several towns, including Gravenstafel and Poelcappelle, were captured. The British had taken more than 20,000 prisoners. General Plumer called it the greatest victory since the Marne. The Germans called it a black day.

In a way, it was a turning point because Germany suffered losses it could no longer afford. Furthermore, Americans would soon be entering the picture with fresh troops. In fact, American destroyers were now plying European waters, but her army troops were not yet sufficiently trained for combat.

Still it rained, as though the heavens themselves wept at the pain and carnage below, where wounded men lay in the mud, soaked to the skin, waiting to be helped or to die; where horse-drawn ambulances slithered into the mud, sometimes dumping their wounded troops; where men and mules slipped off the duckboards into the treacherous slime, sometimes forever.

Sometimes, men struggling to crawl back to their own lines quietly bled to death en route. And sometimes, for a laboring horse hit in the leg by shrapnel, the only recourse would be to shoot the poor creature and shove it off the road.

Passchendaele — The Tragic Victory

By now, even Gough and Plumer, the two most senior British Commanders, had more than enough and wanted to halt the madness in the mud. On 7 October, they tried to persuade their Commander-in-Chief to call off the campaign for the winter. The stubborn Haig refused. He wanted the Passchendaele-Westroosebeke part of the ridge so that his troops would be on higher, drier ground for the season.

The weather deteriorated on 8 October, as the morning sun gave way to clouds. By afternoon, a strong icy wind whipped across the muddy fields, and torrential rains turned the battlefield into a morass.

No matter. Not only would the battle continue, but Haig had another great idea. He would send for the Canadians, still 30 miles or so to the south. So anxious was Haig for the Canadian Corps that he went so far as to personally visit Lieutenant General Currie, who was now being recognized as one of the most competent Commanders in the British army.

Currie was more than reluctant to take his troops to the swamps of Passchendaele. "Let the Germans have it, keep it — rot in it." he argued. "It isn't worth a drop of blood."

But Haig said mysteriously to Currie, "Someday I will tell you why Passchendaele must be taken." The mysterious secret was simply that Haig felt the French army was on the verge of collapse and that an Allied victory was therefore imperative.[7]

And so the Canadian Corps received orders to transfer from the First Army to the Second Army, under General Plumer.

There is some evidence that Haig at one point planned to transfer Currie and his Canadians, then serving with the British First Army, to General Gough and his Fifth Army, but Currie, having lost confidence in Gough at the Somme, preferred to serve with the more competent General Plumer.

While the Canadians prepared to move north, the next battle opened on 9 October, using the same pattern of attack, with the artillery, in the softening-up process, theoretically immobilizing the enemy by cutting his wire entanglements, knocking out machine-gun posts, and generally stunning the German troops long enough to prevent immediate retaliation.

But many of the Allied high-explosive shells merely plopped in the deep mud with muted results. Some even failed to detonate. And wave after wave of British and ANZAC soldiers sank, bullet-ridden, into the vile ooze. "Often a man was indistinguishable from the mud — unless he moved. Many drowned in the mud."[8]

Even behind the line, the scene could have been from Dante's Hell, with dead and dying men and horses lying where they fell, and stranded and broken wagons and ammunition shell casings scattered in chaos. Gunners, some stripped to the waist even in the cold wind, still valiantly fired their armament.

By the end of that October day, for all the valor and casualties, the gain was about 500 yards of muddy No Man's Land. And still the Third Battle of Ypres was not over.

With the rain pelting in almost Biblical proportions, and the battlefield nothing more than a defiled swamp, many Allied Commanders began to give vent to their concerns. A New Zealand Brigadier complained that senior Generals were not familiar with the muddy conditions of the battlefield, the treacherous duckboards, the exhausted horses and mules, and the wet, weary, and, in some cases, demoralized troops, more and more of whom were now debilitated by trench foot, dysentery, and influenza. But Haig, apparently believing that God was at his side, was still not ready to halt the Flanders offensive.

Once again, this time on 12 October, troops from two British Divisions and one Australian were sent forward to fight in pitiful conditions. And once again losses were heavy. In one attack — the Battle of Poelcappelle — the three divisions suffered nearly 7,000 casualties. In another assault, on 12 October, the 2nd ANZAC Corps ran into unforeseen bolts of wire, but nonetheless got within 2,500 yards of the badly battered village of Passchendaele. German casualties were also high and, by 12 October, General Ludendorff was diverting 12 German Divisions en route to the Italian Front to Flanders.

Though British progress was limited, Haig had not despaired. He wanted to press on but finally agreed, somewhat reluctantly, to a delay of further attacks until new roads could be constructed in order to bring forward more artillery.

By 18 October, the Canadians had moved north and were relieving the 2nd ANZAC Corps on the front line. In a strange twist of irony, the front line was almost the same line that the Allies had held before the infamous gas attack so many deadly months and battles before, in April of 1915. But there were differences now. Many of the old landmarks — woods, houses, and even villages — were obliterated.

Lieutenant General Currie, whose painstaking preparation had helped take Vimy Ridge in April 1915, was concerned by what he saw. He noted in his diary, on 17 October, that the battlefield looked bad: "No salvaging has been done and very few of the dead buried."[9] Nevertheless, the methodical General set about his meticulous planning.

Sappers, engineers, and pioneers began the difficult process of constructing roads on the sodden ground, many of which consisted of planks of elm or beech stretched across other planks, wood rails, or rims running along the edges of the "road." Battery positions were built or repaired. And Currie, through liaison with the Australian Corps, advance parties, observation positions, and other Intelligence, quietly gathered all possible information about the German defenses.

Currie would once again rely on the artillery to set the stage for victory. Therefore, to the artillery would fall the responsibility for destroying the enemy's wire, disrupting his defenses, and demolishing his artillery fire. To the artillery would devolve the critical onus of a perfectly timed rolling barrage just in front of the attacking Canadian troops. As one Commander noted, Currie "consistently sought to pay the price of victory in shells and not in the lives of men."[10]

Field Marshal Haig had hoped that the Canadians could take the area around Passchendaele in three separate attacks. Currie, accordingly, planned the first one for 26 October, using his Third and Fourth Divisions (with the First and Second in reserve). But getting the men to the front line proved to be a terrible ordeal, as both men and pack animals would slip off the wet duckboards into the suffocating mud. Nor were the duckways easy to find and follow. They frequently wound around shell holes and more often than not were submerged under water or mud.

Every day, 15 to 20 horses had to be hauled out of water-filled

Mud and Germain-laid wire, through which the Canadians had to advance during the Battle of Passchendaele, Belgium, November 1917. *National Archives of Canada, PA 002167*

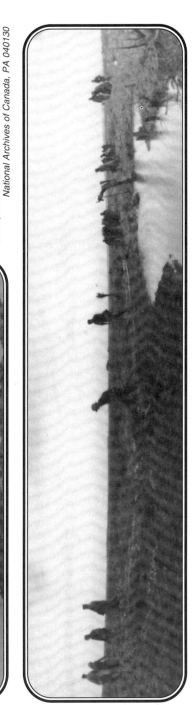

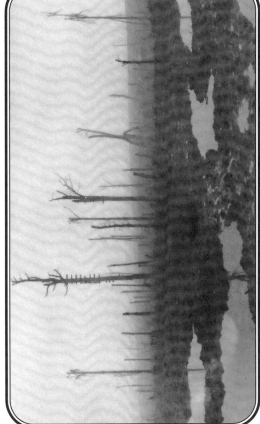

Left: Passchendaele, Belgium, a devastated field of mud in November 1917.
National Archives of Canada, PA 040140

Below: German prisoners and wounded captured by Canadians in the Battle of Passchendaele, November 1917.
National Archives of Canada, PA 040130

shell-holes into which they had fallen; and many of these had to be shot.[11]

The attack by the two divisions went on as scheduled in a wet morning mist that turned into an all-day rain. In spite of the wretched weather, boys of the 52nd (New Ontario) Battalion overtook the German line that had stopped the ANZAC Corps on 5 and 20 October, and took Bellevue and Laamkeek.[12]

Off to their right, the 46th (South Saskatchewan) Battalion of the Fourth Division, along with an Australian battalion, quickly took their objectives on the Passchendaele Road, slogging forward behind the timed barrage that lifted and moved forward 50 yards every four minutes. Battalions of the Third Division, however, managed to struggle through enemy wire only to encounter massive artillery fire. They had to fall back.

Ultimately, Decline Copse, the objective of the Fourth Canadian and 1st Australian Divisions, had to be abandoned. And it was only the determined grenade and bayonet skirmishes of the 44th (Manitoba) and 85th (Nova Scotia Highlanders) Battalions that kept the German forces from recovering lost ground.

The first Canadian assault, therefore, was not entirely successful. And they had suffered another 2,481 casualties in the three days from 26 through 28 October. The troops would have to regroup and prepare for the next assault.

The second of the step-by-step assaults by Currie's forces began in the early morning hours (5:50 a.m.) of 30 October, with the deafening thunder of the Canadian guns and howitzers. By the time the German artillery responded eight minutes later, the troops of the Third and Fourth Divisions had begun to push toward their next objectives.

In the Fourth Division advance, the 85th (Nova Scotia Highlanders) Battalion, though losing half its men, quickly captured enemy strong points. To add insult to injury, the Highlanders used the newly captured machine guns to fire on the retreating Germans. The 78th (Winnipeg Grenadiers) Battalion likewise took its objective, while the 72nd (Seaforth Highlanders of Canada) Battalion captured Crest Farm and, for good measure, sent several patrols into Passchendaele itself.

Meanwhile in the Third Division, the PPCLI had overtaken a nettlesome German pillbox, "Snipe Hall," but was experiencing devastating losses in the process. Nearly all their junior officers were killed by gun fire from hidden enemy machine-gun posts. Casualties also wracked the 49th (Edmonton Regiment), though they succeeded in taking Furst Farm.

As the day wore on and the cold October winds whipped up rain, one battalion after another distinguished itself, and one soldier after another fought with incredible courage.[13] But the casualties mounted for every yard of ground gained. When the day ended, the Canadian Corps had gained about a thousand yards across a 2,800-yard front. But they paid for their success dearly, with 884 killed, 1,429 wounded (including 130 gassed), and 8 taken prisoner of war.

One of those killed was Talbot Papineau, the promising young man from the prominent French-Canadian family of Montreal. Many had believed he would someday be the Prime Minister of Canada, and one of the few seen capable of bringing the two pioneering peoples of Canada together. His body was never found.[14]

Bloodied October of 1917 became November, and it was time to relieve the exhausted troops of the Third and Fourth Division. Accordingly, men of the veteran First and Second Canadian Divisions were moved by rail to an area near Cassel to prepare once more for battle. It would be their role to fully secure the almost-destroyed village of Passchendaele, whose very name was to become synonymous with black-bordered futility and loss. And after four days, they would also be called on to take the crest of the main ridge.

By the morning of 5 November, the relief movements had been accomplished, and on the night of the same day, assault troops moved forward to their jump-off positions. Early the next morning, 6 November, the earth-shattering barrage marked the start of the fateful assault. With Currie's emphasis on training and split-second timing, the troops swarmed forward. Anxious men followed their own artillery's barrage so expertly that "in most cases the Germans could not man their machine-guns before the attackers were on top of them."[15] The elusive village of Passchendaele fell into Canadian hands — specifically the hands of the 27th (City of Winnipeg) Battalion of the Second Division — in less than three hours. And yet another Victoria Cross went to a Canadian soldier, this time to Private J. P. Robertson, who wiped out an enemy post, allowing his platoon to advance into Passchendaele.

As always, the day's success was not without cost. This time, the divisions had lost 2,238 men, including 734 killed or mortally wounded.

Still, a defiant part of the high ground north of Passchendaele, near Vindictive Crossroads and Hill 52, remained to be taken. And Currie, hardly pausing to relish the success at Passchendaele, scheduled the next battle for 10 November. Like so many others before it, it was carried out in heavy rain. And, as in countless times before, troops of the First and Second Divisions[16] plodded through the swampy ground and relentless fire toward their objective, with rain running down their helmets and dripping off their noses. On their left, the First British Division ran into heavy enemy fire and had to withdraw. Some ground, in the form of shell-holes and trenches, was gained and held, but another 1,094 men were lost, including 420 killed.[17]

On 10 November, in wretched weather that saw the cold rain turning to sleet and ice, the Third Battle of Ypres finally limped to an end — about five miles from whence it had started. For the Canadians, a few square miles of mud had been purchased at the cost of 16,404 casualties.

In less than a week, the weary Canadians were being relieved and en route back to the Lens-Arras sector.

It was after the battles were over, that Field Marshal Haig's Chief of Staff, Lieutenant General Sir Launcelot Kiggell made his first visit to the ungodly battlefield. As his staff car inched and slid through the mud, he was overcome by the incredible desolation around him and asked through tears, "Good God, did we really send men to fight in that?" Came the subdued answer, "It's much worse up ahead."[18]

Had the Third Battle of Ypres been the success that Haig had so fervently anticipated?

Many at the time, including Prime Minister Lloyd George, thought not. Certainly the Allies made no breakthrough, as Haig had promised. Winston Churchill called the Battle "a forlorn expenditure of valour and life without equal in futility." The eminent historian B. H. Liddell Hart claimed that it was "so fruitless in its results" that Passchendaele became "a synonym for military failure — a name black-bordered in the records of the British Army."[19] From the advantage point of history, S. L. A. Marshall contends that "not one thing of importance had been achieved" at a cost to Britain and her dominions of 244,897 men, for an advancement of 9,000 yards of marshland.[20] Historian A. J. P. Taylor called the offense at Passchendaele "the blindest slaughter of a blind war."[21] John Laffin, citing 250,000 or more British and Empire casualties for a five-mile advance of no strategic importance called it a "military crime."[22]

On the other hand, the Germans had suffered considerable attrition. German losses were originally listed at about 200,000 but later revised upwards. (Both German and Allied figures are still contentious.[23]) But Germany still held the Belgium ports of Ostend and Zeebrugge. And in spite of Field Marshal Haig's repeated musings, they were not on the verge of collapse, though their morale was indeed affected.

At least one historian, Colonel G. W. L. Nicholson, however, thought the campaign accomplished something.

> The Somme, costly as it was to the Allies, began the destruction of the German Army. Passchendaele carried the process a long step forward.[24]

NOTES

1. General Robert Georges Nivelle, who had flashed across the French military landscape after the Verdun ordeal, had by now flamed out like a nova, and had been replaced by General Henri-Philippe Pétain, on 15 May 1917.
2. Leon Wolff, *In Flanders Fields: The 1917 Campaign* (New York: Ballantine Books, 1958), 83.
3. Colonel G. W. L. Nicholson, C.D., *Canadian Expeditionary Force 1914-1919, Official History of the Canadian Army in the First World War* (Ottawa: Queens Printer, 1964), 307.
4. *Ibid.*, 308.
5. Wolff, *In Flanders Fields*, 164.
6. *Ibid.*, 169; and A. J. P. Taylor, *The First World War: An Illustrated History* (Hammondsworth, England: Penguin Books Ltd., 1963), 192.
7. Recounted in Sandra Gwyn, *Tapestry of War: A Private View of Canadians in the Great War* (Toronto: Harper Collins Publishers Ltd., 1992), 395.
8. John Laffin, *British Butchers and Bunglers of World War One* (Phoenix Mill, Great Britain: Sutton Publishing, 1989), 115-116.

9. Nicholson, *Canadian Expeditionary Force*, 313.

10. *Ibid.*, 315.

11. Colonel G. W. L. Nicholson, C.D., *The Gunners of Canada: The History of the Royal Regiment of the Canadian Artillery, 1534-1919*, Vol. 3 (Toronto: McClelland and Stewart Limited, 1967), 309.

12. Three more Victoria Crosses were won by men of the Third Division in the assault: Lieutenant Shankland, Captain C. P. J. O'Kelly, and Private T. W. Holmes.

13. Three Victoria Crosses were awarded to Canadians that day: Lieutenant Hugh Mackenzie of the PPCLI; Sergeant G. H. Mullin, an American regimental sniper; and Major G. R. Pearkes, a company Commander.

14. His name is among the thousands listed on the Menin Gate at Ypres, where the Last Post is sounded every night at eight o'clock.

15. Nicholson, *Canadian Expeditionary Force*, 324.

16. For the record, they were the 7th (1st British Columbia Regiment), 8th (90th Rifles), 10th (Canadians), and 20th (Central Ontario) Battalions.

17. Nicholson, *Canadian Expeditionary Force*, 326.

18. Wolff, *In Flanders Fields*.

19. B. H. Liddell Hart, *History of the First World War* (London: Macmillan Publishers, 1997), 327; originally published as *The Real War, 1914-1918* (Boston: Little, Brown and Co., 1930).

20. S. L. A. Marshal, *World War I* (Boston: Houghton Mifflin Co., 1992), 105.

21. A. J. P. Taylor, *The First World War: An Illustrated History* (Hammondsworth, England: Penguin Books Ltd., 1963), 194.

22. Laffin, *British Butchers and Bunglers*, 118-120.

23. Martin Gilbert puts German losses (dead and wounded) at 400,000, approximately twice that of Britain. *The First World War: A Complete History*, 2nd ed. (New York : Henry Holt and Co., 1994), 365.

24. Nicholson, *Candadian Expeditionary Force*, 330.

Oh whither are you gone, my company?
— British Poet Herbert Read, an infantry
man who served three years in the trenches

Chapter 22

Cambrai and the Armada of Tanks

*A*S THE COLD NOVEMBER winds whipped across the
face of Europe, and the reality of facing a fourth winter
of war set in, there were misgivings everywhere. Though
the Canadians had taken what was once the insignificant village of
Passchendaele, the cost to them and the Allies had been ungodly.
And now there was deep and growing reluctance within Canada to
serve in the distant war that still seemed to have no end in sight.

There were some bright spots, however. The convoy system
seemed to be working well, and Allied shipping losses were lessening.[1] November saw the smallest number of casualties of the year,
with 126 ships being destroyed. (However, from February to December 1917, subs had sunk 2,966 Allied and neutral ships.) Furthermore, the Americans were finally coming, though they, like the
Canadians before them, were having some trouble in the logistics of
getting men and matériel overseas. But General John J. Pershing was
pushing ahead.[2]

It seemed a good time to call a halt to the offensive. It seemed a good time to give the battle-weary troops time to rest and rehabilitate, while they waited for their American colleagues — and Spring.

It was not to be. There was yet one more battle to be joined on the Western Front in 1917. But this one would feature two surprises for the enemy — seemingly limitless tanks and no advance bombardment. Although some Germans had already experienced the tank, this time a *massive* array of hundreds of the vehicles would lead the assault. And this time there would be no preliminary artillery bombardment to betray the forthcoming attack. A bombardment wouldn't really be needed anyway, because the truculent tanks could simply roll over and destroy the barbed wire, allowing the troops to follow behind.

On 20 November 1917, more than 300 mechanical monsters rumbled forward.[3] On their noses they carried huge bundles of wood, or fascines, which could be used to fill in trenches and ditches, enabling the tanks to more readily pass over. Their objective was the city of Cambrai, about 40 miles southeast of Passchendaele.

In no time at all the lumbering giants crushed the German barbed wire and broke through their front line in a six-mile-wide swath, heading for Cambrai. Troops just behind the tanks surged forward as many Germans, seeing the behemoths bearing down on them, initially fled backwards in holy terror. Victory seemed assured!

Though most Canadian troops had already been moved south for a respite in the winter fighting, some remained behind, and the Canadian Cavalry Brigade (as part of the Fifth Cavalry Division) was by sheer determination about to get closer to Cambrai than anyone else in the assault that day. In a sequence of events worthy of a Hollywood script, their day had started in the early morning darkness when they marched to an assembly area in Dessart Wood, five miles from the Front, to meet the Royal Canadian Horse Artillery. Just before noon, they were ordered to advance toward the St. Quentin Canal, about nine miles away, where an enemy bridgehead had been taken.

The bridgehead had, in fact, not been taken, but the Fort Garry Horse unit, with the help of local inhabitants, managed to cross the canal anyway. By late afternoon, "B" Squadron had galloped ahead, capturing a German engineer staff. In the scuffle, however, several, including their squadron Commander, were hit by machine-gun fire and killed. Still they charged forward, sabers drawn. Suddenly they came upon a German machine-gun battery firing from a sunken road. There seemed no possible escape, until in a flash of quick thinking, their new leader, Lieutenant Harcus Strachan, had the men dismount and stampede their gallant horses toward the German lines. The squadron, greatly reduced in number, then fought its way back to Masnieres. Strachan won the Victoria Cross for his intrepid leadership that afternoon.

By the end of the first day, there was cause for celebration on the Allied side of the line. Much ground, nearly five miles, had been taken. There was a great hole in the German front lines. The Allies had taken 4,000 prisoners. At last, it seemed that 1917 would end with clear victory.

But only the day was over, not the battle. As the hostilities continued the next day, some of the tanks broke down. And the Germans, recovering from their initial shock, began to fight back. By the following day, the Germans had rushed in troops that had returned from the Russian Front. By the 23rd, the British advance was halted at Bourlon Wood. Field Marshal Haig and Lieutenant General Byng, who had counted on a relatively brief attack, had no reserve troops to call on. Too many had already been slaughtered or wounded at Passchendaele.[4]

In an ironical sense of timing, bells rang out triumphantly in Britain to proclaim victory at Cambrai. It was the first time in three years that their sounds had been heard, because pealing bells had been reserved as the warning signal for a German invasion of Britain. But they were rung prematurely. The fighting was not yet over. Victory was not assured. And there was more slaughter to come.

In one instance on 23 November, three Irish battalions managed to drive most of the Germans out of the village of Moevres, but in the process one of their companies was pinned down by German machine-gun fire. Suddenly, overhead, a Royal Flying Corps pilot saw their predicament, and dove straight in to attack the German strongpoint. Though saving them, he was shot down and killed outright. Saddened, the Irish lads remembered the brave but unknown pilot, and ran an "In Memoriam" column in *The Times* of London. It was later learned that he was an American volunteer, Lieutenant A. Griggs, flying with No. 68 (Australian) Squadron.[5]

By 27 November, a week after the battle began, still more tanks had broken down. Some that reached Fontaine were caught awkwardly in the narrow streets (as Colonel Ernest D. Swinton had warned), unable to maneuver. And the Germans had made a new discovery. They learned that although individual grenades tossed on or near the tanks were ineffective, several tied together and thrown under the tanks could bring deadly results.

Halfway to Cambrai, near Flesquieres, the Allied attack faltered. Then the British were forced to halt. Cambrai was not taken.

But now the Germans faced a problem. Undernourished German soldiers, who had pushed the British troops back, were torn between pursuing the enemy or stopping in their tracks to gulp down the food and rum left behind by the British. Many ravenous soldiers succumbed to the temptation and stopped to fill their rumbling stomachs.

It took another week for the battle of Cambrai to peter out.

How successful was it? For the Allies it was like trading a dull nickel for four shiny pennies. On one hand, more ground had been taken by the Allies at Cambrai in six hours than in the whole third Ypres campaign. It had shaken German General Erich Ludendorff to the core. But British momentum had been lost as tanks faltered, more from mechanical failure than from enemy guns. Consequently, the Cambrai attack fizzled out. By 30 November, the Germans, in a massive counterattack, regained most of the ground taken from them just ten days before. The British and Canadians counted 44,000 dead and wounded. They also lost 166 guns and 300 tanks. The Germans suffered about 53,000 losses and the loss of 142 guns.

The stalemate continued.

Other Disturbing Developments in Late 1917

The year 1917 was still not content to fade into history. There were still more heartbreaking events to unfold in various parts of the world, some far from foreign battlefields.

Back in the Halifax (Nova Scotia) harbor, a French merchant ship, the *Mont Blanc*, collided with a Belgian ship on 6 December. The French ship, bound for Europe, was loaded with supplies and munitions. The resulting explosion almost blew the quiet Maritime Province city off the map. More than 1,600 were killed and thousands more injured.

And now there were some compelling new statistics being discussed in Canada. Casualties in the Canadian Corps were outnumbering voluntary enlistments by two to one: 23,939 casualties in April and May, compared with 11,790 enlistments.[6]

On the wider scene, the news was equally depressing as Christmas approached. Although there were reports that thousands were dying of starvation in Germany, there was still no hint of any Allied victory. Russia had been defeated and was out of the picture. Romania had long since fallen, in December 1916. Serbia and Montenegro no longer existed. Italy was defeated. Britain and France were exhausted.

In late December 1917, Winston Churchill, as Minister of Munitions, after serving on the front line in France in 1915, personified the weariness of the nation as he wrote to a friend:

> Thank God our offensives are at an end . . . . Let them rejoice
> in the occasional capture of placeless names and sterile ridges.[7]

To be sure, there were a few bright spots. The British had taken Jerusalem from the Turks. By now about a quarter of a million Americans had landed in France, although they were, understandably, not yet fully trained. Indeed, some of them had been drilling with broomsticks. Even the American ships were in short supply, and more than 50 percent of the troops had to reach France on British ships.[8]

Germany, of course, wanted to finish off the war before the fresh American forces could tilt the odds away from the Central Powers. With Russia out of the picture, such a prospect might finally be possible, and German troop trains began to arrive from the Eastern Front, disgorging troops by the thousands to replace the casualties on the West.

But all was not well with Germany and her allies either. Though they were amassing a million troops at various fronts, most were malnourished and poorly clothed. Even the reserves were in poor physical condition due to malnutrition. More than 70,000 horses had died for lack of food, and countless others had to be sold to butchers. Civilians were also suffering. There were food riots in Vienna and Budapest.

German General Ludendorff pondered the situation. The war must end! He would have to chase the British army back to the Channel, forcing them back to England via the Channel ports. Then he could demolish France once and for all, before the Americans could interfere. He would do so in the operation code-named "Michael."

In the meantime, battle-weary troops on both sides of No Man's Land dug in for another winter of discomfort and discontent. The nightly raids would continue on both sides. So would the casualties. The Canadians would see another 3,552 — 684 of them fatal — before the first day of Spring in 1918.[9]

NOTES

1. Holger H. Herwig offers several insights into the causes for the lessening effect and ultimate failure of the U-boat campaign. He suggests that the Germans did not foresee several factors, including the U.S. shipbuilding potential; England's decision to turn grassland into grain-producing areas; the grain reserves in 1916 in Australia, Canada, South America, and the USA; the British ability to keep its coal mines open with wood from their own forests; and, of course, the successful convoy system. He also notes that Germany was hampered by the lack of U-boats, with only one-third of them in the war zone at any one time, while the other two-thirds were in Germany for repair or en route to or from the war zone. *The First World War: Germany and Austria Hungary 1914-1918* (London: Arnold, 1997), 318-319.

2. Martin Gilbert notes that by November 1917, it was becoming clear that Pershing's hope of having a million armed Americans in Europe by the summer of 1918 was nowhere near realization. The number had been reduced to 525,000 for May. *The First World War: A Complete History*, 2nd ed. (New York: Henry Holt and Co., 1994), 378.

3. The actual number seems obscure. B. H. Liddell Hart and A. J. P. Taylor list 381 tanks; Ian V. Hogg lists 330; and Martin Gilbert gives the figures as 324. B. H. Liddell Hart, *History of the First World War* (London: Macmillan Publishers, 1997), originally published as *The Real War, 1914-1918* (Boston: Little, Brown and Co., 1930); A. J. P. Taylor, *The First World War: An Illustrated History* (Hammondsworth, England: Penguin Books, Ltd. 1963); Gilbert, *The First World War*.

4. Haig critic Denis Winter faults Haig's decision to launch an offensive at Cambrai with a division so badly wounded at Passchendaele, noting that the 29th British Division had "marched ten miles the night before, in full battle order, then another three miles at dawn, just before the attack. They were exhausted before the first shot was fired." *Haig's Command: A Reassessment* (London: Penguin Books, 1991), 122.

5. Gilbert, *The First World War*, 380-381.

6. Colonel G. W. L. Nicholson, C.D., *Canadian Expeditionary Force 1914-1919: History of the Canadian Army in the First World War* (Ottawa: Queen's Printer, 1964), 344.

7. Gilbert, *The First World War*, 389.

8. S. L. A. Marshall, *World War I* (Boston: Houghton Mifflin Co., 1992), 338.
9. Nicholson, *Canadian Expeditionary Force*, 339.

The battle won, the English utterly defeated.
— German Kaiser Wilhelm II,
23 March 1918

Chapter 23

The Winter of Discontent —
1918

CRISIS. EXHAUSTION. DESPAIR.
These were the prevailing feelings, indeed realities, for many leaders both political and military in the Allied camp as 1918 dawned.

It had been a long, ungodly war, and there was still no end in sight. In spite of 40 months of savage warfare and millions of casualties on both sides, the opposing forces still grimly faced each other on the snake-like scar that stretched from the English Channel to the Swiss border. The trench lines were pretty much as they had been in late 1914.

France, holding the greater part of the Allied front line, had suffered losses without surcease, and still hadn't recovered from the human hemorrhage at Verdun. Some soldiers mutinied.

Britain's bloodied efforts on the Somme in 1916 and her protracted battles in Flanders in 1917 had long since depleted, indeed decimated, her armies. Conscripts were replacing the volunteers, who had in turn replaced the original professional soldiers. British shipping losses had been staggering.

Russia was out of the war, thus giving Germany, at least temporarily, numerical superiority. Germany was now able to transfer troops from Italy and the East, trainload after trainload, to the Western Front.

In Canada, the Military Services Act, which had authorized conscription, sadly caused increasing divisions between English- and French-speaking Canadians. Yet Canada had become more mature and self-assured as the war went on, particularly after her soldiers had performed so well at Ypres in the first gas attack of the war, and later at Vimy Ridge. Prime Minister Robert Borden by now had become distressed that his government knew only what it read in the press:

> It can hardly be expected that [*Canada*] shall put 400,000 or 500,000 men in the field and willingly accept the position of having no more voice and receiving no more consideration than if we were toy automata.[1]

Canada also lost one of its most eloquent soldiers. On 28 January 1918, in a military hospital at Wimereux, on the west coast of France, Lieutenant Colonel John McCrae died of pneumonia and meningitis. He had just been appointed consulting physician to the British First Army, the first Canadian to be so honored.[2]

By now, there was also some degree of friction on the Allied side.[3] There was no single overall leader in charge of Allied operations. Unity of command was still to be realized. It would be several months before French Marshal Ferdinand Foch became Commander-in-Chief of all Allied forces (except the Belgians). Field Marshal Haig still commanded the British and Commonwealth troops, and Prime Minister Lloyd George had become increasingly reluctant to give him more, in light of the extraordinary losses in the swamps of Ypres and Passchendaele.

But dissent and disillusionment were not the exclusive properties of the Allies. In Germany there was unrest as well. Both soldiers and civilians had suffered deprivation of colossal proportions, though the citizenry was comforted a bit by news of the end of the war on the Eastern Front. Furthermore, there was the increasing hope that Germany would be triumphant before the American troops would be battle-ready.

For both the Allies and the Central Powers the question was "What will happen next?"

. became obvious to the Allies that one major conclusion could be drawn — Germany was in a position to take the offensive again. *But where?*

On the other side of No Man's Land, General Ludendorff himself was pondering the same question. He had ruled out a second major assault on the Verdun area; the terrain was too rough, and there was no great strategic value there. Flanders was still a possibility, because of its proximity to the Channel ports. But, then again, it would be a sea of mud until midsummer. He looked at the Somme. Now, *that* had possibilities. Though there was nothing of critical strategic value in the area, the stubborn British were there. If they were defeated, the French would collapse.

And so the die was cast. But he would have to move quickly! Uncle Sam was now flexing his muscles to the martial music of John Phillip Sousa. It must all be over before the Americans could tip the scale.

Meanwhile, there was a brief glimmer of hope for peace when President Woodrow Wilson announced his Fourteen Points peace proposal on 8 January. The world listened . . . but the amassing of troops and armaments went on. Lives continued to be lost. And on 18 January, a full American Division entered the front line in the St. Mihiel Salient. Though there were no offensives in the sector at that time, it gave the new Yankee troops some firsthand experience in holding the line.

And, at this same time, even with the German U-boat campaign now held in check, there were still losses at sea, one of which occurred on 5 February, when the British troopship *Tuscania* was sunk en route to Europe. Lost were 166 American servicemen and 44 British crew members.

On 3 March 1918, Russia had signed the Russo-German peace treaty in Brest-Litovsk, the fortress town in eastern Poland, giving up conquests she had made over the course of two centuries, since the time of Peter the Great (1682-1725). Germany was finally free to fight on one front. The German Kaiser was once more confident of victory. But the "short war" — the 42 days Germany had once counted on to knock out her first opponent — had now stretched into more than three years. And it was Russia that was out, not France. No matter. It would not be long now.

Some 44 months after the invasion of Belgium and the outbreak of war,

Germany's General Ludendorff was ready to launch his most massive assault on the Western Front. *He had to!* There were now 325,000 American troops in France, and more on the way. Ludendorff had to strike before they could be used on a large scale.

Operation Michael

Like a soft comforting blanket on a rainy morning, dense fog lay over the devastated Somme battlefields on 21 March 1918. But there was little comfort in store that day for British and French troops holding the line. Indeed, there was little to be sanguine about. General Gough's Fifth Army had only 15 divisions to cover a front that extended some 40 miles. Lieutenant General Byng, commanding the British Third Army, however, was in better shape. His 14 divisions were well dug in over a 28-mile line in front of Arras.[4]

For their part, the Germans had left nothing to chance. Reconnaissance planes, though now temporarily grounded, had already been outfitted with special cameras, and 4,000 cartographers had been employed to analyze the photos. Each regiment had specially trained dogs to carry messages to and from the front. Even pigeons, "housed in hermetically sealed cages to protect them from gas," were available for communication. Some would be released with false messages to confuse the enemy.[5]

The early morning silence was shattered just before 5 o'clock when German high explosives and gas shells began to pierce the fog all along the front line. British and French troops, groping in the darkness, had no way of knowing that there were more than 6,000 German heavy guns in action, and that they'd be subjected to nearly two million gas shells in the next two weeks.[6]

Four hours later, around 9 o'clock, dozens and dozens of German assault divisions, following their own artillery's creeping barrage, stormed the Allied lines between Arras and La Fere.[7]

The meticulous German preparations paid off. Although in some places British regiments fought to the last man, German infantrymen advanced more than four miles on the first day alone. They paid heavily for their success, however, suffering more than 78,000 casualties, the "highest casualty figure for any single day of the war"[8] In some places, the French and British lines simply disappeared.[9]

The second day was no better for the Allies. German soldiers pushed farther, particularly against Gough's thinly held line, where it joined the

French army, taking 45,000 British and French prisoners. On the third day, 23 March, British forces had to retreat to the Somme. To make matters worse, heavy German guns, for good measure, began to bombard Paris from 75 miles away.

The Kaiser was euphoric. He ordered that schools be closed to celebrate the victory, and declared "the battle won, the English utterly defeated."[10] In London, Prime Minister Lloyd George was sufficiently disturbed to telegraph his ambassador in Washington to express to President Wilson the gravity of the situation and ask that American forces already in France be brigaded with British and French troops. The U.S. — specifically Wilson — responded in the affirmative.[11]

Conditions worsened for the Allies on 25 March. German forces broke through British and French lines, capturing Bapaume and Noyon. When the British line east of Amiens was threatened, a special force, including 500 U.S. railway engineers, was summoned to help hold the line. Things were so grim that the war cabinet in London actually discussed the possibility of a British retreat to the Channel ports.

But just as it looked bleakest, the Allies finally held. On 27 March, French forces stopped a German advance near Noyon, and the British took 800 prisoners on the Somme. Though Haig thought Pétain would pull back to guard Paris, and Pétain thought Haig would pull his men back, it was Marshal Foch who stepped in and warned both Allies not to retreat another foot.

Germany, likewise, was now experiencing real problems of its own. In a situation that smacked of its overzealous speed years before at the Marne (1914), General Ludendorff's advances had outrun the supplies. Horse-drawn artillery and matériel couldn't keep up with the infantry over the fractured ground. And instead of breaking through in a clear victory, German forces had created a huge bulge or salient into the enemy lines with its consequent problem of vulnerability on three sides. To make matters worse, German troops became demoralized when they saw the British rations. Many ravenous soldiers simply stopped to gorge on food not seen for years.

By 30 March, British, Australian, and Canadian troops counterattacked the now vulnerable Germans and captured most of Moreuil Wood.[12] It signified the turning of the tide. The German impetus and momentum were broken.

By 5 April, the great German offensive Operation Michael was over. To be sure, General Ludendorff had made enormous gains. In two weeks, the Germans had stormed across 1,250 square miles of French countryside, largely demolished one British army (Gough's Fifth), and sorely wounded another (Byng's Third). They had taken some 90,000 prisoners, captured more than 1,000 guns, and caused the removal of one British Commander (Gough).[13]

But the Germans had paid dearly for every inch of ground gained. They counted losses of 239,000 men — far from a complete victory. Neither the British nor the French had been knocked out of the fighting, and the fresh American troops would soon be on the scene in force, as General Pershing finally agreed to have American troops join the British and French, even if only in small formations.

And there was another significant, unintended ramification. General Ludendorff's great offensive had caused his enemies — finally — to close ranks. They would now operate under one Supreme Commander, Marshal Ferdinand Foch.

Had the whole tide of war finally turned?

NOTES

1. Sandra Gwyn, *Tapestry of War: A Private View of Canadians in the Great War* (Toronto: Harper Collins Publishers Ltd., 1992), 429.
2. McCrae is buried in Wimereux Cemetery, just north of Boulogne, France, not far from Flanders Fields.
3. B. H. Liddell Hart attributes part of the friction to disagreement over the length of line each country should hold. *History of the First World War* (London: Macmillan Publishers, 1997), 364; originally published as *The Real War, 1914-1918* (Boston: Little, Brown and Co., 1930).
4. James L. Stokesbury, *A Short History of World War I* (New York: William Morrow and Co., Inc., 1981), 263.
5. Holger H. Herwig, *The First World War: Germany and Austria Hungary 1914-1918* (London: Arnold, 1997), 396-397.
6. Martin Gilbert, *The First World War: A Complete History*, 2nd ed. (New York: Henry Holt and Co., 1994), 407.
7. B. H. Liddell Hart lists 63 German Divisions, *History of the First World War*, 368.

8. Herwig, *The First World War*, 403.
9. With the benefit of the perspective of history (and the release of war-related documents), Denis Winter claims that the British were driven back 12 (not 4) miles, and lost 600 guns and suffered 40,000 casualties. In another week, the British had been forced back 40 miles, and 25 of Haig's 60 divisions "had become little more than skeletons." Winter calls it the "biggest defeat suffered by an army on the Western Front up to that moment" — with concomitant psychological damage. *Haig's Command: A Reassessment* (London: Penguin Books, 1991), 171.
10. Gilbert, *The First World War*, 407.
11. This was not Lloyd George's first request. He had asked General Pershing for surplus troops on New Year's Day, when he felt Germany was planning a knock-out blow before the American troops could get involved. But Pershing, fearing his troops were not yet ready, refused, though he did agree to a French request from Pétain that four black American regiments then in France could serve with French Divisions.
12. For the most part, the Canadian Corps, with the First Army, was not in the attack, though Canadian cavalry, machine gunners, and some railway troops were called in to help the Fifth Army. The Canadian Cavalry Brigade provided a dismounted brigade of 800 men.
13. S. L. A. Marshall, *World War I* (Boston: Houghton Mifflin Co., 1992), 360.

Say not the struggle naught availeth
The labor and the wounds are vain
The enemy faints not nor faileth
And as things have been remain.
                    — Poet Arthur Hugh Clough,
              "Say Not the Struggle Naught Availeth"

Chapter 24

Germany's
Spring Offensives — 1918

*T*HE SPRING OF 1918 seemed to presage "more of the same." More mud. More casualties. More dreariness. More battles won and lost. More troop and merchant ships sunk. More hope. More despair.

"With Our Backs to the Wall"

There was also more fighting, of course. On 9 April 1918, the first anniversary of the Canadian victory at Vimy Ridge, the Germans struck below Ypres between the town of Armentières and the La Bassée Canal, and by the following day both Armentières and Messines had fallen. Even the imperturbable Field Marshal Haig was so shaken that on 11 April he issued his much quoted Order of the Day:

> Every position must be held to the last man. There must be no retirement. With our backs to the wall and believing in the justice of our cause, each one of us must fight on to the end.[1]

Between the losses of hard-won areas and Field Marshal Haig's words, it seemed that the final curtain, and a somber one at that, was soon to be drawn on the disastrous war. There was not a lot of positive news in April 1918 to indicate otherwise.

On 16 April, more than 1,000 New Zealand troops were gassed.[2] The next day, the eastern side of the hard-won, blood-soaked Passchendaele Ridge fell back into German hands.

By 20 April, Germany's famous "Red Baron," Manfred von Richthofen, so named for his well-known red Fokker triplane, had shot down his 80th Allied aircraft. However, it would be his last victory. The Red Baron was himself shot down the next day by a Canadian airman, Captain Roy Brown.

Eight thousand British troops had been gassed, and on the high seas, another 100 merchant ships were being sent to the ocean floor by German U-boats.

Casualties continued to soar. The two most recent battles had claimed the lives of 56,639 German and 21,128 Allied soldiers. Not only beds, but hallways, doorways, and lobbies of both Allied and German hospitals were clogged with 400,000 wounded, maimed, and dying soldiers. The word "crisis" now routinely appeared in warnings and communiqués of all Allied leaders. In a meeting of the Supreme War Council of Allied leaders at Abbeville, France, on 1 May, French Premier Georges Clemenceau, British Prime Minister David Lloyd George, and Commander-in-Chief of Allied Forces French Marshal Ferdinand Foch all appealed to U.S. General John J. Pershing to bring more American troops into the line. But Pershing, wanting his soldiers to fight under their own flag, replied that he would not be coerced.

Haig, meanwhile, was not particularly pleased with Major General Sir Arthur Currie, Canada's Commander-in-Chief. In March and April, the Canadian Corps had been holding a seven-mile line at Lens and not involved in heavy fighting. They had not, however, been idle. Because the area had strategic importance in mining and communications, the Canadian Corps had spent its time constructing 250 miles of trenches, 300 miles of wire entanglements, and 200 tunneled machine-gun emplacements.[3]

Haig, understandably, once more wanted to switch some Canadian units to the badly depleted British Corps.[4] He didn't grasp, however, that the Canadians — like the Yankees and, long before them, the Pals[5] — desired to fight and die together. Currie protested the removal of his corps from his (and Canadian) control.

The Canadian Corps was ultimately left intact until sent into reserve in early May for a period of rest and training. Even though they hadn't been in the worst scene of the current battle, they had suffered another 5,690 casualties.[6]

Although diaries had long since been forbidden, soldiers were able to express their feeling in letters home. Private Arthur E. Smith, of Hamilton Township, wrote of the changing scene at the front:

> Way back these villages were just as they were in peace, tidy and comfortable. Suddenly you notice that they and the landscape have altered. Trees no longer shade the road. No trees are to be seen, only their stumps and blackened skeletons.
>
> There are no more cultivated fields. The soil is rank and sour. Weeds and grass cover it. It is all holes and mounds. Tangles of barbed wire, reapers or ploughs twisted pitifully into useless shapes of iron, wheels sticking out of rubbish heaps, make desolation eloquent.
>
> In place of tidy, comfortable villages are piles of brick or broken stone, part of a wall here, there a fragment of a church, ruin savage and complete.[7]

In the meantime, American soldiers were proving themselves as something to be reckoned with as they fought and died on French soil. On 20 April 1918, the 26th (Yankee) Division retook the town of Seicheprey near St. Mihiel, suffering 634 casualties. It was hailed as the first American victory of the war. On 28 May, 4,000 soldiers took part in the first full American offensive of the war, and after another grueling battle, took Cantigny village on the Somme.

Canadian Prime Minister Robert Borden, who had expressed his concern about the military situation in France and wondered how quickly American troops could be trained and equipped, finally had a chance to see them firsthand — in fact he had crossed the Atlantic in a convoy of 13 ships carrying 30,000 American troops. He described them as "splendid men and very keen to be in the fight."[8] He had also agreed to an American

Three direct hits on a British gun on Canadian front, June 1918.
National Archives of Canada, PA 003749

request that battle-experienced Canadian officers train some of the American troops.

Thus, in spite of German hopes in 1917 that the Americans would never arrive in time to tilt the scales of battle, they had indeed arrived and were now fighting with élan and spirit. By late June and early July, there were about 800,000 American troops in France, most of them serving under French or British Commanders. Nor were they easy pushovers, as the Germans had anticipated.

A battle that was to become much more famous would begin on 6 June 1918 when Americans rushed Belleau Wood where the Germans had three lines of well-protected trenches. It was there that 10,000 men of the American Marine Brigade of the 2nd Division encountered massive German

I

machine-gun fire and suffered 5,200 casualties, nearly 1,100 of which were fatal. Legend has it that when someone suggested withdrawal, an American officer yelled back, "Retreat hell! We just got here!" It took more than two weeks, until 25 June, before the whole wood was totally secured. In the meantime, the Marines became famous for their bravery and tenacity.[9]

So now it was German General Ludendorff who had growing cause for misgivings. Allied Generals, on the other hand, who had watched their troops toil endlessly in the mud of Flanders, at last took heart when they saw the fighting spirit of the fresh soldiers from America. Canada's Prime Minister Borden continued his high praise for the Americans. He wrote in his diary of 23 August: *The victories of the last four weeks would have been impossible but for the Americans.*

NOTES

1. B. H. Liddell Hart, *History of the First World War* (London: Macmillan Publishing, 1997), 339; originally published as *The Real War, 1914-1918* (Boston: Little, Brown and Co., 1930).
2. Martin Gilbert, *The First World War: A Complete History*, 2nd ed. (New York: Henry Holt and Co., 1994), 415.
3. Colonel G. W. L. Nicholson, C.D., *Canadian Expeditionary Force 1914-1919: Official History of the Canadian Army in the First World War* (Ottawa: Queen's Printer, 1964), 378.
4. Denis Winter charges that "whenever Haig planned a breakthrough or came upon a particularly obdurate German position, British units were pushed aside and Dominion troops put in charge." To make his point, he cites Haig's use of the ANZACs at Pozières, Canadians at Vimy, Australians at Bullecourt, and Canadians and Australians at Passchendaele. His claims may have merit, but it is also true that the British forces suffered fiercely time and time again, sometimes almost to the last man. After all, there are 2,500 British cemeteries in France and Belgium. *Haig's Command: A Reassessment* (London: Penguin Books, 1991), 144.
5. Pals were battalions of Lord Kitchener's men who volunteered from the same area, town, or factory. For example, there were the Liverpool Pals consisting of more than 2,500 men from the Liverpool area, who joined together, served

together, and too often died together. J. M. Winter writes that the Pal's battalion was a quintessential British institution of World War I. *The Experience of World War I* (New York: Oxford University Press, 1988).

6. One of the casualties was Corporal Joseph Kaeble of the 22nd (French Canadian) Battalion. On 8 June, he was the last defender of a Lewis gun section in the front-line trenches near Neuville-Vitasse. When about 50 Germans approached his post, he climbed over the parapet, and, though dying from his wounds, fired repeatedly at the attackers, repelling them. He received the Victoria Cross posthumously. Nicholson, *Canadian Expeditionary Force*, 385.

7. Reprinted in Percy L. Climo, *Let Us Remember: Lively Letters from World War One* (Coburg, Ontario: Haynes Printing Co., 1990), 280.

8. Gilbert, *The First World War*, 435.

9. Gilbert, *The First World War*, 430-435; Marshall, *World War I*, 379-386; and Ian V. Hogg, *Dictionary of World War I* (Lincolnwood, IL: NTC Publishing Group, 1997), 26.

*The infinite value of surprise . . . for
3,000 years of recorded warfare has
proved the master key to victory.*
— B. H. Liddell Hart,
History of the First World War

Chapter 25

Amiens and the
Turning of the Tide

*T*OWARD THE END OF July 1918, Marshal Foch met with
the Allied Commanders-in-Chief southeast of Paris. For
once, they had cause for cautious optimism. The German
offense at Reims had been repulsed, and with the almost daily arrival
of fresh American troops, the Allies could claim some degree of
numerical superiority on the Western Front.

It was now the Allies' turn to think of a major offensive, and Foch
had a plan. There would be, in fact, several offensives by Allied
forces, each one following the other so closely as to disorganize the
enemy and baffle him as to where to send his reserves.

Inter-Allied Attacks
In describing the inter-Allied August offensive on the Western
Front, historians generally show the British forces on the north,
the Americans on the south,[1] and the French in between. That is

essentially correct, of course. But it is incomplete. Significantly, the British forces of 17 divisions would include 4 Canadian and 5 Australian Divisions, all destined to play a critical role in the operation.

The first assault would take place in the Amiens area, and its most significant feature would be the "element of surprise" — since time immemorial, a critical component of battle strategy. But how could they pull it off? Tanks would be unleashed in large numbers; yet how could these huge armored weapons be moved in secrecy? Canadians and Australians, by this time renowned for their fighting expertise, would be sent in as shock troops, as part of the British Fourth Army. But how could the movement of troops be kept secret?

To disguise the roar of the tanks, the Royal Air Force (formerly the Royal Flying Corps) increased its flying activity and staged its own "noise barrage," in the hopes of deceiving the enemy. And although the Germans were not totally deceived, General Ludendorff seemed more concerned with his troops' morale. Perhaps he should have been more concerned with his own personal problems. By now he appeared to some as though having a nervous breakdown, sometimes frozen in indecision, sometimes raging about the incompetence of others, often looking for scapegoats. Unlike others in the German High Command, Ludendorff refused to acknowledge that the diabolical flu — Spanish influenza — that was sweeping around the globe was also afflicting his soldiers. (It is estimated that in July 1918, there were about half a million soldiers wallowing in the trenches with the deadly sickness. Another 80,000 soldiers were languishing in hospitals.) Historian A. J. P. Taylor described Ludendorff as by now "punch drunk making mechanical gestures of menace like a stunned boxer."[2]

To solve troop and supplies logistics, all Allied movement in the Amien offensive took place at night. G. W. L. Nicholson notes that trains were loaded and unloaded under cover of darkness, while decoy movements were staged in the light of day, accompanied by much noise, dust, and dummy wireless traffic, to a feigned concentration area some twenty miles northwest of Arras."[3] In the night hours prior to the planned attack on 8 August, the roads were clogged with troops, horses, lorries, guns, tanks, and inevitably, of course, ambulances.

Under the cloak of secrecy, Canadian troops moved forward in the dark, predawn hours, with no moon to guide them to their assembly area. In poignant deference to the memory of recently lost fellow Canadians, the operational instructions were code-named Llandovery Castle, or "L.C." for the British hospital ship *Llandovery Castle*, which had been hit and sunk by a German U-boat torpedo some weeks earlier, on 27 June. Only 20 of the 283 on board the ship had been saved. Passengers were fired on as they struggled in the water, and all 14 Canadian Nursing Sisters with the ship had perished.

Within the British Fourth Army that August night, the Canadians were on the right, the Australians in the center, and the British on the left. As zero hour approached, a heavy mist settled over the entire area, making it imperative that troops move forward in single file to maintain contact.

In a major reversal of past trends, where soldiers had courageously fought for a few yards with incredible numbers of casualties, the Allied assault troops smashed right through the German lines. Part of the success was due to the "swarm" of 456 tanks bearing down on the German lines, in place of the usual "softening up" preliminary bombardment. Part of the success was due to the element of surprise itself — the extraordinary care that had been taken to move troops and artillery at night had paid off. And part was due to the arrival of the Canadians and Australians — "matchless attacking troops" who had "surged irresistibly over the enemy's forward divisions."[4]

By the end of the day, Germany had suffered its greatest defeat of the war. The Canadian Corps had pushed the German line back as much as eight miles, and the Australians had almost equal success. On their flanks, the French had advanced about five miles, and the British two — all despite the fact that the Australians had been hampered somewhat by British reverses north of the Somme and the fact that the British Third Corps had been handicapped by the loss of experienced infantry officers and NCOs since the opening of the German offensive in March!

The assault continued for two more days, before running out of steam, with additional prisoners and ground taken. After Field Marshal Haig visited the Front on 10 August, he prevailed upon Marshal Foch to break off the Fourth Army's assault (of which the Canadians and Australians were a part), and let the British Third and First Armies begin their successive battles.

Allied losses were considered light in terms of the gains made. Of 8,800 casualties in the British Fourth Army, Canadians accounted for 3,868 — 1,036 killed, 2,803 wounded, and 29 taken prisoner. German casualties were put at 650 to 700 officers and 26,000 to 27,000 other ranks, including more than 15,000 prisoners. The Allies also captured or destroyed more than 400 enemy guns, numerous trench mortars, and machine guns. The Canadian Corps alone took 12 villages, more than 5,000 prisoners, and 161 guns. The Australians took 7 villages, nearly 8,000 prisoners, and 173 guns. Even the Americans got into the act. In spite of heavy machine-gun fire, American engineers bound tree trunks together to enable troops to cross the river Vesle at Bazoches. Though it was only five feet deep, it had been filled with barbed wire.

As was becoming commonplace, several Canadians displayed extraordinary courage in the face of certain death. Among them were Corporal H. G. B. Miner of the 58th (Central Ontario) Battalion, who twice rushed enemy posts singlehanded and captured an enemy machine gun, and Private J. B. Croak and Corporal H. J. Good, both of the 13th (Royal Highlanders of Canada) Battalion, and Lieutenant J. E. Tait of the 78th (Winnipeg Grenadiers) Battalion, who rushed machine-gun nests ignoring their own safety. Miner and Croak died of their wounds. Tait was killed in action three days later. All won the Victoria Cross. And once again, the Canadian operations brought praise. Lieutenant General Byng who had commanded the Canadians much earlier, said that their performance at Amiens was "the finest operation of the war."[5]

Though this had not been the most dramatic of Western Front operations, it marked a significant change of fortunes, and a major psychological shift.

Was the tide indeed finally turning?

~·~

German Morale Plunges

Over behind the new German lines, Ludendorff was stunned. He later described 8 August as "the black day of the German Army in the history of the war." On 11 August, Field Marshal von Hindenberg said, "We have reached the limit of our power to resist. The war must be ended."

German morale plunged for other reasons, of course. Her war-weary people in August had entered their fifth year of the conflict, and the average citizen had suffered major deprivation. Due to the British blockade and the sealing off of Germany from the world's markets, Germany had to impose severe rations. Butter or margarine allowances, for example, had fallen to two ounces a week. So scarce were everyday goods and necessities that in any city "one could see automobiles and bicycles moving on hinged metal rims, emaciated horses on the verge of collapse." Paper was substituted for cloth. "Citizens learned to be careful when it rained, running for cover so their paper-made clothing didn't disintegrate."[6]

And one Allied success followed another, until even the dour Field Marshal Haig began to think not only of an Allied victory, but of victory in 1918, not 1919. By 21 August, the French captured Lassigny, and British forces advanced more than two miles, taking 2,000 German prisoners into the bargain. Thiepval Ridge was taken on 24 August, and Mametz Woods the next day. The Germans began a withdrawal along ten miles of the Front on 26 August, and the next day surrendered Delville Wood, which they had taken in 1916. General Ludendorff then began to pull his troops out of Flanders, in order to hold his Hindenburg Line — whatever the cost.

Still the Allies attacked. Even the battle-worn French, British, Canadian, and Australian troops fought with renewed vigor and élan, partly because of the turning tide, but also in large part because of the arrival of their American allies. On 30 August, the Americans captured Juvigny. Then the Australians, still not content with their conquests in August, ended the month by capturing Peronne.

August 1918 had indeed signaled the turning of the tide. British — including Canadians and Australians — French, and the American forces had captured 150,000 German soldiers, 2,000 guns, and 13,000 machine guns.[7]

Nor were the Canucks finished. Although troops are normally given an opportunity to rest and regroup after a major operation, they had no such respite here. On the contrary, the pace was stepping up. French Marshal Foch wanted continuing attacks along the *whole* Western Front. With the Allies now pounding enemy lines at every possible opportunity, the Canadians were handed a new challenge — hitting the Drocourt-Queant (D-Q) Line, which blocked the approach to Cambrai in the Arras sector. It was one of the strongest German positions on the Western Front.

Drocourt-Queant Line

In three days of fighting, from 28 through 30 August, the Canadians advanced more than five miles, taking more than 3,300 prisoners, 53 guns, and 519 machine guns. They also seized a critical part of the enemy's Fresnes-Rouvoy defense system. And, as usual, the success came with a human price tag. The Second and Third Divisions suffered more than 5,800 casualties. Every officer of the 22nd (French Canadian) Battalion had been killed or wounded. One of the wounded (who lost a leg) was Major Georges Vanier, a future Governor General of Canada.

But they had to press on toward the Drocourt-Queant Line and its heavily fortified defense system. Major General Currie decided to hit it at its most critical point, the Arras-Cambrai road. This time Currie sent in his oldest (First) and newest (Fourth) Divisions. Shortly after dawn on 2 September, accompanied by the thunder of the opening barrage, the troops swarmed forward. In no time at all, battalions of the First Division began to make their objectives. The 13th (Royal Highlanders of Canada) soon captured part of the D-Q Line, while the 14th (Royal Montreal Regiment) took Cagnicourt. While they were at it, they "captured in the village cellars enough Germans to make a full battalion."[8] Not satisfied, the Montrealers pressed on and reached their objective in front of the village of Buissy.

The 16th (Canadian Scottish) Battalion, however, was experiencing more difficulty, having encountered ferocious machine-gun fire. Man after man defied the odds and bitter fire to break forward at all costs. Two received the esteemed Victoria Cross within hours of each other. One was Lance Corporal W. H. Metcalf, an American serving with the 16th Battalion. In an extraordinary display of fortitude, he stood out on open ground ignoring a rain of machine-gun fire to direct a tank's firepower against an enemy stronghold. Another was Lieutenant Colonel Cyrus W. Peck, Commanding Officer of the 16th (Canadian Scottish) Battalion, who also faced machine-gun fire while making a reconnaissance to show tanks where to protect the battalion's open flank. Incredibly, on 2 September, seven Victoria Crosses were won by troops in the Canadian Corps. The others were Captain B. S. Hutcheson, Sergeant A. G. Knight, Private C. J. P. Nunney, Private W. L. Rayfeld, and Private J. F. Young.

Everywhere, sister battalions pushed, plodded, and worked their way forward, some with more success, some with less. The 5th (Western Cavalry) was engaged in frantic hand-to-hand fighting when the 7th (1st British Columbia Regiment) leapfrogged through to continue the attack and reach the D-Q line. Then the 10th (Canadians) stormed through, only to be caught in massive machine-gun fire and exploding trench mortars. But by 11:00 that night, battalions of the veteran First Division had taken the Buissy Switch.

Meanwhile, the Fourth Division had faced its own set of difficulties. The 72nd (Seaforth Highlanders of Canada), 38th (Ottawa), and 85th (Nova Scotia Highlanders) Battalions all faced heavy machine-gun fire, but nonetheless stormed and captured their objective, a sunken road joining Dury to the Cambrai road. Not far away, the 47th (British Columbia) and 50th (Calgary) Battalions ran into wire that had to be cut by hand. Nonetheless, they were able to let the 46th (South Saskatchewan) troops leapfrog through their position to take the village of Dury.

By the end of the day, 7,000 yards of the critical D-Q Line had been taken, as well as the Buissy Switch and two villages. It was a major achievement.

The assault continued the next day with the determined Canadians taking even more territory. Currie was elated by the performance of his troops, particularly those of the First Division whose success he termed "one of the finest performances in the war."[9]

Sometimes a linchpin is the key to a well-swinging gate. Such was the case with the capture of the Fresnes-Rouvroy and Drocourt-Queant Lines by the Canadian Corps. It cleared the way for the whole British Third Army to advance. It affected the whole Western Front from Ypres to the Oise River.[10]

The Yankees, too, had been far from idle. They were prepared to shove the Germans out of the St. Mihiel Salient, southeast of Verdun. Their assault began in a driving rain on 12 September when more than 200,000 American troops — supported by 48,000 French troops — attacked along a 12-mile front. Though they didn't have all the tanks they had requested, the Americans were supported overhead by the largest number of aircraft ever assembled up to that time. Nearly 1,500 American, French, Italian,

Belgian, Portuguese, and Brazilian planes were there to help the ground troops.[11]

The Americans rushed to victory, stunning the German High Command. The offensive at St. Mihiel had flattened out the Salient, which had been in German hands for four years, and freed about 200 square miles of French countryside. About 15,000 German prisoners were taken, as well as more than 250 guns.

But as always, the victory had a sad price. The victory that had enabled the French troops to enter St. Mihiel on 13 September had cost the Americans about 7,000 casualties.[12] Nonetheless, the swift success of the Americans on the St. Mihiel Salient was the first major victory by the First American Army, gaining the American troops widespread admiration. Even French President Raymond Poincaré and Minster Clemenceau personally came to congratulate them.[13]

NOTES

1. By this time, General Pershing had his own First U.S. Army fighting as a unit.
2. A. J. P. Taylor, *The First World War: An Illustrated History* (Hammondsworth, England: Penguin Books, Ltd., 1963), 230.
3. Colonel G. W. L. Nicholson, C.D., *Canadian Expeditionary Force 1914-1919: Official History of the Canadian Army in the First World War* (Ottawa: Queen's Press, 1964), 390.
4. B. H. Liddell Hart, *History of the First World War* (London: Macmillan Publishers, 1997), 429; originally published as *The Real War, 1914-1918* (Boston: Little, Brown and Co., 1930).
5. Nicholson, *Canadian Expeditionary Force*, 424.
6. Laurence V. Moyer, *Victory Must Be Ours: Germany in the Great War 1914-1918* (New York: Hippocrene Books, 1995), 264.
7. Martin Gilbert, *The First World War: A Complete History*, 2nd ed. (New York: Henry Holt and Co., 1994), 457.
8. Nicholson, *Canadian Expeditionary Force*, 436.
9. *Ibid.*, 440.
10. Denis Winter credits the leadership of Major General Currie for much of the success. "His capture of the Drocourt-Queant Switch in autumn 1918 remains the British army's single greatest achievement on the Western Front." *Haig's Command: A Reassessment* (London: Penguin Books, 1991), 271.
11. Gilbert, *The First World War*, 458.
12. S. L. A. Marshall, *World War I* (Boston: Houghton Mifflin Co., 1992), 430.

13. For a full account of the American victory on the St. Mihiel Salient, see Gilbert, *The First World War*, 457-460, or Marshall, *World War I*, 421-432.

For while the tired waves vainly breaking
Seem here no painful inch to gain
Far back through creeks and inlets making
Comes silent flooding in the main
— Poet Arthur Hugh Clough, "Say Not the
Struggle Naught Availeth"

Chapter 26

The Collapse
of the Central Powers

*J*UST AS AT NEAP TIDE, when the change in direction of
ocean movement seems almost imperceptible, so too were
changes in the direction of the war in August and September of 1918. Indeed, the changes were so gradual that some,
fearing the war would continue indefinitely, were making strategic
plans for 1919.

But changes there were, and once turned, the tide's movement
became more and more pronounced.

On 3 September, Marshal Foch outlined his plans for the rising
tide of the Allied assault. *"Tout le monde a la bataille"* [All the
world is at war], he proclaimed. There would be a whole-scale offensive on the entire Front from the English Channel to the Meuse
River, more than 200 miles away. On the northwest, King Albert
would lead his Belgian forces in Flanders in his own country's Ghent
and Bruges areas. The British and Commonwealth troops would
attack at Cambrai and St. Quentin. In the southeast, the Americans
would try to reduce still farther the St. Mihiel Salient and, with the
French army, strike toward Mezieres.

The big offensive would come in late September. But much would occur before then.

The Canadian Corps would be involved in the next major push, but first would be given a brief respite. The bitter fighting that had enabled them to penetrate nearly five miles into the Drocourt-Queant Lines had cost them more than 5,600 casualties in the first three days of September alone.

But the respite was hardly that. There was too much to do. First, the careful Currie directed his troops to "reverse" or convert the newly captured German front-line trenches, with their fire steps facing the wrong way. Additionally, new communication lines had to be installed to the rear. Even in the relatively quiet period, casualties continued to mount — as a rule, about 100 a day.

Meanwhile, Field Marshal Sir Douglas Haig met with the Commanders of the British First, Second, and Third Armies in mid-September, after which Major General Currie learned of his next role: the Canadian Corps was assigned the capture of Bourlon Wood (not to be confused with Belleau Wood already taken by the Americans), about three miles west of Cambrai. As a strong defensive position and outpost of the Hindenburg Line, Bourlon Wood was crucial to the taking of Cambrai.

It wouldn't be easy. To get there, the troops would have to face another obstacle first — the Canal du Nord and the swampy area around it. The Germans had flooded the marshland area, making it totally impassible. Farther south, where the ground was dry, they had fortified their positions with machine-gun posts. Currie was between a rock and a hard place, but really had no choice. He could only go for the dry area near the village of Inchy-en-Artois.

Once again Currie carefully mulled over his circumstances. Enemy positions were studied from the air. One small scouting party climbed into a church tower that would later serve as an aiming point. Ammunition was brought forward at night. Even in the cool night air of late September, gunners sweated as they unloaded wagon after wagon of ammunition and stacked deadly rows of shrapnel and high explosives on the ground. Then the big 18-pounder guns were secretly brought up to positions within 150 yards of the enemy line, with their wheels, harnesses, and even the horses' hooves wrapped in sacking to muffle the noise.

Death was never far away. Bursting shells continued to fall all around them.

[N]ot a night passed without one or more of the wagon lines
becoming the target of a low-swooping aeroplane's load of
bombs. There would be the confused din of bursting charges,
shouting men, and the cries of stricken horses. Then would
come the distressing count of casualties — some drivers killed,
more wounded, and perhaps a third of the battery's horses and
mules that had to be destroyed.[1]

Would Currie's meticulous planning pay off again?

As Major General Currie made his plans, battles continued elsewhere. Farther south, at Havrincourt and Epehy, the French and British
armies continued to push the enemy back. The eager Americans were
doing just what the British and French had hoped they'd do. Now fighting
together as a national army, they wiped out a six-mile nettlesome salient
between the Meuse and Moselle Rivers that had plagued the Allies for
years.

The Franco-American Assault — Meuse-Argonne

Day by day, Commanders and troops alike were anxious to get on with
the *big push*. Foch himself was now more than ready, knowing he had a
clear superiority of men and matériel. He was eager to unleash the south-
eastern pincer of his great plan, the Franco-American assault.

In the early morning hours of 26 September 1918, the Battle of the
Meuse-Argonne got underway just above and west of the battle-scarred
city of Verdun. It would severely test the Allied forces. The Germans
would fight bitterly because a major defeat here would kill their last hope
of victory.

The course of history could have changed during those same early
morning hours of 26 September had not an American battery Commander
arisen at 4 a.m. to begin firing 3,000 rounds of ammunition. Shortly after
he had moved from his sleeping place at the edge of a wood, a German
barrage hit it. But Captain Harry S. Truman was unhurt.

Following a heavy, six-hour bombardment during the night, more than

700 tanks rumbled toward the German lines, followed by 37 divisions of the First U.S. and French Fourth Armies. By the following morning they had advanced more than three miles and captured more than 23,000 prisoners.

Their remarkable initial progress, however, slowed to a crawl on the following days. By 29 September, the fourth day of the battle, it ground to a halt.

There were several critical reasons for the holdup. It wasn't just because the Germans fought back fiercely. It was also because the territory to be covered was murderous even in the best of conditions and described by historian S. L. A. Marshall as "wrapped in perpetual gloom."[2] Much of it was full of ridges and ravines, most of them riddled with enemy strongholds. Thus, not only was the fighting made more difficult, but supplies couldn't reach the troops; some went hungry for days in the front-line trenches.

And there were other causes. Because of the difficulty of bringing experienced troops up from St. Mihiel, some 50 miles away, many of the new troops were green, so much so that they were called by some "the thin green line."[3] Years later, in 1940, American Chief of Staff General George C. Marshall spoke of their lack of organization.

I discovered that of the 200 men to a company, approximately 180 were raw recruits. I found that some of these new units not only did not have their weapons but the men themselves had never heard of them.[4]

Opposite them, the German army threw in more and more experienced divisions.

There was, perhaps, yet another problem. More than one historian has indicated that General Pershing had badly overextended himself, allowing considerable disorganization to occur. Pershing had a full-strength army fighting a desperate battle itself, but also had by now ten divisions fighting with the French and British armies. Yet, states S. L. A. Marshall, "he initially insisted on personally commanding that army, which meant making main decisions about reinforcements, reliefs, corps boundaries, changes in plans, shifts in direction, the replacement of Commanders who proved unfit," among other things.[5]

The young Americans were also handicapped by the "haste of

preparation, by the exiguity of their communications and by their own dense numbers. The traffic congestion became fearful."[6]

Even the young green soldiers spoke of mismanagement. However, the situation was remedied on 16 October when General Pershing relinquished command of the First Army, to Major General Hunter Liggett, and created the Second Army.

Nevertheless, the young Americans fought fiercely and valiantly, suffering dreadful losses — more than 100,000 casualties — at the hands of Germans determined to hold on at all costs.

It was during the Meuse-Argonne struggle that the 1st Battalion of the 308th U.S. Infantry Regiment quickly forged ahead of its sister battalions, on 2 October, and took a ravine more than a mile beyond the front line. Before long, all contact with them was lost. Not only were the isolated men completely surrounded by German machine-gun fire but were shelled by their own artillery. After two days, their food ran out and they released their last carrier pigeon. Finally, however, the Germans withdrew after using flamethrowers against the stranded soldiers. Both Germans and Americans assumed the whole battalion was lost.

Not all had died, however. Five days after having lost contact, 194 survivors of "the Lost Battalion" crawled and limped to safety. But 360 had perished.[7]

On 10 October, the First Army, still under Pershing, finally routed the Germans from the Argonne Forest, but didn't achieve a breakthrough. A week later, in spite of a shortage of supplies and horses, they advanced along a ten-mile front, south of Le Cateau. And still another offensive was planned for the first day of November on the Meuse.

～·～

The British Assault —Verdun to the English Channel

By now, as the inter-Allied offensive struck all along the Western Front from Verdun to the English Channel, Germany was frantically shifting and shunting troops from one hot spot to another.

At the south end of the British line, the British Third Army (to the right of the Canadians who were in the middle of the British armies) had broken through the Hindenburg Line southwest of Cambrai. The British Fourth Army (with two American Divisions) had also penetrated Hindenburg defenses north of St. Quentin.

About 200 miles to the northwest, the British Second and Fifth Armies were pushing forward in the Ypres Salient, providing the other side of Foch's pincers movement. Like giant forceps, the two prongs were tightening. On 28 September, 4,000 prisoners were taken.

The next day, another 5,000 were captured, and Passchendaele was back in Allied hands, having been recaptured by Belgian troops. That same evening, though unknown to the Allies, Ludendorff told Hindenburg that Germany must seek an armistice. And it was on this day, 28 September 1918, that a seemingly insignificant event in the annals of war occurred. But it would change world history — forever. Victoria Cross recipient Private Henry Tandey, one of Britain's most decorated heroes, was serving with the Duke of Wellington's regiment at Marcoing, near Cambrai. Suddenly he had an enemy soldier in his rifle sight at point-blank range. But he couldn't pull the trigger because the man was wounded. Only much later did he learn that the wounded German corporal was Adolf Hitler.[8]

At this same time, all four divisions of the Canadian Corps, now back in the thick of battle, were running into deadly German defense systems as they tried to protect the flank of the British Third and Fourth Armies. (It will be recalled that the Canadian Corps was with the First British Army, roughly in the center of the British forces. The Second and Fifth British Armies were on their left (north) and the British Third and Fourth were on their right (south), where they hooked up with the First French Army.)

Sometimes little ground was gained in spite of heavy casualties. On 27 September alone, there were more than 2,000 casualties, with many battalions losing most or all of their officers and senior NCOs. One of the wounded that day was the much beloved Canon Scott, senior Protestant Chaplain of the First Division, whose candles had kept blowing out on Easter Sunday, 1917.

With German resistance, progress was slow, and setbacks were many. (Though the Canadians didn't know it at the time, the Germans, respecting the Canadian fighting reputation, had used nine full divisions and parts of three others to fend them off.) But by 2 October, after five days of bitter fighting, the weary troops had taken 7,000 prisoners and 205 guns, and had broken through the last organized defense system before Cambrai.

The Canadians Take Cambrai

A renewed assault on Cambrai began on 8 October by the British First Army (including the Second and Third Divisions of the Canadian Corps) in conjunction with the British Third Army. Initial progress was slow, and by evening sudden cold showers soaked the troops. Pressing forward in spite of the rain, they attacked at 1:30 in the morning on 9 October and found the enemy preparing to withdraw. Later that morning, the 27th (City of Winnipeg) Battalion captured Ramillies, and other western battalions (Vancouver and Alberta) found several villages (Blecourt, Batigny, and Cuvillers) deserted. But it was by no means a pushover. At Pont d'Aire, the retreating Germans had attached explosives to the girders of the main bridge. In a scene reminiscent of the story of the 6th century B.C. Roman Hero, "Horatio at the Bridge," Captain C. N. Mitchell held off advancing Germans until his men of the 4th Battalion Canadian Engineers were able to find and disarm the explosives. The bridge was saved for the advancing Allies, and for his daring, Mitchell won the Victoria Cross.

By nightfall of 8 October, the 25th (Nova Scotia Rifles) Battalion had captured Escaudoeuvres, and the 26th (New Brunswick) Battalion was on the outskirts of Cambrai. Finally, on 9 October, in spite of sporadic German fire, the 4th and 5th Canadian Mounted Rifles entered Cambrai itself, dousing fires that were raging in many areas. The Germans hadn't had time to torch the whole city, though unignited combustible materials were evident everywhere.

There would be, of course, more casualties and more selfless acts of bravery before the Canadians were relieved at 5 p.m. on 11 October. In one instance, Lieutenant W. L. Algie of the 20th (Central Ontario) Battalion led a handful of men who volunteered to rush two machine-gun nests in the village of Iwuy. He was killed while bringing up reinforcements, and was awarded the Victoria Cross posthumously. And once again the young, but now-seasoned, citizen soldiers had forged another remarkable record of accomplishment.

In the 47 days of the Arras-Cambrai campaign, from 26 August through 11 October, the Canadian Corps had fought and hammered their way

Canadians (barely visible at far end of street) entering Cambrai, east of Arras, France, 9 October 1918.   *National Archives of Canada, PA 003273*

forward through thundering guns, rain, mud, and fire. They had taken 18,585 prisoners, 371 guns, and nearly 2,000 machine guns. More important to the French, the Canadians had liberated 54 towns and villages and 116 square miles of French soil.[9]

As always, there was another statistic to add — 3,806 casualties, killed, gassed, wounded, and missing.

For several days after the capture of Cambrai, Canadian troops pursued the retreating Germans. Sometimes artillery had to be brought forward into unknown areas in the middle of the night. But advances in daylight hours brought out cheering civilians who plied the liberating troops with what little scraps of food they had. The Canadian advance also brought a new problem: how to help feed some of the liberated but destitute civilians.

As Canadian troops surged forward in the month of October, the tide of events was swelling elsewhere, one momentous wave crashing after another. On 17 October, while Americans were advancing south of Le Cateau, British troops entered the city of Lille. On the same day, the German navy evacuated Ostend and Zeebrugge. The next day, German U-boats were ordered to return to their German bases. The Belgian coast was now in Allied hands, though the seas weren't safe yet, however, for on 21 October, a German sub sank a British ship, the *Saint Barcham*, in the Irish Sea. And still more were to meet the same fate.

On 25 October, German General Ludendorff — who had sometimes spoken of a negotiated peace only to change his mind and threaten to fight on endlessly — resigned, close to a nervous breakdown. Three days later, Austria asked the Allies for an armistice which would take effect on 4 November. On 30 October, Turkey capitulated, and the Kaiser fled Berlin.

As October ended, while talks of Armistice continued, everywhere the Germans and Austrians retreated farther.

NOTES

1. Colonel G. W. L. Nicholson, C.D., *The Gunners of Canada: The History of the Royal Regiment of the Canadian Artillery 1534-1919*, Vol. 1 (Toronto: McClelland and Stewart Limited, 1967), 362.
2. S. L. A. Marshall, *World War I* (Boston: Houghton Mifflin Co., 1992), 436.
3. *Ibid.*, 436.
4. Denis Winter, *Haig's Command: A Reassessment* (London: Penguin Books, 1991), 216-217.
5. Marshall, *World War I*, 445.
6. C. R. M. F. Cruttwell, *A History of the Great War 1914-1918* (Oxford: Clarendon Press, 1934; 2nd ed., 1936), 567.
7. Martin Gilbert, *The First World War: A Complete History*, 2nd ed. (New York: Henry Holt and Co., 1994), 470; James L. Stokesbury, *A Short History of World War I* (New York: William Morrow and Co., 1981), 290; and Marshall, *World War I*, 436.
8. *London Daily Telegraph*, July 28, 1997, 3.
9. Colonel G. W. L. Nicholson, C.D., *Canadian Expeditionary Force 1914-1919: Official History of the Canadian Army in the First World War* (Ottawa: Queen's Printer, 1964), 460.

*If the stones could talk and could repeat
what they have witnessed, and the thoughts
they had read on dying men's faces, I wonder if there would ever be any wars.*
— Artilleryman Major Alan Brooke,
on his visit to Lens, 1918

Chapter 27

The Distant Thunder Ceases

S THE FIFTH LEADEN November of the war grimly
dawned in 1918, events trivial and momentous tumbled
on each other's heels in rapid succession. It was clear that
the Central Powers were, in fact, on the verge of collapse — clear
even to the German civilian population who, up until October, had
been told by German newspapers that all was well. Whispers of an
end to hostilities grew louder. Letters and notes regarding a cease fire
sped from one nation's capital to another.

General Ludendorff and Field Marshal von Hindenburg had asked
for an armistice back on 29 September at the Council of War in Spa,
Germany, and German and Austrian notes were sent to President
Wilson on 4 October. But it was not yet to be. On 12 October, a
young German U-boat Commander fired two torpedoes into the liner
Leinster on its regular route between Britain and Ireland, and 450
passengers perished, including women and children. In the revulsion
that followed, many people, including former President Theodore
Roosevelt, asked Wilson to halt any negotiations, other than those for

complete surrender. When the Allies demanded an unconditional surrender, Germany refused.

On 2 November, many of the German reinforcements that had been transferred from the Eastern Front to the West began to mutiny, rather than go into action. The next day, the Austrian armistice was signed, to take effect the next day. Also on 4 November, all fighting on the Italian Front ceased at 3:00 p.m.

But Peace would not make her appearance for several more days, and in those diminishing hours, countless more soldiers would continue to die. Nonetheless, the clock was ticking as the entire Allied line moved forward, liberating French and Belgian soil that had been in enemy hands for more than four years.

The Americans Advance

The Americans had remounted their assault on the Meuse on the first day of November. There had been much preparation. Three batteries of 14-inch naval guns (standard armament for a battleship) had lobbed shells weighing more than 1,000 pounds, from railway wagons, into German defenses. Then artillerymen had fired 36,000 rounds of mustard gas shells at the opposing German Divisions. Those who survived the mustard gas were then strafed by low-flying aircraft.

Still, there was a degree of lethargy in the American ranks, which some historians attribute to the terrible casualties of the previous weeks. Nonetheless, the U.S. Army broke through the German line with alacrity, and for the next five days pushed forward relentlessly. By 6 November, however, military history repeated itself, and the rapidly advancing troops outdistanced their ability to bring up critical supplies. In the confusion that followed, several mistakes and ironies played havoc with their progress. Some units marched into each other as conflicting orders piled confusion on chaos. In one instance, Colonel Douglas MacArthur, then commanding an infantry brigade, was taken prisoner by his own side. In another battalion, soldiers had to be harnessed to wagons because horses were in such short supply.[1]

Undaunted, however, the Americans pressed on, and in the first week of November advanced for 24 miles on either side of the Meuse River. The French troops, on their left, kept pace with them, taking Mezieres and Charleville. Both armies headed toward the symbolic Sedan.

Sedan, a fortified town and major rail junction in Northern France lying astride the Meuse five miles from the Belgian border, had been the site of French humiliation during the 1870-1871 Franco-Prussian War. In the disaster, Napoleon III was captured, as were more than 100,000 French troops. It was at Sedan in 1870 that Germany became a unified country, and Germans celebrated every 2 September as "Sedan Day," a national holiday.

In a curious turn of events in 1918, U.S. General Pershing, ignoring or unaware of French emotion, wanted "the honor of entering Sedan," though it was in the French army's sector. General Hunter Liggett, Commander of the U.S. First Army, fortunately showed more sensitivity, and approached Sedan with the French but then stood aside to allow them to re-take the city.

Valenciennes

While the Americans were charging forward in that first week of November, British and Canadian forces were mounting a strong offensive along a 30-mile front near Valenciennes, between the Scheldt and the Sambre Rivers. New Zealand troops had as their objective the walled town of Le Quesnoy, near the Belgian border. Even though the war was in its dying days, men battled on with courage and imagination.

The Battle of Valenciennes was the last major attack by the Canadian Corps, and, as usual, the careful Currie used the artillery extensively to purchase "victory, as far as possible, with shells rather than with the lives of men."[2]

The Canadian bombardment had actually begun well before dawn on 1 November. There was no preliminary registration to warn the enemy of the impending attack. The artillery, instead, used old French cadastral survey maps drawn up in the previous century, together with aerial photographs, to plot their targets. The bombardment that day (shrapnel, machine-gun bullets, and high-explosive shells) "was the heaviest weight of fire ever to support a single infantry brigade in the entire war."[3]

German soldiers, stunned by the torrent of fire and tempest, surrendered dejectedly, and the 44th (Manitoba) Battalion quickly took Mount Houy.

The 47th (British Columbia) Battalion took Le Poirier Station, and the 46th (South Saskatchewan) Battalion, as planned, leapfrogged the 44th to head toward Valenciennes.

The enemy had reason to be dejected. On 1 November alone, the Canadians took 1,800 prisoners and counted more than 800 enemy dead. Canadians suffered fewer than 400 casualties, including 80 killed.

The last Victoria Cross awarded to a Canadian went to Sergeant Hugh Cairns of the 46th (South Saskatchewan) Battalion on 1 November. He singlehandedly rushed a German post, killed a crew of five, and captured a Lewis gun. He repeated the act a short time later. Then once again, when his battalion was held up by German fire, he led a small party to outflank the machine-gun posts. Though his party forced the Germans to surrender, he was severely wounded in the process and died the following day.

Valenciennes lay ahead, still to be liberated. It presented several problems, however. The city couldn't be bombarded because of the large number of French civilians there. Furthermore, the Escaut Canal constituted an effective barrier on two sides of the city, both of which were heavily wired. To make matters worse, the Germans had opened the sluice gates and flooded many square miles of land.

Nonetheless, after a crushing barrage on the enemy's assembly positions, British and Canadian troops on 4 November broke through the German line, completely routing the German rearguard beyond recovery. Canadians had broken Germany's hold on Valenciennes, and the British First Army could again surge forward.

As always, individual acts of imagination and bravery stood out. New Zealand troops, embroiled in the battle for Le Quesnoy, were stymied by the defenses of the walled town. But not for long. Not to be denied, in almost medieval fashion they propped a single 30-foot ladder against the ancient ramparts and, soldier-by-soldier, climbed it in the only way they could — in single file. The New Zealanders finally penetrated the city, taking 2,500 prisoners and 100 guns.[4]

British troops likewise were attempting the almost impossible. On the Sambre Canal, near the village of Ors, troops tried desperately to construct a bridge over the waters but were repulsed repeatedly by machine-gun fire. Nearly all the engineers were wounded or killed. Still, the canal was unbridged. Finally, one officer tried to help his men use rafts, or even duckboards wired together, to cross the canal. It would be his last contribution to the war, however, as he was hit and killed trying to urge on his troops. He was Wilfred Owen, the poet.

On the wider stage of the final days, one last-gasp development succeeded another.

While British, Canadian, ANZAC, American, and French soldiers were pursuing the retreating German forces, Vice Admiral Reinhard Scheer ordered the German High Seas fleet to battle. It would go down fighting! But disillusioned crews had other ideas. They mutinied, killed some of their officers, and turned the ships around, hoisting red flags to indicate their opposition to the war and to the German regime and their support of the revolutionary fervor at large. At Kiel, Germany, on 4 November, thousands of sailors, garrison troops, and factory workers jumped headlong into the mushrooming mutiny against the war and the German regime. Ironically, on the same day, Allied Commanders were meeting to decide on their next offensive, which was to get underway in ten days.

On 6 November, while French and American troops were nearing Sedan, the King of Bavaria lost his throne. Two days later, Marshal Foch met with the German Armistice Commission in a railway car on a siding in the Compiègne forest. At the same time, crowds were rioting in Germany's major cities, setting fire to government buildings, mobbing officials, and in some cases shooting at each other.

On 9 November, Kaiser Wilhelm II, told that his army was no longer behind him, began to draft the details of his abdication. The next day, the Imperial train rolled out of Spa in southwest Belgium, toward Holland. Wilhelm II, who four years before had told his soldiers they would be home before the leaves fell, had abdicated.

In 1918 alone, 380,000 German soldiers lost their lives in combat. The total number of German war dead was now more than a million and a half men.[5]

On the same day the Kaiser abdicated, Canadian troops (the Royal

CASUALTIES BY COUNTRY

Country	Killed/Died	Total (Including Wounded/Missing	% Mobilized
Russia	1,700,000	9,150.000	76.3
France	1,357,800	6,160,800	73.3
British Empire	908,371	3,190,235	35.8
(Incl. Canada)[1]	(66,655[2])	(239,605)	(38.6)
Italy	650,000	2,197,000	39.1
USA	126,000	350,000	8.0
Japan	300	1,210	0.2
Romania	335,706	331,706	71.4
Serbia	45,000	535,706	46.8
Belgium	13,716	93,061	34.9
Greece	5,000	27,000	11.7
Portugal	7,200	33,291	33.3
Montenegro	3,000	20,000	40.0
Allied Total	**5,152,115**	**22,089,709**	**52.3**
Germany	1,773,700	7,142,558	64.9
Austria-Hungary	1,200,000	7,020,000	90.0
Turkey	325,000	975,000	34.2
Bulgaria	87,500	266,919	22.2
Central Powers Total	**3,386,200**	**15,404,477**	**67.4**

1. Approximately 1,600 Canadian airmen flying with the Royal Flying Corps (later RAF) also lost their lives.
2. Source: *Valour Remembered: Canada and the First World War* (Canada: Minister of Supply and Services, 1982).

Source: Funk and Wagnalls New Encyclopedia, Vol. 27 (except Canadian statistics).

Note: Anyone who searches for war statistics will find extraordinary variations in casualty numbers. For example, Ivan V. Hogg, *Dictionary of World War I*, show the U.S. with 58,480 deaths, 189,955 wounded, and 14,290 missing. He lists Canada with 56,600 dead, 149,700 wounded, and none missing. The *Encyclopedia Americana* shows the American Army casualties as 36, 926 killed in action, 13,628 died of wounds, 23,853 died of disease, and about 3,000 from various other causes for a total of 77,889 deaths and 275,948 casualties (including dead and wounded). In its chart on "Armies Mobilized and Casualties in World War I," Canada is not listed. C. R. M. F. Cruttwell, in *A History of the Great War 1914-1918*, lists 115,660 American dead but includes in that figure those who died of disease in the U.S. More recent books show the U.S. with 114,000 deaths and 324,170 total casualties (which included wounded). Often, Canada is not listed.

Whatever the cold statistics, most of the men were young citizen soldiers who left ordinary jobs to serve their country in an extraordinary war. The numbers are staggering. More than 70 million men were in uniform, of whom 9 million died. Approximately one in eight who served was killed. Countless more suffered debilitating wounds. Final figures will never be known.

The author knows of no chart that shows the percentage of men killed based on their country's overall population. Perhaps some student of the First World War will compile yet another significant statistic of the war.

Canadian Regiment, and the 42nd Battalion) entered the ancient town of Mons, Belgium, the memorable spot where the British Expeditionary Force had first entered the line in 1914. It was the fateful place where the British, with the French on their left and right, were to try to envelop General von Kluck back on 22 August 1914. But the French force on the left never arrived, and those on the right had to retreat, leaving the British vulnerable with open flanks. The British had been forced to retreat, and Mons had been in German hands ever since.

But no more. That evening, the skirl of the bagpipes could be heard as the Royal Highlanders of Canada marched in.

At 5:00 a.m. on 11 November, Matthias Erzberger, head of the German delegation, and other officials inked their signatures to the terms of the Armistice scheduled to take effect six hours later. Four years, three months, and 27 days after it had begun, the great conflagration was about to end.

A few hours later, just east of the now-historic Mons, near the village of Ville-sur-Haine, Private George Price of the 28th (Northwest) Battalion was, like every other war-weary soldier, anxiously awaiting the end of the war. He was admiring some flowers just given to him by Belgian civilians, grateful for their liberation.[6] It was not quite 11 o'clock in the morning. In but two more minutes there would be peace.

Just then, a German sniper took one last shot, and young George Price fell dead. He was the last casualty of the long, sorrowful war, and one of the more than 60,000 Canadian dead.[7]

Finally — at the eleventh hour of the eleventh day of the eleventh month of 1918, all hostilities ceased.

And the thundering guns fell silent.

NOTES

1. Martin Gilbert, *The First World War: A Complete History,* 2nd ed. (New York: Henry Holt and Co., 1994), 494.
2. Colonel G. W. L. Nicholson, C.D., *The Gunners of Canada: The History of the Royal Regiment of the Canadian Artillery, 1534-1919*, Vol. 1 (Toronto: McClelland and Stewart Limited, 1967), 366.

3. *Ibid., 368.*

4. Gilbert, *The First World War*, 492.

5. Laurence V. Moyer, *Victory Must Be Ours: Germany in the Great War 1914-1918* (New York: Hippocrene Books, 1995), 292. Moyer also notes that 1918 witnessed the largest one-year number of German deaths on the Western Front during the entire war. The war total for other nations was by then equally disastrous. France, with a smaller population, had also lost a million and a half men. Great Britain's losses were about three-quarters of a million. Russian losses are hard to identify. Gilbert, in *The First World War*, lists Russian dead at 1,700,000, whereas A. J. P. Taylor claims the Russian losses were probably more than all the rest put together.

6. Tonie and Valmai Holt, *Battlefields of the First World War: A Traveler's Guide* (London: Pavilion Books Limited, 1993), 13.

7. This figure does not include those who died after the war as a result of their wounds or gas poisoning. The Canadian Department of Veterans Affairs publication, by Patricia Giesler, *Valour Remembered: Canada and the First World War* (Ottawa, 1995), lists 619,636 Canadian men and women in the services in World War I, of whom 66,655 gave their lives, and of whom 172,950 were wounded. It notes (and it is widely acknowledged) that it was Canada's remarkable war effort that gained for her a separate signature on the Peace Treaty at the end of the war.

Epilogue

*G*UNNER ROBERT JAMES KENNEDY survived his wounds and, when fully recovered, was promoted and assigned to the Canadian Military Police Special Services for the remainder of the war. He received an honorable discharge from the Canadian Expeditionary Force on 22 January 1919, with three medals — the 1914-1915 Star and the British War and Victory medals. (The British and Canadian Expeditionary Forces had no equivalent to the American Purple Heart for wounds.)

Kennedy still had to wait for his beloved Eva, however, who was completing her R.N. studies in New York City, where she thought of going to France in 1918 with the American or Canadian Red Cross. He prevailed on her not to go. Robert and Eva were married on 23 July 1919, in St. Mark's Anglican Church, Cumberland, Ontario, where she had served as church organist before the war and where he had so often envisioned her while in ravaged France and Belgium.

Robert ultimately became township Clerk and Treasurer (akin to County Administrator) for the Township of Cumberland, while Eva

The Public Memorial in the village of Cumberland, Ontario. Robert and Eva's son is listed under the 1939-1945 conflict.

Hap Kennedy

continued with her nursing profession, ministering to the sick and delivering countless babies, many of them in their large family home. She continued as the church organist for nearly 50 years until suffering a stroke in 1969.

Robert and Eva had four sons and two daughters (including the author). The three eldest sons were of war age in the second great conflict of the century, World War II, and all saw active service overseas in the Royal Canadian Air Force. The eldest son, Robert, served with Wireless Communication in Bomber Command. "Hap," became a renowned Spitfire pilot. Carleton was killed on his first mission on 30 August 1944.

Robert died on 24 June 1970. He and Eva had been married for more than 50 years. Eva died in 1978.

The large brick home that Robert purchased for his new bride in 1919 still anchors the center of the village of Cumberland in the Ottawa Valley, not far from the community memorial that honors the names of the war dead, including his son. The local community center is named in Robert's memory, in recognition of his devoted service to the community.

Sources

Aitken, Sir Max (Lord Beaverbrook). *Canada In Flanders*, Vol. 1. London: Hodder and Stoughton, 1916.

Ashworth, Tony. *Trench Warfare 1914-1918, The Live and Let Live System*. New York: Holmes and Meier Publishers, Inc., 1980.

Ballard, Robert D., with Spencer Dunmore. *Exploring the Lusitania*. Toronto: Madison Press Books, 1995.

Barnett, Correlli. *The Swordbearers: Supreme Command in the First World War*. New York: William Morrow and Company, 1964.

Bernhardi, General Friedrich von. Allen H. Powles, transl. *Germany and the Next War*. London: E. Arnold, 1914.

Berton, Pierre. *Vimy*. Markam, Ontario: Penguin Books Canada Ltd., 1987.

Bird, Will R. *Ghosts Have Warm Hands: A Memoir of the Great War, 1916-1919*. Nepean, Ontario: CEF Books, 1997; originally published by Clarke, Irwin and Company, 1968.

Black, Ernest G. *I Want One Volunteer*. Toronto: Ryerson Press, 1965.

Blake, Robert, ed. *The Private Papers of Douglas Haig, 1914-1919*. N.P., 1952.

Brown, Malcolm. *The Imperial War Museum Book of the Somme*. London: Pan Books, 1997.

Burns, General E. L. M. *General Mud: Memoirs of Two World Wars*. Toronto: Clarke, Irwin and Company, 1970.

Canada in the First World War and the Road to Vimy Ridge. Canadian Veteran Affairs Publication, 1992.

Cassar, George. *Beyond Courage: The Canadians at the Second Battle of Ypres*. Ottawa: Oberon Press, 1985.

Christie, Norm. *For King and Empire — The Canadians on the Somme*. Winnipeg: Bunker to Bunker Books, 1996.

_____. *For King and Empire — The Canadians at Vimy*. Winnipeg: Bunker to Bunker Books, 1996.

_____. *For King and Empire — The Canadian at Ypres*. Winnipeg: Bunker to Bunker Books, 1996.

Churchill, Winston S. *The World Crisis*, 5 vols. London: Thornton Butterworth, 1923-1931.

Clare, John D., ed. *First World War*. London: Gulliver Books, Harcourt Brace and Company, 1994.

Clark, Alan. *The Donkeys*. London: Pimlico, 1961.

Clausewitz, Karl von. *On War*. Ed. by Michael Howard and Peter Paret. Princeton, NJ: Princeton University Press, 1984.

Climo, Percy L. *Let Us Remember: Lively Letters from World War One*. Coburg, Ontario: Haynes Printing Co., 1990.

Coombs, Rose E. B. *Before Endeavours Fade: A Guide to the Battlefields of the First World War, Battle of Britain*. London: Prints International Ltd., 1976.

Cooper, Bryan. *The Ironclads of Cambrai*. London: The Souvenir Press, 1967.

Crozier, Emmet. *American Reporters on the Western Front 1914-1918*. New York: Oxford University Press, 1959.

Cruttwell, C. R. M. F. *A History of the Great War 1914-1918*. Oxford: Clarendon Press, 1934, 2nd Ed. 1936.

Currie, Colonel J. A., M.P. *"The Red Watch" with the First Canadian Division in Flanders*. London: Constable and Company, Ltd., 1916.

Dancocks, Daniel G. *Welcome to Flanders Fields: The First Canadian Battle of the Great War, Ypres, 1915*. Toronto: McClelland & Stewart, Inc., 1989.

Davy, Major F. *Canada in Khaki*. London: The Pictorial Newspapers Co. Ltd., 1910
1917.
Der Weltkrieg, 1914-1918. Berlin: *Reichsarchiv*, 1932.
Dolden, A. Stuart. *An Infantryman's Life on the Western Front, 1914-1918*. Poole,
Dorset, England: Blandford Press, 1980.
Duguid, Colonel A. Fortescue. *Official History of the Canadian Forces in the Great
War 1914-1918*, Vol.1. Ottawa: Minister of National Defence, 1938.
Dyer, Geoff. *The Missing of the Somme*. London: Penguin Books, 1994.
Ellis, John. *Eye-Deep in Hell: Trench Warfare in World War I*. Baltimore: The Johns
Hopkins University Press, 1976.
Evans, Martin Marix. *The Battles of the Somme*. Osceola, WI: Motorbooks Interna-
tional Publishers & Wholesalers, 1966.
_____. *Passchendaele and the Battles of Ypres 1914-1918*. London: Osprey (Reed
Books), 1997.
Falkenhayn, General Erich von. *General Headquarters and Its Critical Decisions*. Lon-
don: Her Majesty's Stationery Office (HMSO), 1919.
Frothingham, Thomas G. *A Guide to the Military History of The World War, 1914-1918*.
New York: Little, Brown, and Company, 1920.
Fussell, Paul. *The Great War and Modern Memory*. Oxford: Oxford University Press,
1975.
Gardner, R. B. *The Big Push*. London: Cassell & Company, Ltd., 1961.
Giesler, Patricia. *Valor Remembered: Canada and the First World War*. Ottawa: De-
partment of Veterans Affairs, 1995.
Gilbert, Martin. *Atlas of World War I — The Complete History*, 2nd ed. New York: Ox-
ford University Press, 1994.
_____. *The First World War: A Complete History*. 2nd ed. New York: Henry Holt and
Company, 1994.
Goodspeed, D. J. *The Road Past Vimy: The Canadian Corps, 1914-1918*. Toronto:
Macmillan Publishers, 1969.
Griffith, Paddy. *Battle Tactics of the Western Front: The British Army's Art of Attack
1916-1918*. New Haven: Yale University Press, 1944.
Gwyn, Sandra. *Tapestry of War: A Private View of Canadians in the Great War*. Toron-
to: Harper Collins Publishers Ltd., 1992.
Halsey, Francis Whiting. *The Literary Digest History of the World War*, Vol 3. New
York: Funk & Wagnalls Co., 1919.
Haythornwaite, Philip, J. *A Photohistory of World War One*. London: Arms and Ar-
mour, 1989-1990, 1995.
_____. *The World War One Source Book*. London: Arms and Armour Press, 1994.
Herwig, Holger H. *The First World War: Germany and Austria Hungary 1914-1918*.
London: Arnold, 1997.
Hogg, Ian V. *Battles — A Concise Dictionary*. Orlando: Harcourt Brace & Co., 1995.
_____. *Dictionary of World War I*. Lincolnwood, IL: NTC Publishing Group, 1997.
Holt, Tonie and Valmai. *Battlefields of the First World War: A Traveller's Guide*. Lon-
don: Pavilion Books Limited, 1993.
Horne, Alistair. *The Price of Glory, Verdun, 1916*. London: Penguin Books, 1962.
Johnson, J. H. *1918: The Unexpected Victory*. London: Arms and Armour Press, 1997.
_____. *Stalemate! The Great Trench Warfare Battles of 1915-1917*. London: Arms and
Armour Press, 1995.
Keegan, John. *The Face of Battle*. New York: Penguin Books, 1976.
_____. *The First World War*. London: Alfred Knopf, Inc., 1998.
King, Jere Clemens, ed. *The First World War*. New York: Walker and Company, 1972.

Laffin, John. *British Butchers and Bunglers of World War One*. Phoenix Mill, Great Britain: Sutton Publishing Ltd., 1989.

_____. *Jackboot: A History of the German Soldier 1713-1945*. New York: Barnes and Noble Books, 1964.

Liddell Hart, B. H. *History of the First World War*. London: Macmillan Publishers, 1997; originally published as *The Real War 1914-1918*. Boston: Little, Brown, and Company, 1930.

Lloyd, Alan. *The War in the Trenches*. New York: David McKay Company, Inc., 1976.

Lloyd George, David. *War Memoirs of David Lloyd George, 1915-1916*. Boston: Little, Brown, and Company, 1933.

Macdonald, Lyn. *1915: The Death of Innocence*. London: Penguin Books, 1993.

March, Francis A., in collaboration with Richard J. Beamish. *History of the World War, An Authentic Narrative of the World's Greatest War*. Philadelphia: The United Publishers of the United States and Canada, 1919.

Marshall, S. L. A. *World War I*. Boston: Houghton Mifflin Co., 1992.

McCarthy, Chris. *The Third Ypres — Passchendaele — The Day by Day Account*. London: Arms and Armour Press, 1995.

McClure, S. S. *Obstacles to Peace*, Boston: Houghton Mifflin Company, 1917.

McWilliams, James L., and R. James Steel. *Gas! The Battle for Ypres, 1915*. St. Catherines, Ontario: Vanwell Publishing Limited, 1915.

Middlebrook, Martin. *The First Day on the Somme*. New York: W. W. Norton and Company, Inc., 1972.

Montgomery, L. M. *Rilla of Ingleside*. Toronto: McClelland and Stewart, Ltd., 1920; Seal Books, 1992.

Morton, Desmond. *When Your Number's Up: The Canadian Soldier in the First World War*. Toronto: Random House of Canada, 1993.

Morton, Desmond, and J. L. Granatstein. *Marching to Armageddon: Canadians and the Great War 1918-1919*. Toronto: Lester and Orpen Dennys, 1989.

Moyer, Laurence V. *Victory Must Be Ours: Germany in the Great War 1914-1918*. New York: Hippocrene Books, 1995.

Murray, Colonel W. W. *The History of the 2nd Canadian Battalion (Eastern Ontario Regiment) in the Great War, 1914-1919*. Ottawa: Mortimer Ltd., 1947.

Nicholson, Colonel G. W. L., C.D. *Canadian Expeditionary Force 1914-1919: Official History of the Canadian Army in the First World War*. Ottawa: Queen's Printer, 1964.

_____. *The Gunners of Canada: The History of the Royal Regiment of the Canadian Artillery, 1534-1919*, Vol. 1. Toronto: McClelland and Stewart Limited, 1967, 1976.

Noyes, Frederick W. *Stretcher-Bearers...at the Double! History of the Fifth Canadian Field Ambulance Which Served Overseas During the Great War of 1914-1918*. Toronto: Hunter-Rose Company, Ltd., undated.

O'Shea, Stephen. *Back to the Front: An Accidental Historian Walks the Trenches of World War I*. Vancouver: Douglas & McIntyre, 1996.

The Oxford Dictionary of Quotations, 3rd ed. New York: Oxford University Press, 1980.

Panichas, George A., ed. *Promise of Greatness: The War of 1914-1918*. New York: The John Day Company, 1968.

Prior, Robin, and Trevor Wilson. *Passchendaele: The Untold Story*. New York: Yale University Press, 1996.

Rawling, Bill. *Surviving Trench Warfare: Technology and the Canadian Corps, 1914-1918*. Toronto: University of Toronto Press, 1992.

Reeder, Colonel Red. *Bold Leaders of World War I*. Boston: Little, Brown, and Company, 1974.

Remarque, Erich Marie. *All Quiet on the Western Front.* Boston: Little, Brown and Co., 1929. New York: A Fawcett Columbine Book, Ballantine Books, 1996.
Russenholt, E. S. *Six Thousand Canadian Men: Being the History of the 44th Battalion, Canadian Infantry 1914-1919.* Winnipeg: DeMonfort Press, 1932.
Schreiber, Shane B. *Shock Army of the British Empire: The Canadian Corps in the Last 100 Days of the Great War.* Westport, CT: Praeger, 1997.
Scott, Canon Frederick George C.M.G., D.S.O. *The Great War as I Saw It.* Vancouver: The Clark & Stewart Co., Ltd., 1934.
Simmons, Dan. "The Great Lover," in John Betancourt, ed., *New Masterpieces of Horror.* New York: Barnes & Noble Books, 1966.
Smith, Aubrey. *Four Years on the Western Front: By a Rifleman.* Long Acre, England: Odhams Press, Ltd., 1922.
Stokesbury, James L. *A Short History of World War I.* New York: William Morrow and Co., Inc., 1981.
Swettenham, J. A. *Valiant Men: Canadian Victoria Cross and George Cross Winners.* Toronto: Hakkert, 1973.
Taylor, A. J. P. *The First World War: An Illustrated History.* Hammondsworth, England: Penguin Books Ltd., 1963.
Tuchman, Barbara W. *The Guns of August.* New York: Ballantine Books, 1962.
_____. *The Proud Tower: A Portrait of the World Before the War 1890-1914.* New York: The Macmillan Company, 1966.
_____. *The Zimmerman Telegram.* New York: The Viking Press, 1958.
Tucker, A. B. *The Battle Glory of Canada.* London: Cassell, 1915.
Tucker, Spencer C. *The Great War, 1914-18.* Bloomington: Indiana University Press, 1998.
War Diary of the 1st Canadian Field Artillery Brigade. Ottawa: National Archives of Canada.
White, Stuart N. *The Terrors, 16th (Pioneer) Battalion Royal Irish Rifles.* Belfast: The Somme Association Limited, 1966.
Wilson, Barbara M., ed. *Ontario and the First World War, 1914-1918: A Collection of Documents.* Toronto: University of Toronto Press, 1977.
Winter, Denis. *Death's Men: Soldiers of the Great War.* London: Penguin Books, 1978.
_____. *Haig's Command: A Reassessment.* London: Penguin Books, 1978, 1991.
Winter, Jay, and Blaina Baggett. *The Great War and the Shaping of the 20th Century.* New York: Penguin Studio, 1966.
Winter, J. M. *The Experience of World War I.* New York: Oxford University Press, 1988.
Wolff, Leon. *In Flanders Fields: The 1917 Campaign.* New York: Ballantine Books, 1958.

VIDEOS AND FILM

Lusitania: Murder on the Atlantic
WWI: The Death of Glory
The Battle of the Somme, Cromwell Productions, 1996
Cat.#HW011, Sports Business & Leisure Ltd., United Kingdom
Vimy: The Birth of a Nation, Vimy Productions, Inc., Vancouver, B.C.

CREDITS

Chapter heading quotes are from the following sources:
Chapter 1 — Barbara Tuchman, *The Proud Tower: A Portrait of the World Before the War 1890-1914.* New York: The Macmillan Company, 1996.

Chapter 2 — General Friedrich von Bernhardi. Allen H. Powles, transl. *Germany and the Next War*. London: E. Arnold, 1914.

Chapter 3 — Francis Whiting Halsey. *The Literary Digest History of the World War*, Vol. 3. New York: Funk & Wagnalls Co., 1919.

Chapter 4 — Alistair Horne, *The Price of Glory, Verdun, 1916*. London: Penguin Books, 1962.

Chapter 5 — Martin Gilbert. *The First World War: A Complete History*, 2nd ed. New York: Henry Holt and Company, 1994.

Chapter 6 — Colonel G. W. L. Nicholson, C.D. *Canadian Expeditionary Force: Official History of the Canadian Army in the First World War*. Ottawa: Queen's Printer, 1964.

Chapter 7 — Daniel G. Dancocks. *Welcome to Flanders Fields: The First Canadian Battle of the Great War, Ypres, 1915*. Toronto: McClelland & Stewart, Inc., 1989.

Chapter 8 — A. J. P. Taylor, *The First World War: An Illustrated History*. Hammondsworth, England: Penguin Books Ltd., 1963.

Chapter 9 — Percy L. Climo, *Let Us Remember: Lively Letters from World War One*. Coburg, Ontario: Haynes Printing Co., 1990.

Chapter 10 — Robert D. Ballard, with Spencer Dunmore. *Exploring the Lusitania*. Toronto: Madison Press Books, 1995.

Chapter 11 — Erich Marie Remarque. *All Quiet on the Western Front*. Boston: Little, Brown and Co., 1929. New York: A Fawcett Columbine Book, Ballantine Books, 1996.

Chapter 12 — General Erich von Falkenhayn. *General Headquarters and Its Critical Decisions*. London: Her Majesty's Stationery Office (HMSO), 1919.

Chapter 13 — Alistair Horne. *The Price of Glory, Verdun, 1916*. London: Penguin Books, 1962.

Chapter 14 — Karl von Clausewitz. *On War*. Ed. by Michael Howard and Peter Paret. Princeton, NJ: Princeton University Press, 1984.

Chapter 15 — Erich Marie Remarque. *All Quiet on the Western Front*. Boston: Little, Brown and Co., 1929. New York: A Fawcett Columbine Book, Ballantine Books, 1996.

Chapter 16 — S. L. A. Marshall. *World War I*. Boston: Houghton Mifflin Co., 1992.

Chapter 17 — Prior, Robin, and Trevor Wilson. *Passchendaele: The Untold Story*. New York: Yale University Press, 1996.

Chapter 18 — Barbara W. Tuchman. *The Zimmerman Telegram*. New York: The Viking Press, 1958.

Chapter 19 — D. J. Goodspeed. *The Road Past Vimy: The Canadian Corps, 1914-1918*. Toronto: Macmillan Publishers, 1969.

Chapter 20 — General E. L. M. Burns. *General Mud: Memoirs of Two World Wars*. Toronto: Clarke, Irwin and Company, 1970.

Chapter 21 — Leon Wolff. *In Flanders Fields: The 1917 Campaign*. New York: Ballantine Books, 1958.

Chapter 22 — Martin Gilbert. *The First World War: A Complete History*, 2nd ed. New York: Henry Holt and Company, 1994.

Chapter 23 — Martin Gilbert. *The First World War: A Complete History*, 2nd ed. New York: Henry Holt and Company, 1994.

Chapter 24 — *The Oxford Dictionary of Quotations*, 3rd. ed. New York: Oxford University Press, 1980.

Chapter 25 — B. H. Liddell Hart. *History of the First World War*. London:

Macmillan Publishers, 1997; originally published as *The Real War, 1914-1918*. Boston: Little, Brown and Company, 1930.

Chapter 26 — *The Oxford Dictionary of Quotations*, 3rd. ed. New York: Oxford University Press, 1980.

Chapter 27 — Martin Gilbert. *The First World War: A Complete History*, 2nd ed. New York: Henry Holt and Company, 1994.

Glossary

AEF American Expeditionary Force.

Alberich (Operation) Code name for the systematic German retreat to the Hindenburg Line in 1917, just before the battle at Vimy Ridge, and the wanton destruction of what was left behind. Named after the malicious, "deceitful" dwarf in the Nibelung Legend.

ANZAC Australian and New Zealand Army Corps.

Bandolier A belt worn over the shoulder and across the breast, sometimes for supporting some article (such as cartridges) or as part of official dress.

Barrage Shelling for a pre-arranged period. A creeping barrage was a rolling or creeping wave or curtain of shell fire in front of your own advancing infantry designed to keep the enemy down until the last possible moment.

Battalion An infantry unit of three or four companies, with about 1,000 men.

Battery A small artillery unit of 4 to 16 men.

BEF British Expeditionary Force(s).

Big Berthas German guns with a caliber of 17 inches that launched 420- millimeter mortars. Developed by Krupp, they were the largest guns in the Great War, with a firing shell weighing more than a ton, and nearly as tall as a man. To be transported, they had to be dismantled into 172 pieces, and required 12 wagons. They were used to shatter Liége, and 13 were used at Verdun.

Breastwork A temporary defense or fortification, often a parapet just a few feet high.

Brigade A brigade in the British army is equivalent to a U.S. regiment. In 1914, three brigades of four battalions made one division. (From Middlebrook, 1972).

CEF Canadian Expeditionary Force.

Central Powers The German and Austro-Hungarian Empires, later joined by Turkey and Bulgaria.

CFA Canadian Field Artillery.

CMR Canadian Mounted Rifles.

Communication trench A trench that connected the front line of trenches with the support and rear lines.

Duckboards Strips of wood laid parallel to each other over a muddy trench floor.

Dugout An excavation — a shelter — dug into and below the side of a trench; a resting spot.

Dump In military terms, a temporary depot of munitions.

FOO Forward Observation Officer — an artillery battery officer with the infantry, reporting targets to his battery and signaling ongoing target corrections.

GGFG Governor General's Foot Guards.

GOC General Officer Commanding.

HMCS His Majesty's Canadian Ship.

Howitzer An artillery weapon able to fire at elevations greater than 45 degrees (so as to pass over intervening obstacles) to destroy roads and railway spurs. The 4.5-inch howitzer could fire a 35-pound shell 7,200 yards. Its muzzle velocity was more than 1,000 feet per second.

Limber Detachable front of a gun carriage (two wheels, axle, pole, and ammunition box).

Listening Post A sap running out toward the enemy, terminating in a rifle pit capable of holding three or four men, and used to eavesdrop on enemy conversations.

Mortar A muzzle-loaded artillery cannon fired at high angles, usually into enemy trenches.

Mustard gas Smells like mustard, generates both internal and external blistering and sores.

No Man's Land The deadly area between the enemy and your own lines.

Outflank To move or maneuver around and behind the enemy's flank or side, for tactical advantage.

Parados An elevation of earth behind a fortified place — especially the mound along the back of a trench — to protect men from rear attack or fire.

Parapet A defense of earth or stone to conceal and protect troops; a mound along the front of the trench.

Pals Battalions or regiments comprised of men from the same region or business who had joined together to serve together. (As in the Liverpool Pals, with more than 2,500 men from the Liverpool area.)

Phosgene A highly poisonous, colorless, odorless heavier-than-air gas that quickly causes unconsciousness and death.

Pincer A military maneuver in which the enemy is attacked (or pinched) from two flanks and the front.

Pioneer From the French word *pionnier*, or foot soldier. In the military, one of a body of foot soldiers — some construction engineers, marching in advance with spades, etc., to prepare the road for the main body of troops.

Plan XVII A French war plan adopted in 1913 (and preceded by 16 earlier versions) that called for a general offensive in an east-northeast direction from Alsace by the French Armies. It was destined to fail.

PPCLI Princess Patricia's Canadian Light Infantry.

Puttee A long strip of cloth wound spirally around the leg from the ankle to the knee, for protection and support.

Rampart A fortification consisting of an elevation or embankment.

Redoubt A small, often temporary defensive fortification. An enclosed earthwork or protected place of siege or defense.

Regiment An infantry unit of three or four battalions.

Revetment A stone, cement, or sandbag facing to protect a wall or bank of earth.

RFC Royal Flying Corps (British).

Rifle grenade Small missile similar to hand grenade but fired from a rifle.

RMS Royal Mail Ship (British).

Salient A jutting out, conspicuous projection or bulge beyond a line. An outwardly projecting part of a fortification, trench system, or line of defense, which by its very nature was excessively vulnerable, being exposed on three sides. The Ypres Salient was apparently about nine miles wide at the largest point, and projected about four miles from Ypres itself into the German line. It was, of course, vulnerable from three sides.

Sap A trench or tunnel, usually covered; a kind of *cul de sac* trench or hole jutting out from other trenches into No Man's Land, usually to serve as a listening post on the enemy. (*v.* To make a trench or cover the enemy's approach to a besieged place.)

Schlieffen Plan The elaborate plan, named for its creator, German Field Marshal Graf Alfred von Schlieffen, and adopted by the German General Staff in late 1905, proposing to hold the Russian army in the East as the larger part of the German army moved against France to take Paris. The Geman army would then use the French rail network to move German troops eastward, to conquer the menacing Russians. The plan was predicated on the ability to knock out France in 42 days. It would be later modified by Chief of the German General Staff Helmuth von Moltke, during the three years preceding World War I, and although it came close to success, it eventually failed, and with it the notion of a "short war."

Shrapnel Bullets or pieces of metal contained in a shell timed to burst slightly short of objective and let them fly on in shower. Part of bomb so scored as to break and scatter. Named after its inventor.

Stollen A large, underground, shell-proof gallery burrowed out by the Germans along the attack zone, specifically at Verdun. Some of the concrete shelters could hold half a battalion.

Very light or Very flare A pyrotechnic signal using white or colored flares, fired from a special pistol for signaling or temporarily illuminating part of a battlefield. So named for its inventor.

Whizbang A nickname for the Canadian Field Service postcard, which troops were encouraged to use, pre-printed with essentially optimistic of messages, from which soldiers could choose. Probably so-named for the "Whizz Bang" high-velocity German shell that usually arrived without warning.

Chronology

1831
Belgium wins independence from Netherlands.
1839
England, France, Russia, Prussia, and Austria sign a pact that guarantees the sovereignty of Belgium.
1870-1871
Franco-Prussian War.
1871
In defeat, a humiliated France cedes its western provinces of Alsace-Lorraine to the newly unified Germany which emerges as a world power. King William I of Prussia is crowned Emperor of Germany on French soil at Versailles. Bismarck foresees that France will never forgive Germany.
1879
Germany and Austria-Hungary sign Dual Alliance, which Italy later (1882) joins, making it the Triple Alliance.
1882
Germany, Austria-Hungary, and Italy form Triple Alliance through which one party would defend the other if attacked.
1888
The 29-year-old Wilhelm II becomes ruler of Germany.
1890
Wilhelm II dismisses Otto von Bismarck.
1891
Russia and France agree to consult if either is attacked, and Franco-Russian Alliance is signed the following year.
1901
Queen Victoria dies and Edward VII becomes King.
1904
England becomes somewhat allied with the Franco-Russian pact through its *entente cordiale* with France.
1905
Germany's Schlieffen Plan is born.
1908
Austria-Hungary annexes the Turkish province of Bosnia and Herzegovina. England, France, and Russia form Triple Entente.
1909
Nations (including Germany) ban use of asphyxiating gas at the Hague Convention.
1910
Edward VII dies and George V become King of England.
1911
Prince Arthur, Duke of Connaught, and youngest son of Queen Victoria, is appointed Governor General of Canada.
1912
The *Titanic* sinks.
1914
June 28 Assassination of Archduke Ferdinand, heir to the throne of Austria-Hungary.

1914 *(continued)*

July 23 Austria sends ultimatum to Serbia.

July 25 Serbia concedes most of Austria's demands, but Austria is not satisfied.

July 28 Austria-Hungary declares war on Serbia.

July 29-31 Russia mobilizes troops for Austrian frontier.

August 1 Germany declares war on Russia. France orders mobilization.

August 2 Germany demands free passage through Belgium. Germany invades Poland.

August 3 Germany declares war on France. Belgium refuses Germany's demand. German troops enter Luxemburg.

August 4 German troops cross into Belgium at 8:02 a.m., and Belgians resist at Liége. England declares war with Germany. Lord Kitchener becomes Secretary of War. Canada enters war.

August 5 First American electric traffic light system is installed in Cleveland, Ohio.

August 6 Holland declares neutrality.

August 7 Germans take Liége. French forces invade Alsace. Britain's forces land at Ostend, Calais, and Dunkirk. Russians invade East Prussia.

August 7-16 The BEF lands in France.

August 11 Germans penetrate France.

August 12 Britain at war with Austria-Hungary.

August 15 The Panama Canal opens to shipping. Japanese give ultimatum to Germany.

August 17 Belgian capital removed from Brussels to Antwerp. Germans in Louvain.

August 19 Canadian Parliament authorizes an expeditionary force.

August 20 Germans take Brussels.

August 20-25 Germans capture Namur.

August 23 Battle of Mons. Japan enters the war against Germany.

August 24 Allies retreat across the Meuse River. Germans enter France near Lille.

August 25 Louvain destroyed by Germans.

August 26 Battle of Tannenburg begins. Battle of Le Cateau.

August 27 Allies retreat to Somme.

August 28 Austria declares war on Belgium.

August 29 New Zealanders occupy German Samoa.

August 30 Germans capture Amiens. Allies retreat.

September 3 Paris in state of siege; government transferred to Bordeaux. Germans at the Marne River.

September 5-10 First Battle of the Marne. Von Kluck is beaten back by Joffre, and Germans retreat from Paris to Soissons-Reims line.

September 14-15 First trenches of the Western Front are dug.

September 17-October 18 The "race to the sea."

September 23 Germans take St. Mihiel.

October-November First Battle of Ypres. Battle of Arras.

October 1 Antwerp surrenders. Government moved to Ostend.

October 3 British Army moves to Flanders.

October 14 Canadian Expeditionary Force of 35,000 men lands at Plymouth. Allies in Ypres.

October 15 Germans occupy Ostend and Zeebrugge. Belgian government removed to Le Havre, France.

October 16 Battle of the Yser River begins.

October-November First Battle of Ypres.

October 31 Crisis at Ypres. British line forced back.

1914 *(continued)*
November 1 British cruisers *Monmouth* and *Good Hope* sunk by German squadron off Chile. Germans take Messines.
November 5 Great Britain and France declare war on Turkey.
November 9 German cruiser *Emden* destroyed by Australian cruiser *Sydney.*
December 5 Russians driven from Lodz.
December 17 Egypt declared a British protectorate.
December 25 Unofficial Christmas truce by soldiers in the trenches.

1915
January 19 First German Zeppelin air raid on England.
February 10 Russians defeated by Germans in Battle of Masurian Lakes.
February 26 Germans use flamethrowers for first time near Verdun.
March 1 Britain declares blockade of German coast.
March 10-13 British take Neuve Chapelle in Flanders.
March 14 German raiding cruiser *Dresden* is sunk by British off Chile.
April 5 America demands reparation from Germany for sinking of the *William P. Frye.*
April 17 British offensive in Flanders (Hill 60) begins.
April-June Second Battle of Ypres. Germans begin bombardment of Ypres and ultimately destroy it.
April 22 First gas attack on French territorial and Canadian troops holding the line near Bikschote. The French were pushed back to Steenstraat but the Canadians held the line at St. Julien.
April 25-26 Landings at Gallipoli with severe British losses.
May 1 American tanker *Gulflight* torpedoed by Germans.
May 7 Cunard liner *Lusitania* sunk off Irish coast by German U-boat, with 1,152 lives lost.
May 16 Battle of Festubert begins.
May 23 Italy declares war on Austria-Hungary.
May 24 American steamer *Nebraskan* torpedoed off Irish coast but reaches Liverpool safely.
May 25 Allies begin assault on Gallipoli.
May 31 German Zeppelins bombard London suburbs.
June 26 Battle of the Argonne.
July 25 American steamer *Leelanaw* torpedoed off Scotland.
August 5 Warsaw captured by Germans.
August 19 White Star liner *Arabic* sunk by U-boat.
August 25 Brest-Litovsk, Russian fortress, captured by Austro-Germans.
September 1 Tsar Nicholas II takes control of Russian troops.
September 25 Allies open offensive on Western Front and occupy Lens. Battle of Loos begins.
September 30 Critical losses at the Battle of Loos.
October 12 English Nurse Edith Caval shot by Germans for helping Allied prisoners escape from Belgium.
October 13 London bombarded by Zeppelins: 55 killed, 114 injured.
October 14 Bulgaria at war with Serbia.
October 15 Britain declares war on Bulgaria.
December 19 General Sir Douglas Haig succeeds Field Marshall Sir John French as Commander-in-Chief of British forces in France.
December 19 Germans use phosgene gas mixed with chlorine.
December A third Canadian Division begins to form (to be completed in March 1916).

1916
January 29-31 German Zeppelins bomb Paris and towns in England.
February 21 Battle of Verdun, which will become the longest battle of the war, begins. Germans capture Haumont.
February 3 A fire of questionable origins destroys Centre Block of Canada's Parliament Buildings.
February 19 Germany declares waters around British Isles a war zone where all ships will be sunk on sight.
February 25 Germans take France's Fort Douaumont at Verdun.
March 9 Germany declares war on Portugal.
March 24 French cross-Channel passenger ship, *Sussex*, torpedoed.
April 19 American President Woodrow Wilson warns Germany not to pursue submarine policy.
April 24 Rebellion begins in Ireland on Easter Monday.
May 8 White Star liner *Cymric* torpedoed off Ireland.
May 15 General Nivelle superseded by General Pétain.
May 23 Italy enters the war.
May 31 British and German naval fleets suffer losses in the Battle of Jutland in North Sea.
June 4 Brusilov Offensive begins against Austria-Hungary.
June 5 Lord Kitchener en route to Russia is lost at sea when the cruiser *Hampshire* is sunk off Orkney Islands.
July 1 The Battle of the Somme begins north and south of Somme River in France. British suffer 60,000 casualties the first day.
August A fourth Canadian Division (formed from units already in England) crosses the Channel.
August 28 Italy at war with Germany; Germany at war with Rumania.
September 2 First Zeppelin shot down over Britain.
September 15 Tanks are introduced to war by on the Somme at Flers by Winston S. Churchill; British capture Flers, Courcelette.
October 13 Germans invade Rumania.
October 24 Fort Douaumont recaptured by French.
November 9 Battle of River Ancre.
November 21 British hospital ship *Britannic* is sunk by mine in Aegean Sea.
December 7 David Lloyd George succeeds Herbert Henry Asquith as Prime Minister.
December 15 French recapture Verdun.
December 31 Self-avowed Russian "holy man" Rasputin, is murdered by relatives of Tsar Nicholas II.
1917
January 1 Cunard liner *Ivernia* is sunk in Mediterranean.
January 16 Zimmerman telegram is intercepted by British.
January 22 President Woodrow Wilson suggests "peace without victory."
January 31 Germany announces plan to sink all vessels in war zone around Britain.
February 1 Germany again declares unrestricted submarine warfare.
February 3 United States severs diplomatic relations with Germany.
February 7 Anchor liner *California* is sunk off Irish coast without warning.
February 13 White Star liner, *Afric*, is sunk by submarine.
February 21 Germans retreat to Hindenburg Line.
February 24 Britain releases Zimmerman telegram to U.S.
February 25 Cunard liner *Laconia* is sunk off Irish coast.

1917 *(continued)*
February 26 President Wilson requests Congressional authority to arm U.S. merchant ships.
February 28 U.S. makes public the contents of Zimmerman telegram.
March 3 British advance on Bapaume. Zimmerman admits Mexican plot.
March 11 Russian revolution begins. British capture Baghdad.
March 15 Tsar Nicholas II abdicates, ending Romanov reign of three centuries.
March 18 American ships *City of Memphis, Illinois,* and *Vigilancia* torpedoed.
March 21 American tanker *Healdton* is sunk.
April German U-boats take heavy toll, more than 880,000 gross tons, 500,000 of which are British.
April 16-29 Mutiny among French troops.
April 1 American ship *Aztec* sunk.
April 5 American steamer *Missourian* sunk in Mediterranean.
April 6 United States declares war on Germany.
April 7 Cuba and Panama at war with Germany.
April 9 20,000 Canadians launch massive, text-book assault at Vimy Ridge.
April 10 Canadians capture Hill 145 placing Vimy in Canadian hands.
April 13 Vimy, Givenchy, Bailleul, and positions around Lens taken by Canadians.
April 16-May 15 Nivelle offensive suffers heavy losses.
May 4 U.S. Navy destroyers land in Ireland.
May 15 Pétain succeeds Nivelle as Commander in Chief of French armies.
June 6 British capture Messines-Wytschaete Salient, using a million pounds of explosives in the greatest mining operation in history.
June 12 King Constantine of Greece abdicates.
June 13 General John J. Pershing arrives in Paris. Gotha bombing raid on London.
June 27 American Expeditionary Force reaches France.
July 6 Canadian House of Commons passes Compulsory Military Service bill.
July 12 Germans use mustard gas.
July 16-November 10 Third Battle of Ypres (and Passchendaele).
July 16-23 Russians retreat along a 155-mile front.
July 26-31 British advance on Cambrai.
July 31 Third Battle of Ypres, a major British offensive.
August 8 Canadian conscription bill passes third reading in Senate.
August 14 China at war with Germany.
August 15 Canadian troops capture Hill 70, dominating Lens.
September 16 Russia proclaimed a republic.
October 6 Peru and Uruguay break with Germany.
October 17 American transport *Antilles* sunk by submarine.
October 23 American troops in France fire their first shots in trench warfare.
October 26 Brazil declares war on Germany.
November 5 General Pershing leads American troops into first action against the Germans.
November 6 Passchendaele captured by Canadians.
November 16: Bolshevik government formed in Russia.
November 24: British troops approach Cambrai with massed tanks, but Germans counterattack and regain much territory.
December 6 Steamer *Mont Blanc*, laden with munitions, explodes in Halifax Harbor after colliding with the *Imo*, killing 15,600 people. American destroyer *Jacob Jones* sunk by U-boat.
December 7 Finland declares independence from Russia.

1917 *(continued)*
   December 8 Jerusalem, held by Turks for 673 years, surrenders to British.
   December 11 United States at war with Austria-Hungary.
   December 15 Armistice signed between Germany and Russia at Brest-Litovsk.
   December 17 Coalition government of Sir Robert Borden is returned to office in
      Canada and conscription is confirmed.
1918
   January 8 President Wilson offers the Fourteen Points for world peace.
   February 21 British forces in Palestine capture Jericho.
   March 3 Treaty of Brest-Litovsk signed.
   March 21 Last German offensive on Western Front.
   March 26 Marshal Foch appointed overall Commander of Allied armies.
   March 28 Germans repulsed at Arras.
   April 1 Royal Air Force formed.
   April 15 Germans capture Messines Heights.
   April 25 British and Australian troops stop Germans near Amiens.
   May 23 German shells land on Paris.
   May 25 German U-boats make first appearance in U.S. waters.
   May 28 First American Division engaged at Castinuy.
   May 29 German troops are stopped by U.S. troops at the Marne.
   June 3 U-boats raid American shipping off New Jersey coast.
   June 4-7 American Marines engaged at Belleau Woods.
   July 15 General Ludendorff launches final offensive (Second battle of the Marne).
   July 16-17 Former Tsar Nicholas II, his wife, children, and members of his entourage
      are murdered by Bolsheviks.
   August 8 Second Battle of Amiens. German army's "Black Day."
   August 8 (to November 11) "Canada's Hundred Days" in which her troops advanced
      130 kilometers, captured 31,537 prisoners, and suffered 45,830 casualties.
   August 28-29 Germans retreat in Flanders.
   September 12-13 St. Mihiel Salient captured by Americans. U.S. forces take 15,000
      German prisoners.
   September 26 Major offensive by Americans in Meuse-Argonne. Second Battle of
      Cambrai.
   September 29 Allied troops break through the German fortifications at the Hinden-
      burg Line.
   September 30 Bulgaria surrenders.
   October 1 British troops occupy Damascus.
   October 9 Allies capture Cambrai.
   October 11-18 German defenses weaken.
   October 26 German General Ludendorff resigns.
   October 28 Mutiny at Kiel by German soldiers.
   October 29 Austria seeks armistice.
   October 31 Turkey surrenders.
   November 1 American break through German defenses at Meuse.
   November 3 Austria-Hungary surrenders. German navy mutinies.
   November 9 Kaiser Wilhelm II abdicates.
   November 10 The German Republic is founded.
   November 11 10:58 a.m. Canadian Private J. L. Price is last soldier to be killed in the
      war. The Armistice is signed at the 11th hour of the 11th day of the 11th month.
1919
   June 28 The Treaty of Versailles is signed in Hall of Mirrors at Versailles, France.

Index

by Sonie Liebler

— A —

Airplane
  American, 289-290
  Belgian, 289
  Brazilian, 290
  Fokker triplane, 278
  Gotha G IV bombers, 230
  Italian, 288-289
  Spitfire, 311
Alderson, General E. A. H.,
  58, 67, 74, 87, 90, 99, 107,
  113, 139, 144
Albert, King, 8, 31, 32, 40, 292
Albrecht, Duke of Württem-
  berg, 77, 92, 95
Algerians, 81, 83, 85-87
Algie, W. L. (Lieutenant), 298
Allenby, Sir Edmund (Gener-
  al), 154, 197
Allied
  artillery and guns, 96, 106,
    159, 178
  casualties, 278, 286
  Commanders-in-Chief, 263
  forces, 94, 109, 136, 154,
    184, 229, 283
  line, 43, 45-46, 84, 94, 98,
    154, 270
  offensive, xiii, 198, 224
  operation, 199
  shipping, 282
  Supreme War Council, 278
Allies, 36, 40, 46, 77, 98, 104,
  137, 146, 152, 175, 194,
  202, 220, 250, 260-261, 263,
  265-266, 271-272, 283, 286-
  287, 294, 297, 300
Alps, 43
Alsace-Lorraine, 2, 31
American, 42, 104, 191, 263,
  267, 281, 286, 290, 292-293,
  295, 300, 302-303, 305
  casualties, 290
  government, 104, 190, 193
  neutrality ends, 187
  offensive, 279
  ships, 192-193
  troops, 273, 275, 279, 283,
    287, 289
Andrews, _____, 69
Anglo-French
  forces, 197
  line, 46

ANZAC (Australian and New
  Zealand Army Corps), 170,
  248, 252, 254, 251, 304
Arizona, 193
Arthur, Prince, 21, 54
Ashworth, Tony, 117
Atlantic Ocean, 1, 4, 28, 52-
  53, 102, 111, 134, 154, 189,
  191, 279
Australia, xiv
Australian, 58, 169-170, 274,
  285-287
  casualties, 170
Austria, 6-8, 300
  Vienna, 267
Austria-Hungary, 3, 5, 188-189
Austrian, 267, 301
  armistice, 302
  howitzers, 40
Austro-German forces, 137

— B —

Balfour, Earl Arthur James,
  191
Balkans, 6
Baltic coast, 188
Baltic Sea, 4
barbed wire, 42, 46, 48, 128,
  132, 137, 152, 154-155, 158,
  163, 179-179, 198, 204, 227,
  235-236, 254, 264, 278
Barker, William G. (Lieutenant
  Colonel), 209
batmen (message carrier), 96
Battle of
  Aisne River
    Second Battle of, 220
  Arras, 218, 220
  Aubers Ridge
    Duck's Bill, 108-109
    H.2., 108-109
    H.3., 108-109
    K.5., 106-107
    K.10., 106-107
  Cannae, 29, 40
  Hill 52, 260
  Hill 60, 74-75, 87, 90, 96,
    149-150
  Hill 70, 197, 233-234, 236,
    243-245
  Hill 135, 198, 201
  Hill 145, 198, 201, 210,
    217-219

Battle of *(continued)*
  Hill Top Ridge, 90
  Hooge, 127
  Jutland, 155
  Loos, 234
  Marne, 28, 30, 34-37, 42,
    187, 252, 274
    Second Battle of, 37
  Menin Road, 257
  Messines Ridge, 229-233,
    236-237, 242-243
  Meuse-Argonne, 294-299
    Arras-Cambrai   Cam-
      paign, 298-299
  Mons, 33-34
  Neuve Chapelle, 69-70
  Passchendaele
    see Third Battle of Ypres
  Pilckem Ridge, 250
  Poelcappelle, 254
  Scarpe River, 227
  Somme, 153-167, 169-185,
    206, 261
  St. Eloi, 137-143
    Crater 2, 141-143
    Crater 3, 141-143
    Crater 4, 140-143
    Crater 5, 140-143
    Crater 6, 140, 142-143
    Crater 7, 140, 142-143
    "The Mound," 138-139
    Salient, 138
  St. Mihiel Salient, 272, 289
    290, 292
  Tannenberg, 33
  Valenciennes, 303-304
  Verdun, 125-134
  Vimy Ridge, 196-221, 224
  Waterloo, 33
  Ypres
    First Battle of, 41, 77
    Second Battle of, 73,77,
      80-90, 103
      gas attack, 77-84, 86-
        87, 92-93, 95-96, 98-
        99, 136
    Third Battle of (Passchen-
      daele), 238-239, 248,
      250, 253-261, 266, 271
      Salient, 41, 49, 72, 75, 77,
        80, 85, 87, 92, 95-96,
        98, 105, 137, 164, 166,
        229, 233, 297

Bavaria, 192
Bay of Biscay, 62
Beaverbrook, Lord, Max Aitken, 137, 139, 144
Belgian, 31-32, 72, 271, 297, 302-303
    army, 31-32, 40, 74
    coast, 188, 197
    forces, 292
Belgium, 3, 7-8, 28, 31, 33, 36, 39-40, 72, 77, 111, 127, 137, 146, 230, 249, 272, 309
    Bruges, 188, 292
    Brussels, 32
    Fort Pontisse, 32
    Frezenberg, 96
    Ghent, 292
    Liége, 31-32, 126
    Louvain, 32
    Namur, 34
    Nieuport, 40, 46
    Ostend, 153, 188, 249, 261, 300
    Passchendaele, 254-255, 257-261, 263-264, 297
        Passchendaele Ridge, 278
        Passchendaele Road, 258, 264
    Passchendaele-Westroosebeke sector, 253
    Ploegsteert ("Plug Street"), 109
    Poelcappelle, 252, 254
    Pozières, 169-170
    Pozières Ridge, 169-171, 181
    Spa, 301, 305
    Ypres, 40-41, 69, 72-75, 77, 80-83, 85, 89, 92, 95, 98-99, 102, 105-106, 113, 136-137, 143-144, 146, 149, 163-165, 172, 219, 229, 231, 249-250, 271, 277, 289
        Cloth Hall, 40, 72
        Menin Gate, 219
        Menin Road, 96
    Zeebrugge, 153, 188, 249, 261, 300
Bellew, Edward (Lieutenant), 93
Bermuda, 154
Bernhardi, Friedrich von (General), 5, 11-12
Berton, Pierre, 122, 203-205
Bethmann-Hollweg, Theobald von (Chancellor), 189
Birchall, Arthur P. (Lieutenant Colonel), 90-91
Bishop, Billy (Major), 208-209
Bismarck, Otto von, 2-3, 7, 28
Black Hand, 6
Bloch, Ivan, 42
Bolsheviks, 197

"bombers," 71, 88, 107
Borden, R. L. (Prime Minister), 110, 119, 271, 279-281
Bosnia
    Sarajevo, 6
    Bosnia-Herzegovina, 6
Boulter, _____, 69
Boyle, Russell (Lieutenant Colonel), 87-89
Bragg, Lawrence, 204
Bristol Channel, 62-63
British, 1, 33-34, 37, 40-41, 72,75, 93, 105, 108-109, 113-114, 125, 138-140, 142-144, 149, 153-158, 162, 167, 169-171, 175, 184, 180-190, 196-198, 204, 207, 209-210, 220, 225, 229, 231, 234, 236, 248, 250-254, 261, 266, 271-275, 278, 280, 285-287, 294-298
    Admiralty, 53
    Air Services, 209
    Army
        Medical Corps, 158
        New, 152
        Regular, 91, 152
        Reserve, 154, 169
        Territorial, 59
    casualties, 114-115, 152, 159, 162, 221, 251, 261
    Commonwealth, 8, 271, 292
    Empire, xiv, 164, 184, 187, 203
    Expeditionary Force (BEF), 69, 96-97, 117, 138, 123, 307, 309
    forces, 283-284, 286, 303-305, 307
    government, 7
    Guards, 49
    Heavy Groups (artillery), 227
    House of Commons, 54
    Intelligence, 213
    military units, 66, 69-70, 106-107, 113, 197-198
        divisions, 157, 248
        Pals, 278-279
        Royal Flying Corps (RFC), 147, 207, 210, 220, 265, 284
            No. 16 Squadron, 221
            No. 68 Squadron (Australian), 265
        Royal Horse Artillery, 227, 264
        trenches, 43-46, 96, 157, 162-163, 167
        troops, 33, 35-36, 75, 87, 90, 94-95, 140, 162, 278, 292, 300
        tunneling companies, 206
    War Cabinet, 274
    War Council, 32

British (continued)
    War Office, 57, 62, 112
    Yorkshire Battalions, 94
British Isles, 103
Britton, R. H. (Lietuenant Colonel), 227
Brooke, Alan (Major), 301
Brown
    Harry (Private), 243
    Roy (Captain), 278
Brutinel, Raymond (Brigadier General), 204-205
Bull, Lucien, 204
bully beef, 118
Burns, Martin, 24
Burstall, H. E. (Brigadier General), 108, 149
Butler
    H. C. (Lieutenant), 148
    J. A. (Gunner), 84
Byng, Sir Julian H. (Lieutenant General), 144, 148, 175-176, 197, 199-200, 206, 209, 218, 234, 265, 273, 275, 286
Byng Trophy, 144

— C —
Caesar, Julius, 151, 197
Campbell, F. W. (Lieutenant), 109
Cairns, Hugh (Sergeant), 304
California
    Los Angeles, 43
    San Francisco, 43
Canada, xiii-xiv, 1, 8, 11, 14, 17-18, 26-28, 52, 58, 60-61, 104, 107, 119, 137, 140, 144, 146-147, 183, 187, 219-221, 246, 259, 271, 281
    Alberta, 89, 176
        Calgary, 13, 87, 91
    British Columbia, 11, 26, 111, 155
        Esquimalt, 12
        Vancouver, 11, 67, 116
    Manitoba, 89
        Winnipeg, 11, 87
    New Brunswick, 13, 94
    Ontario, 25, 105, 108
        Berlin, 144
        Cumberland, 68, 70, 82, 309-311
            Public Memorial, 310
            Township of, 309
        Guelph, 23, 82
        Haileybury, 18
        Orleans, 17
        Ottawa, 17-18, 55, 80, 84
            Peace Tower, 209
            Valley, 18, 108, 311

Canada *(continued)*
Ontario *(continued)*
Toronto, 11, 43, 67, 81, 87, 102, 136
Windsor, 27
Saskatchewan
Regina, 144
Quebec, 14-17, 23, 57
Lachute, 217
Montreal, 11, 13, 43, 81, 86, 208, 259
Quebec City, 13, 23-24
Valcartier, 13, 23-24
Canadian, xiv, xvi, 11, 18, 26, 55, 58, 62, 67, 70, 72, 80, 84-85, 88-91, 93-94, 98, 106-109, 120, 125, 136-138, 140, 144, 146-150, 160, 170-176, 178-184, 193, 200-203, 205-207, 209-212, 215-216, 218, 221, 224-225, 227, 231, 234-236, 240, 243-245, 253, 255-260, 263-265, 271, 274, 278-280, 284-289, 304-305, 307
army, 12, 67, 99
Service Corps, 13
Cavalry Brigade, 264
Artillery, 181, 183, 207-208, 224-227, 229, 231, 233, 236-239, 241-245
Cabinet, 25
casualties, 92, 97, 143, 179, 202, 221, 259-260, 266- 268, 299, 304, 307
Casualty Clearing Station, 155, 158, 198, 245
Dressing Station, 158
Corps, 113, 137-138, 144, 148, 150, 170, 175-176, 197, 199, 201, 205, 207-208, 213, 220, 234, 245, 248, 254, 259, 278, 283, 286, 288-289, 293, 297-298, 303
Heavy Artillery, 227
Dominion government, 54, 220
Expeditionary Force (CEF), 14, 22, 26
Field Artillery (CFA), 81, 86, 148, 214, 220, 237
Field Post Office, 69
Field Service, 71
Governor General's Foot Guards (GGFG), 17-18, 21
Intelligence, 116, 143, 213
Military Department, 112
Military Police Special Services, 309
Mounted Rifles (CMR), 176
Non-Permanent Active Militia (NPAM), 12

Canadian *(continued)*
Parliament, 12
Permanent Force, 12
Princess Patricia's Canadian Light Infantry (PPCLI), 13
Reserve
Divisional Artillery, 227
Militia, 18
Reserves, 17
Royal Canadian
Air Force, 309
Highlanders, 307
Horse Artillery (RCHA), 116
Marine Artillery, 206
Navy, 11-12
Regiment, 305, 307
submarines, 12
Class C, 12
C.C. 1, 12
C.C. 2, 12
troops, 20, 23, 58, 62-63, 66-67, 73-75, 80-81, 105, 111-113, 116, 172-176, 213, 285, 287, 304
training in England, 59-61
Bustard Camp, 58
Pond Farm Camp, 58
Shorncliffe Camp, 112
West Down North Camp, 58
West Down South Camp, 58
trenches, 73-74, 85, 115-117, 147-149, 172, 200, 206, 230-231, 278
Canadian Convalescent Hospital (Bear Wood, England), 246
Canadian Gazette (Extra Edition), 8
Canadian National Vimy Ridge Memorial, 219
Canadian Pacific Railway, 27
Canal de l'Yser, 90
Central Powers, 36, 40, 43, 137, 197, 267, 271, 292, 301
Chapman, Bombardier, 180
Chemin des Dames Ridge, 197, 220
Chile, 12
Chotek, Sophie, 5-6
Churchill, Winston S., 36-37, 52, 134, 171, 173, 175, 184, 260, 267
Civil War (American), 42
Clarke, Leo (Corporal), 170
Clausewitz, Karl von, 136
Clemenceau, Georges (Premier), 278, 290
Clough, Arthur Hugh (poet), 277, 292

Clyne, Harry (Captain), 207-208
Coburg World, 118
Collishaw, Raymond (Major), 209
Colt machine gun, 86
Continuous Wave (CW) wireless set, 236, 243
Council of War at Spa, 301
Crimean War, 162
Croak, J. V. (Private), 286
Croft, Earl (Lieutenant), 118
Costigan, Captain, 137
Coutanceau, General, 126
Cunard line, 102, 192
Currie
Sir Arthur W. (Lieutenant General), 67, 80, 99, 106-107, 113, 149, 199, 210, 234, 236, 241, 243, 245, 253, 255, 258-260, 278-279, 288-289, 293-294, 303
J. A. (Colonel), 52, 62, 65, 93

— D —
Dante, 169, 254
Dardanelles expedition, 152
Darwin, Charles Galton, 204
Day, Gunner, 180
da Vinci, Leonardo, 171
Desire and Desire Support Trenches, 183
Deville, Captain, 21
Driant, Emile (Colonel), 126
Drocourt-Queant (D-Q) Line, 287-289, 293
Drummond, Guy (Captain), 86
duckboards, 44, 48, 252, 305
Duguid, A. Fortescue, 26, 98
Duke of Wellington, 297
Dutch frontier, 230

— E —
Eastern Front, 113, 137, 250, 267, 271, 302
Eckhardt, Heinrich von (German Imperial Minister to Mexico), 189-191, 193
Edmonds, J. E., 225, 229
Egypt, 58
Ellis, John, 45
England, 14, 62, 91, 94, 102, 107, 111-112, 119, 144, 181, 188-189, 193, 245, 267
Amesbury, 57
Amesbury Station, 57-58
Avonmouth, 62-63
Berkshire
Wokingham
Bear Wood, 246
Devonshire, 159

England *(continued)*
  Folkestone, 112, 230
  Hampshire
    Boscombe, 245-246
  Liverpool, 102, 246
  London, 32, 156, 252, 274
    No. 10 Downing Street, 233
  Plymouth, 55, 57
    Harbor, 57
  Portsmouth, 32
  Salisbury Plain, 57-61, 63, 112, 144, 203
  Shorncliffe, 230
  Southampton, 32, 55, 57
English, 58, 77, 270, 274
English Channel, 9, 35, 40-41, 46, 55, 72, 113, 151, 156, 230, 249, 267,270, 272, 274, 292, 296
Erzberger, Matthais, 307
Europe, 2, 5, 8, 20, 26, 33, 112, 188, 263, 266
Eye Deep in Hell, 45

— F —
Falkenhayn, Erich von (General), 39-40, 46, 77, 111, 127, 132-134, 167
Farmer
  Eva, 18-25, 58, 60-61, 68-69,71, 110, 118-120, 122, 180, 245-246, 309-311
  Walter, 82
Ferdinand, Francis (Archduke), 5-7
Fernie, Bombardier, 180
fire step, 44, 47, 293
Fisher, Frederick (Lance Corporal), 86-87, 98
flamethrower, 127, 131-132, 236, 244, 296
Flanders, 16, 40-41, 43-44, 49, 69, 72, 97-98, 125, 153, 170, 196, 240, 254, 270, 272, 281, 287, 292
  Offensive, 248, 252, 254
flash spotting (artillery), 203-204
Foch, Ferdinand (General), 95, 99, 249, 274-275, 278, 283, 285, 287, 292, 305
Forward Observation Officer (FOO), 118-119, 148
Fourteen Points, 272
France, 2-4, 7-9, 11, 14-15, 17, 26, 28-29, 31-32, 34, 39, 59, 61-62, 64, 70, 111-113, 127, 131, 134, 137-138, 144, 146, 151, 154, 163, 181, 187-188, 196-197, 219, 221, 267, 271-273, 278-280, 303, 309

France *(continued)*
  Abbeville, 278
  Albert, 156, 182
  Amiens, 274, 283-284, 286
  Arleux, 225, 227
    Arleux Loop, 225
  Armagh Wood, 149
  Armentières, 66-67, 109, 277
  Arras, 94, 114, 154, 181, 196-197, 229, 234, 273, 284, 287, 298-299
  Artois, 109, 152
  Aubers Ridge, 105
  Avion, 237
  Bapaume, 152, 157, 184, 274
  Batigny, 298
  Bazoches, 286
  Beaumont-Hammel, 155, 161-162
    Caribou Memorial, 161
  Bec de Canard, 46
  Belleau Wood, 280-281, 293
  Bethune, 108
  Blecourt, 298
  Bois de la Ville, 201
  Bois Dixhuit, 242
  Boulogne, 113
  Bourlon Wood, 265, 293
  Briey Basin, 127
  Buissy, 288
  Cagnicourt, 288
  Camblain, 184
  Cambrai, 164, 263-264, 287, 292-293, 296-299
  Canal du Nord, 293
  Cassel, 68, 72, 95, 113
  Champagne, 69, 114, 152
  Charleville, 39, 303
  Chipilly, 228
  Cite du Grande Conde, 241
  Cite St. Auguste, 241
  Compiègne forest, 305
  Courcelette, 169, 174-176, 179
  Cuvillers, 298
  Delville Wood, 287
  Dessart Wood, 264
  Douai Plain, 105, 196, 213, 234
  Epehy, 294
  Escaudoeuvres, 298
  Escaut Canal, 304
  Farbus, 207
  Farbus Wood, 201, 210, 215
  Festubert, 105, 152
  Flesquieres, 266
  Fontaine, 265
  Fort Douaumont, 126, 128-129, 131, 133
  Fort Souville, 132-133
  Fortuin, 73

France *(continued)*
  Fort Vaux, 126, 131-133
  Fresney, 227, 229
  Ginchy, 169
  Givenchy, 105, 108, 207, 217
  Gommecourt, 154
  Gravenstafel, 95, 252
  Havrincourt, 294
  Hawthorne Ridge, 162
    Hawthorn Redoubt Mine, 162
  Hazebrouck, 113
  Inchy-en-Artois, 293
  Iwuy, 298
  Juvigny, 287
  Kitchener's Wood, 87-90, 92, 98-99
  La Bassée Canal, 107, 114, 277
  La Folie Farm, 201
  Lassigny, 287
  Le Cateau, 34, 95, 296, 300
  Le Havre, 62
  Lens, 114, 181, 184, 196, 233-234, 244, 248, 301
  Le Quesnoy, 303-304
  Lille, 46, 114, 196, 300
  Loos, 114-115, 152, 154, 233, 244, 248
    Elvaston Castle, 244
  Mametz Woods, 287
  Maple Copse, 148
  Marcoing, 297
  Masnieres, 265
  Maubeuge, 126
  Mauser Ridge, 80, 90
  Messines, 230, 277
  Messines Ridge, 41
  Mezieres, 292, 303
  Moevres, 265
  Moreuil Wood, 274
  Morval, 169
  Mount Houy, 303
  Mount Sorrel, 146, 148-149
  Mouse Trap Farm, 85-86, 94
  Nancy, 125
  Neuve Chapelle, 152
  Noyon, 274
  Nubecourt, 36
  Ors, 304
  Paris, 28, 35-36, 125-126, 129, 131, 274, 283
  Peronne, 287
  Petite Douve Farm, 116
  Picardy, 15
  Pilckem, 97
  Pilckem Ridge, 80, 250
  Pont d'Aire, 298
  Ramillies, 298
  Reims, 283
  Roubaix, 46

France *(continued)*
Sallaumines, 234
Sambre Canal, 304-305
Samogneux, 129
Sanctuary Wood, 146, 148-149, 160
Sedan, 303, 305
Seicheprey, 279
Serre, 155, 184
Soissons, 197
Steenstratt, 72
Steenvorde, 68
St. Eloi, 72, 136-137, 143-144, 149-150, 138
St. Julien, 80, 82, 85, 87, 90, 92, 95
St. Michael, 279, 290, 295
St. Nazaire, 62, 64, 66
St. Omer, 113, 170, 245
St. Quentin, 151, 292, 296
St. Quentin Canal, 264
Thélus, 198, 201, 207
Thiaumont Works, 132
Thiepval, 169-170, 175
Thiepval Ridge, 287
Turcoing, 46
Valenciennes, 303-304
Verdun, 125-134, 137-138, 153-154, 167, 184, 187, 197, 199, 234, 270, 272, 289, 294, 296
Versailles
  Hall of Mirrors, 2
Ville-sur-Haine, 307
Vimy Ridge, xiii, 105, 114, 196-198, 200-201, 205, 234, 255, 271, 277
Vlamertinghe, 74
Voie Sacree, 130
Wimereux, 271
Wytschaete Ridge, 140
Zillebeke, 239
Franco-British
  Front, 137
  Offensive, 152
Franco-Prussian War (1870-1871), 303
Franz Josef I, Emperor, 5
Frederick III, 3
French, 5, 29, 31, 36-37, 41, 43, 49, 72, 74, 77, 83, 85, 90, 95, 108, 113-114, 125, 127-129, 131-134, 138, 151, 153-154, 164, 196-199, 218, 220, 248, 250, 271-275, 278, 280, 283, 285, 292, 294, 299, 303-305, 307
  army, 87, 248, 258
    Headquarters, 74
    Intelligence, 127, 199

French *(continued)*
  casualties, 92, 97, 115, 133-134, 152, 184, 254
  forces, 69, 105
  High Command, 126
  troops, 33-34, 36, 72, 81, 87, 287, 290, 302-303, 305
French, Sir John (Commander), 36, 41, 69, 72, 95, 99, 109, 115
French-German border, 28-29, 40
Fresney-Rouvoy Line, 288-289

— G —
Galicia, 249
Gallipoli Campaign, 114, 137
Gambeth, Leon, 2
Gallieni, Joseph Simon (General), 35-36, 126
Gaspé Bay, 26, 52, 54, 120
Gaspé Harbor, 1
Gault, A. Hamilton (Captain), 13, 96
Geddes, John (Captain), 89
George V, King, 18, 60, 62, 99, 113, 163, 220, 234
German, 2-5, 22, 31-32, 35, 41-42, 45, 62, 67, 74-75, 77, 80, 83-84, 86, 89-90, 92-96, 98, 105, 109, 114, 120, 125-133, 137, 139, 141, 143, 147-160, 162-163, 167, 169-170, 173, 175-176, 178-179, 181-182, 184, 191-192, 194, 196-198, 200-205, 208, 210, 213, 215, 217-218, 220, 225, 229-231, 233-235, 243-244, 249-250, 252, 256-259, 261, 264-266, 271-275, 277-278, 280-281, 284, 293-305, 307
  Admiralty Staff, 181
  Armistice Commission, 305
  army, 29, 32, 40,74
  artillery, 107
  Campaign of 1914, 36
  casualties, 97, 115, 150, 152, 184, 261, 266, 275, 278, 286, 305
  cavalry, 31
  Foreign Office, 27
  General Staff, 4
  High Command, 77, 284, 290
  High Seas Fleet, 4, 305
  morale, 286-287
  navy, 2, 9, 300
    cruisers, 26
  offensive, 283, 285
  Reichsarchiv, 98
  Secret Service, 26-27
  Storm Troopers, 127

German *(continued)*
  submarines (U-boats), 55, 55, 62, 64, 103-104, 180-190, 192-194, 197, 249, 285, 300-301
  bases, 249
  campaign, 272
  U-20, 103
  trenches, 43, 45-47, 69, 75, 110, 147-149, 155-156, 159, 162-163, 175-184, 206-208, 213, 215, 227, 293
Germany, 2-5, 7-8, 17, 26-29, 36-39, 46, 72, 74-75, 103-104, 109, 127, 187-191, 193, 251-252, 267, 271-274, 285, 287, 296-297, 303-304
  Berlin, 8-9, 190, 300
  Kiel, 305
  Munich, 5
  Nauen, 9, 190
Gibson
  (Gunner), 180
  R. B. (Sergeant), 171
Good, H. J. (Corporal), 286
Goodspeed, D. J., 196
Gordon, H. (Brigadier General), 158
Gough, Sir Hubert (General), 154, 164, 169-171, 183, 250, 273, 275
Great Britain, xiv, 3, 7-9, 11, 13, 15, 26, 29, 31-32, 54, 57, 103, 163-164, 180, 187-188, 190, 265, 267, 301
Great War, xiii, 1-2
  see also World War I
Greek Battle of Marathon, 131
Greek, 60
Grey, Sir Edward, 8
Griggs, A. (Lieutenant), 265
Gulf of St. Lawrence, 54
Guthrie, Percy (Major), 94
Gwyn, Sandra, 184

— H —
Hague, the, 74
Hague Conference, 5
Haig
  A. G. (Colonel), 204
  Sir Douglas (General), 69, 95, 106-107, 113, 115-116, 138, 152-153, 159, 169-171, 173, 175, 181, 184, 197-198, 204, 211, 220, 225, 227, 229, 234, 236, 248-252, 254-255, 260-261, 265, 271, 273, 277-278, 285, 287, 293
Haley, _____, 119
Hall
  F. W. (Sergeant Major), 93

Hall *(continued)*
 Sir William Reginald, 190-191
Halsey, Francis Whiting, 17
Hanley, Gunner, 180
Hannibal, 29
Helmer
 Alexis (Lieutenant), 82, 97
 R. A. (Colonel), 82
Hemming, Harold, 203
Herr, Colonel, 129
Herwig, Holger, H., 43
"Hessian" Line Trench (Somme),
 175
Hindenburg Line, 191, 197, 293,
 296
Hindenburg, Paul von (Field Mar-
 shal), 33, 133, 189, 286, 297
Hitler, Adolf, 297
Hobson, Fred (Sergeant), 244
Hoffman, _____, 111
Holland, 28, 305
Holtzendorf, Henning von (Ad-
 miral), 188-189
"Horatio at the Bridge," 298
Horne, Sir Henry (General), 198,
 234, 236
Horses, 12, 15, 23, 24, 26, 34-35,
 59, 64, 80-82, 128-129, 133,
 159, 184, 188, 203, 224-228,
 250, 252, 255-258, 265, 267,
 284
"Hotel De Buzz," 119
Hötzendorf, Franz Conrad von
 (General), 6-7
Hughes
 Garnet (Lieutenant General), 67
 Sam (Colonel), 12-14, 21, 52,
 62, 67, 144
Hugo, Victor, 2
Hungary
 Budapest, 267
Hutcheson, B. S. (Captain), 288

— I —
Imperial German Government,
 103
Indian Corps, 41
Industrial Revolution, 2
"In Flanders Fields," 23, 97
International Declaration, 74
Ireland, 103
 Kinsdale, 103
 Old Head, 103
Irish, 265
 battalions, 265
 Guards, 115
 1st Battalion, 115
 2nd Battalion, 115
 Royal Irish Regiment, 93
Irish Sea, 300

Italy, 3
 Caporetto, 197
 Italian, 197
 Front, 137, 254, 302
Irving, T. C. (Captain), 73

— J —
"Jack Johnson's" shells, 80
Japan, 190, 193
Japanese, 193
Jellicoe, Sir John R. (Admiral),
 249
Jerusalem, 267
Joffre, Joseph (General), 29, 36,
 69,74, 95, 105, 114, 126-127,
 129-130, 152-153, 197
Johnson, H. (Lieutenant), 241
Joubaire, Alfred, 39

— K —
Keegan, John, 170, 184
Kemball, A. H. G. (Lieutenant
 Colonel), 203
Kennedy
 Carleton, 311
 "Hap," xvi, 311
 Robert, xvi, 311
 Robert James, ix, xiii, 17-26,
 53, 55, 58, 60-62, 64, 67-69,
 71, 80, 82-83, 92, 96, 107-
 108, 110, 118-122, 149-150,
 170, 180-181, 184, 206-207,
 237, 245-246, 309-311
 Thurlow, 17
Kenora Trench, 176-178
Kerry, Sergeant, 180
Kiel Canal, 4
Kiel Institute for World Econ-
 omy, 189
Kiggell, Sir Launcelot (Lieuten-
 ant General), 248, 260
King of Bavaria, 305
King
 Mackenzie (Prime Minister), 2
 William B. M. (Major), 86-87,
 98
Kipling
 John (Lieutenant), 115
 Rudyard, 60, 115
Kitchener armies, 114, 184
Kitchener, Lord Horatio H., 8, 55,
 60, 113-114, 144, 153, 155, 167
Kluck, Alexander von (General),
 33-35, 133, 307
Knight, A. G. Sergeant, 288
Korean War, 162
Kriegsbrauch im Landkriege, 4
Krupp "Big Bertha" Howitzer,
 32, 127, 132
Kultur, 5

— L —
Laffin, John, 3-4, 60, 261
Lahore artillery groups and bat-
 teries, 149
"La Marseillaise," 11
Lanrezac, Charles (General), 34
Learmouth, O. M. (Major), 244
Leckie, R. G. E. (Lieutenant), 88-
 89, 91-92
Lee-Enfield Rifle, 14-15, 109,
 141, 150
Lewis gun, 244, 304
Liddell Hart, B. H., 35, 37, 260,
 283
Liggett, Hunter (Major General),
 296, 303
Llandovery Castle ("L.C.") Oper-
 ational Instructions, 285
Lloyd George, David (Prime
 Minister), 164, 173, 175, 233,
 252, 260, 271, 274, 278
Loomis, Frederick (Lieutenant
 Colonel), 85
Ludendorff, Erich (General), 111,
 184, 189, 192, 251, 254, 266-
 267, 272-273, 275, 281, 284,
 286, 297, 300-301
Luxembourg, 8, 39

— M —
"MacAdam" shovel, 15, 67
MacArthur, Douglas (Colonel),
 302
MacDonald, Harold (Captain),
 94
MacDowell, Thane (Major), 217
MacLaren, Joseph (Major), 89
Maine, 26-27
 Vanceboro, 27
March, Francis, xiv
Marshall
 George C. (General), 295
 S. L. A., 5, 261, 295
Mary, Queen, 60
Maxim, Hiram, 42
McCrae, John (Major), 23, 69,
 82-83, 97-98, 271
McDougall, A. A. (Lieutenant),
 202
McGill University (Montreal),
 203
McKenna, W. J. (Private), 88
McIntosh, Norman, 109
McNaughton, A. G. L. (Major),
 59, 203-204, 213
Medal
 Distinguished Conduct Medal,
 109
 Distinguished Service Order,
 217

Medal *(continued)*
Grand Cross of the Legion of Honor (French), 32
Legion d' Honneur, 131
Military Medal (French), 32
Purple Heart (American), 309
Victoria Cross, 85-86, 93-94, 109, 170, 209, 211-212, 217, 243-244, 260, 265, 286, 288, 297-298
Melvin, Tom, 24
"Memorandum on Training," 71-72
Mercer, Malcolm S. (Major General), 67, 75, 99, 136, 147, 150
Metcalf, W. H. (Lance Corporal), 288
Mexico, 190-191, 193
Mexican, 193
Middlebrook, Martin, 158
Milne, W. J. "Bill" (Private), 211
Miner, H. G. B. (Corporal), 286
Mitchell, C. N. (Captain), 298
Moltke
Helmuth von (General), 27, 34
Helmuth von (the younger), 27, 29-30
Montenegro, 267
Montreal Light, Heat, and Power, 27
Moroccan, 81
Morrison, Edward W. B. (Lieutenant Colonel), 68, 81, 96-97, 205, 236
Morton, Desmond, 117
Muggleton, George, 24

— Military Units —
1st Battalion (Western Ontario), 20, 87, 90, 91-92, 99, 109
1st Canadian Divisional Artillery, 225, 227
1st Essex Regiment (British), 162-163
1st Field Artillery Brigade (Canadian), 22, 67, 68, 81, 96-97, 116, 237, 243-245
1st Battery, 244
2nd Battery, 244
3rd Battery, 243-245
4th Battery, 243-244
1st Infantry Brigade (Canadian), 71,74-75, 80, 99, 107-108, 136, 227, 229
Ammunition Column, 22, 80, 82
1st Lincolns (Canadian), 154
1st Motor Machine Gun Brigade (Canadian), 204
2nd ANZAC Corps, 254-255, 258

— Military Units *(continued)* —
2nd Battalion (Eastern Ontario), 21, 87, 89
A Company, 88-89
2nd Canadian Divisional Artillery, 227
2nd Canadian Pioneer Battalion, 140-141
2nd Corps (British), 175
2nd Division (U.S.), 280
Marine Brigade, 280-281
2nd East Yorkshire Battalion (British), 87
2nd Field Artillery Brigade (Canadian), 68, 93
2nd Battery, 69, 110, 119, 237
2nd Field Company (Canadian), 73
2nd Infantry Brigade (Canadian), 59-60, 69, 71, 73-74, 80, 94, 99, 106, 113, 242
1st Battery, 208, 211
2nd Howitzer Battery, 237, 241-242, 245
3rd Battery, 242
4th Battery, 242
3rd Battalion (Toronto), 87, 89, 149, 178-179
3rd Canadian Divisional Artillery, 227
3rd Canadian Tunneling Company, 139
3rd Corps (British), 285
3rd "Diehard" Brigade (British), 90
3rd Infantry Brigade (Canadian), 59-60, 69, 71, 74, 80, 94, 99, 106
4th Battalion (Central Ontario), 87, 90-92, 99, 142, 178-179
Engineers, 298
4th Canadian Mounted Rifles, 147-148, 175, 298
4th Infantry Brigade (Canadian), 140
5th Battalion (Western Cavalry), 210, 264, 289
5th Canadian Mounted Rifles, 298
5th Cavalry (Western Canadian), 176
5th Corps (British), 72, 137
5th Infantry Brigade (Canadian), 140, 178, 208, 229
6th Infantry Brigade (Canadian), 140-142, 227, 229
7th Battalion (1st British Columbia), 113, 116, 201, 210, 289
7th Infantry Brigade (Canadian), 143

— Military Units *(continued)* —
8th Cavalry (Canadian), 176
8th Infantry Battalion (90th Rifles) (Canadian), 92-93, 99, 176, 242
9th Brigade (British), 139
10th Battalion (Canadian), 87-90, 94, 97-98, 106-107, 137, 243, 289
10th Cavalry (Canadian), 176
10th Infantry Brigade (Canadian), 183, 207
11th Division (French), 74
11th Infantry Brigade (Canadian), 181, 183, 201, 203, 218
13th Battalion (Royal Highlanders of Canada), 81, 85-86, 91, 93, 98-99, 149, 175, 179, 286, 288
13th Brigade (British), 221
14th Battalion (Royal Montreal Regiment), 176, 210, 288
15th Battalion (48th Highlanders of Canada), 52, 92-93, 99, 210
15th Battery (Canadian), 1487
16th Battalion (Canadian Scottish), 82, 88, 92, 98-99, 106, 149, 178-179, 210-211, 288
17th Infantry Brigade (Canadian), 208
18th Battalion (Western Ontario), 113, 142
18th Reserve Jager Battalion (German), 139
20th Battalion (Central Ontario), 142, 298
21st Battalion (Kingston and Eastern Ontario), 142
22nd Battalion (French Canadians), 175, 178, 288
24th Battalion (Victoria Rifles of Canada), 178
25th Battalion (Nova Scotia Rifles), 137, 142, 175, 178, 298
26th Battalion (New Brunswick), 142, 175, 227
26th Yankee Division (U.S.), 279
27th Battalion (City of Winnipeg), 140-142, 259, 298
27th Division (British), 67
28th Battalion (Northwest Canada), 137, 142, 176, 227, 307
29th Battalion (Vancouver), 137, 141-143, 176, 207, 298
29th Division (British), 154, 162
31st Battalion (Alberta), 140-142, 176, 298
38th Battalion (Ottawa), 217, 289
39th Battery (Canadian), 224
42nd Battalion (Royal Highlanders of Canada), 307

— **Military Units** *(continued)* —
44th Battalion (Manitoba), 181-182, 218, 258, 303
45th Division (Algerian), 77, 85, 90
45th Division (French), 87, 90
46th Battalion (South Saskatchewan), 183-184, 218, 258, 288,307
47th Battalion (British Columbia), 183, 289, 304
49th Edmonton Regiment (Canadian), 175, 259
50th Battalion (Calgary), 218, 289
51st Highlander Unit (British), 220
52nd Battalion (New Ontario), 258
54th Battalion (Kootenay), 183-184, 203, 215, 217
58th Battalion (Central Ontario), 149
70th Brigade (British), 159
72nd Battalion (Seaforth Highlanders), 217, 227, 258, 289
78th Battalion (Winnipeg Grenadiers), 217, 258, 286
85th Battalion (Nova Scotia Highlanders), 289
87th Battalion (Canadian Grenadier Guards), 181
87th Grenadier Guards (British), 213-214
87th Territorial Division Artillery (French), 77, 81
102nd Battalion (North British Columbians), 181, 183
308th Infantry Regiment (U.S.), 296
1st Battalion, 296
Allied Forces
First Army, 229
Third Army, 229
American
First Army, 134, 295
Second Army, 295
Australian
Corps, 255
Division, 254, 284
First, 169, 258
Second, 170
Imperial Force (AIF), 169
Reserve Army, 170
tunnelers, 231
British
Fifth Army, 251, 253, 273, 275, 297
Fifth Division, 198, 229
First Army, 234, 253, 255, 267, 271, 286, 293, 297, 304

— **Military Units** *(continued)* —
British *(continued)*
First Division, 107, 260
Fourth Army, 154, 159, 173, 255, 285-286, 297
Middlesex Regiment, 90
Second Army, 72, 229, 251, 253, 255, 293, 297
Third Army, 154, 197, 234, 255, 273, 275, 286, 289, 293, 296-298
Third Division, 139
Canadian
"C" Company, 23
First Division (First Contingent), 1, 13, 52-54, 60-62, 88, 109, 111-113, 140, 143, 146-147, 170, 176, 179, 183, 208, 210-213, 236, 259-260, 288-289, 297
Fort Garry Horse unit, 264
"B" Squadron, 264-265
Fourth Division, 170, 181-184, 202-203, 213, 217-218, 220-221, 236, 243-244, 258-259, 288-289
Second Division (Second Contigent), 111-113, 138-140, 143, 146, 170, 173, 211-213, 236, 259-260, 288, 298
Third Division, 136, 146-147, 170, 175, 179, 183, 213, 236, 258-259, 288, 298
Artillery, 140
French
Fifth Army, 33
Fourth Army, 295
Sixth Army, 154
Tenth Army, 74
German
First Army, 32
Second Army, 31
Fourth Army, 72, 77
Fifth Army, 127
Russian
Second Army, 33
Eleventh Army, 249

— **N** —
Napoleon, 164
Napoleon III, 303
Nasmith, George (Colonel), 81
National Hockey League, 144
New Mexico, 193
New York, 2, 26
New York City, 102, 245, 309
New York Times, 191
New Zealand, xiv, 58, 254, 304
contingent, 58
troops, 278, 303-304

Newfoundland, 11, 154, 162-163
British colony, 162
Newfoundland Regiment, 161-163
Nicholas II, Tsar, 7
Nicholson
G. W. L. (Colonel), 196-197, 220, 261, 284, 220
Nathaniel (Private), 82
Nivelle, Robert Georges (General), 125, 131, 133, 197-198, 220
Niven, H. W. (Lieutenant), 96
Nobel Prize, 203-204
No Man's Land, 44-46, 48, 70, 81, 85, 117,137, 152, 156-159, 163, 178, 202-203, 207, 241, 254, 267, 272
North Africa, 9
North Sea, 4, 8, 40
North Sea Cables, 8-9
Norsworthy, Edward (Major), 85-87, 98
Nova Scotia
Cape Sable, 12
Halifax, 112, 266
Nunneg, C. J. P. (Private), 288

— **O** —
Observation balloons, 203
Observatory Ridge, 146, 148-149
"O Canada," 55, 88, 91
Odlum, Victor (Brigadier General), 93, 201-202
Odysseus, 53
On War, 136
Operation Alberich, 191-192, 197
Operation Michael, 267, 273-275
Oppy-Mericourt line, 225
Ormond, Dan (Major), 89-91
Ottawa Citizen, 81
Owen, Wilfred (poet), 305

— **P** —
Pacific Ocean, 111
Panama, xiv
Papineau, Talbot, 259
parados, 44, 72
parapet, 44, 72-73
Pershing, John J. (General), 263, 275, 278, 295-296, 303
Pétain, Henri-Philippe (Marshal), 128-131, 248, 273
Peter the Great, 272
Pheidippides, 131
pigeons, carrier, 131, 143, 163, 171, 296
Pikelhaube (spiked helmet), 41
Pilckem, 87
Pilckem Ridge, 250

Pioneers, 19, 96, 140-141, 255
Plan XVII, 29
Plumer, Sir Herbert (General), 72, 87, 95, 229, 251, 253
Poincaré, Raymond (President), 290
Poincaré family, 36
poison gas, 74, 77, 90, 94, 102, 109, 132, 236, 243-244
  chlorine gas, 84, 92, 114
  phosgene gas, 132-133
  teargas, 90
  "yellowcross" mustard gas, 236, 243-244, 302
Poland, 272
  Brest-Litovsk, 272
  Grunwald, 32
Price
  George (Private), 307
  H. (Captain), 155
Prince Edward Islands, 11, 111
Princip, Gavrilo, 6
Prior, Robin, 169
Prussia, 2, 8
  East, 33
Prussian, 60
  Guard, 217

— R —
"race to the sea," 40
Rawling, Bill, 199, 227
Rawlinson, Sir Henry (Lieutenant General), 153-154, 157, 163
Rayfield, W. L. (Private), 288
Read, Herbert (poet), 263
Red Cross
  American, 245
  Canadian, 235, 245, 309
    Society, 102
Regina Trench (Somme), 175-184
Reims-the Argonne area, 114
Remarque, Erich Marie, 105, 146, 188, 225
Reynal, S. E. (Major), 131-132
Richardson, Piper James, 179
Richthofen, Manfred von (Red Baron), 278
Ripley, A. (Major), 227
River
  Aisne, 39, 220
  Douve, 116, 137
  Jacques Cortier, 17
  Marne, 34-35, 39, 126, 133
  Meuse, 114, 125, 292, 294, 296, 302-303
  Moselle, 294
  Sambre, 303
  Scarpe, 197, 225

River *(continued)*
  Scheldt, 303
  Somme, 125, 133-134, 149, 151-154, 163, 169-170, 181, 184, 187, 192, 197, 203, 210, 217, 228, 234, 253, 270, 272, 279
  Souchez, 237
  St. Lawrence, 13, 26
  Vesle, 286
  Yser, 40, 72
Robertson, J. P. (Private), 260
Rockefeller Foundation, Department of Industrial Relations, 2
Romania, 267
Romanov dynasty, 197
Roman, 29
  times, 151
Romer, C. F. (Colonel), 71
Roosevelt, Theodore (President), 104, 301
Ross, Sir Charles, 14-15
Ross Rifle, 14-15, 62, 67, 93, 99, 109, 141, 144, 150
  Mark I, 15
  Mark II, 15
  Mark III, 15, 20
Royal
  Air Force
    see British, Royal Flying Corps
Royal Victoria Hospital of Montreal, 81
"Rule Britannia," 11
runners, 94, 130, 142-143, 170, 213, 217, 224, 243
Rupprecht, Crown Prince of Bavaria, 192, 245
Russia, 3-4, 6-8, 11, 29, 33, 127, 152, 155, 187-188, 267, 270, 272
Russian, 77, 98, 137
  Empire, 187
  Front, 114, 137, 265
  Infantry, 33
  Revolution, 197
Russo-German peace treaty, 272
Russo-Japanese conflict (1904-1905), 42
Rutherford, Ernest, 203
Ryerson
  Arthur (Lieutenant), 91-92, 102
  George (Captain), 91-92, 102
  Mrs. G. Sterling, 91, 102, 104

— S —
San Marino, xiv
Samsonov, Alexander (General), 32-33

sap, 45-46
"T," 147
sapper, 231, 255
Sassoon, Siegfried, 151
Schlieffen, Alfred von, 28-29, 39-40
Schlieffen Plan, 31, 36-37
Schwieger, Walter (Lieutenant Colonel), 103
Scott, Canon F. G. (Major), 88, 208, 297
Scottish, 77
Scrimger, F. A. C. (Captain), 81, 94
"Sedan Day," 303
Serbia, 7
Scylla, 53
Shaw, Harry (Major), 213-215
ship
  Alaunia, 53
  Arcadian, 53
  Athenian, 53
  Bermudian, 53
  Birmingham, 57
  Canada, 53
  Caribbean, 53
  Cassandra, 53
  Charybdis, 52-54
  Column X, 43-54
  Column Y, 53
  Column Z, 53-54
  Corinthian, 53
  Cushing, 104
  Diana, 52-54
  Eclipse, 52-54
  Falaba, 104
  Franconia, 53
  Glory, 53
  Grampian, 53
  Gulflight, 53
  Hampshire, 155
  Ivernia, 53
  Laconia, 53, 192
  Lapland, 53
  Leinster, 301
  Llandovery Castle, 285
  Lusitania, 92, 102-104, 107
  Majestic, 53
  Manhattan, 26
  Manitou, 26, 53, 55, 57, 246
  Mauretania, 103
  Megantic, 52-53
  Monmouth, 53-55
  Mont Blanc, 266
  Montezuma, 53
  Montreal, 53
  Mount Temple, 62, 64
  Niobe, 12
  Pancras, 64
  Rainbow, 12

ship *(continued)*
  Royal Edward, 53
  Royal George, 53
  Ruthenia, 53
  Saint Barcham, 300
  Saxonia, 24, 53, 246
  Scandinavian, 53
  Scotian, 53
  Silician, 53
  Talbot, 52-54
  Teleconia, 8-9, 190
  Titanic, 202
  Tryolia, 53
  Tunisian, 53
  Tuscania, 272
  Zeeland, 53
Smith-Dorrien, Horace (General), 34, 69, 72, 87, 90, 95, 112
Smith, Arthur E. (Private), 279
"Snipe Hall," German pillbox, 259
Sousa, John Phillip, 272
South African Boer War, 85, 88, 162
South African artillery groups and batteries, 149
Spain, 9
Spanish influenza, 284
Stafford, A. B. (Major), 225
Steele, S. B. (Major General), 113
Stengel, Baron von, 5
Stevenson, Charlie (Sergeant), 91
St. Eloi-Wytschaete Road, 141
St. John's Road (Trench), 162-163
St. Mark's Anglican Church (Cumberland, Ontario), 309
St. Martin's Cathedral (Ypres), 40, 72, 164-165
Stoddart, _____, 69
Stokesbury, James L., 164
Stollens, 126
Strachan, Harcus (Lieutenant), 265
Swinton, Ernest D. (Colonel), 171, 173, 175, 265
"subway" trench line, 176
"subway" tunnel, 206, 209
Sudbury Trench, 176
Swiss border, 46, 270
Switzerland, 249

— T —
Tait, J. E. (Lieutenant), 286
Tandey, Henry (Private), 297
tank, 171, 173, 175, 264-266, 284, 295

Taylor, A. J. P., 66, 184, 261, 284
Teasdale, George (Driver), 205
Texas, 193
The Book of Remembrance, 209
The First Day of the Somme, 158
The Literary Digest History of the World War, Vol. 3, 17
"The Maple Leaf Forever," 55
"The Pimple," 217-218
The Times (London), 265
Tirpitz, Alfred von (Admiral), 4
trench warfare, 42, 46
  communication line, 48, 209
  development of, 42
  front line, 46
  life in, 47-50, 117-122, 138
  lines, 270
  reserve line, 46
  support line, 45-46
  system, 43-46
trench foot, 49, 117
Triple Alliance, 3-4
Truman, Harry S. (Captain), 294
Turkey, 114
  Gallipoli, 114
Turner, R. E. W. (Major General), 67, 80, 85, 99, 140, 144, 173
Tuchman, Barbara, 1

— U —
U-boats
  see German submarines
"Uncle Sam," 272
United Kingdom, 61, 138, 164
  also see Great Britain
United States, 2, 9, 15, 27, 104, 134, 189, 192-194, 275
  Army, 302-303
  Congress, 193-194
  National Guard, 58
unrestricted submarine warfare, 62, 189-191, 193-194

— V —
Vanier, Georges (Major), 288
Varett, Captain, 119
Vermont, 26
Very flares, 89
Victoria, Queen, 21
Vimy, 122, 205
Vincent, H. (Private), 109

— W —
War Diary of the 1st Canadian Field Artillery Brigade, 208, 237, 241-243, 244-245

Washington
  Seattle, 12
Washington, D.C., 103, 274
Watson, David (Major General), 202
Wemyss, Sir Rosslyn (Rear Admiral), 52-53
Western Front, xiii, 28, 32, 62, 64, 66, 77, 84, 95, 109, 113, 115, 118, 125, 152, 157, 184,188, 197, 199, 225, 245, 250-251, 264, 267, 271, 273,283, 286-287, 289, 292, 296
Wharton, Edith, 192
"Where Duty Leads," 52
"Whizbang" postcard, 71
Wilhelm I, Emperor (Prussia), 2-3
Wilhelm II, Kaiser, 3, 5-6, 36-37, 39, 41, 57, 127, 129, 133, 144, 187, 189, 191, 270, 272, 300, 305
Wilken, A. G. (Captain), 143
Wilks, _____, 119
Williams, V. A. S. (Brigadier General), 147
Wilson
  Trevor, 169
  Woodrow (President), 104, 187, 190-191, 193-194, 272, 274, 301
Winter, Denis, 117, 167
Wolff, Leon, 249
World War I, xiv, 42, 49, 209, 218, 226, 228, 233
  casualties by country, 306
  see also Great War
World War II, 36, 311

— Y —
Yankees, 278
Young, J. F. (Private), 288

— Z —
Zeppelin airships, 230
Zimmerman, Alfred (German Foreign Secretary), 189-191, 193
Zimmerman Telegram, 189-193
Zollern Graben Trench (Somme), 175-176